(2597)

4

CULTURE CHANGE

This is one unit in a series of co-ordinated studies of culture in its dynamic aspects being carried on within the Department of Sociology and Anthropology, Stanford University. These studies form part of a more comprehensive interdisciplinary program of research on "social change" being developed by the Stanford Committee for Research in the Social Sciences, and made initially possible by a grant from the Ford Foundation for work in the behavioral sciences. A further grant from the Wenner-Gren Foundation for Anthropological Research enabled this unit of work to be completed and published.

STANFORD ANTHROPOLOGICAL SERIES

NUMBER ONE

CULTURE CHANGE

An Analysis and Bibliography
of Anthropological Sources
to 1952

Felix M. Keesing

Committee for Anthropological Research

Department of Sociology and Anthropology

Stanford University

STANFORD UNIVERSITY PRESS, STANFORD, CALIFORNIA

LONDON: GEOFFREY CUMBERLEGE, OXFORD UNIVERSITY PRESS

STANFORD UNIVERSITY PRESS
STANFORD, CALIFORNIA

Published in Great Britain, India,
and Pakistan by Geoffrey Cumberlege,
Oxford University Press,
London, Bombay, and Karachi

The Baker and Taylor Company
Hillside, New Jersey

Henry M. Snyder & Company, Inc.
440 Fourth Avenue, New York 16

W. S. Hall & Company
457 Madison Avenue, New York 22

Printed and bound in the United States
of America by Stanford University Press

Library of Congress Catalog Card Number: 53-10842

PREFACE

This analysis and bibliography of anthropological studies dealing with culture in its time-dimensional aspects is essentially a work tool. It presents in chronological order (for the most part on a yearly basis) significant works written in the fields variously called cultural dynamics, culture change, culture growth, culture process, culture contact, acculturation, and (as relating to attempted control and direction of culture) applied anthropology. As such, its prime purpose is to reveal in as comprehensive fashion as possible the development of theory and method by anthropological workers, and also give access to significant case materials in regional and cross-cultural contexts.

The bibliography does not purport to contain all references which would be used by students of what may be called here for brevity "culture change." The criteria of selection are as follows:

1. Works by professional anthropologists or else oriented closely to the professional interests of anthropologists. This excludes a vast quantity of source materials often very important in the study of particular instances of change, such as official documents or missionary records for overseas countries. Also excluded in general are works by scholars in related disciplinary fields such as psychology, sociology, or economics, though a few exceptions are made where the subject matter is of direct relevance to the anthropological problem concerned. One of the tests used, especially prior to the twentieth century when professional training and standards become fixed, is whether the item concerned appears in some technical journal or bibliography of anthropology (see below). Necessarily an arbitrary margin of selection is involved here, but the attempt has been made to be consistent throughout in terms of the compiler's sense of the problems under scrutiny.

2. Works focused primarily or importantly upon phenomena of change and having, directly or inferentially, some theoretical or methodological significance. Here again an arbitrary margin of selection is involved. For example, an archaeological work recording changes in a local ceramic style, or an analysis of phonetic modifications in a particular language, would have too limited a frame of reference to justify being included. Also excluded are a vast number of minor or incidental references to change contained virtually throughout the massive technical literature which focuses on standard ethnographic, archaeological and linguistic description.

The method of compilation gives some further clues as regards these criteria. As a beginning, early in 1952, the compiler used his own bibliographic file of sources accumulated over nearly three decades, and to these were added items from personal files and class bibliographies of Stanford anthropology colleagues. Two graduate students were then enlisted to help check, after the establishment of what seemed reasonable criteria, the references and bibliographies in important books and articles on this initial list, and to do the same with several of the most important technical journals. (To a remarkable degree, as anthropologists working in this field well know, there are a comparatively small number of pioneer or key works which get cited again and again, whether in relation to theoretical problems or to particular regions being studied.) Standard anthropological bibliographies were also searched, e.g., regional bibliographies such as those of Hambly, Schapera, and Wieschhoff on Africa; Embree on Southeast Asia; Kennedy on Indonesia; Mandelbaum on India; Murdock on North America; and topical and general bibliographies such as those of Dieserud (1908), Steinmetz (1911), Thomas (1937), and Meggers (1946).

By this time, the outward push of the project became virtually irresistible. New sources came into sight continuously, yet no compilation was found which could serve in any comprehensive way to cover the field. The compiler therefore devoted much of the summer of 1952 to the work, with two part-time student helpers (his sons Donald and Roger), and brought the bibliography close to its present form. Completion of the list approximately to cover the year 1952, and writing of the interpretive introduction, followed along.

A key decision was to carry the bibliography back into the nineteenth century so as to show the mood and content of early work. As will be seen, enough sources appeared to justify pushing back the year by year listing to 1865, by which time anthropological-type reporting was becoming standardized and the first professional journals were appearing. It should be frankly noted here that searching was limited to serials in English, French, German, and (to a smaller extent) Spanish, and also that many of the minor regional series which span the earth in many languages could not be examined: minor serials purporting to be anthropological are legion. The situation here is somewhat saved, however, by the fact that the more important technical journals in the languages mentioned often contain notices and reviews of works by the important writers in these other media, so that the bibliography includes some items in Scandinavian, Slavic, Italian, and other languages. To this may be added the point that interest in culture change as a subject for anthropological research has been limited mainly to the Western European countries with their overseas offshoot countries and territories.

Of invaluable aid in the compilation work have been various quarterly and annual listings of contemporary sources in several of the older serials, often not only with titles but also with descriptive summaries of the works involved. Notable were the systemic compilations from 1866 on in the German serial Archiv für Anthropologie; from 1872 in Revue d'Anthropologie; from 1879 to 1892 by O. T. Mason in Smithsonian Institutions Reports; and in the American Anthropologist first by R. Fletcher (1888 to 1899), and then by A. F. Chamberlain (1900 to 1913). In addition to such technical bibliographies, standard book and periodical lists were examined. Nearly all anthropologists have written for more general scientific, and even popular serials, so these were searched in relation to names of the contemporary professionals as well as to subjects, and in this way many interesting items found, as in <u>Science</u>, <u>Nature</u>, <u>Scientific</u> <u>Monthly</u>, <u>Dial</u>, <u>Open</u> <u>Court</u>, <u>Southern</u> <u>Workman</u>, and many others. Where available the listed works of deceased professionals as given in necrological notices were examined for items which might otherwise have been missed.

The decision was made quite early to structure the bibliography primarily on a chronological basis. As the introductory interpretation shows, the chronological presentation reveals the rise (and often the fall) of theoretical and methodological preoccupations not only as regards culture change but also more broadly within cultural anthropology in general. Interest in particular problems and regions is also revealed in a significant historical sequence.

A numbering system has been devised to give ready placement of each bibliographic entry. The first two numbers indicate the year (e.g., 87- is 1887, 19- is 1919), though in the first few items the full year is given for identification (i.e., prior to 1865). Within each year the authors are put in alphabetical order, and in turn identified by the second group of numbers (e.g., -1, -23). This coding system is used in the interpretive survey.

Undoubtedly the bibliography still has many gaps. The compiler is particularly conscious that his selection was exercised rather rigidly in the decades from about 1880 to 1910, for which numbers of items were omitted in marginal fields such as criminal anthropology, folk psychology, archaeological perspectives of culture growth, or in the case of regional studies historically oriented materials on European, Asian, and Latin American groups. Significant references which come to light later, together with new items from 1952 on, may be compiled in supplementary bibliographies. The compiler would welcome, on behalf of the Stanford group, information on omissions noted.

Acknowledgments are due to Stanford anthropological colleagues, particularly Drs. Bernard J. Siegel and George D. Spindler, for use of personally compiled materials, and for critical advice relating to the bibliography and text. Important help was received in the compilation work from my wife, Marie Keesing; the secretary of the Department of Sociology and Anthropology, Elizabeth Ireland; and also the following students: James Bosch, Roland Force, Donald Keesing, Roger Keesing, Louise Spindler, Florence Stanley. Appreciation is due to the Ford Foundation and Wenner-Gren Foundation for Anthropological Research for financial grants which made the project possible.

F. M. K.

STANFORD UNIVERSITY
CALIFORNIA

TABLE OF CONTENTS

PART I

CULTURE CHANGE— AN ANALYTICAL SURVEY

PART II

CHRONOLOGICAL BIBLIOGRAPHY

ix

Part One

CULTURE CHANGE–
AN ANALYTICAL SURVEY

CULTURE CHANGE— AN ANALYTICAL SURVEY

1. GENERAL PERSPECTIVES

Studies of culture in its time-dimension aspects are as old as cultural anthropology itself. Yet, paradoxically, this field of theory and method is currently weak and not well integrated. Only in the last handful of years has it been undergoing the complete rescrutiny it deserves in the light of newer approaches to the study of behavior which have been developing both within anthropology itself and in collateral behavioral science fields as well as in certain aspects of study in the humanities.

The history of studies of culture change, or cultural dynamics, within anthropology shows with particular vividness the major theoretical "sets" which have emerged within the science during the period of its organized existence. As even a casual scrutiny of the bibliography will show, the earlier work, particularly throughout the second half of the nineteenth century, was dominated by long-term considerations of cultural origins and development, particularly within the theoretical set of "evolutionism," of which more below. With the early twentieth century, a burgeoning trend toward "historicalist" and "diffusionist" approaches takes the spotlight, with the emphasis on treating specific events and items of custom in their time and space sequences, both long-term and short-term. Then from the 1920's fresh theoretical sets tend in turn to take over: so-called "functional," "configurational," "psychological" and other approaches. Time-dimensional phenomena are here not the main interest of the pioneer workers and the prevailing mood is of total-culture, societal, and personality analysis, as in the works of Malinowski, Radcliffe-Brown, Sapir, Benedict, Mead, Linton, Warner, and others. Major dynamic interests are focused on motivational or "covert culture" dimensions, together with sub-adult conditioning or learning.

Throughout the whole period, however, a thin but consistent thread of interest has continued in study of what are variously called culture contact, acculturation, and "applied" problems: these go back to the 1850's. By the 1930's, as will be seen, these shorter-term phenomena of the culture process are becoming recognized as particularly significant for anthropological theory, and works dealing with them assume more scientific guise. In the 1940's, as the number of entries in the bibliography shows, studies with this emphasis expand sharply. They also become conjoined with the newer theoretical interests spoken of above. For contemporary cultural or "social" anthropology, therefore, time-dimensional phenomena have become a major concern. Even longer-term studies of culture growth, which had tended to wither away for want of scientifically controlled data, were being revived, especially in the light of the increasing body of data from world-wide archaeological studies. The entries for the years 1945 to 1952 show a sharply increasing emphasis on theoretical and methodological problems which will undoubtedly continue in future years.

1

In the sections which follow, a brief analysis is given of the early works to 1869, and then of the references located for each subsequent decade. The major sets of theory referred to above will be placed, and their durability reviewed critically through the eyes of both contemporary and later scholars. Sources from which the compilations were made will also be discussed.

2. NINETEENTH-CENTURY WORKS

Studies in which a dominant emphasis is upon culture in its time-dimensional aspects are rare among the pioneer books and articles dealing with anthropological subjects, even though there is much incidental reference of an unsystematic nature. The emphasis, indeed, in anthropological works up to about the mid-century is upon the fields now classed as physical anthropology and archaeology. Even ethnology, as it comes somewhat more slowly into focus by way of the records of travelers, officials, missionaries, and others, consists predominantly of descriptive accounts of the non-Western peoples in terms of their traditional settings.

Early Works to 1869

The works listed in the bibliography up to 1870 show the expectedly meager findings from a careful search which included the anthropological journals of the time and their book review and bibliography sections, e. g. , The Anthropological Review and Journal of the Anthropological Society of London and associated British journals; Archiv für Anthropologie. It should be noted, however, that there was a deliberate exclusion of rather profuse writings of the period in philosophical, theological, governmental, and other fields in which the mood did not approach that counted "anthropological." Only where recognized anthropological compilers of the time admitted such works into their bibliographies were they included.

A major emphasis in the works listed is upon culture "history" in various regions, e. g. , Asia (1820—1, 66-10, 67-5, etc.), America (1821-1, 1854-1, 66-6, etc.) Going beyond this, regional history is generalized in a series of pioneer experiments in delineating total culture history, foreshadowing a major trend of scholarship in the further decades of the nineteenth century. Of these, the most significant appear to be compilations by Klemm (1843-1), Lubbock (1855-1), Buckle (1857-1), Waitz (1858-1), Bastian (1860-1, 68-1), and Tylor (65-8, 67-7). These and others were attempting to classify the various levels of cultural development or "progress" from postulated origins, or from the types of life of contemporary "savage" and "barbaric" peoples, to "civilization," i. e. , the European cultural "stage." They were also trying to isolate dynamic factors at work in building up, retarding, or bringing about "degeneration" in such long-term developmental processes.

Klemm, for example, saw man as variously at stages of "savagery," "tameness," and "freedom." Waitz pictured all mankind as having essentially the same mental potential but being variously influenced by favorable and unfavorable circumstances of geography, accessibility, and other historical and social factors. Lubbock attempted, though with the characteristic naïveté and ethnocentrism of the time, to analyze "savage" customs so as to give a reconstruction of cultural origins. Bastian was exploring the importance of what he called "elementary ideas" (elementargedanken) as the common mainsprings of culture. Buckle speculated on the varying

3

influences of climate, soil, diet, and other factors on cultural growth.
The references also show others analyzing such dynamic influences as
climate, "race," "hybridity," and psychological potential (e. g. , 1861-2,
1863-1, 65-1, 68-6, 68-11).[1]

A first series of experiments were also tried out during this time in
documenting historically and comparatively various more specific aspects
of culture, society, and language. Notable were studies by Bachofen and
McLennan on aspects of marriage and kinship (1861-1, 65-4); Maine on
law (1861-3); Galton on animal domestication (65-3); Fergusson and Harris
on art and architecture (1862-1, 69-3); Jackson, Gerland, and Baring-Gould
on religion (67-4, 68-5, 69-2); Riecke and Brinton on mythology (67-6,
68-2); and Brodie, Crawfurd, Riecke, and de Rosny on language (66-7,
67-1, 67-6, 69-6). These foreshadow a very extensive literature of this
type in subsequent decades.

Again, certain phases of modern studies in so-called culture contact,
or acculturation, and in applied anthropology are interestingly anticipated.
Several papers discuss the influence of missions on indigenous cultures
(65-2, 65-5, 65-6, 66-1), a "nativistic" movement (66-12), and factors
making for depopulation and extinction of indigenous groups (66-13, 66-14,
69-7). The position of the Negro, and also slavery, topics of great public
interest and controversy at the time, are also subjects of analysis (1864-
2, 66-2, 68-3, 69-5). Relevant early discussions likewise occur of "social
innovation" and "anthropology as a practical science" (66-3, 66-4). Finally,
several papers involve discussions of methodology in part relevant to cultural dynamics (1854-2, 1862-2, 1864-1).

1870—1879

In this decade a number of new technical serials were started, with
corresponding expansion in the number of book reviews and bibliographies
available for search. But the number of items focused on aspects of culture change remains very few in spite of the rapidly expanding amount of
work being published in ethnology, as in the other fields of anthropology.

As adumbrated in earlier years, the main stress in this decade is upon
studies of longer-term cultural "origins" ("genesis," etc.), "history,"
"development," "evolution," seen from varied points of view. Secondarily
there is a growing emphasis on shorter-term change through intergroup
contacts in various parts of the world, especially as between indigenous
peoples and Western expansionism.

Of the longer-term studies, one type of materials tends to stress the
specific factual history and geography of culture. Included are: (1) attempts
to reconstruct origins or "prehistoric" conditions (e. g. , 70-1, 70-9, 70-14,

---

[1]More detailed discussion of these early ideas can be found in various
histories of anthropology, notably in Lowie, R. H. , The History of Ethnological Theory, Chapters II—IV.

72-11, 73-1, 73-12); (2) extensive regional surveys of the rise, spread, and relationships of culture (e.g., 70-3, 71-2, 71-9, 71-12, 72-4); (3) more intensive delineations of the specific history of some locality or ethnic group, as with the Jews (70-5, 71-5, etc.), Puerto Rico (72-3), Ashantis (73-2), Madagascar (76-11), and others; (4) histories of some broad aspect of culture, such as the family and kinship (72-12, 76-18), religion (71-17, 79-12), law (73-17, 76-10, 76-18), art (76-24), and language (74-8, 76-13, 76-16, etc.); and (5) reconstructions of the story of some specific cultural item, e.g., the alphabet (73-7) fire (77-12), numerals (77-20), the week (79-13), the game of patolli (79-15). The emphasis is for the most part on what was later to be called "historicalist" in stressing the unique item or event in its time and place setting. It will be noted that German scholars were especially active in these types of study, and this foreshadowed major sets in German cultural anthropology which were to be labeled "geographical" and "culture-historical."

All such longer-term studies of culture history within the scientific setting of anthropology tended, however, to take on an additional flavor of generalization, particularly through comparison of the more specific events or items of custom from group to group: the so-called "comparative method." This generalizing approach, as it became more systematized, involved attempts to isolate explanatory processes, even "laws" of development and change. Perhaps inevitably, considering the dominant scientific theme of the time, Darwinian evolution, they were increasingly cast in a conceptual mold which is known in the history of anthropology as cultural or social "evolutionism."

The evolutionary approach, with its particular terminology and its explicit and implicit assumptions, provides the main body of theory and method relating to culture in its time-dimensional aspects for this and the next two decades, and so deserves somewhat fuller analysis. It may be introduced by a quotation from what anthropologists generally would recognize as the outstanding work of the 1870's, Tylor's study of "primitive culture" (71-18, vol. 1: 1, 26—27):

> The condition of culture among the various societies of mankind, insofar as it is capable of being investigated on general principles, is a subject apt for the study of laws of human thought and action. On the one hand, the uniformity which so largely pervades civilisation may be ascribed, in great measure, to the uniform action of uniform causes: while on the other hand its various grades may be regarded as stages of development or evolution . . .
>
> [By] simply placing [the European] nations at one end of the social series and savage tribes at the other, [and] arranging the rest of mankind between these limits . . . ethnographers are able to set up at least a rough scale of civilisation . . . [representing] a transition from the savage state to our own.

Tylor, associate of Darwin, Galton, Spencer, and other British scientists

of the time, was the first scholar to bring into disciplined order within
such a framework the desultory bodies of data and theory extant to this
time: hence his appellation of "father of modern ethnology." Another definitive work by Morgan, the only American scholar of the time seriously interested in evolutionary interpretation, states its basic assumptions as
follows in his volume on "ancient society" (77-11: 3, 7):

> As it is undeniable that portions of the human family have ex-
> isted in a state of savagery, other portions in a state of barbarism,
> and still other portions in a state of civilization, it seems equally
> so that these three distinct conditions are connected with each other
> in a natural as well as necessary sequence of progress . . . [The]
> domesticated institutions of the barbarous, and even of the savage,
> ancestors of mankind are still exemplified in portions of the human
> family with such completeness that, with the exception of the
> strictly primitive period, the several stages of this progress are
> tolerably well preserved.

Culture, or society, is here considered to evolve comparably with organic
life; its pathway is marked by "survivals" in custom comparable with the
rudimentary organs of physiology; progress is generally upward, though
perhaps with some localized "degeneration"; a general "psychic unity"
is assumed, i.e., the capacity to evolve through the same stages; European civilization is assumed without question to be at the top of the scale,
and other peoples lower proportionately to the degree of difference in
their customs from those of Europeans; and the whole is fitted together as
a kind of generalized superhistory or theory of progress without much regard to the specific realities of regional and local events and customs in
past or present. These ideas will be seen additionally in writings by Lubbock, Spencer, Pitt-Rivers, Maine, Denis, Girard-Teuton, and Müller,
among others (e.g., 70-9, 70-14, 72-12, 74-5, 75-10, 75-12, 78-14).

Later scholars, starting particularly with Boas (see discussion of 96-2
on the "limitations of the comparative method"), were to wreck the great
superstructure built up on these assumptions. The confident reconstruction of origins and early cultural history, apart from the limited data and
inferences which archaeological research could provide, was discredited,
especially as many of the supposed "survivals" (e.g., primitive sex
promiscuity, the primacy of animism) did not stand the test of more accu-
rate field work. The ethnocentric assumptions of superior civilization and
inferior savage could not hold up in the face of scientific study of the
amazing array of different cultural systems. The unilinear schemes, the
arbitrary and atomistic juggling of cultural elements in tracing supposed
lines and stages of evolution, the lack of concern for the specifics of the
history and geography of culture, were attacked. Vague assumptions of
"psychic unity" were psychologically quite inadequate. As will be seen,
the debacle of this "school" was so complete among professional scholars
(however much it lingered otherwise) that the term "evolution" as applied
to culture and society became practically taboo to a generation or so of

twentieth-century English-speaking anthropologists. But meantime evolutionism is in the saddle of theory.

As regards the studies of shorter-term contact and change in the decade under consideration, it will be noted that these refer to peoples and situations widely scattered over the world. A number deal with the acculturative impact of the West upon indigenous peoples: in the Americas, Africa, Asia, and the South Pacific. Others deal with immigrant groups in North America (the Negro, Japanese, Chinese, Irish); the history of Mormonism; the Hispanic-American traditions of Middle and South America; Islamic expansionism in Asia and Africa; adjustments of India to the West; the Russians in Siberia; Chinese relations with Central Asia; revival of Shinto in Japan. Among topics covered are population dynamics including migration and depopulation, warfare, slavery, miscegenation, the influence of missions, religious movements, the development of pidgin English, aptitude for agriculture of Indian groups, utensils, and bead ornaments of western Indians.

Several papers will be seen presenting specific discussion of the methods of research characteristic of the time, notably Pike on "methods of anthropological research" (70-12), Wake on "the aim and scope of anthropology" (70-16), Schaaffhausen in German on methods of cultural reconstruction (72-17), and Hovelacque in French on ethnology and ethnography (76-12). Two additional papers worthy of note as somewhat anticipating later theoretical interests are Westropp on "analogies and coincidences among unconnected nations" (72-23) and Dunn on "ethnic psychology" (75-4).

1880—1889

A dominant theme in this decade continues to be attempted reconstructions of the origin and evolution of culture. This was a main preoccupation of European scholars, such as Tylor, Maine, McLennan, Wake, Balfour and Pitt-Rivers in England, Letourneau, Hovelacque, Giraud-Teulon and d'Alviella in France, and Lippert, Meyer, Post, and Friedrichs in Germany. Most discussed subjects were religion, marriage and the family, government, the arts, language, and particular items of material culture. In the United States little interest was generated in this approach, though Powell discussed the stages of "savagery," "barbarism," and "civilization," (85-29, 88-29), and Hough the criteria for classifying "civilization" (80-13).

With less flavor of evolutionary theory, numbers of writers worked on aspects of culture history both in general and for particular peoples and regions. Bastian in Germany continued to write prolifically along his rather individualistic lines of theoretical interest. Ratzel produced a monumental work on the history and geography of culture (85-30) which provides a kind of base line for a "culture-historical" school of German theory with strong geographical emphasis, of which more later. At an even more factual level, archaeological workers were elaborating and clarifying their schemes of prehistoric classification.

A subject on which interest begins to focus in this decade is "invention."

Notable discussions are by Seely (83-25, 85-32), Wilkie (84-33), Smith (86-32), Boas (88-8), and Mason (88-25). The paper by Boas mentioned here, titled "the occurrence of similar inventions in areas widely apart," foreshadows his critiques of unilinear evolution, to be discussed in the next section. Various dynamic factors considered influential in culture growth and change are also the subject of special papers: diet (82-12), idiosyncrasy (83-1), mental stimulus (85-38), antagonism (88-16), competition (88-28), and imitation (89-15). A group of early American scholars whose work was centered particularly in the Bureau of American Ethnology and in museums, notably Powell, Hough, Mason, Holmes, Matthews, Dorsey, Brinton, and Hale, made generally hardheaded contributions on the historical development of particular cultural items or of peoples among whom they were doing field work.

An important continuing aspect of historical survey work was a series of culture-contact, or acculturation, studies. The largest number related to interaction of peoples on the American continent, particularly North American Indian groups, with incoming "whites." The adjustment of the Negro in the New World is also featured, and there are scattered studies relating to Asia, Africa, and the South Pacific. Most are descriptive accounts, yet they also show significant treatments of topics of interest to scholars today such as population dynamics, miscegenation, political adjustments, the influence of missions, education, language change, and personality adjustment. Several papers deal with biographical materials on indigenous leaders, including a "messiah" in Mexico (80-7, 85-18, 85-19, 89-9) Several papers attempt more general analyses of cultural change, including problems of directed change, notably by Mason on the "savage" in relation to "civilization" (81-8, 82-10), Frere on "the laws affecting relations between civilised and savage life" (82-7), Wilson and Withington on problems of "civilizing" indigenous peoples (82-16, 84-34), Cowles on "insistent and fixed ideas" (88-11), and Gomme on "the conditions for survival of archaic customs" (89-17).

Criminal anthropology emerged as a special interest in this period, notably in France and Italy, but has not been emphasized in this selection of references. Folk-lorists wrote on the dynamics of their materials, though mostly in very specific contexts. An incipient interest in methodology also continued, but was only rarely separated out as a topic for special discussion (e.g., 80-12, 84-12).

1890–1899

The interests shown in the previous decade were in general continued and elaborated. But several highly significant shifts in approach can be noted which lay the basis for future theoretical and methodological concerns.

The evolutionary approach continues as the dominant theoretical set, with numerous books and papers on general and specific topics, and with European rather than American scholars involved. To older names, such as those of Tylor, McLennan, Balfour, and Letourneau, are now added new writers, e.g., Haddon, Lang, and Westermarck in England, Lefevre, Reclus, and Mauss in France, Achelis, Cunow, and Vierkandt in Germany, Argancelli in Italy, and Stolpe in Sweden. Religion in its various aspects continued to head the list of subjects, with marriage and family, morals, the arts, technology, and language also emphasized. An article by Caillard on personality in evolution (94-9) foreshadows important modern interests. Of American writers, Brinton, in several broadly interpretive works on peoples and cultures, approached an evolutionary viewpoint in some of his writings (e.g., 90-10, 93-7, 96-4); Powell had some leaning in that direction, but generally kept to a historical approach (e.g., 94-27, 98-27); and McGee also stressed on the whole a historical viewpoint in several broadly titled papers on development and progress (e.g., 95-17, 95-18, 98-20, 99-10).

It was this more "historicalist" view, with its insistence upon checking speculative reconstructions against archaeological and other factual evidence, which was to prove the downfall of the great facade of evolutionary theory erected to this time. Two main centers of scholarship were nurturing most overtly the critical ideas involved: the United States and Germany. In both, works of the decade show a notable turn toward realistic examination of the evidence available (and not available) for long-term reconstruction of cultural growth. In Germany this built upon the original historical-geographical compilation work of Ratzel (85-30), and even back of him Bastian, as discussed previously. The new approach is perhaps best seen in Ratzel's continuing work, and in that of Frobenius and Hahn just before the turn of the century (e.g., 96-10, 98-9, 98-10, 99-18). These are representative of what is often now called the German "geographical" school. Hahn, for example, on the basis particularly of his studies of animal domestication, rejected the evolutionary three-stage hypothesis of hunting-herding-agriculture, and attempted instead to define a more realistic economic typology. The elaboration by Frobenius and others of a "culture-historical" method opposed to the older evolutionism will be discussed in later sections.

In the United States the intellectual atmosphere of anthropology, described in the last section as "hardheaded," was perhaps even more favorable to realistic assessment of the proliferating evolutionary theories. The "professionals" of the time (i.e., more or less full-time workers) came in many cases from the natural science fields, and continued to be based in government or at museums. Their "field work" understandably stressed descriptive rather than theoretical interests, c.f. the works cited, in addition to those of the three American scholars mentioned above, of Mason, Chamberlain, Holmes, Bandalier, Grinnell, Cushing, Mooney, Fewkes, Hodge, Hoffman, Dorsey, and Hewitt. Mason, for example, rounded out his interest in invention with a careful book-length work on "the origins of invention," stressing known data from archaeology (95-20). Holmes wrote on the "natural history of flake stone implements" (94-14, 94-15).

Even more directly than the German scholars of the "geographic" school such American workers were realistically aware of the influence of the physical environment or habitat in cultural development. The American Indian peoples lived in widely differing geographic settings, and showed many varieties of technology, economy, and society. The extensive ethnographic records of the time, few of them cited as they usually did not feature strongly the matter of change, reveal this awareness, and here and there it provides the theme of a chapter or paper, e.g., studies by McGee and Powell on relations of culture to environment (95-18, 95-24). Problems of the distribution and "diffusion" of specific cultural elements was also becoming an absorbing topic as workers compared one Indian culture with another. Resistance was also being erected at this time to easy European-based theories of Old World origins for the New World civilizations which archaeology was bringing to light: this problem again induced a careful mood of historical analysis opposed to that of the grand evolutionary generalization.

The two more or less separate scholarly traditions here summarized became conjoined in this period in the work of an anthropologist who took the discipline for the first time strongly into the university academic atmosphere in the United States and was to become its leading figure for several decades: Boas. This highly creative scholar, after working in physics and geography in Germany, established himself in the United States by way of field work among Eskimos and northern Indians and a geography post at Clark University; subsequently by way of a position at the American Museum of Natural History he became lecturer in 1896 at Columbia University and in due course established there the first important anthropology department and training center. Though concentrating on ethnographic description, Boas was strongly interested in distributional problems, e.g., his paper on "dissemination of tales among the natives of North America" (91-1). In 1896 a paper by him on "the limitations of the comparative method of anthropology" (96-2) presented a first comprehensive attack upon the assumptions and methods of evolutionism. It also gave a rationale for the hitherto mainly implicit assumptions and methods of the American "school" of workers: Boas gave it a name which was to stick, namely, "the historical method," or "historicalism." To quote Boas:

> [Supporters of evolutionism], while not denying the occurrence of historical connections, regard them as insignificant in results and in theoretical importance . . . But the discovery of [uniformities in universal ideas] is only the beginning of the work of the anthropologist. Scientific inquiry must answer two questions in regard to them: First, what is their origin? and second, how do they assert themselves in various cultures? . . . [This calls for] another method, which in many respects is much safer. A detailed study of customs in their relation to the total culture of the tribe practising them, in connection with an investigation of their geographical distribution among neighboring tribes, affords us almost always

with a means of determining with considerable accuracy the historical causes that led to the formation of the customs in question
and to the psychological processes that were at work in their development . . . We have in this method a means of reconstructing
the history of the growth of ideas with much greater accuracy than
the generalizations of the comparative method will permit.

Boas was to elaborate these initial ideas in much further writing. With
his students he was to set virtually a new course in theory and method,
opening the way to many new types of study in culture change as in other
fields. But discussion of these developments can rightly be held over to
the next decades, where the further fate of evolutionary studies will also
be examined.

The emphasis placed here upon the German and American scholarly
traditions needs in fairness to be rounded out by reference to incipient
tendencies toward a historical rather than an evolutionary stance in British
work of the time. The key person here was Tylor, whose introduction to
an English translation of Ratzel (96-26) shows an awareness of geographic
and diffusionistic phenomena of culture beyond what is usually credited to
him in anthropological histories. His studies of the distribution of games
(79-14, 79-15, 96-27) also demonstrate this interest. An important step
toward greater realism was the sending of a team of British scientists
into the field, the so-called "Torres Straits Expedition," in 1898, to explore anthropological and other phenomena; the publication of results,
however, does not start until the next decade.

The period is also marked by a continuation of more specific historical
studies of peoples and regions, including acculturation phenomena. Besides
American Indian and New World Negro materials there is a growing emphasis on culture-contact studies in various zones of Africa, and scattered
case materials on the South Pacific, India and some other sections of
Asia (e.g., "Russia as a civilizing force in Asia"—95-11). Subjects again
emphasized are population dynamics including depopulation, miscegenation,
economic and social adjustments, religion and missions, and language
changes. Two papers deal with the trade "jargon," Chinook (90-23, 94-12).
But most emphasized are studies of new American Indian cults and their
leaders ("messiahs"), a subject of keen interest to contemporary students
of culture change (90-7, 90-34, 91-9, 91-19, 91-21, 93-12, 94-11, 94-25,
96-17, 97-4, 98-7). Of this group the best known is Mooney's classic study
of the Ghost Dance religion (96-17). A somewhat comparable paper is
Risley's study of political movements in India (90-47). Studies by Culin
and Chapman of the Chinese in the United States give materials on immigrant group adjustments. Of more general materials analyzing culture
change McGee's paper on "piratical acculturation" (98-21) is particularly
notable.

Criminal anthropology reaches a crescendo of interest in the anthropological literature of this decade, with French and Italian writers in the
forefront; a review of this field by an American scholar is noted (91-6).

Folklore students put a growing emphasis upon realistic study of the development and diffusion of tale materials, notably in works by Boas (91-1, 96-3), Mason (91-17), Grinnell (91-9), Mooney (91-19), and Newell (95-21). A paper by Fellows on the relation of anthropology to history is a useful attempt at methodological review (96-6). An interesting example of prescience is Powell's paper on "seven venerable ghosts" (96-20), which anticipates the modern "operational" treatment of scientific concepts ("these are the seven ghosts of science: substrate . . . substance . . . essence . . . space . . . force . . . mind . . . cause . . . reified words, seven voids, seven nothings").

In this period the term "acculturation" is becoming used in the English language to refer to the transfer of cultural elements through contact between groups. As early as 1880 Powell had spoken of "the force of acculturation under the overwhelming presence of millions of civilized people" as changing indigenous traditions.[1] Powell, Holmes, McGee, and probably others used the term sometimes more in the sense of the narrower process of "diffusion," and sometimes as implying a continuing front of intercultural contacts. McGee, in his paper on "piratical acculturation" states (98-21: 243):

> Human development . . . may be measured by the degree in which
> devices and ideas are interchanged and fertilized in the process of
> transfer, i.e., by the degree of acculturation. In the higher cul-
> ture-grades . . . the interchange is friendly and purposive; this
> is amicable acculturation. In the lower culture-grades . . . the
> interchange is largely inimical and adventitious; this may be called
> piratical acculturation.

Scientific usage, as would be expected, soon brought such a term into the dictionary. Where, for example, the 1906 Century Dictionary and Encyclopaedia does not have it listed, it appears in a "New Volume" for 1909, defined as "the process of adopting and assimilating foreign cultural elements"; under "acculturize" it gives as an example "the partly acculturized Papago" (from Smithsonian Institution Report, 1895: 44). Webster's dictionary defines "acculturation" in its 1914 edition as: "the approximation of one human race or tribe to another in culture or arts by contact." The term also had some currency in Germany back at least as far as 1910.[2] As will be noted, more modern usage is not to develop until the 1920's (e.g., Gifford, 24-7), and careful technical definition came only in 1936 (36-54).

---

[1] Powell, J. W. Introduction to the Study of Indian Languages. Bureau of American Ethnology, 1880: 46; see also SIR, 1895: 44; BAER, 1897–98: xxi.
[2] Noted in Beals, R. "Acculturation," in Anthropology Today, Kroeber, A. L. (ed.): 621. Chicago, 1953.

3. EARLY TWENTIETH-CENTURY WORKS

The opening decade of the twentieth century is a period of transition in theory and method in relation to cultural dynamics, as to cultural anthropology generally. On the one hand, the evolutionary set which has been dominant in this period continues strongly, and particularly so in the United Kingdom and France. On the other, a series of works are pioneering new approaches which are to come into full development during the following two decades. The period is also marked by an increasing emphasis upon professional training and scientifically modeled "field work." Non-Western peoples, hitherto regarded as "savages," "barbarians," etc., are being looked at as "people," and their systems of life seen as having their own integrity rather than as being curiosa representative of stages and survivals on the pathways of progress to superior civilization.

1900—1909

More modern-sounding names were being added in this decade to the roster of writers generally following the evolutionary framework. Among them were Marett, Hobhouse, Crawley, Frazer, Hartland, Keane, and Rivers, in the United Kingdom; Rivet, Mauss, Foucart, and Guibert in France; Preuss, Schurtz and Kohler in Germany; Vecchio and Rostagno in Italy; and Landtman in Sweden. In Germany, however, a new theoretical approach was now being welded out by way of the writings of Graebner, Foy, Schmidt, Ankermann, and Thomas (05-2, 05-15, 05-30, 08-21, 09-5, 09-6, 09-8, 09-28) around concepts of "culture-history" and "culture-complex" (kulturkreis) which were rooted in the historical-geographical tradition spoken of earlier. This "German diffusionist" school as it was later to be called will be analyzed in due course. Similarly in England a paper by Petrie on migrations of culture (06-14) foreshadowed an English "diffusionist" school to be discussed later. In both cases, however, these new approaches had in common with evolutionism the objective of trying to reconstruct the total history of culture from its beginnings, and so interpreted culture processes in an extensive rather than intensive frame of reference.

Besides this continuing preoccupation of European scholars with comparative and reconstructional studies, a fresh emphasis shows in this decade upon scientific field work. Haddon was publishing field materials from the important British Torres Straits Expedition of 1898; in 1906 Rivers published his classic monograph on the Todas; Rivet's work on the Jibaro was being issued; Kramer and Hambruch were publishing on Oceania: these just a few examples.

It was, however, in the United States that the new trends showed most clearly. Along with the older voices of Powell, Mason, Brinton, Fewkes, Matthews, Mooney, Chamberlain, and others were now sounding those of younger men, most of whom had received professional training from Boas

13

at Columbia: Kroeber, Wissler, Dixon, Tozzer, and before the decade
had run out Lowie, Sapir, and Speck. Boas continued to elaborate his
"historicalist" viewpoint in ways destructive of key assumptions of evolutionism, e.g., in his initial generalized formulations on "the mind of
primitive man" (01-1), which was to become a decade later the title for
one of his key books. Wissler, in a paper on "ethnic types and isolation"
(06-20) foreshadowed later theoretical interests on processes of culture
growth and diffusion. But most of the younger men mentioned were settling
into solid field work activities in their chosen settings, as indicated by
the titles of their early papers which are relevant here, e.g., Dixon on
the mythology of the Maidu (03-6), Tozzer on the Maya (07-19). The
American "historical" and "diffusionist" approaches can best be discussed
in a later decade when their theoretical frame has become more clarified.

So-called "primitive" peoples and cultures were by now emerging, as
indicated above, into more realistic perspective in relation to "civilization."
This shows strongly, for example, in writings by Boas (e.g., 01-1, 04-2,
04-3), and appears to provide the impulse to papers such as those by
Chamberlain on "contributions of the American Indian to civilization"
(03-4) and Whitley on "the high intellectual character of primeval man"
(09-34). Naive ethnocentrism, even when couched in a theory of progress,
was breaking down before the new mood of scientific "objectivity." If
anything, the newly fledged anthropologist was now likely to weigh the
chips a little romantically to the side of his primitives.

Localized historical studies, including varied acculturation situations,
continued in this decade. American, African, Asian, and South Pacific
case materials are included, with the familiar wide range of subjects:
population dynamics, folklore, the rise of jargons, etc. Again various
cult phenomena were of special interest, including peyote and the Shaker
faith of Puget Sound (00-15, 00-16, 00-17, 07-3). Persistence of "paganism" among "civilized" Iroquois is described by Boyle (00-1). An article
by Singh discusses "the Americanization of Oriental women" (09-31). More
general discussions of contact between non-Western and Western peoples
include papers on this topic by Chamberlain, Gollier, and Hall (02-6,
05-14, 06-7). A paper by Matthews on the "American character" (05-24)
presages recent studies of this subject.

1910—1919

The newer trends spoken of in the previous section gather momentum
in this decade. Its mood was well struck in a paper by the British anthropologist Rivers in 1911 in which he publicly "recanted" his earlier evolutionary ideas (11-45):

The theoretical anthropology of this country [has been] inspired
primarily by the idea of evolution . . . Where similarities are
found in different parts of the world, it is assumed almost as an

axiom that they are due to independent origin and development, and this in its turn is ascribed to the fundamental similarity of the workings of the human mind all over the world . . . [But] evolutionary speculations can have no firm basis unless there has been a preceding analysis of the cultures and civilizations now spread over the earth's surface.

The emphasis is now upon study of cultures, the distribution in time and space of their specific elements or "traits," their origin through "invention," and their transmission through "diffusion." While the problem of generalizing culture history remained a valid scientific goal, it had to await the much fuller availability of specific data on the history and geography of culture over the world such as scientifically controlled field work could produce.

Not all scholars in the United Kingdom were prepared to shift their position so fully. Frazer, Lang, Hartland, and some others kept to the evolutionary framework. But Haddon (10-12), Westermarck (11-60), Seligman (16-33), and Marett (19-13), are among those showing awareness of the "historicalist" trend, and Continental scholars such as van Gennep (10-8), Thurnwald (12-43, 13-55), Birket-Smith (15-3), and Nordenskiöld (17-15), to mention just a few of the new important names appearing in this decade. But it is in the United States that the new approach and its theoretical and methodological implications were being most fully worked out.

Boas, as indicated earlier, was taking the lead here. In a variety of statements on the historical method in this and the next decade he insisted on "the consideration of every cultural phenomenon as the result of historical happenings . . ."

Each culture can be understood only as an historical growth determined by the social and geographic environment in which each people is placed and by the way in which it develops the cultural material that comes into its possession from the outside or through its own creativeness (27-4).

It will be noted in the latter part of this quotation that Boas puts "diffusion" from outside ahead of "invention" within a culture in assessing processes of cultural growth. The mood is strictly empirical, "behavioral," in accordance with interpretations of "objective" scientific method current in this early twentieth-century period. Cultures are analyzed into their constituent traits ("units of observation") much as anthropologists of the time were ranging objects on their museum shelves, their localization in time and space plotted and counted ("distribution" studies, "age-area" analyses, etc.), the processes of invention and diffusion traced or hypothecated so far as specific data allowed, and their associations in a given culture or at a particular time level within a region noted ("trait-complex," "culture-pattern," "culture area," etc.).

Boas, for all his resistance to generalization, inevitably was advancing in this decade toward more systematic theory, such as is now associated with historicalism, and in this some of his associates and students even moved out ahead of his cautious approach. Two influences were at work here: first, recognition, even if almost reluctantly, of positive theoretical implications of the materials and terminology, and second, opposition often of heated character by these workers to interpretations put on their materials and on human culture generally by a number of scholars (and sometimes pseudo scholars) in other fields. This period saw the heyday of various theories with which anthropologists disagreed, especially schools of thought which overstressed one or another of the dimensions which enter into cultural life or even gave them the character of "single determiners": geographic, biological, racial, psychological (e.g., "instinct" theory), psychoanalytic ("infantile" determinism), materialistic or economic, or sociological (e.g., the "group mind"). In laying upon them lustily Boas and others were forced into positive formulations relating to habitat-culture relationships, biology-culture relationships, racist theories, and a range of other topics, including cultural growth and change.

Boas, in his "mind of primitive man" and other writings (10-4, 11-6, etc.) insisted, for example, on "the fundamental sameness of mental processes in all races and in all cultural forms of the present day." Kroeber and others insisted that culture was capable of description and analysis in terms of its own processes or laws ("the superorganic," "universal culture pattern," etc.) without reference to the individual, who was left for psychology to handle. Lowie's small book on "culture and ethnology" (17-11) provided one of the earliest systematic presentations. The following list of scholars and titles reveals more fully something of the American historicalist preoccupations of the time in the field of general theory and method:

Lowie: Methods of American ethnologists (11-32); On the principle of convergence in ethnology (12-22); Oral tradition and history (17-12); Survivals and the historical method (18-15); Economic interpretation of history; a footnote (19-12).

Goldenweiser: The principle of limited possibilities in the development of culture (13-18); Culture and environment (16-5); Diffusion versus independent origin (16-6); Reconstruction from survivals . . . (16-8); History, psychology, and culture (18-4).

Wissler: The relation of culture to environment from the standpoint of invention (13-58); The aboriginal maize culture as a typical culture-complex (16-44); Psychological and historical interpretations of culture (16-46).

Wallis: Individual initiative and social compulsion (15-36); Similarities in culture (17-25); Psychological and statistical interpretations of culture (17-26); The influence of anthropology on history (17-26).

Sapir: Time perspective in aboriginal American culture (16-28); Civilization and culture (19-21).

Kroeber: The superorganic (17-9); Heredity, environment, and civilization; factors controlling human behavior . . . (18-9); On the principle of order in civilization as exemplified by changes in fashion (19-8).

In addition to these more general works, these and other American writers applied historical analysis to more specific cultural phenomena, e.g., totemism (10-10, 11-31, 15-12, 16-3, etc.), language (11-28, 11-46, 12-31, 12-33, 13-31, etc.), and to regional studies, e.g., Dixon on "the independence of the culture of the American Indians" (12-8), Goldenweiser on "diffusion of clans in North America" (18-3).

Study of the time-dimension aspects of culture was obviously inherent in the historicalist approach, both specifically in shorter term known data and hypothetically in longer term process. The concepts of "invention" and "diffusion" are central, and are supplemented by associated concepts of "parallelism" or independent invention, "divergence," and "convergence." In addition to relevant works listed above, further items will be noted in the period in which phenomena of innovation and change are explicitly analyzed: Kroeber on "Eskimos as aboriginal inventors" (14-15), and Wissler on "the influence of the horse in the development of Plains culture" (14-36), and Boas on folklore dynamics (reviewed in 16-2) are notable examples, and also acculturation studies to be discussed below.

In the United Kingdom, Rivers wrote on various diffusionistic problems: the "disappearance of the useful arts," "contact of peoples," his monumental "history of Melanesian society," and "sun cults and megaliths in Oceania" (12-29, 13-41, 14-26, 15-28). Hocart also wrote in this mood (12-15, 14-9, 14-10). As anticipated in the last section, however, English "diffusionism" tended to become merged with the Egypt-centered interests of Flinders-Petrie and other archaeological scholars. Mainly responsible for this are Elliott Smith, professionally a specialist in brain anatomy, and Perry. Smith in this decade starts a spate of writing which purports to interpret cultural growth in total diffusionistic perspectives, with Egypt as providing at practically all levels the dynamic for invention and dissemination of important cultural elements. His Egyptians provide the outlying parts of the world with agriculture, megalithic building, sun worship, cults of kings and priests, mummification, and so on, throughout a list of supposingly matching elements of "civilization" wherever they are located, even reaching the Americas as they voyage after gold and pearls across the South Pacific (15-31, 15-32, 16-37, 16-38, and on into the next decade). This flight of fancy actually begins to reach the proportions of a minor school of theory as the ideas are taken up and popularized by a plausible writer, Perry (18-19, and next decade). It is usually referred to as the "English diffusionist," "heliolithic," or "Egypt-centric" school, when not called by scholars less polite names, as will be seen in a critique in the next section.

In Germany, too, as indicated in the last section, another "diffusionist" approach involving an interpretation of total culture history is gathering strength. In this decade both regional and general interpretation of the so-called "culture-historical" or kulturkreise school are being consolidated, especially through the works of Foy (10-7, 13-15), Graebner (10-11, 11-21), Father Schmidt (10-28, 12-35, 12-36, 13-43, 19-22), and Father Koppers (15-20, 16-15). A major theoretical and methodological exposition is given in Graebner's Methode der Ethnologie (11-21). On the basis of detailed regional studies of the distribution and possible relationship of cultural elements among the more isolated "primitives" of today, a series of kulturkreise or "culture complexes" ("strata," "circles") were postulated as having developed which singly or in combination account for the total "culture-history" of man. The various primal strata are most clearly represented in the modern cultures of the tropical forest pigmies, the arctic hunters, and certain Australian Aborigine groups; next come complexes of various simple cultivators and herders; and so on to civilization. The "scientific" tests used to establish the postulated relationships include "irrelevant form" (i. e. , formal similarities which have no functional reason to exist), "quantity," "contiguity" and other methodological criteria.

Though exponents of this theoretical system disclaimed any relationship with evolutionism, the resulting total-history interpretation shares the same great construct character. The postulated strata, like the evolutionary stages, bear no demonstrated relationship to specific culture history, and give what in terms of even the archaeologically known data of today is a vastly oversimplified picture of the story of regional growth and differentiation in culture. Furthermore, this whole approach touches upon a very circumscribed and stilted range of culture change phenomena. As will be seen, it failed to get any strong adherence outside the German-Austrian group of scholars among whom it was developed, and came under strong criticism as a rather deviant "school" of diffusionism.

In France this general period was noted for work of a "sociological" group following up the creative thinking of Durkheim and using anthropological materials extensively. The scholar most oustanding here is Lévy-Bruhl, whose initial work on "primitive mentality" was issued in this decade (10-18). His interpretations of the "savage" mind as "prelogical" and hence different from the "logical" civilized mind were strongly resisted, however, especially by American field workers who, as Lévy-Bruhl never did, knew non-Western peoples and their modes of thought at first hand.[1]

In Germany a long-term interest in "folk psychology," which also tended to have this same broadly speculative character, finds expression at this

---

[1]Of many definitive critiques of this French approach, the most comprehensive is perhaps that by Lowie in his History of Ethnological Theory, Chapter XII.

time in increasingly realistic work, based on field data, e.g., Wundt (12-48). Thurnwald (13-55), Krueger (15-21). This parallels an incipient interest in psychologically oriented problems shown in some of the titles listed for American historicalists. This was to gather momentum in the next decade and to produce strong psychologically oriented approaches in the 1930's. Because a pioneer in the latter type of work was to be Sapir, whose interests became strongly psychoanalytic, it is worth noting that he had in this decade a first paper adumbrating this concern and titled "psychoanalysis as a pathfinder" (17-19). Another worker who was to be influential in bringing together psychoanalysis and anthropology, Róheim, also has a first set of significant publications in this decade (12-30, 14-28, 18-22).

Studies in localized culture history and acculturation expand considerably in number. Again they cover varied topics, and widely scattered zones of the world, though particularly the American Indian peoples. Cult and messianic phenomena, for example, are well represented, including first reports from New Guinea where they proliferate from this time on (13-36, 17-3). A noteworthy group of studies relate to India, some by Indian scholars (11-37, 11-49, 12-5, 12-24, etc.). Significant use is made of verbal documentation from the indigenous peoples as relating to change (11-13, 11-27, 11-39, 12-10, 12-16, 12-20, 13-11). A notable record is the story of Ishi, last of a California Indian tribe, and his adjustment from a wild habitat to life centered in the University of California anthropology department (12-20, 17-27). Among "professional" anthropologists shaping up specific analyses of local acculturation data in a "historicalist" manner are Parker (10-24, 11-40, etc.), Barrett (11-4), Evans (11-15), Skinner (13-48), Hocart (14-9, 14-10), Jenks (14-13), Radin (13-38, 13-39, 14-23), Speck (13-52, 16-39), Hrdlička (17-7), Jenness (18-7), and Parsons (18-18). More general discussions of cultural dynamics include Sergi on "differences in customs and morals, and their resistance to rapid change" (11-47); Chamberlain on "some influences of race contact upon the art of primitive peoples" and "some interesting phases of the contact of races individually and en masse" (11-8, 13-5); Triggs on the "decay of aboriginal races" (12-44); and Marett on "the psychology of culture-contact" (18-16).

Some of this acculturation material has an "applied" emphasis, and this shows in a number of other works. Several deal with policies relating to the American Indian, e.g., Brownell (10-5), Stefansson (11-53), Speck (13-51). A significant paper by one of the early "government anthropologists," Chinnery, is on the "application of anthropological methods to tribal development in New Guinea" (19-5). This, too, was a decade marked by World War I and varied socially dynamic phenomena which stimulated anthropologists to turn the scientific eye away from "primitives" to their own cultural milieu: Chamberlain on the "antagonism of city and country" (13-6); Parsons on "feminism and conventionality" and "social freedom" (14-21, 15-25); Goldenweiser on "Atlanta riots and the origin of magic" (15-10); Sapir on "culture in the melting-pot" (16-27); Boas on "nationalism"

(19-2); Hrdlička on "effects of the war on the American people" (19-6);
and Rivers on "psychiatry and the war" (19-19). More generally Temple
wrote on "anthropology as a practical science" and "the value of a training
in anthropology for the administrator" (14-34, 14-35), the latter a subject
of great interest today, and Lowie on "anthropology put to work" (18-14).

1920–1929

This is par excellence the decade of historicalism, with its varied diffusionistic offshoots. The voice of evolutionism is muted to the work of a
few diehards, notably Frazer. Yet new tendencies in theory and method
are also showing, and are justifying their later general labels of "functional"
and "psychological" schools. As with the first decade of the twentieth
century this is a transitional period, as will be seen below. It may be
noted that a marked distinction shows in this decade, having its main initiative among British scholars, between "ethnology" and a newer term, "social
anthropology." The former continues to stress study of cultural differences,
with their historical relationships, and tends to have a museum atmosphere.
The latter focuses upon "scientific study of behavior," attacking problems
and seeking generalizations from cross-cultural contexts, and is more
aligned with the other "social" sciences, particularly psychology and sociology.[1]

The German "culture-historical" approach, dealt with critically in the
last section, continued to build up its data and theory, notably through the
work of Schmidt, Koppers, Graebner, Ulrich, and Heine-Geldern (21-6,
21-11, 21-19, 22-10, 23-24, 24-9, etc.). Most monumental of the studies
involved is Father Schmidt's "origin of the idea of God," ten volumes of
which have been issued up to 1952. In France, too, Lévy-Bruhl issued
more of his peculiar theory on primitive "mentality" (22-12), without much
response other than criticisms, e.g., by Goldenweiser (22-7).

In England this was the heyday for the Egypt-centric writings of Smith,
Perry, and a few others, with popular titles including Perry's "children
of the sun" and "the growth of civilisation" (23-16, 24-18), and Smith's
"elephants and ethnologists" (trying to justify his claims that elephant
motifs showed in Middle American art), "ancient mariners and the spread
of civilisation," and "the migrations of early culture" (24-25, 26-31, 29-41).
But controversial exchanges, especially with American scholars, were
already riddling the pseudoscientific guise of these writings, as seen notably
in a joint volume to which Smith, Malinowski, Spinden, and Goldenweiser
contributed on "culture, the diffusion controversy" (27-39). Opponents of
the school pointed to the weakness of equating, without regard to space
and time over the world, artifacts and customs identical only in the broadest

---

[1]An account of the discussions among British scholars leading to this
distinction is given by Radcliffe-Brown, A.R., "Historical note on British
social anthropology," American Anthropologist, 54: 275–77. 1952.

sense but differing vastly in detail, e.g. , pyramid-shaped structures,
mummification of the dead, a centering of interest on the sun in religious
belief, and having a godlike leader or king. Even the supposed priority
of Egypt in basic inventions was being cast into doubt by archaeological
finds in Mesopotamia and zones still further east in Asia, including evidence of development of "dry cultivation" ahead of the intensive "wet" agriculture of the river valleys. The Nile region was being relegated by these
new data into the position of a marginal rather than a central area as regards development of "early civilization." American scholars particularly
attacked claims made by these British theorists, and also by a French
group of whom Rivet was the most outstanding (25-21, 26-27), that Middle
American civilizations received their creative stimulus from the Old World
by way of the South Pacific islands: a thesis, indeed, which keeps bobbing
up again even into the 1950's. The American viewpoint of the time is well
summed up by Boas in a paper on migrations from Asia to America (29-6).
At least such oversimple diffusionist ideas and total-history interpretations,
for all their plausibility and some lay popularity, have gone for scientific
purposes into the same category as theories of the Atlantis and Mu "lost
continents" and of Kon-Tiki-like Pacific voyagings from America to settle
Oceania: they are not taken seriously by professional specialists who are
informed on racial, archaeological, linguistic, and other scientifically
valid data.

British scholars of the decade were also publishing more controlled
work along historicalist lines, though always colored with the strong tendency
toward generalization (the mood of social anthropology). Among titles of
the time are Marett on "psychology and folk-lore" and "the diffusion of culture" (20-17, 27-26); Rivers on "history and ethnology," and "psychology and
ethnology" (20-23, 26-26), Hocart on "convergence of customs" and "kingship"
(23-6, 27-19), Hobhouse on "social development" (24-11), three important
papers on "invention" by Harrison (25-11, 26-10, 26-11), including useful
classificational concepts ("obtrusive," "directional," "independent," etc.);
Malinowski, writing with Smith, on "is civilisation contagious?" (26-32), and
the psychologist Bartlett's influential book on "psychology and primitive culture" (23-1). Examples, too, of more ethnically localized work with dynamic
emphasis are Torday's "culture and environment: cultural differences among
the various branches of the Batetela" (22-24), and Seligman's "temperament,
conflict and psychosis in a stone-age population" (29-40). The tendencies
toward psychological orientation spoken of in the beginning paragraph show
in a number of these titles. The German scholar Thurnwald was also showing at this time an especially strong turn of interest out of the older "folk
psychology" channel toward realistic psychological, combined with historical, investigation which makes him in the next decade one of the most creative thinkers in the field of cultural dynamics (20-26, 21-24, 22-23, 29-52).

In the American setting of the time, historicalist and diffusionist studies
dominate the scene, and psychological interests stir more slowly. The
professional ethnologists are mostly "head down" to orthodox descriptive

field and museum work. They write discernibly less for nonprofessional journals and on marginal subjects, including the more casual accounts of acculturation such as were rather numerous in the previous decades. At the same time, a number of the scholars concerned write theoretical and methodological works which, accompanied by considerable verbal controversy, bring out the full implications of the American historicalist-diffusionist approach. Of major books the following may be cited: Goldenweiser on "early civilization" (22-7); Kroeber on "anthropology" (23-8); Wissler on "man and culture," perhaps to be counted the classic work (23-29), and on "introduction to social anthropology" (29-58); Dorsey on "why we behave like human beings" (25-7); Tozzer on "social origins and social continuities" (25-25); Boas on "anthropology and modern life" (28-6); Dixon on "the building of cultures" (28-9); Lowie on "are we civilized?" (29-25). Of shorter general papers a considerable number appear by Boas, e.g., "the methods of ethnology" (20-2), Goldenweiser, Hrdlička, Lowie, Wissler, Dixon, Wallis, and Steward.

American scholars in this decade also contribute numerous studies in the historicalist manner focused upon particular ethnic groups or aspects and items of culture. Old and new names appear here, e.g., Spier on the development and differentiation of the "sun dance of the Plains" (21-22); Cushing, Fewkes and Parsons on "contributions to Hopi history" (22-5); Speck on "Algonkin influence upon Iroquois social organization" (23-21); Linton on "the degeneration of human figures used in Polynesian decorative art" (24-14); Cooper on "culture diffusion and culture areas in southern South America" (25-4); Goldfrank on "Isleta variants: a study in flexibility" (26-7); Hallowell on "bear ceremonialism in the northern hemisphere" (26-9); Herskovits on "the cattle complex in east Africa" (26-12); Hawley on "Pueblo social organization as a lead to Pueblo history" (28-13); Hough on "development of culture in relation to population" (29-16); Lesser on "kinship origins in the light of some distributions" (29-23); the Lynds pioneering with the first objective study of an American community, "Middletown" (29-26); Mead on "an inquiry into cultural stability in Polynesia" (28-25); and more general studies of social organization (20-16, 27-17), political development (24-8, 24-17, 27-24), education (27-16), and other topics, of which three books by Lowie on "primitive society," "primitive religion," and "the origin of the state" are classics. A similarly definitive work by Boas on "primitive art" (27-4) is important for general theory as well as for its specific subject matter.

Historicalism, with its "objective" recording and even counting of cultural traits in time and space, appeared at the time to represent the acme of scientific method. Yet science in this decade was becoming profoundly modified by new views, summarized by the philosopher of science Whitehead as "organismic." These were shifting emphasis from atomistic study of unit phenomena as such to the dimensions of "organization" and "wholeness," with new key concepts to the fore, such as "structure," "interrelationships," "relativity," "complementarity," "integration." Impinging upon fields of knowledge all the way from the physical sciences to the humanities, these were inevitably seeping into anthropological minds.

By the end of the decade, therefore, the historicalist theory and method was starting to come under attack, and studies were beginning which stress this newer holistic approach. Historicalists, critics said, in reducing observed behavior to "objective" trait units, were moving far from the realities of such behavior. Not only did this produce a fragmented, atomistic, and mechanistic result, but also it involved naïvetés in isolating, manipulating, and at times reifying such traits without full realization of their construct character. Furthermore, by shutting out the problems of the relation of culture to its individual carriers, or merely regarding them as passively stamped with the culture in its generation, the historicalist theory had in it at least implicitly a kind of "cultural determinism" unacceptable to many later scholars. The "descriptive" or "historical" approach, though still essential to observation and analysis, had to become handmaid to scientifically oriented problems and overtly formulated methodology if it was to be more than what Benedict was to call "anecdotal." Historicalists, defending themselves, replied that the newer ideas were implicit in their work, and so taken for granted, e.g., the terms "trait-complex" and "culture pattern" anticipated study of integrative tendencies in culture. Kluckhohn writes later of this:

> Precisely the great objection to the work of the followers of Boas is that they have taken too much for granted . . . The work of the Boas group was too much in the family tradition— it was not necessary to set down certain things of absolutely fundamental importance (such as techniques of field work) because these were handled largely on the basis of implicit agreement or on the basis of informal, oral, discussion. Such a tradition may achieve quite good results in practice as long as work goes on in the teacher-apprentice framework, but when the time comes for the general conclusions to be communicated to a larger intellectual fellowship (especially that of the other disciplines) it is most inadequate . . . We do need to make our abstract procedures as explicit as our evidential critiques or anthropology tends to be a little more than obscure antiquarianism. [1]

Because the newer ideas undergo their main development after this decade they will be discussed in a comprehensive way later. But two main streams of creative thought may be distinguished as starting here, one in British settings usually summed up in the term "functional," the other in the United States and called broadly "psychological." The two great figures in British functionalism, Malinowski and Radcliffe-Brown, each started his important work with a field monograph published in the same year,

---

[1]Kluckhohn, C., "Bronislaw Malinowski 1884–1942," Journal of American Folklore, 56: 209. 1943.

1922: <u>Argonauts</u> <u>of</u> the <u>Western</u> <u>Pacific</u>, and <u>The</u> <u>Andaman</u> <u>Islanders</u> respectively (not listed in bibliography as not strongly concerned with dynam-
ics). Malinowski's beginning conceptual system is best seen in an <u>Encyclo-
paedia</u> <u>Britannica</u> article on "anthropology" (26-19), while the markedly
different system of Radcliffe-Brown, often called a "neo-Durkheim" school
is foreshadowed in "the methods of ethnology and social anthropology"
(23-19). In the United States, pioneering work is shown in writings by
Sapir, who has been referred to as the one "genius" to appear in anthropology to date, in a book on "language" and papers on "culture, genuine
and spurious," and "the unconscious patterning of behavior" (21-17, 24-
20, 27-37); also works by Benedict on "psychological types in the cultures
of the Southwest" (28-4), Mead on "coming of age in Samoa" (28-24),
Róheim with a more marginal psychoanalytic emphasis on various topics
(21-14, 25-22, 26-28, etc.), and White on "personality and culture" (25-28
    Shorter-term historical, acculturation, and applied studies assume in-
creasingly scientific guise in this period. A selection of those worth special mention is somewhat arbitrary, but the following appear to be those
with most theoretical and methodological significance: Parson's "Pueblo
Indian journal" (20-20); Hewitt on changes in the Southwest art (20-11,
25-12, 25-13, 26-13); Radin's autobiography of an Indian "Crashing Thunder
(20-21); Jenness on "cultural transformation of the Copper Eskimo" (21-10)
Roy on "a new religious movement among the Oraons" in India (21-16);
Sapir's "life of a Nootka Indian" (21-18); "essays on the depopulation of
Melanesia," edited by Rivers (22-17); Papuan studies by Williams (23-27,
28-43, 28-44); Gifford on "Euro-American acculturation in Tonga" (24-7);
papers by Spier and Waterman on new religious movements in American
Indian groups (24-30, 27-40); two French papers on the psychology of religious conversion among non-Western peoples (25-1, 26-24); Herskovits
on "acculturation and the American Negro" (27-18); Pitt-Rivers on general
"contact" phenomena (27-32, 27-33); Keesing on "the changing Maori" (28-
15, 28-16, 29-18); Parsons on Spanish elements in Pueblo religion (28-29);
Redfield, anticipating his later "folk culture" concept in a study of "materia
culture of Spanish-Indian Mexico" (29-36); Schrieke in the volume he
edited on "western influence . . . in the Malay archipelago" (29-39); and
Thurnwald on "social problems of Africa" (29-51). A Bantu African speaking through the pen of Junod raises one of the many applied problems in
such contacts: "should heathen games be preserved?" (20-15). Two important items with longer-term perspective can also be singled out by
Nordenskiöld on American Indian inventiveness (20-19, 29-34), as well
as other materials on South American Indian acculturation (22-14, 22-15).
    Several works again focus anthropological attention upon the western
society of the period, e.g., Jenks on the "relation of anthropology to
Americanization" (21-8), Goldenweiser on "immigration and national life"
(26-6), and Wallis on "contemporary society as a culture phenomenon"
(29-56). More general items on applied anthropology are Haddon on "the
practical value of ethnology" (21-4), Jenks on "the practical value of an-

thropology to our nation" (21-9), Malinowski on "anthropology and administration" and "practical anthropology" (26-20, 29-29), and "anthropology
and government" by Sir Apirana Ngata, the New Zealand Maori statesman-
scholar, in a paper full of insights (28-28).

The compiler cannot pretend that this section gives a full review of the
proliferating works of this decade, and the same will apply even more to
the decades that follow. Sources are being expanded widely over the world
at this time, e.g., establishment of new journals such as _Africa_ and
Oceania. The emphasis is being put in this analysis upon significant theoretical and methodological trends, and the works that in the judgment of
the compiler carry them forward most definitively.

1930–1939

The best way to grapple with some 650 references found for this decade
will be to trace first the main works which are characteristic of each
school. Special problems of significance for culture change, e.g., acculturation, applied anthropology, will then be discussed.

Writings in the evolutionist tradition are thinned to a trickle, and are
marginal to professional work in anthropology (e.g., 37-17). The vocabulary and assumptions involved continue to make anthropologists unhappy
by having some vogue in works by occasional students especially in other
fields when they write on so-called primitives or cultural origins and
early development, e.g., the Yale "science of society" group carrying on
the Sumner-Keller tradition. By this time, however, use of the term "evolution," shorn of its old unilinear framework, occasionally creeps back
into the vocabulary of some anthropologists to express the larger perspectives of culture process (see 30-13).

The British Egypt-centric school, which was so vocal in the last decade,
vanished almost wholly with Smith's death. The French Durkheimian tradition, particularly the work of Lévy-Bruhl, also came largely to a dead
end in theoretical terms, except as it had derivative vigor in the Radcliffe-
Brown functional systematics (below). The German-Austrian _kulturkreise_
approach, however, continued with some vigor, particularly centered in
the journal _Anthropos_ and the work of Schmidt and Koppers, at Vienna
(30-25, 31-19, 31-38, etc.); most notable is Father Schmidt's _Handbuch
der Methode der kulturhistorischen Ethnologie_ (37-55), with its English
equivalent (39-79). A critique by Kluckhohn, who worked for a time at
Vienna, should be read with this (36-30).

More in the historicalist tradition, but with the expected generalizing
tendencies, Old World scholars continued to produce considerable work
involving time-dimensional approaches to cultural study. In the United
Kingdom, Harrison does further writing on "invention" (30-17, 30-18);
and Marett (32-31, 33-26), Westermarck (32-58, 33-40, 36-71), Sayce
(33-34, 38-69), Forde (34-12, 39-31), Hornell (34-21), Seligman (34-50),

and the archaeologist Childe (35-13, 35-14, 37-6, etc.), were among
other creative writers. In Germany the publications of Thurnwald, marked
by strong interest in sociological and psychological dimensions, as well
as sound field work in Oceania and Africa, is outstanding (31-43, 31-44,
31-45, 31-46, etc.); most notable of his theoretical and applied works relating to change is his highly important paper on the "psychology of acculturation," and "contributions toward analysis of the mechanism of culture"
(32-51, 36-66, 37-62). Examples of the relevant writings of other German
scholars are Dempwolff (32-12), Plischke (32-42), Weinert (32-57), Mühlmann (34-40, 38-58, 38-59), and Cunow (37-8). Among other professional
names of significance are for Europe Birket-Smith (30-6), Nordenskiöld
(30-34, 38-61), Métraux (31-31, 34-37), Mus (33-28), Karsten (35-31),
Shirokogoroff (37-57); in India Chattopadhay (31-4), Mills (31-32), Ghurye
(32-18), and Hutton (37-25); and in Indonesia Schrieke (37-54). But the
main historicalist-diffusionist work was still being done in the American
setting, where it was being modified only slowly by the newer creative
traditions.

United States scholars, broadly speaking, in this decade tended to
stress the historical method in field work and museum settings, but in
their university contacts to veer toward more theoretically oriented studies
in "social anthropology," not least of all with an eye on, and eyed by, colleagues in interested collateral disciplines. Again the list of historicalist
studies is far too long to cover, but some key items may be listed for special reference and illustration: Kroeber on "diffusion," the "culture-area
and age-area concepts," "historical reconstruction of culture growths,"
"history and science in anthropology," "area and climax" with reference
to extensive "culture element distribution" studies on Western Indian peoples
being carried on under his leadership at the time in the University of California, "cultural and natural areas in North America" (30-26, 30-27, 31-20,
31-21, 35-34, 36-32, 39-52), and with Driver a statistically oriented study
of "quantitative expression of cultural relationships" (32-14); Lowie on
"inventiveness of the American Indian," and discussions of historicalism
in his "history of ethnological theory" (31-25, 37-35); Nelson on "the origin
and development of material culture" (32-38); Cole on "the long road . . .
to civilization" (33-6); Goldenweiser on "history, psychology, and culture,"
"theory on the individual, pattern, and involution," and "the concept of
causality" (33-12, 36-16, 38-29); Boas on "the tempo of growth of fraternities," "history and science in anthropology," and "invention" (35-5, 36-4,
38-10); Linton on "errors in anthropology," and also an important general
text on "the study of man" (36-35, 36-36); Strong on "anthropological theory
and archaeological fact" (36-62); Hart on "the culture-complex as a research tool" (39-39); Radin on "the mind of primitive man" (39-71); and
Swanton on "some thoughts on the problem of progress and decline" (39-88).

In addition to general works there are a considerable number of more
specific studies dealing in a dominantly historicalist manner with long-
or short-term changes in particular ethnic groups or aspects of culture.

Perhaps most notable are studies on Negro groups in the New World by
Herskovits (30-19, 32-21, 33-15, etc.); on history and acculturation in
Pacific island areas by Handy (30-15, 31-8, 31-9, etc.), Keesing (30-24,
31-15, 32-25, etc.), Buck (31-3, 36-6, 38-13, etc.), Dixon on distribution
of the sweet-potato (32-13), Burrows (38-14), and Thompson (38-76, 38-
85); on diffusion of Asian cultural elements by Laufer (30-28, 31-23); on
California Indian cultures by Klimek (35-33); on Hispanic and modern influences in Middle America and the Southwest by Parsons (30-35, 30-36,
32-39, etc.), Redfield (30-41, 33-30, 33-31, etc.), Beals (32-3), Bennett
and Zingg (35-4, 39-99), Haines (38-31, 38-32), Woodward (38-90),
Luomala (38-53), and Hill (39-42); on history and acculturation of other
Indian groups by Swanton (30-46, 30-47, 39-87), Barbeau (31-1, 33-4,
36-2, etc.), MacLeod (31-26, 31-27, 33-25, etc.), Speck (31-40, 33-36),
Boas "on current beliefs of the Kwakiutl" (32-8), Mekeel (32-34, 32-35,
36-43, etc.) Cooper (33-7, 34-7, 39-15, etc.), Hewitt (33-16, 34-19, 38-
39), Lesser (33-23, 33-24), Jacobs (34-24), Wissler (34-54, 36-75, 36-76,
etc.), Spier (35-49), Ray (36-53), Hawley (37-20), Densmore (38-21),
Keesing (39-47), Lips (39-56), and Steward (39-85); on "culture migrations
and contacts in the Bering Sea region" by Collins (37-7); on cultural chronology in the Australian region by Davidson (35-18, 38-18); on changes
among the Toda of India by Emeneau (38-23, 39-27); on "culture contact
without conflict" between Tungus and Cossacks in Manchuria by Lindgren
(38-50); on long-term changes in various cultural elements by Hough (30-
22, 30-23, 31-13, etc.); and on religion by Radin (37-48) and Wallis (39-
95).

In this decade, for the first time, attempts were made to define more
systematically the field of culture contact or acculturation. This came into
initial focus, so far as American historicalists were concerned, in a
classic delimitation and analysis of "acculturation" prepared by a committee of the Social Science Research Council consisting of Redfield, Linton,
and Herskovits (36-54):

> Acculturation comprehends those phenomena which result when
> groups of individuals having different cultures come into continu-
> ous first-hand contact, with subsequent changes in the original
> cultural patterns of either or both groups. Under this definition,
> acculturation is to be distinguished from culture-change, of which
> it is but one aspect, and assimilation, which is at times a phase
> of acculturation. It is also to be differentiated from diffusion,
> which while occurring in all instances of acculturation, is not
> only a phenomenon which frequently takes place without the oc-
> currence of the types of contact between peoples specified in the
> definition given above, but also constitutes only one aspect of the
> process of acculturation.

Linton elaborated his ideas further in his "study of man" (36-35), and
Herskovits followed up with a small book on "acculturation" (38-38; see

also 37-23). Further general and methodological statements were offered
by Keesing (39-48), and by a number of other workers in the next decade.

The work of one scholar listed above, Redfield, may be singled out for
additional discussion as being associated with a special conceptual framework summed up in the term "folk society." Though having earlier usage
in sociology, this was applied by Redfield to categorize the type of fused
Hispanic-American peasant community which he first described in his
study of the Mexican village of Tepoztlan (30-41). Such a type stood historically and culturally between the indigenous Indian society of pre-Columbian
days and the modern metropolitan elements which were penetrating particularly around the central plaza area. Redfield continued to develop the
theme in additional studies of Yucatán and Guatemalan communities (33-
30, 33-31, 34-44, 37-49, 39-73), including experiments with equating
historical processes of transition from folk to urban society with the geographic distribution of older and more modern cultural elements as between
the remote village by way of transitional communities to the town center.
Redfield's work also represents a milestone in "community studies" which
in this decade begin to assume theoretical importance as one of the many
approaches in understanding group behavior. With Redfield's work might
be mentioned the study of the sociologist Lynd and his wife of "Middletown,"
which, with its sequel on changes in this Midwestern town during the depression of the 'thirties, was made in the historicalist manner with guid-
ance from Wissler (29-26, 37-36).

Redfield's work, and increasingly that of others who had originally been
trained in the historicalist tradition, was being influenced by the integrative "holistic" tendencies, referred to briefly in the previous section as
"functionalism" and the "configurational" or so-called "psychological"
approach. These may be introduced by way of the British "functional"
schools, which reach their main theoretical and methodological formulation in this decade.

Already reference was made to the initial work of Malinowski. This
brilliant Polish scholar turned Englishman was based for most of his career
at the London School of Economics and Political Science, but at the end
of the decade transferred to Yale University for a brief period until his
death in 1942. The rounding out of the very distinctive Malinowskian systematics may perhaps be seen best by comparing his definitive statement
on "culture" in the Encyclopaedia of the Social Sciences (30-31), with his
final posthumously published works to be noted later. His ideas were focused on developing a "scientific theory of culture" looked at in its totality,
and drawing its case materials from contemporary field observation; for
this purpose data from the past could not in his thinking be full and controlled enough to yield scientifically valid conclusions. Malinowski, indeed,
purported to make an entirely fresh start with what he called the "functional
method" of social anthropology, and took every opportunity to pour ridicule
on evolutionary, historicalist, diffusionist, and other approaches. Every
element in human culture has its "function," i.e., it is meaningfully related

to all other elements in the culture concerned, and has a purpose in meeting needs. Furthermore, culture everywhere has the same universal aspects — a material substratum, economics, social organization, political organization, law, religion, aesthetics, language — which are based variously upon the same biological, derived (instrumental), and integrative (synthetic) needs or imperatives. The effective elements of culture are not isolated "traits" but "institutions": organized systems of activity involving personnel, an ideology, a legal charter, continuity, needs.

Malinowski's earlier formulations tend to represent the analysis of culture under static conditions. Later he takes more account of the "laws" of "culture process," examining "not only what cultural varieties are but how they work and how they change." His writings throw up numerous statements which could be worked on as hypotheses to be tested through research: fundamental changes come through "increasing differentiation of form in accordance with an increasingly definite function": the vanguard of change is often found in "works of leisure and supererogation"; "what diffuses are institutions and not 'traits,' 'forms,' or 'fortuitous complexes' " — these examples out of many. Malinowski failed, however, to face definitively the theoretical problems of (a) lack of functional consistency in a given cultural setting, or (b) change of function. A posthumous book was published in the next decade on "the dynamics of culture change" (45-79), but deals rather superficially with acculturation and applied phenomena.

The impact of Malinowski's creative insights was very great both in and outside anthropology. The "functional method," overtly formulated or otherwise, became accepted as part of the necessary sphere of reference for both field work and theory. But by the later 1930's his conceptual system was already proving too rigid and idiosyncratic to carry forward the research problems of the time, even among his British pupils, e.g., his scheme of needs, inadequate in terms of the newer psychological approaches, his lack of interest in "form," his overstress on functional consistency, his contempt for historical and distributional studies. Subsequent ramifications of the Malinowski ideas will be discussed in the next section.[1] But he will be referred to again in connection with acculturation studies below.

Radcliffe-Brown, the second great creative figure in British functionalism, has held academic posts not only in England at the beginning and later stages of his academic career but also in South Africa, Australia, the United States (University of Chicago), and briefly China, South America, and the Near East. His conceptual system might alternatively be called "social structuralism" because of the primacy given to behavior in terms of the social structure or interrelations among members of any group, or of "society" more generally. (He was noted earlier as being labeled a "neo-Durkheimian.")

---

[1]An important recent analysis of the significance of the functional dimensions in sociocultural theory is by the sociologist Robert K. Merton, Social theory and social structure: 21-82. New York, 1949.

Radcliffe-Brown's influential teaching in varied settings, backed up by relatively rare written materials, followed somewhat the evolutionary approach in looking on a society as analogous to an organism. The task of the social anthropologist is to study the social "morphology" (physiology, structure, etc.) and "functional" interrelations of the parts (i.e., individuals and groups), from which he can ascertain the contributions they make to the total integration, hence to the survival interests of the society.

> The function of any recurrent activity, such as the punishment of a crime, or a funeral ceremony, is the part it plays in the social life as a whole, and therefore the contribution it makes to the maintenance of the structural continuity (35-44).

Like Malinowski, he believed that research in contemporary settings should precede historical reconstruction, or in his vocabulary "synchronic" (cross-sectional) studies should come before "diachronic" (time-dimensional) studies. But he also believed that his systematics could be applied in time to dynamic, even long-term cultural processes, e.g., see his biting critique of Davidson's diffusion studies on Australian Aborigines and his classic reconstructions of Australian social organization (30-38, 30-40). Also going beyond Malinowski he laid emphasis on studies of society (he uses the term "culture" sparingly in his work) as an "adaptive" system, ranging in particular cases from being well integrated to the other extreme of having its survival threatened or undermined through "dysfunction." To express the concept of "healthy integration" he adopted from Durkheim the term "eunomia," but with its opposite "dysnomia" to express conditions of relative functional inconsistency rather than Durkheim's anomie. Corresponding categories in terms of feelings of well-being or malaise are "euphoria" and "dysphoria."

Even with this greater emphasis on dynamics, however, the Radcliffe-Brown system as such provides the student of culture process with only a very general and highly categorized frame of reference. It passes over, for example, many of the key concerns of the newer American theorists in by-passing the study of the individual as such with the assumption that he can be "left to the psychologist." Even his closest students found need to break through into newer dimensions of analysis and to develop more precise terms and categories. But as with Malinowski his overtly formulated ideas on scientific standards and methods, and particularly his "social structure" and "social integration" concepts, helped to create great dissatisfactions with the older historically oriented approaches.

Malinowski's students went particularly into the British African areas by way of the International Institute of African Studies, Rhodes-Livingstone Foundation, and other institutional sponsorship, as will be seen from works by Evans-Pritchard, Perham, Richards, Mair, Read, Fortes, Nadel, Wagner, Hofstra, Wilson, Hunter, and others, mostly including a strong acculturation emphasis and often applied anthropology dimensions. But others worked elsewhere, e.g., Firth and Piddington in the Pacific area, Fei in China, and Majumdar in India. In a number of instances such younger British scholars came under influence both from Radcliffe-Brown and Malinowski, as with Firth, Evans-Pritchard, Piddington, Bateson, Fortune, Beaglehole. The Radcliffe-Brown training shows particularly in the work of Schapera in South Africa; Elkin, Hogbin, Kaberry, Wedgwood, Blackwood, the American scholar Warner, and numbers of others by way of his Australian period; and in the United States Eggan, Embree, Nash, Tax, and others. Derivative influences of the Radcliffe-Brown systematics within American social anthropology, particularly by way of Warner, will be traced in the next decade.

It is impossible within the space available to analyze at all fully the rich and varied materials on cultural dynamics being worked on by scholars of these two "functional" traditions. But a selection of references may indicate something of the emphasis and range of topics, and the theoretical and methodological approaches involved. Malinowski himself writes on anthropology's contributions to colonial administration and education, changes in African culture, "the present state of studies in culture contact," and "the dynamics of contemporary diffusion" (30-30, 36-38, 38-56, 38-57, 39-58, 39-59); Radcliffe-Brown on "applied anthropology" (30-39). Of others, Piddington writes on "the psychology of culture-contact" (32-41); Elkin on acculturation and policy matters relating to the Australian Aborigines (33-9, 34-10, 35-21, 35-22, etc.); Hunter on methods of study of culture contact, and a major study of change among the African Pondo (34-23, 36-28); Mair on culture-contact studies in terms of method (34-34, 38-54, 38-55); Schapera on field methods, and changes in South Africa (34-48, 34-49, etc.); Bateson on "schismogenesis" and other dynamic processes (35-1, 36-3); Brown and Hutt on "anthropology in action," in which experimental situations of applied anthropology are discussed (35-9); Evans-Pritchard and Richards on "witchcraft" and culture change (35-23, 35-45); Richards on "the village census in the study of culture contact" (35-46); Firth on initial reactions to contact in Tikopia (36-12); Fortes on "culture contact as a dynamic process" (36-14); Perham on Nigerian peoples (36-52); Eggan on kinship change (37-13); Majumdar on culture change situations in India (37-37, 39-57); Nash on a case of religious revivalism (37-44); Tax on Guatemalan communities (37-59, 39-89); Read on "standards of living and African culture change" (38-66); Embree on immigrant Japanese in Hawaii (39-26); Hogbin on rapid change in the Solomons (39-43); and Wagner on a case study of African family change (39-94).

In the United States the "functional" approach tended in this same creative decade to be conjoined with more comprehensive "psychological" and other approaches noted incipiently in the last section. The recognized pioneer here was Sapir, trained originally in the Boas tradition, and developing his insights particularly through his early studies of language. Sapir came to see "culture" not as having a separate, more or less reified, existence but as the largely unconscious patterned behavior of individuals based on common conditioning to the same communicative symbols.

That culture is a superorganic, impersonal whole is a useful
enough methodological principle to begin with, but becomes a seri-
ous deterrent in the long run to the more dynamic study of the
genesis and development of cultural patterns because these cannot
be realistically disconnected from those organizations of ideas and
feelings which constitute the individual . . . The true locus of culture is in the interactions of specific individuals, and on the subjective side, in the world of meanings which each one of those individuals may unconsciously abstract for himself from his participation in these interactions (32-48).

Sapir's brilliant mind, influencing students particularly at the University
of Chicago and later, until his death in 1939, at Yale, and combining
aesthetic with scientific interests, is seen in retrospect as anticipating
practically the whole range of modern theory. He traced, often well ahead
of both controlled data and method, great consistencies in language and
culture. His later work stressed particularly the relation of culture to the
individual, e. g., personality formation, normality and abnormality, and
the potentialities more generally of interdisciplinary co-operation among
cultural anthropologists, psychologists, psychiatrists, psychoanalysts,
and other workers in this great common field of problems. Nowhere in
his scattered writings, for all their many important insights and hypotheses
which bear upon culture in time-dimensional aspects (30-44, 32-48, 34-46,
etc., and most accessible in his "collected writings" edited by Mandelbaum,
1949), did he offer any comprehensive formulation apart from an early
classic on criteria of historical reconstruction (16-28). Sapir's conceptual-
izations, however, affected profoundly such studies not only by his immediate pupils and associates (Mekeel, Opler, Dollard, and others to be noted)
but also less directly virtually all others working with theoretical and
methodological problems in mind.

    At Columbia University another Boas-trained scholar, Benedict, was
working along rather closely related pattern-function lines of thought.
Poet as well as scientist, she became interested by way of American Indian case materials in delineating cultural systems in terms of their
"psychological types," or dominating and pervasive "configurations." The
early phases of her work culminated by 1934 in the small but highly influential book on "patterns of culture," and an article published in the same
year on "anthropology and the abnormal" (28-4, 31-2, 32-4, 34-4, 34-5).
Benedict's theory, as that of other systematizers of this period, grappled
with the problem of a scientific delineation of culture in its totality. For
such analysis she treated her materials for the most part synchronically,
holding them stationary in time while examining them as wholes.

A culture, like an individual, is a more or less consistent pattern
of thought and action. Within each culture there come into being
characteristic purposes not shared by other types of society . . .
[Cultures] differ from one another not only because one trait is

present here and absent there . . . [but] still more because they
are oriented as wholes in different directions . . . [The significant
unit is] the cultural configuration (34-4).

Following leads already extant to a degree in the work of such social
philosophers as Dilthey and Spengler, and also using some of the behavioral
categories recognized in psychology, she characterized dominant "configurations" in cultures with which she was experimenting as variously
"Dionysian" (individualistic, aggressive, introvert, etc.) or "Appolonian"
(conforming, ceremonious, extrovert, etc.), or again "paranoid," "melago-
manic," et al. By way of their preadult conditioning, individuals in each
society become normal or deviant in the degree that their behavior ap-
proximates to the particular configurations (purposes, values, ideals,
goals, etc.) represented in the culture concerned.

Benedict's approach provoked vigorous initial criticism, both from
many American historicalists and from the British functionalists. The
methods by which her generalizations, or constructs, were reached were
said to be too subjective and selective, involving the intuitions of art
rather than science. But even cautious scholars had to acknowledge that
she was touching upon "covert" dimensions of group behavior and motivation which could not be by-passed or dismissed as mysticism even if not
yielding to "overt" observation and measurement. Neither of the British
functional systems delineated above, for all their theoretical emphasis
on cultural or social integration, had worked strongly upon these differences among cultures treated as wholes which make each more or less
unique.

Benedict made a few sketchy points in her "patterns of culture" on
time-dimensional phenomena, especially in a final chapter emphasizing
fluidity of culture and personality in the American setting. In considerable
further work, particularly in the next decade up to her death in 1948, she
paid sporadic attention to culture dynamics in both its theoretical and
appli d settings, as in various "national character" studies relating to
modern states. Her general ideas on "culture change" are set out in two
later articles (42-12, 43-3). The direct or indirect influences of her work
on that of others, as will be seen below, was to be very great. More
widely the further development of configurational theory, and the quest
for greater scientific control in the study of patterns, orientations, values,
or whatever other concepts particular scholars choose to apply to inte-
grational phenomena, form one of the major preoccupations of contemporary social anthropology, as indeed of cultural studies in other disciplines.

Mead, Benedict's first graduate student, had struck out during the
last decade in the then novel direction of studying child development in a
cultural setting, Samoa, extremely different from that familiar in Western
countries (28-24). She followed up with widely read studies of preadult
conditioning in a series of other societies as correlated with adult "character structure." Mead's work merged closely in its further development

with that of Benedict, and was to range particularly in the next decade
across a wide zone of educational, governmental, psychoanalytic, and other
problems. Specific time-dimensional studies in this period include a book
on "the changing culture of an Indian tribe" (31-29, 32-32, 35-38, etc.).

The strong psychological orientations of Sapir, Benedict, and Mead
included growing liaisons with psychiatry and psychoanalysis, particularly
with reference to child rearing and dynamic social conditions in cross-
cultural contexts. Their work, and that of other anthropologists stimulated
by them and to be mentioned below, rounded out rather more exotic materials being tried out by Róheim and a few others (32-47, 33-33, 34-44,
etc.), following up earlier, none too successful, attempts by Freud, Jung,
Adler and other pioneers of psychoanalysis to weave anthropological data
into their systems.[1] Another strong lead in developing anthropological-
psychoanalytic collaboration in this decade came from an interdisciplinary
group working at Columbia University from 1936 on, under joint leadership
of Linton and Kardiner.

Linton, previously working at the University of Wisconsin, had written
an influential introductory text on "the study of man" (36-35). This bridged,
more than any previous work, between the older historicalist approach
and psychological-sociological interests of generalizing social science,
e. g. , culture growth, personality formation, participation, status and role,
integration, to mention a few of the topics looked at with a rather fresh
view, and welded into a consistent system. Linton was appointed to head
the Columbia department when Boas retired. Collaboration with psychoanalyst Kardiner started by way of a joint seminar in which, over the years
to World War II, a series of anthropologists were used as informants on
the minutiae of child rearing and other significant behavior in societies
which they had studied. Out of this material, Kardiner took the main lead
in trying out what might be called a kind of "culturoanalysis" for the group
concerned, with special reference to what became conceptualized as the
"basic personality structure" or "modal personality" characteristic of each
culture, produced by the particular conditioning processes in childhood,
and consistent with the institutions and values of the adult society. Linton,
dissatisfied with Kardiner's Freudian emphasis upon a kind of infantile
determinism, added further dimensions in his complementary concept of
"status personality": child and adult alike continue to develop secondary
personality characteristics by way of sex, age, class, occupation, and
other group and individual roles in which they participate (38-51, 38-52,
39-55). The first major report on this Columbia seminar work appears in
1939 (39-46), and it has an important continuing literature in the next decade,
including fuller consideration of dynamics beyond the short-run period of
preadult conditioning.

Another "psychological" lead of markedly different character was becoming influential in social anthropology at this time: the Yale "learning

---

[1]See, for example, Freud's Totem and Taboo.

theory" approach. Formation at Yale University of the Institute of Human Relations brought cultural anthropologists into close contact with an experimental group of psychologists and others working on learning experiments, particularly with laboratory animals (the group had included for some time already Yerkes and some other physical anthropologists working with anthropoids). Particularly under leadership from Dollard (e.g., 34-9, 39-20), and with tangential encouragement from Sapir, a general conceptual system being developed in relation to learning was applied to man's cultural learning, and to cross-cultural reference.

Reduced to its main categories, this approach looks at cultures as "adaptive" systems of behavior based on learned "habits," and "personality" development as the training of individuals in such standardized habits. Habit formation starts from "drives," either "primary" as with the biologically given tensions such as hunger, sex, and excretion, or "acquired" ("secondary") as with food tastes, sleeping habits, and fears specifically defined in a particular cultural setting. Drives involve anxieties, dilemmas, and also anticipation and generalization in terms of a context of prior learning. "Cues" provided variously by the external habitat and the somatic, cultural, and social situations lead to "responses" directed toward reducing drive tension. These may take random or trial-and-error form in man as with a rat in a maze. But because culture normally provides standardized responses for almost all situations the individual will meet (especially in a stable society), humans tend to follow previous learning or to proceed by "imitation" or "identification": in the case of a child, parents or parent substitutes are usually there to point to the acceptable goal responses. Suitable responses bring "reward," that is, relief from tension, with attendant cultural or other specific benefits. From this comes "reinforcement" of the existing habit or "readaptation" in the case of a new response. Should, however, a response bring "punishment," or denial of reward, it tends to inhibit the existing habit or cut off the potential new behavior. Persisting inhibition or punishment, or indeed, anticipatory fear of it, increases anxiety, leads to "frustration," which in turn may find outlet in "aggression" or in various other forms of neurotic or psychotic behavior.

The Yale learning theory is counted by social scientists as only one of a number of systematic approaches to learning, and the very precision of its categories tends not only to order but also to limit its usefulness in analyzing the many variables in dynamic human experience. Focused on observation of specific behavior, as in laboratory animals, it still leaves a large place for other theoretical approaches to fill in the totality of cultural contexts, including the functional-configurational levels of analysis and total-personality data. Furthermore, though it goes further than any other systematic approach to data in defining actual contexts and processes of the learning situation, it tends to have a somewhat mechanical ring when applied to actual case materials of culture change and resistance to change in human societies. Culture change involves much more complex dimensions than merely the individuals concerned unlearning one set of habits and learning another, or adding new habits to prior habits. Fortunately the Yale-inspired group, as will be seen particularly in works of the next decade, has been extending its field studies and theory to work on wider and less atomistic dimensions of culture process, while still using this conceptual system for the main guide points.

Before evaluating specific time-dimensional works with these psychological emphases, still other theoretical leads must be noted in this highly productive decade as meshing themselves more or less with such psychological approaches yet in themselves perhaps best called "sociological." The pertinent interests of Redfield ("folk society") and of Radcliffe-Brown and his students ("social structure") at the University of Chicago have already been discussed. Additionally, one of Radcliffe-Brown's American protégés who worked with him in Australia, Warner, was having a marked influence upon theory and method in both social anthropology and sociology, first at Harvard and later at Chicago.

Starting essentially with the social structure approach of Radcliffe-Brown, Warner and a group of student associates undertook a succession of studies in modern Western communities, notably in this period a peasant group in Ireland (37-1, 40-2), "Yankee City" (Newburyport, Mass., 41-77, 41-78, etc.), and "Deep South" community (Natchez, Miss., 41-16, etc.), in the last-named unit using separate White and Negro field work teams. While Warner's work became best known for its delineations of American class structure, it also presented important leads for the study of social mobility and cultural change. To Warner, "society" is a group of "mutually interacting individuals," and "events or activities, to be understood, must be placed in an immediate social relational context." The "total system of interaction" is made the basis of analysis, with all its "interpersonal relations," "interdependent statuses" (class, age, etc.), and other dimensions, including consideration of the individual in terms of the "equilibrium of the social structure." These concepts were to undergo further operational definition by some of Warner's associates of the time, especially Chapple (39-14) and Arensberg, in works of the next decade, and to provide the basis for something of a "school" of highly quantified "interaction" studies dealing primarily with industrial and other dimensions of contemporary American society. Though the main emphasis of Warner and his associates was on the stabilities of social structure, integration, the equilibria of interaction, account was also taken of changes as expressed in dysnomic conditions, disequilibria, with possible attendant neurotic and psychotic manifestations in individuals. The strengths of working with such a definite set of concepts and constructs, however, had as with other highly systematized approaches corrollary limitations that go with forcing the rich and variable texture of human behavior into one particular set of molds— even in the name of science.

Tracing now the ramifications of these new trends in the writings of other scholars, it must be noted that most of the workers to be referred to came under multiple influences from these creative new systems, not least of all because some of them studied in several of the institutional settings concerned. Most of the individuals mentioned took their first formal training in the Boasian tradition, and then branched out into problem-oriented studies in which they experimented with these fresh ideas. Cooper shows the new trend with papers on a "psychosis" among the Cree, and "mental disease" and "adjustment" in cross-cultural contexts (33-7, 34-7, 39-16). Hallowell writes on "culture and mental disorder" (34-15) and Morris Opler on "the psychoanalytic treatment of culture" (35-41). Then from 1936 to the end of the decade a small flood of papers come out. Without attempting a complete inventory the following works appear to the compiler to have most significance for studies in the culture change field: Gillin on "the configuration problem in culture" and "some unfinished business in cultural anthropology" (36-15, 39-34); Hallowell on "psychic stresses and culture patterns," "fear and anxiety . . . in a primitive society," "Shabwan: a dissocial Indian girl," "the child, the savage, and human experience," and several more ethnographically oriented papers (36-19, 37-19, 38-33, 38-34, etc.); Mekeel on social science approaches to psychiatric and other applied problems (35-40, 36-42, 36-43, 37-41); Morris Opler especially on the significance of the peyote cult among Apache groups (36-47, 38-62, 38-63, etc.); Beaglehole on "cultural compensation" and other psychologically oriented phenomena in various Polynesian groups (37-3, 37-4, 38-6, etc.); DuBois on "some psychological objectives and techniques in ethnography," "some anthropological perspectives on psychoanalysis," and a study of the Indian ghost dance of 1870 (37-10, 37-11, 39-21); Erickson with a most provocative study of Sioux child rearing in an acculturation context (37-14); Landes on delineation of Ojibwa culture and personality (37-30, 38-45, 38-46, etc.); Mandelbaum on "boom periods" of a tribe in India (37-38); Aginsky on "psychopathic trends in culture" and an analysis of time levels in the role of the family (39-1, 39-2); Devereaux on "maladjustment and social neurosis" (39-18); Ford of the Yale learning group on "society, culture, and the human organism" (39-30); Kluckhohn on "theoretical bases for and empirical methods of studying the acquisition of culture by individuals" and a further methodological study (39-50, 39-51); also studies of particular groups involving psychological dimensions by Kennard (37-29), Leighton (37-34), Erminie Voegelin (37-64), Dyk (38-22), Holden (38-40), La Barre (38-44); Miner on a French-Canadian parish (39-64); Powdermaker in a study of Negroes in the Deep South (39-70); and the English scholars Bateson (35-1, 36-3, 37-2), and Gorer (38-30).

A notable feature of this decade is a strong interest shown by archaeologists in the theoretical implications of their methods, not only in relation to long-standing historical-diffusionist concerns characteristic of the meticulous work of professionals in this field of anthropology, but also as regards the implications of the functional and psychological approaches for reconstruction of cultural dynamics of the past. This can perhaps be

seen best in Strong's discussion of "anthropological theory and archaeological fact" (36-62), Steward and Setzler on "function and configuration
in archaeology" (38-73), Gifford on "typology for archaeology" (39-33),
and a general discussion of the archaeologist's opportunities and potential
contributions in the field of culture dynamics by Rouse (39-77). Examples
of other works involving such dimensions are by Kidder (31-17), Roberts
(32-46), Gorodzov (33-13), Childe (35-14, 37-6), and Mera (39-63). As
pointed out in the preface, however, this bibliography does not attempt to
be comprehensive in relation to more detailed archaeological contributions
to cultural dynamics.

A last group of anthropological studies worth selecting out consists of
works by anthropologists employed by governments overseas, mainly with
an applied emphasis. Notable examples are the New Guinea studies of
Williams (30-49, 33-42, 33-41, etc.), Chinnery (32-10), Todd (35-59),
and Groves (36-17, etc.); also studies by Mills (31-32) and Hutton (38-41)
in India, Noone in Malaya (39-67), and Brown and Hutt (35-9) and a number
of others in Africa (see under "functionalism" above). Studies of this type
proliferate greatly in the next decade.

A selected group of writings highly relevant to the anthropological frame
of reference and done by scholars in collateral professions has been included in this part of the bibliography. The work of Hodgen on "survivals"
relates to the "social institutions" approach of Teggart (31-11, 33-17,
36-26). Of works by sociologists, psychologists and others the following
are illustrative of the interests involved: Price on "culture conflict" (30-
37); LaPiere and Wang on "incidence and sequence in social change" (31-
22); Becker on population movement and culture contact (33-5); Klineberg
on the Huichol (34-30); Cantril on "cultural lag" (35-11), Gilfillan on "invention" (35-24); Lasswell on "collective autism" resulting from culture
contact (35-35); Pemberton on "a curve of culture diffusion" (36-51, 37-46,
38-64); Bowers on "the direction of intra-societal diffusion" (37-5); Murphy
on "personality and social adjustments" (37-43); Sorokin on "social and
cultural dynamics" (37-58); Anderson on "change and personality" (38-3);
and Stern on the family and social change (39-84).

4. RECENT WORKS

For this latest period, with its very extensive and expanding coverage, the materials are so complex that they can best be dealt with in a year-by-year summary. But this will be preceded by a brief general exposition of the major theoretical currents so as to give continuity to the preceding sections.

1940–1952

From about 1940 on, studies in the area of culture change, culture contact, and acculturation are being given increasingly the more general label of "cultural dynamics," and textbooks of the period usually have a special section on this topic. The number of regional and topical serials is expanding, including several emphasizing applied problems, e.g., Applied Anthropology (later called Human Organization), American Indigena, South Pacific. In 1941, a Society for Applied Anthropology was formed in the United States, mainly under the influence of the Chapple "interaction" group centered at Harvard, and the great intensification of applied studies especially during World War II made this approach much more "respectable" academically. Anthropological theory and technique now use as their starting points of reference not only problems emerging within the scientific frame of reference but also a wide range of practical issues: colonial and minority administration, agricultural extension, education, social service, industrial organization, military intelligence needs, psychological warfare, morale, military government, Japanese war relocation on the Pacific coast, relief and rehabilitation, and in due course ECA, MSA, "Point Four," United Nations trusteeship, UNESCO studies—and even this list is not exhaustive.

On the theoretical side, "evolutionism," apparently long since dead so far as professional anthropologists were concerned (though the term "evolution" was now being used again somewhat by some scholars for the generalization of history), undergoes a surprising one-man revival in the United States. White, of the University of Michigan, became interested in trying to justify the main approach of the early American scholar, Morgan (77-11). The latter, though relegated to the classics in his home country, had a continuing vogue in Russia as having been used by Engels as a basis for Soviet dialectics relating to cultural growth and primitive society.[1] Starting in 1943, as will be seen, White writes a whole series of works spelling out his revisions of evolutionary theory, and in doing so attacks virtually all the later approaches from Boasian

---

[1]The place of Morgan's ideas in contemporary Soviet thought is discussed by Tolstoy (52-208). He considers that only recently has their hold begun to wane in terms of the accepted "scientific" interpretations, though they are likely to be given "continuing honor."

historicalism to the "psychological" schools. For purposes of anthropological theory, he tries to insist, the individual is "irrelevant," because
"culture can only be explained in terms of culture," i.e., "culturologi-
cally." White goes beyond the older evolutionism in setting up what he
considers an objective criterion for evaluating evolutionary progress: the
"amount of energy harnessed by man per capita per year . . . [or] the
efficiency of the technological means of putting this energy to work . . .
[or] both factors . . . simultaneously" (43-103, 45-109, 45-110, etc.).
Though White's views become considerably publicized by vigorous presentation, no professional following has fallen in behind him.

In the United Kingdom a few scholars, notably Childe, still tend to use
the old terminology of "savagery" and "barbarism," along with "evolution,"
in which they encapsulate sound factual data from archaeology and ethnology.
But the dominant theory, now that extremes of "diffusionism" are moribund, is a "social structure" approach in which concepts and ideas from
both Malinowski and Radcliffe-Brown have tended to fuse, e.g., as seen
in general works on "social anthropology" by Evans-Pritchard (51-60),
Firth (51-64), and Nadel (51-132). For long critical of the "configurational"
and varied "psychological" approaches rampant in American theory, British scholars tend themselves to shift in the latest years toward more psychologically oriented interests, as will be seen.

As regards countries on the Continent, academic scholarship is largely
in eclipse during World War II, except as refugee scholars work abroad.
Afterward, with help from the United States, Britain, Canada, and other
overseas countries, a considerable revival occurs in spite of desperately
low numbers of trained personnel. Notably, in Germany, Thurnwald continues his important sociological-psychological writing, in Vienna Schmidt
and Koppers provide the rallying point for the culture-historical school
groups, and Rivet gives leadership to French anthropology, with a field
work and diffusionistic emphasis that has no place for the now moribund
Levy-Bruhl type of theory. Scholars from the European centers also work
overseas, with Africa and South America particularly strong fields for
their researches; and university centers in such localities as South Africa,
Australia, and Japan resume student training. Academic centers and government agencies in Latin America and Asia (especially India) show a
growing vitality and some disposition to contribute creatively to theory in
such fields as culture change.

But it is in the United States that interest in theory and method appears
to hold the attention of scholars most fully and creatively, even if some
of the leads are highly experimental. The historical method still has its
vogue, particularly in dominantly descriptive studies and museum oriented
work where it provides materials for overt, "first level," analysis.[1]

---

[1]Notable here is the gigantic compilation work of the "Human Relations
Area Files" project, started by Murdock at Yale in the 1930's and now a
co-operative enterprise of a number of institutions; see Murdock and others,
Outline of Cultural Analysis (revised 1950). Yale University Press.

Even here, however, historicalist studies tend to be permeated by the newer theory and method. Even when units of observation in behavior or material objects are isolated for investigation, they are assumed to have a functional context and to play a part within the total integrated system of the culture and society concerned. Anthropology is now being strongly influenced, along with science as a whole, by so-called "operationism" as first strongly formulated by the physicist Bridgman, by which terms and abstractions used for scientific purposes are seen to have no more reality or validity than is provided by the "operations" of observation and experiment which went to their making and measurement. This viewpoint is particularly formulated in relation to anthropology by Chapple in a general work on his "interaction" theory (42-15), and also by Kluckhohn in studies of "patterning" and other abstractions, including the basic concept of "culture" itself (41-48, 43-43, 45-66, etc.). From another tangent, influences sometimes subsumed under the new label of "meta-anthropology" enter by way particularly of more philosophically oriented questions raised by Bidney (44-12, 46-13, 46-14, etc.), and provoking important theoretical discussion by Kluckhohn, Bateson, Kroeber, and others as to the levels of abstraction centered around the concept of "culture" and their relation to observed behavior. Still further self-questioning by anthropologists arises in relation to method, especially under influences from psychology and sociology, abetted by specialists in statistics, symbolic logic, communications research, model delineation, and other techniques relating to accuracy and use of symbols. The older historicalist has had to take account of the implications of controlled interviewing, life history analysis, sampling and validation of data, use of highly structured tests such as the Rorschach technique, and other dimensions of work that go far beyond merely "getting informants to talk."

While general trends of this kind are the special mark of the 1940's, rendering inadequate the older "culturological" approaches, and permeating the scientific atmosphere in which time-dimensional studies are being carried on, these latter studies are also given much more formulation and precision. The older historical-diffusionist frame of reference, centered around the concepts of "invention" and "diffusion," while still generally valid, is too sparse and mechanistic to bear the newer needs for operationally valid constructs relating to behavior in dynamic situations. Barnett, Kroeber, and others now explore the contexts of "innovation." Linton, Hallowell, Herskovits, Keesing, and others, including younger scholars for whom this field becomes a prime theoretical interest, elaborate greatly the body of abstractions concerned with "cultural transactions": e.g., circumstances surrounding selectivity when cultural alternatives are presented (i.e., accepting or rejecting the new, conserving or discarding the old), the contextualization of new elements and reformulation of traditional elements in a changing culture, the variable phenomena of disintegration and reintegration (as for example "nativistic" movements), the dynamics of personality and its formation in situations of change, group and individual stresses involved in unlearning and relearning, differential tendencies to "adaptability" inherent in given cultures, differential "compatability" of cultural systems interacting with one another, the significance of variables such as numbers, mobility, and momentum (e. g. , aggressiveness or passivity), characteristic of the society involved in contact and change. The great range of titles in the important literature reviewed in the sections which follow give clues to these many burgeoning ideas, even though fuller discussion of them is not possible here.

Several of the newer lines of thought in the United States may be singled out as having particular significance, notably formulations in theory and method beyond those analyzed in the last section. It may be noted, first, that the "configurational" approach of Benedict and the "character structure" approach of Mead tend to converge, as already indicated, particularly in studies of the "national character" of contemporary states or ethnic groups including inevitably dimensions of change. Called for first by governmental needs during World War II (i. e. , studies both of the enemy countries, notably Germany and Japan, and of friendly countries and groups over the world about which behavioral knowledge was required), these become elaborated in the postwar period. But the great constructs offered by some of the scholars concerned on national behaviors, with attendant materials on personality (character) and its infant to adult formation, as in the work of Gorer and of Mead on the Soviet Union (49-40, 51-123), have also evoked criticism, at least to the extent that they have been allowed so to speak "out of the laboratory" and into general publication before adequate testing of their validity.

At the more theoretical level a great amount of new work is done on "patterning" and "configurational" phenomena in culture, and their important roles in shaping conservatism and change in overt behavior. Notable are extensive delineations of the concept of "value"; a scheme by Kluckhohn to classify varied dimensions and levels of patterning, and his later amendments of it, including recent use of the concept of "enthymemes" (or "unstated premises"); Morris Opler's concept of "themes"; Linton on "style"; LaBarre on "social cynosure"; Herskovits on "focus"; Thompson on "logico-aesthetic integration"; Kroeber's classification into "systemic," "style," and "total-culture" patterns; even these merely a few out of quite numerous concepts being tried out to refer to regularities of motivation and consistency in culture.

Another main concern, as witness the proliferation of relevant titles, is with further delineation of personality (character) structure, its development and dimensions. Social anthropologists team up here in thinking, and in some instances in active research, with psychologists, psychiatrists, psychoanalysts, specialists in psychosomatic medicine, sociologists, educators, and others in continuing exploration of child development, learning and interaction theory, psychopathology, and other aspects of so-called "culture and personality" studies. Anthropological protagonists of "depth" psychologies battle it out, still by no means conclusively, with those leaning more on controlled observation of explicit behavior, and considerable common ground is found by workers such as Hallowell, the Oplers, and Gillin who are cognizant of both starting points of reference. Kluckhohn and Murray also try to bring "personality" into a common universe of discourse in a volume of readings (48-62). Personality studies assume relevance as regards the individual as conservative or innovator, personality development in stable and dynamic situations, problems of adult unlearning and relearning, psychopathological responses to change, and similar problems, few of which have gone far beyond being spelled out conceptually, with accumulation of some usually sketchy case materials.

Taking up further some of the more specific theoretical leads discussed in the last section, it will be noted that anthropological-psychoanalytic workers such as Roheim, Erickson, Devereux, and Bateson continue with research on child conditioning, communication, national character, and other fields. The Yale "learning theory" group translates its ideas more fully into anthropological contexts, as in work by Dollard, Hallowell, Gillin, Murdock, and Ford, including culture change as a main field of interest. Linton and Kardiner from 1941 on follow up rather separately the interests of the Columbia group, with the former particularly emphasizing "status personality" dimensions additive to the latter's "basic personality structure." The somewhat newer concept of "modal personality," more sensitive to the approximations of variables of individual training and experience to the common mode or norm, tends to be used to overarch both. From the viewpoint of method, special note may be taken of further significant use of projective test materials (Rorschach, TAT, etc.) in cross-cultural and dynamic situations by such workers as Hallowell, the Henrys, Joseph, Hsu, the Spindlers, and Anthony Wallace, with the results generally checked against orthodox ethnographic materials. Examples are the work of Hallowell and his students on Ojibwa Indian groups and Hsu's attempts to interpret contrasts between traditional Chinese behavior and the puritan model of Western behavior, e.g., as between the typical use of "suppression" or external controls and "repression" or internalized controls in the respective systems of child conditioning (49-48).

With greater societal orientation, Redfield at the University of Chicago refines his concept of the "folk society" (47-112) and Warner at the same institution works especially on rank and class among ethnic groups in North America (41-77, 41-78, 42-107, etc.). At Harvard, the incipient offshoot of Warner's ideas represented in "interaction" and "equilibrium" theory undergoes considerable further development. A major work by Chapple in collaboration with Coon (42-15) gives a first total interpretation of this fresh theoretical position. Chapple himself largely leaves the university setting to take his chronological measurement of interaction behavior into industry by way of an industrial consultant business which he establishes with interested colleagues, using an interviewing device called the "chronograph" for personnel rating, and following up other applied problems. But he retains scientific interests, and Arensberg, Coon, Oliver, Homans, and others follow his general approach.

Homans, a sociologist rather than an anthropologist, demonstrates in

a recent book (50-71) how behavior in three contrasting social situations
may be processed through a few great constructs, notably the central concept of "interaction," and without reference to the traditional one of "culture": culture change here resolves itself essentially into shifts in interaction systems. With its emphasis on social process rather than the almost
endlessly variable detail of cultural content, this interaction approach
appears in itself, for all its precision, to yield only limited insights. Recent stress, however, particularly by this group, upon the idea of delineating "significant systems" as the effective units or "living models" for
analysis seems particularly important in dynamic situations where the
traditional concept of "a culture" may become operationally less realistic
in the face of complex assemblages and fusions of varying behavioral elements, especially in large heterogeneous societies, or under conditions
of extensive contact and dysfunction.

A significant trend especially of the post-World War II period is a growing rapprochement of cultural anthropology at the theoretical level with the
humanistic disciplines, just as earlier it developed liaisons with other social sciences. Common interests begin to come into focus, not only in
more obvious fields such as cross-cultural studies in the arts, religion,
and linguistics, but also in formulations, for example, relating to personality (or "character" as the dramatist and novelist calls it), the basic
"philosophies" permeating different behavioral systems, values and their
evaluation, change and development in values through individual interaction,
the circumstances of individual creativity, and phenomena of conservatism
and change generally. Discussions are under way in a number of institutional settings in the attempt to reach some common frame of discourse.
Among anthropologists making notable contributions have been Benedict,
Kroeber, Kluckhohn, Redfield, Herskovits, Thompson, and Bernard Siegel;
and of others the name of the philosopher Northrop stands out.

Archaeologists in this period continue to examine their theoretical and
methodological assumptions regarding historical reconstruction, and contribute materials within the limits of their data on dynamics. Their contributions to generalization of the larger perspectives of culture history are
also increasingly definitive and important. Among the more notable works,
particularly involving self-criticism, are items by Brew (46-17), Taylor
(48-101), and Steward (49-112). Linguistic specialists also write occas-
sionally on broader facets of theory and method relevant to culture change,
e.g., Whorf (41-80), Hoijer (48-50), Voegelin (51-196). Also included in
the year-by-year analysis which follows are a continuing selection of what
appear to be the most important works by writers in collateral fields dealing with theory and case data which come closely within the anthropological
frame of reference.

1940

Linton edits an important book on "acculturation in seven American

Indian tribes," for which seven field works contribute the constituent papers; Linton's final three chapters provide a definitive theoretical statement on processes of acculturation (40-41). Barnett also breaks theoretical ground in a paper on "culture process," particularly factors surrounding innovation (40-5).

Kroeber writes on a concept of "stimulus diffusion," and with Richardson explores the possibility of establishing longer-term regularities relating to women's dress fashions (40-38, 40-39). Redfield generalizes his "folk society" concept as a part of cultural dynamics theory (40-55). Malinowski writes on "transculturation" (40-44), a term coined by Ortiz and having some currency among Latin-American scholars as an alternative to "acculturation."[1] Hallowell discusses "aggression" in the changing Salteaux Indian society (40-25), and Henry "some cultural determinants of hostility" among the Pilagá (40-27).

Focusing more on the individual, Beaglehole discusses some of the dynamics of "interpersonal" theory, and also a case study of "psychic stress" in a Tongan village (40-6, 40-7). Devereux writes on "social negativism and criminal psychopathology" (40-16). Gillin and Raimy relate current "personality" studies to "acculturation" (40-22). Kroeber writes on "psychosis or social sanction" (40-37). Mead has a provocative paper on "education and cultural surrogates," including some comments on personality formation in the changing Western society (40-47). Elkin in Australia sets out his views on "society, the individual and change," with an applied emphasis (40-18). Wagley gives a case study of the "effects of depopulation upon social organization" as illustrated in an Amazonian tribe (40-71).

Of more general theory relevant to dynamics, Chapple discusses personality in terms of his "interaction" theory, and with Arensberg reports on their pioneering study of interaction as measured chronologically in the behavior of Boston shipyard workers; he also has a paper with Harding on related emotional activity (40-11 to 40-13). Evans-Pritchard reviews the merging in British social anthropology of theoretical currents to date (40-20), and Gluckman demonstrates its dominant "social structure" approach as applied to change in a study of the modern Zulu (40-24). Linton discusses definitively the relations between psychology and anthropology (40-40). Radcliffe-Brown publishes one of his rare papers, on the concept of "social structure" (40-54). Thurnwald summarizes his highly creative ideas relating to "function" in cultural theory (40-66). White discusses "symbols" as basic to behavior throughout man's cultural development (40-73).

The year is marked by expansion of acculturation studies of primarily descriptive character relating to particular peoples and problems, e.g., Barbeau on Indian trade silver and Northwest Indian totem poles (40-3, 40-

---

[1]Malinowski also contributes an introduction to Ortiz' book (40-53), in which he offers a critique of the term "acculturation," mainly on the grounds that it expresses a one-sided emphasis in contact dynamics, and claiming that "transculturation" is a more precise concept for documenting the process involved.

4); Carneiro on African cults in Bahia (40-10); Hill on two centuries of
changing Navaho life (40-29); Hunt on Indian intertribal war and trade (40-
32); Kinietz on Delaware Indian acculturation (40-35); Mandelbaum on the
Plains Cree (40-46); Marvin Opler on Ute peyotism (40-52); Richards on
marriage and economics among the African Bemba (40-56); Sutherland
editing a volume on the modern Polynesian Maori (40-64); Tschopik on
changes in Navaho basketry (40-68); and papers by Elkin, Goldman, Harris,
Joffe, Opler, Smith, and Whitman in the Linton volume (40-41). Works of
special significance relating to longer-term archaeological and historical
trends are those by Lowie on "American culture history" (40-42), Mera
on population dynamics as seen through archaeological reconstruction (40-
49), and Strong on the Great Plains area (40-63). Examples of "applied"
studies are Thompson's analysis of culture change and administration in
the Lau islands of Fiji (40-65), and Tindale on the "half-caste problem"
in South Australia (40-67).

1941

Redfield, in a study of three Yucatán communities in different stages of
the acculturation process, extends his analysis of culture history (41-65).
Herskovits shows expanding insights regarding "culture contact" beyond
his earlier theoretical statements on acculturation (41-37). Barnett has an
important paper on "personal conflicts and cultural changes" (41-3). Hallowell gives an important critique of the usefulness of the Rorschach test for
study of personality in cross-cultural situations (41-33).

Wartime problems of "morale building" are given both theoretical and
practical formulation by Bateson and Mead (41-6, 41-57), and Bateson also
writes on the "frustration-aggression hypothesis" (41-5). Kardiner with
Spiegel writes on "the traumatic neuroses of war" (41-45). Barber discusses
"acculturation and messianic movements" (41-2). Dollard and Miller write
on "social learning and imitation" (41-19). Fenton takes Iroquois suicide
as the basis of a "study in stability of a culture pattern" (41-26). Ford experiments usefully with "life history" techniques in a study of a Kwakiutl
chief against the backdrop of modern changes (41-28). Cooper discusses
"temporal sequences and the marginal cultures" on the American continent
with a critical eye on problems of historical-diffusionist reconstruction
(41-15). Keesing offers comparative and generalized materials on culture
change in the South Pacific (41-46).

In the linguistic field, Jesperson follows up earlier work on language
growth with a study of "efficiency in language change" (41-44). Whorf lays
the basis for his important theoretical work on the relation between language
categories and the organization of experiences represented in the culture
concerned (41-80). Herzog writes on language change as illustrated from
Pima Indian materials (41-38).

Of relevant general works, Kluckhohn offers an important systematiza-

tion of concepts relating to pattern and configuration which are significant
in relation to stability and change (41-48). Humphrey writes on "social
insight, nuance, and mind-types: a polar hypothesis," and also the "concept of culture in social case work" (41-40, 41-41). Linton discusses
"culture and personality" for an educator audience (41-54). Whiting tests
the Yale learning theory concepts in a Melanesian community setting (41-
79).

The year sees a sharp growth in the number of well-documented studies
of culture in time-dimensional aspects which, while primarily descriptive,
have importance for theory and method. The following may be singled out:
Bascom on Gullah Negroes (41-4), Beaglehole's village study in Tonga
(41-7), Debo on Creek Indians (41-17), Eggan on Philippine mountain
peoples (41-20), Embree on immigrant Japanese (41-22), Farmer and
also Kluckhohn on the Navaho (41-23, 41-49), Fenton on the Iroquois (41-
25, 41-27), Greenberg on Negro-Mohammedan contact in an African group
(41-31), Henry on a Brazilian tribe (41-35), Honigmann on an isolated
Canadian Indian group (41-39), Mandelbaum on Nilgiri hill tribes in India
(41-56), Olen and Loomis on a Mexican community (41-60), Perham on
British administration in Africa (41-62), Rainey on changing Eskimo culture (41-63), Siegel and also Tax on Guatemalan groups (41-70 to 41-72,
41-75), Steward on British Columbian Indians (41-74), Wieschoff on the
Ibo in Africa (41-81), and Wilson on "economics of detribalization" in
Northern Rhodesia (41-82).

Several archaeological studies deal with broader aspects of change,
especially Byers (41-11), Childe (41-14), Jenness (41-43), and Rogers
(41-66). Keur uses archaeological data to reconstruct early Navaho acculturation (41-47). The year is also marked by the appearance of important
works dealing with the contemporary American setting: Warner with Lunt
reporting on "Yankee City" (41-77), with Junker and Adams on Negro personality development (41-78), and with Davis, Gardner, and Gardner on
"Deep South" (41-16); Herskovits on "the myth of the Negro past" (41-36);
and Kluckhohn on the American "way of life" (41-50).

1942

Ruth Benedict writes in this year one of her few systematic presentations
on "culture change" (42-12). Lowie also gives his general views on stability
and change in an important paper titled "the transition of civilizations in
primitive society" (42-61). Aginsky discusses "acculturation" (42-1), and
Barnett has two important articles on acculturation processes, particularly
phenomena of innovation (42-7, 42-8). Gillin writes on "acquired drives in
culture contact," drawing upon the conceptual system of the Yale learning
group (42-34).

With more applied emphasis, Arensberg writes broadly of "the nature
of the world equilibrium" (42-3), and Chapple on how a world equilibrium

"can be organized and administered" (42-17). Arensberg and Macgregor
present a study of "industrial morale" (42-4) and Bateson of "morale and
national character" (42-11). Focused more upon the individual, Bateson
is also breaking ground on the concept of "deutero-learning" in relation to
social planning (42-9), and Hallowell writes on personality dynamics in
relation to acculturation processes, with emphasis on techniques of measur-
ment (42-37 to 42-39). Devereux discusses "mental hygiene" with reference
to the North American Indian (42-24), and the Leightons "some types of
uneasiness and fear" characteristic of the modern Navaho (42-55). Mead
and others discuss "culture and the purposive cultivation of democratic
values" (42-67). Tannous analyzes emigration as a force of social change
with reference to an Arab village (42-104).

Of more general relevance, Bateson analyzes "some systematic approaches to the study of culture and personality" (42-10). An important
general work by Chapple and Coon sets out the "interaction" theory develop-
mainly by the former from the Warner approach (42-15); Chapple also continues his analysis of measurement as applied to "interpersonal behavior"
(42-16). Ford demonstrates some of the findings of the Yale learning group
on "culture and human behavior" (42-30). Herskovits writes on "values,"
now becoming a particular reference point for study of configurational
phenomena (42-41). Kluckhohn reviews certain aspects of mythology and
religion in the light of new theory, particularly using Navaho field material
(42-50, 42-51). Mead and Warner participate in a symposium on "environment and education" (42-14). Marvin Opler reviews the worth of psychoanalytic techniques in social analysis (42-73). Warner and Lunt discuss the
status system of "Yankee City" (42-107). Webster writes in the evolutionary
manner on "taboo" (42-108). Zingg, following up an early concept of Sapir,
attempts to delineate "genuine" and "spurious" values in a changing Mexican Indian culture (42-113).

Again there are a number of more descriptive studies of change relating
to peoples and problems, notably by Arensberg relating to a Japanese relocation camp (42-2), Buck on "disappearance of canoes in Polynesia" (42-
13), Cooper on age-area studies in South America (42-19, 42-20), Malouf
on Gosiute peyotism (42-62), Mead on "the family in the future" (42-66),
Métraux on a Peruvian Indian messiah (42-69), Nadel on an African "Byzantium" (42-70), Oliver on "a case of a change in food habits" in the Solomons
(42-72), Opler on Ute peyotism (42-74), Passin on "culture change in southern Illinois" (42-76), Pierson on Negroes in Brazil (42-78), Read on effects
of migrant labor on tribal life in Africa (42-81), Shimkin on "dynamics of
recent history" in a Shoshone group (42-96), the autobiography of a Hopi
Indian recorded by Simmons (42-98), Stout on San Blas Cuña acculturation
(42-102), Thompson's study of Guam (42-105), Wagley on changes in Tapira
social organization (42-106), Willems and Baldus on Japanese immigrants
in Brazil (42-110), and Yount on the Hopi in 1942 (52-112).

Important works on change from the archaeological viewpoint are method-
logical discussions by Colton (42-18) and McKern (42-65), while Steward

(42-101) centers on problems of historical reconstruction. Studies in related social science fields include Hirsch on "assimilation" (42-43), Hodgen on the age-area hypothesis (42-45), the compilation by Locke and Stern on "when peoples meet" (42-59), Ogburn on "inventions, population and history" (42-71), and Parsons on "anthropology and prediction" (42-75).

<u>1943</u>

Benedict contributes an additional paper analyzing "two patterns of Indian acculturation"; this, together with her paper of the previous year, presents her mature ideas on culture change (43-3). She also writes on the need for "recognition of cultural diversities in the postwar world" (43-2). Devereux and Loeb discuss a type of culture contact situation which they call "antagonistic acculturation" (43-16). Humphrey writes on "assimilation and acculturation" (43-39), and on "accommodation and assimilation" (43-63).

Linton writes an important theoretical paper on "nativistic movements" (43-47), and Wallis on the role of "messiahs" in civilization (43-101). Devereux and Loeb have an additional paper on "criminality" in the context of Apache life (43-15). Eggan writes on "the general problem of Hopi adjustment," and Goldfrank on "historic change and social character" among a Dakota group (43-17, 43-24). A posthumous work by Malinowski discusses "pan-African culture contact" (43-51), and Schapera analyzes "the mechanism of culture change" in terms of a Bechuanaland group (43-76). Powdermaker writes on the "channeling of Negro aggression by the cultural process" (43-66). Beals, Redfield, and Tax collaborate to analyze time-dimensional and other problems for research in contemporary Mexico and Guatemala (43-1). Steward and also Titiev attempt similar reviews for Latin America as a whole (43-84, 43-86, 43-94).

Methods relevant to culture change studies are discussed by Herskovits and by Mead (43-31, 43-54). Lee, Spicer, and Thompson develop various linguistic aspects of acculturation (43-46, 43-83, 43-91). Slotkin has a work on the sociological concept of "the marginal man" (43-80). Róheim develops his psychoanalytic views further relating to the "origin and function of culture" (43-73). White makes his first bid to rehabilitate the evolutionary viewpoint in discussing "energy and the evolution of culture" (43-103).

Applied problems are being brought to the forefront more urgently, particularly as being stimulated by war needs, e. g. , intelligence work, military government and other training, morale studies, relief and rehabilitation, Japanese relocation, though only a small fraction of the materials prepared by anthropologists are given public distribution. Chapple writes on "anthropological engineering" and administration within the context of his interaction theory (43-12); Elkin on applied anthropology with special relation to Southwest Pacific peoples then becoming freed from Japanese occupation (43-18), and Mead on policy for the South Pacific peoples more

generally (43-55); Haring on the Japanese and the war (43-26); Herskovits
on "education and cultural dynamics" (43-30); Honigmann on "what anthropology indicates as the best colonial policy" (43-35); Kennedy on "accultura
tion and administration in Indonesia" (43-41, 43-42); Kluckhohn on "covert
culture and administrative problems" (43-43), indicating the importance of
configurational dimensions of cultural analysis for applied anthropology;
Embree on Japanese relocation on the Pacific Coast (43-19 to 43-21); Mead
on American character in relation to the war (43-56); Reed on "the making
of modern New Guinea" with an applied anthropology emphasis (43-68);
Ritzenthaler on the impact of the war on an American Indian group (43-71),
and John Useem, Macgregor, and Ruth Useem on a similar topic (43-96);
Loomis and Grisham on an experiment in village rehabilitation in New
Mexico (43-48); Rojas on the problem of indigenous groups in Argentina
(43-74), and Steward on "acculturation and the Indian problem" (43-85).

Primarily descriptive studies of special significance are those by Botell
de Magalhães (43-9), Fenton (43-22), Heizer on an Eskimo invention in
historic times (43-29), Herskovits (43-32), Hsu (43-37), a volume edited
by Loram and McIlwraith on "North American Indians today" (43-49),
Malouf (43-52), Mekeel (43-57), Morris Opler (43-59), Ortiz (43-61),
Raper and Tappan (43-67, on "Georgia share croppers"), Richardson (43-
70), Siegel (43-78), Slotkin (43-79, on "jazz" as exemplifying acculturation
Speck (43-81, 43-82), Tannous (43-89, 43-90), Wagley (43-100), and Whyte
(43-105). Archaeologists continue to discuss theory and method, as in thre
papers by Bennett (43-4 to 43-6), and also Colton (43-14), and Steward
(43-86). Birket-Smith attempts to reconstruct the origin of maize cultivation (43-7). Among papers in collateral fields are Bogardus on "culture
conflicts" in Japanese relocation centers (43-8), Furnivall and also Vanden
bosch on Southeast Asia (43-23, 43-97), and a Javanese, Supatmo, on the
merging of different religious traditions in the "animistic beliefs and practices" of his people (43-87).

1944

A major work analyzing long-term trends in culture process, using rich
data from the history of Western civilization, is Kroeber's "configurations
of cultural growth" (44-54). A posthumous volume by Malinowski, titled
"freedom and civilization," goes further than his earlier theory in attempting some total interpretations of cultural development, and also in analyzin
the newer concept of "value," in an at times passionate attempt to formulat
the case for freedom and democracy in the face of Nazi aggression (44-59).
Another influential scholar, Thurnwald, discusses the dynamics of cultural
origins (44-73).

Gillin has a general paper on "cultural adjustment," and one on "houses
food, and the contact of cultures in a Guatemalan town" (44-27). John
Bennett writes on "culture change and personality in a rural society," and

also "interaction of culture and environment in the smaller societies" (44-7, 44-9). Pierson discusses "symbolic" and "non-symbolic" interaction (44-64). Kelly presents data on culture change phenomena in the extreme dimensions represented by Aborigine-white contact in Australia (44-47). Bonfante and Sebeok discuss the age-area hypothesis in relation to linguistic data (44-13).

Of more general works, Bateson contributes an important statement on "cultural determinants of personality," Beaglehole reviews critically the main literature on "character (or personality) structure," with some case materials on stability and change, and Kluckhohn with the psychologist Mowrer experiments with a conceptual scheme for comprehensive analysis of culture and personality (44-5, 44-6, 44-49). The philosopher-anthropologist Bidney writes the first of his theoretically provocative articles on "the concept of culture and some cultural fallacies" (44-12). The Henrys contribute a study of "doll play" among Pilagá children which has methodological significance for personality dynamics (44-32). Honigmann discusses "morale in a primitive society" (44-41). Morris Opler writes on "cultural and organic conceptions in contemporary world history" (44-61). Thompson and Joseph interpret "the Hopi way" through an integration of various ethnological and psychological approaches, this being the first of a series of reports on tribal studies of Indian personality initiated by the Office of Indian Affairs (44-72).

The applied emphasis is again strongly represented. Brown writes on "missions and cultural diffusion" (44-15); Elkin on "citizenship for the Aborigines" and the "future of Australian territories" in the light of anthropology (44-20, 44-21); Embree on "community analysis" in Japanese relocation centers, and problems of a postwar Japan (44-22 to 44-24); Grigson on "the aboriginal in the future of India" (44-29); Herskovits on "self-government" and other problems of Africa (44-33, 44-35); Hogbin on indigenous councils and courts in the Solomons (44-40); Kluckhohn on "anthropological research and world peace" (44-48); Krige on "the magical thought pattern of the Bantu in relation to health services" (44-53); Lester on the "effects of war on Fijian society" (44-57); Mekeel on "an appraisal of the Indian Reorganization Act" (44-60); Thompson on "some perspectives in applied anthropology" (44-71); Vivo on the indigenous problem in Hispanic America (44-77); and a posthumous paper by Williams on mission influences in a Papuan group (44-81).

More descriptive papers of importance are various studies of North and South American groups by Adair (44-1), Barbeau (44-4), Herskovits (44-34), Hill (44-39), Knowlton (44-50), Kraus (44-51), Kuer (44-55), Orozco (44-62), Reed (44-66), Sanchez (44-68), Stewart (44-69), Titiev (44-74), and Willems (44-79, 44-80); on African groups by Culwick (44-18), Francolini (44-26), Harris (44-30), Hopgood (44-42), Jeffreys (44-46), and Winterbotham (44-82); on Asian groups by Aiyappan (44-2), and Majumdar (44-58); and on Oceania by Buck (44-16), Hawthorn (44-31), and Inselmann (44-44). Archaeological studies are by Childe (44-17), Ischer (44-45), Krieger (44-52), and Rouse (44-67).

1945

A distinct upturn shows in this year in the number of theoretical works focused on change. A posthumous work by Malinowski gives his matured views on "the dynamics of cultural change" from both theoretical and applied viewpoints (45-79). Broom discusses "a measure of conservatism" (45-10). Herskovits essays a general formulation of "the processes of cultural change," and also writes on "problem, method, and theory" with special relation to Afro-American studies (45-45, 45-46). Kimball discusses "diversity and change in the culture of non-literate peoples" (45-62). Demonstrating British approaches Kuper writes on "social anthropology as a study of culture contacts," and the Wilsons on "the analysis of social change" (45-69, 45-114).

With the psychological viewpoints more to the fore, Dollard demonstrates the Yale learning approach to the "acquisition of new habits" (45-19). Hallowell gives an important statement on "sociopsychological aspects of acculturation," and reformulates his views on use of the Rorschach technique in the study of personality and culture (45-42, 45-43). Goldfrank uses Indian tribal materials to illustrate "changes in configuration," and "socialization, personality and . . . structure" (45-34, 45-35), Greenman discusses innovation, with emphasis on individual creativity (45-38).

Fortes writes on "the dynamics of clanship" in an African society, showing a social system in action by way of the British type of "social structure" analysis (45-24). Gillin discusses "inhibitions to acculturation" in a Guatemalan community (45-30). Guthe, Mead, and others prepare for the National Research Council a definitive analysis of the "problem of changing food habits" (45-39). Radin documents a major Indian religious ceremonial, taking account of dynamic factors (45-84). Ransom discusses "writing as a medium of acculturation," using Aleut data (45-86). Reay analyzes the cultural adjustments of a "half-caste aboriginal community" in Australia (45-87). Speck writes on the "historical versus the ethnological view" in Iroquois studies (45-95). Wallis offers a critique of age-area distributional studies (45-105). Widengren harks back to older approaches in discussing "evolutionism" (45-112), and White continues his neoevolutionary interpretations (45-109, 45-110).

Of more general works, Gillin writes on "personality formation from the comparative point of view" (45-31). Kardiner brings up to date his theory and method relating to the "basic personality structure" concept, including a major book on "the psychological frontiers of society" covering the Kardiner-Linton collaboration at Columbia University as discussed in the last section (45-55, 45-56). Linton also writes a tightly argued little book on the "cultural background of personality," and edits a general survey volume on "the science of man in the world crisis" (45-75, 45-76). A chapter by Linton in the latter volume attempts a general survey of total culture growth, based on archaeological and other evidence.

Kluckhohn discusses the use of personal documents in anthropological science and demonstrates by analysis of a Navaho personal document; he

also contributes to a symposium on "group tensions," and essays with
Kelly a definition of culture as seen through the eyes of different theorists
(45-63 to 45-66). Kroeber also writes on the "use of autobiographical evidence" (45-67). Murdock gives a provocative paper on "the common denominator of culture," drawing upon concepts of the Yale learning approach
(45-81). Morris Opler tries to achieve greater methodological control
over configurational phenomena by use of a concept of "themes" (45-82).
Thompson also experiments with total-culture dimensions which she calls
"logico-aesthetic integration," using Hopi case materials (45-101).

Works with an applied orientation also expand in number. General definitions and critiques of applied anthropology are offered by Embree (45-21),
Keesing (45-57), Kennedy (45-61), Lantis (45-70), and Tax (45-100). Several specific studies will be mentioned as illustrating the range of topics:
Ballinger on "a scientific approach to post-war unemployment" among
non-Europeans in South Africa (45-3); Capell on "the future of education
in Papua" (45-12); García on "el indigenismo" in Colombia (45-28); the
Honigmanns on "alcoholic drinking in an Indian-White community" (45-50);
Keesing on agricultural extension work in Pacific islands (45-59); Leighton
on "the governing of men" as demonstrated in a Japanese evacuation camp
(45-73); Redfield on "ethnic groups and nationality" (45-88); Smith on "the
missionary and anthropology" (45-93).

Again there are useful case materials of which the following are singled
out for their importance to theory and method: Austin on cultural changes
in the Trobriand islands where Malinowski did his classic ethnographic
work (45-1); Beals on contemporary Cáhita Indian culture (45-6); Carr and
Westez on survival of culture elements among the Shinnecock Indians of
Long Island (45-13); Fortes on "the impact of the war on British West
Africa" (45-25); Fürer-Haimendorf on acculturation of an Asian group (45-
26); Geddes on "acceleration of social change in a Fijian community" (45-
29); Hall on English "loan-words" in Micronesian languages (45-41); Hsu
on "influence of South-Seas emigration in certain Chinese provinces" (45-
52); Jeffreys on "the death of a dialect" in Africa (45-54); Lowie on Lapp
culture history (45-78); Useem on "the changing structure of a Micronesian
society" (45-103); and Watson on acculturation in rural Brazil (45-106,
45-107).

Archaeological works worth special note are by Ekholm (45-20), Goodwin (45-36), Haury (45-44), and Strong (45-98). Carter writes on plant
geography and culture history in the American Southwest (45-14). Among
collateral works are Cressey on Chinese traits in European civilization
(45-17), Hodgen on acculturation as illustrated by glass and paper (45-48),
La Violette on Americans of Japanese ancestry (45-71), and Woolston on
"assimilation" (45-115).

1946

White's neoevolutionary writings, continued in this year (46-102),
evoke vigorous rebuttals by Bidney, Kroeber, and Lowie (46-14, 46-63,

46-69, 46-70). Bidney also continues his philosophical-anthropological analyses with a paper on the concept of "culture in crisis" (46-13). Angel writes on the "social biology of Greek culture growth" (46-4). In a dominantly historicalist manner Birket-Smith presents a major work in German on the "history of culture" based on archaeological and ethnological data (46-15). The archaeologist Garrod writes on "environment, tools and man,' Hornell on early development of water transport, and Lips on "the origin of things" (46-38, 46-55, 46-68).

Hawley analyzes "group designed behavior patterns in two acculturating groups," and also Pueblo social organization in relation to religious acculturation (46-49, 46-50). Kluckhohn and Leighton write of persistence and change in personality and society among the Navaho (46-60, 46-62). Macgregor has a book on "warriors without weapons," analyzing modern changes in a Plains Indian society (46-71). Morris Opler discusses the "creative role of shamanism" in Apache mythology, and Quimby the social structure of the Natchez as an "instrument of assimilation" (46-78, 46-85). Green discusses "social values and psychotherapy" (46-41). In India, Datta-Majumdar writes on the "malaise" of culture, and Rao on the "cause and cure" of culture conflicts (46-27, 46-87).

The year is more marked by descriptive items than by theory. Altman writes on a Navaho wedding (46-1); Amoo on the effect of Western influence on marriage in an African tribe (46-2); Baldus on acculturation in a South American group (46-6); Bastide on "Catholic-fetichistic syncretism" (46-8); the Beagleholes on contemporary Maori death customs (46-10); Beals on a rural Mexican community (46-11); Childs on Christian marriage in Nigeria (46-19); Cook on human sacrifice and war as affecting demography in pre-Colonial Mexico (46-23); Eduardo on "three way religious acculturation" in a Brazilian city (46-29); Forde and Scott on indigenous economics in Nigeria (46-35); Fuchs on tribal changes in India (46-36, 46-37); Geddes on a contemporary Fijian village (46-39); Greenberg on "the influence of Islam on a Sudanese religion" (46-42); Honigmann on acculturation of a Canadian Indian group (46-54); Malherk on bilingualism in South Africa (46-73); Philipps on a contemporary African culture (46-82); Radin on Japanese ceremonial life in California (46-86); Spicer on change in an Arizona Yaqui village (46-92); Willems on acculturation of a Brazilian group (46-103); and Wonderly on a case study of linguistic acculturation (46-104).

Applied studies are well represented, perhaps most notably by the Beagleholes' book on change and education in a highly acculturated Maori community (46-9); Comas on "social service and anthropology in Mexico" (46-22); Cooper on anthropology as relating to peace and to international understanding (46-24, 46-26); Elkin on "conservation of aboriginal peoples" (46-30); military government problems in Micronesia as viewed by Embree (46-31, 46-32), Thompson (46-96) and Useem (46-99, 46-100); Evans-Pritchard giving one British view on applied anthropology (46-33); Goldfrank on Navaho agricultural adjustment and leadership (46-40); Haring on "Japan's prospect" (46-46); Hogbin on local government in New Guinea

(46-53); Hutton on "problems of reconstruction in the Assam hills" (46-56);
Mead on "education in dependent countries" (46-74); Herskovits and Montagu
on "anthropology and social engineering" (46-52, 46-76); Pijoan on medical work among a Nicaragua Indian group (46-83); and Shropshire on "primitive marriage and European law" in South Africa (46-90).

Notable among archaeological works is an important discussion by
Brew of typology (46-17), Childe and also Clark on early cultural development (46-18, 46-20), Griffin on "culture change and continuity" in eastern
United States archaeology (46-43), and Osgood on Caribbean-South American
contacts (46-79).

1947

At the theoretical level, Bidney discusses cultural processes in various aspects (47-17 to 47-19). Gluckman gives an important critique of
Malinowski's "functional" analysis of social change (47-44). Laviosa Zambotti gives an Italian view on the origin and diffusion of civilization (47-80).
Patai reviews various theoretical approaches in relation to a study of culture contact in modern Palestine (47-106). Radcliffe-Brown writes on
"evolution" in terms of a distinction between historical and scientific analysis, and Redfield reviews again his "folk society" concept (47-109, 47-
112). Bernard Siegel discusses the "meaning of history in anthropology"
as exemplified by Near Eastern case materials (47-125). White writes
three items in the attempt to advance his "culturological" approach as
over against the newer "psychological" interests (47-148 to 47-150).

Interest in culture change and the individual strengthens, with several
important works. Erikson combines psychoanalytic and anthropological
viewpoints in an analysis of "ego development and historical change" (47-
34). Mead contributes an important paper on "the implications of culture
change for personality development" (47-93). Thompson and Joseph write
on "white pressures on Indian personality and culture" (47-138). Dyk tests
out the worth of an autobiographical approach, using Navaho materials
(47-32). Henry writes on "cultural discontinuity and the shadow of the past"
(47-56). Honigmann writes on "a new attack on cultural lag; the significance
of anthropological knowledge for problems of the psychiatrists" (47-62).
Kroeber presents "a Southwestern personality type" (47-73). LaBarre discusses "primitive psychotherapy" in American Indian cultures (47-78).
Leighton and Kluckhohn continue to report on Navaho personality development (47-82). Molina gives a case study of a "psychopathic personality"
in Guatemala (47-96).

Among other works with marked theoretical bent, the Aginskys discuss
changes in Pomo Indian culture (47-3, 47-4). Benedict has a major work
on Japanese culture and personality which includes discussion of stability
and change — one of the pioneer studies of the "national character" type
(47-14). Childe discusses "history" from anthropological and other viewpoints (47-25). Cook writes on food and other factors relating to "survivor-

ship in aboriginal populations" (47-27). Goto writes on the old problem of
"diffusion or independent invention" (47-46). Honigmann discusses "the
cultural dynamics of sex" (47-60). Kardiner and Spiegel report on "war
stress and neurotic illness" (47-67). Pierson and Cunha outline research
possibilities relating to culture change in modern Brazil (47-108). Spoehr
has an important analysis of "changing kinship systems" (47-131), and
Warner and associates again demonstrate their "social structure" approach
as applied to American institutions (47-145, 47-146).

It may be noted in these titles that the narrower concept of "acculturation" is tending to be replaced by the wider concepts of "change," "contact,"
"process," or "dynamics," covering not only contact phenomena but also
all dimensions of cultural-social-psychological process. This likewise
shows in more descriptive and applied studies, though "acculturation"
still has full usefulness within its defined scope. A list of descriptive items
can only sample the growing list of systematic studies, e.g., Adams on
acculturation of the Delta Negro (47-2), the Berndts on "card games" in
an Australian Aborigine group (47-15), Burrows on intercultural contacts
in Hawaii (47-23), Flannery on "the changing form and functions" of an
Indian dance (47-37), Garfield on Tlingit clan history (47-40), Gillin on
a Peruvian community (47-42), Goldschmidt on an American farming
community in transition (47-45), Herskovits on a Trinidad village (47-57),
Hogbin on "native Christianity in a New Guinea village" (47-59), Honigmann on witchcraft in a modern Indian group (47-61), Hulse on changing
Japanese culture (47-63, 47-64), Lewis on wealth differences in a Mexican
village (47-85), Little on an African tribe in transition (47-86), Ortiz on
African music in Cuba (47-104), Read on effects of the war on New Guinea
groups (47-111), Speck on modern Creek Indians (47-127, 47-128), Spencer
on Spanish "loanwords" in an Indian language (47-129), Stout on San Blas
Cuna acculturation (47-134, 47-135), Whitman on change in a Pueblo culture (47-151), and Willems on changes in Brazilian groups and in Japanese
migrants to Brazil (47-152, 47-153).

Applied studies, too, can only be named selectively, e.g., studies of
African government, economy, and society by Ashton (47-7), Batten (47-9),
Firth (47-36), Kuper (47-77), Lambert (47-79), Nicholls (47-100), Schapera (47-122); of Oceanic groups by Beaglehole (47-10, 47-11), Belshaw
(47-13), Elkin (47-33), Keesing (47-68), Marie Keesing (47-70), Thompson (47-138), and Useem (47-140); of South Asia by Bhargava (47-16),
Fürer-Haimendorf (47-39), Grigson (47-48), Mukerji (47-98), and Somasundaram (47-126); of various American zones and problems by de la
Fuente (47-38), Loomis (47-88), Oberg (47-102), Sady (47-120), Villa
Rojas (47-142); also more general papers by Jacobs on "cultures in the
present world crisis" (47-66), and Morris Opler on "cultural alternatives
and educational theory" (47-103).

Of archaeological works the following may be noted: Cook on "population,
food supply, and building in early Mexico" (47-26), Duff on the "evolution"
of culture in pre-European New Zealand (47-31), Heizer on Drake and

California Indians (47-54), Hesselberth on "the fall of a culture" (47-58),
Lewis on "the beginning of civilization in America" (47-84), Rouse on
ceramic sequences in New England (47-118), Steward on "American culture history" (47-133), and Swanton on the "primary centers of civilization" (47-136).

1948

Anthropology texts are published by the Gillins (48-41, 48-42), Herskovits (48-54), and Kroeber (48-64), each containing important general
statements on culture in time-dimension aspects. In India, Aiyappan
writes on "theories of culture change and culture contact" (48-2), and a
Netherlands scholar, van Baal, discusses "the acculturation process,"
with special reference to New Guinea case materials (48-5). Gillin writes
on "race relations without conflict" as exemplified in Guatemala (48-40).
Thompson discusses "attitudes and acculturation" (48-103). The neoevolu-
tionistic views of White, written up still further in three items (48-110
to 48-112), are again targets of critical comment: by Jacobs and Kroeber
(48-58, 48-65).

With the individual more in focus, Billig, Gillin, and Davidson present
materials on personality and culture in a Guatemalan community, using
both "ethnological and Rorschach approaches" (48-12). Carothers writes
of "mental derangement in Africans" (48-16). Green discusses "culture,
normality, and personality conflict" (48-46). Hsu essays an analysis of
Chinese culture and personality (48-56). Kluckhohn joins with the psychoanalyst Murray in editing an important volume on "personality" which has
much material relevant to culture process (48-62). Trager discusses "a
status symbol and personality" at Taos Pueblo (48-102), and Voget analyzes "individual motivations" in the known diffusion of an Indian dance
(48-107).

Other more theoretical works focused on change include Eisenstadt
on "demographic factors in a situation of culture contact" (48-27); French
on "factionalism" in a Pueblo under conditions of change (48-35); Gibson
on "the probability of numerous independent inventions" (48-39); Goldschmidt on the dynamics of California Indian social organization (48-44);
Hawley on "problems basic to acculturation" among certain Pueblo groups,
and also the "adaptation to American individualism" of some Indian "Holy
Roller" converts (48-48, 48-49); Hoijer on "linguistic and cultural change"
(48-50); Róheim on "the origin of the ideal" (48-91); and Smith on "synthesis and other processes" in Sikhism (48-96).

In a more general setting, Benedict has a relevant paper on the relationships of anthropology to the humanities (48-10). Cohen discusses the
"place of 'themes' and kindred concepts in social theory" (48-22). Firth
has a provocative paper on "religious belief and personal adjustment"
(48-32). Goldfrank analyzes the impact of "situation and personality" on
four Hopi myths (48-43). Greenman discusses a concept of "the extra-

organic" (48-47). Kosven in the Soviet Union writes on the historical problem of the "matriarchate," harking back to Morgan's theory of the evolution of the family (48-63). Lowie issues important revisions of his historical and comparative studies on religion and social organization (48-74, 48-
75). Morris Opler writes on "recently developed concepts relating to culture,
and "theories of culture and the deviant," both emphasizing the newer
"psychological" approaches (48-82, 48-83). Bernard Siegel writes on
"value concepts" (48-93). Wallis discusses "presuppositions in anthropological interpretations" (48-108). Webster presents, with a generally
evolutionary emphasis, extensive materials on "magic" (48-109).

Primarily descriptive works continue to contribute case materials virtually worldwide in scope, notably by Aiyappan (48-1), Chêng (48-18),
Codere (48-21), Drucker (48-26), Foster (48-33), Gondal (48-45), Hill
(48-55), Huot (48-57), Kirchoff (48-61), Lewis (48-70), Little (48-71),
Loomis and Schuler (48-73), Mair (48-76), Miller (48-78), Mills (48-79),
Quain (48-87), Quimby (48-88), Reay and Sitlington (48-89), Spencer (48-
97), Stewart (48-99), Underhill (48-106), and Willems (48-113). Among
applied anthropology studies Beaglehole and Belshaw write on the Cook
and the Solomon islands respectively (48-7, 48-9); Davidson on missions
and marriage in the Belgian Congo (48-24); Gamio on "the indigenous problem" in Mexico (48-37); Hellman on "an African slum" (48-51); Little on
Negroes in Britain (48-72); Mair on policies in New Guinea (48-77); Smith
on "a dynamic science of man" as relating to "plans and people" in Africa
(48-95); Stent on migrancy and urbanization in South Africa (48-98); and
Sundkler on Bantu prophet movements (48-100).

In the archaeological field, Taylor's "a study of archaeology" (48-101)
is an outstanding critique of method. Additionally, Beardsley writes on
cultural sequences in California archaeology (48-8), and Bullen those in
Massachusetts (48-14); Braidwood gives a popular summary of Old World
prehistory (48-13); Childe reviews the "dawn of European civilization"
(48-19); Cline writes on "cultural innovations" in dynastic Egypt (48-20),
and Jeffreys on early diffusion in Africa (48-59). Of collateral studies,
Palmer writes on "culture contacts and population growth" (48-84), and
Rose on "innovations in American culture" (48-92).

1949

Of theoretically oriented works on change, Hoebel includes general
delineations of culture history and change in an introductory text (49-45).
Adair and Vogt analyze "contrasting modes of culture change" in terms
of the impact of war veterans returning to adjacent Navaho and Zuni communities (49-2). Keesing essays a broad characterization of the whole
field of cultural dynamics, contributed to a symposium on culture change
and administration (49-51). Kluckhohn writes on "adaptation and adjustment" as concepts for understanding behavior, and also has a prize-
winning volume on anthropology titled "mirror for man" with much relevant

material (49-53, 49-54). Leighton writes on "human relations in a changing world" (49-62). Mühlmann in Germany discusses some aspects of "ethnic assimilation" (49-80). The psychoanalyst Ruesch joins with Bateson in a provocative formulation on "structure and process in social relations" (49-97). Thurnwald presents his mature views on "innovation" (49-116).

Emphasizing change and the individual, Abel and Hsu present projective test results from studies of Chinese Americans (49-1). Barnouw explores the "phantasy world" of a modern Ojibwa woman, and Caudill the "psychological characteristics of . . . acculturated children" in an Ojibwa group (49-9, 49-15). Gorer and Rickman present an interpretation of child development, and of related cultural stability and change, in Great Russia (49-40). Joseph, Spicer, and Chesky contribute another tribal unit to the series of studies of Indian personality (49-49). LaBarre plays with the problem of building a personality type appropriate to life in the contemporary world (49-59). Leighton writes on a Navaho "hand-trembler" as a "psycho-biological personality study" (49-63). Mead discusses "character formation and diachronic theory" (49-72). Spiro analyzes psychological-anthropological dimensions in a small and remote Pacific island society (49-110).

Culture change in its sociological dimensions is also becoming well represented. The Aginskys discuss the "process of change" in family types (49-3). Fortes deals with "time and social structure" in the setting of African Ashanti (49-33). The French scholar Lévi-Strauss takes an important fresh look at the dynamics of family structures (49-64). Mead writes on "male and female . . . in a changing world" (49-73). Murdock demonstrates use of the great compilations of ethnographic data in the Human Relations Area Files developed at Yale University in a significant book on "social structure" (49-82). Warner reviews his methodology for the study of "social class" and continues with collaborators to apply it to contemporary American society (49-124 to 49-126).

On the Continent, Koppers and Schmidt continue to write in the culture-historical tradition (49-56, 49-100). White sets out his evolutionary views at book length (49-129), and Radcliffe-Brown, besides offering a critique of White's ideas, restates his "functional" position (49-92, 49-93). Shimkin lifts the curtain on "recent trends in Soviet anthropology," including the orthodox evolutionary dialectic, as analyzed from Russian language sources (49-105). Steward tries out a provocative reinterpretation of "cultural causality and law" in the development of early civilization, showing the important newer approach of combining sound archaeological data with scientific generalization on total culture process (49-112). In Argentina, Massini traces the history of art in its larger cultural context (49-71).

Other works of special theoretical importance include a paper by a Netherlands scholar, de Bruyn, analyzing cult phenomena with special reference to a recent movement in Netherlands New Guinea (49-21); Digby in England on the influence of "primitive techniques . . . upon economic

organization" (49-25, 49-26); Eisenstadt on "the perception of time and
space in a situation of culture-contact" (49-28); Honigmann on "culture
and ethos" with reference to an acculturating Indian group (49-47); Sereno
on "language, transculturation and politics" (49-103); Bernard Siegel with
an anthropological study of "shared respect" as part of an interdisciplinary
research on "revolution" (49-106); and Zipf on "human behavior and the
principle of least effort" (49-132).

Significant works with an applied emphasis include a discussion by
Shapiro of the "responsibility of the anthropologist" in the face of contemporary problems (49-104); Hawthorn on "administration and primitive
economy" (49-42); van Baal on "national movements and the problem of
acculturation" (49-119); studies of United States Navy administration in
Micronesia from the anthropological viewpoint by Embree (49-29), Keesing
and others (49-52) and Murdock (49-83), of Southeast Asia by DuBois
(49-27), of American Indian self-government by Embree (49-30), of indigenous groups in Mexico by Gamio (49-36), of New Guinea by Hogbin
(49-46) and Reed (49-94), and of occupied Japan by Montgomery (49-78).

Again descriptive studies are too numerous to list, but the following
may be noted: Barnett on Palau society (49-8); de la Fuente on a Mexican
town (49-24); Fenton on Iroquois history (49-31, 49-32); Kurath on Mexican dance acculturation (49-58); Miner on a corn-belt county in the United
States (49-75); Montgomery, Smith, and Brew on a pueblo in mission days
(49-79); Oliver on a Solomon island group (49-88); Reichard on Navaho
Christianity (49-96); Siegel on Taos pueblo (49-107); Smith on "Indians
of the urban northwest" (49-108); Spoehr on a Marshall island community
(49-111) Wagley and Galvao on an isolated Brazilian culture in transition
(49-122); Weitzel on a Yucatán group (49-128); and Willems on religious
acculturation in Brazil (49-130). Notable collateral studies are those by
Altus (49-4), Cavan and others (49-16), Davis and McDavid (49-20), and
Gordon (49-39).

1950

In this year, studies of time-dimensional phenomena branch out in
increasingly numerous directions, following the research interests of the
scholars concerned. Most general in scope from the viewpoint of theory
are Hallowell on "values, acculturation, and mental health," and more
broadly on "personality structure and the evolution of man" (50-61, 50-
62); Heinrich on "some present-day acculturative innovations in a non-
literate society" (50-65); Honigmann on "culture patterns and human
stress" (50-72); Loomis on "studies in applied and theoretical social
science" (50-96); Mühlmann in Germany on "social mechanisms of ethnic
assimilation" (50-106); Pederson on the concept of culture as applying to
contexts of change (50-111); Slotkin on cultural dynamics in a general
work on social anthropology (50-130); and Wagner, trained in the Malinowski tradition, on whether directions of culture change can be anticipated
(50-156).

Again an emphasized theme is that of the individual in situations of change: Barnouw writes on "acculturation of personality" among an Indian group (50-6); Erikson on "childhood and society" with special reference to two changing Indian tribes (50-52, 50-53); Spiro on "a psychotic personality" on a Micronesian island (50-134); Voget on a Shoshone Indian "innovator" (50-155).

Various works stress aspects of culture history or process. Brandon reviews "the problem of change in the ancient world" (50-22). Embree reports from the anthropological viewpoint on an interdisciplinary round-table discussion of "social forces" in the contemporary world setting (50-49). In the older historicalist manner, Erasmus writes on distributions of certain games (50-51), and Gunther on the "westward movement of some Plains traits" (50-59). Heine-Geldern reviews the old problem of "cultural connections between Asia and pre-Columbian America" (50-64), and Hocart follows up British diffusionist studies with a comparative work on "caste" (50-67). The historian-anthropologist Hodgen has a critical essay on "similarities and dated distributions" (50-69). Kern gives another reminder of European tradition in discussing evolutionism and "mother right" (50-80, 50-81). Rinaldo analyzes culture change as demonstrated through archaeological case materials (50-122). Thurnwald writes on the origin and development of political structures and other problems of culture history (50-143 to 50-145). White examines "ethnological theory" from his special viewpoint (50-158).

Of more specialized works on aspects of change, some deal with religious phenomena: Bascom on Cuban "santeria" (50-7); Belshaw on "modern cults" with special reference to Melanesian development (50-14); Collins on "continuity and change in religion" as illustrated by the Indian Shaker church (50-35); Radin on problems of reconstructing historically an Indian rite (50-118); Schlosser on prophet movements (50-127). Bidney writes on "the concept of myth and the problem of psychocultural evolution" (50-18), Muensterberger discusses "some elements of artistic creativity among primitive peoples" (50-105). Spencer gives case materials on Japanese-American language behavior (50-133).

Redfield demonstrates the methodological importance of documenting stability and change by revisiting a group periodically, a field work practice by now being done by a number of the pioneers in acculturation studies (50-120). Majumdar in India, for example, resurveys what in 1937 he called a "tribe in transition" (50-97). In other field studies, Pehrson documents "culture contact without conflict" in Lapland (50-112). Thompson writes on "culture in crisis," showing contemporary stresses within a hitherto very conservative Hopi community; she also attempts to set anthropological research within a larger framework of scientific conceptualism with both theoretical and applied significance (50-139 to 50-142). Tumin discusses "dynamics of cultural discontinuity in a peasant society" (50-147).

Of applied works with additional significance to theory, the following may be noted from the ever increasing number of studies with this orienta-

tion: Almond on "anthropology, political behavior and international relations" (50-2); Bowles on "Point Four and improved standards of living"
(50-20); Carvalho on "problems of assimilation" in Latin America (50-30);
Dube on tribal planning in India (50-44); Embree on the UNESCO exchange
of persons program (50-47); Firth on the peasantry of Southeast Asia
(50-54); Gladwin and Hall on military government on a Micronesian island
(50-57, 50-60); Hanks and Hanks on a Canadian "tribe under trust" (50-63);
Kimball on Navaho administration (50-82); Mason on the transplanted Bi-
kini islanders (50-100); Stroup on "the contribution of anthropology to
social work education" (50-137); Thompson on "action" (or "operational")
research (50-140, 50-141); an interdisciplinary UNESCO study of the
"preservation and development of indigenous arts" (50-149); Van der Kroef
on Indonesian nationalism and minority problems (50-150 to 50-152);
Wedgwood on "the contribution of anthropology to the education and development of colonial peoples" (50-157); and Yole and Mandelbaum on pacification in Burma (50-162).

It becomes invidious here, as indeed it has perhaps become earlier,
to single out special archaeological, historical, and descriptive studies.
They are almost world-wide in scope, and where written by professional
anthropologists or other social scientists they are particularly likely to
be cast into careful methodological molds.

1951

The British approaches to time-dimensional phenomena are well represented in three general works on social anthropology by Evans-Pritchard,
Firth, and Nadel (51-60, 51-63, 51-132). Of other more general theoretical
works, Childe surveys the total perspectives of culture growth, using the
title "social evolution" (51-32). DuBois writes on "use of social science
concepts to interpret historical materials" (51-50). Kroeber has a paper
on "configurations" and "causes" in culture process (51-109). Steward
writes on "levels of cultural integration as an operational concept" (51-
174), and Stewart on "some determinants of social change" (51-175). Tax
analyzes principles of "selective cultural change" (51-181).

Emphasizing more the individual, Aberle makes a "psychosocial analysis"
of an Indian life history (51-1). Adams writes on "personnel in culture
change" (51-2). Devereux gives psychoanalytically oriented case materials
on "reality and dream" in a study of "psychotherapy of a Plains Indian"
(51-45). Hallowell again reviews the use of projective techniques in the
"socio-psychological study of acculturation" (51-73). Henry writes on
"family structure" in relation to the transmission of neurotic behavior
and to psychic development (51-78, 51-79). Joseph and Murray combine
psychological and ethnographic data in analyzing the reactions of the Saipan-
ese under traumatic conditions of Japanese evacuation and early American
occupation (51-96). Kardiner and Ovesey analyze the "basic personality
structure" of the American Negro (51-100). Mead and Macgregor interpret

a pictorial record of "growth and culture" among the Balinese (51-124). Slotkin presents a general work on "personality development," and Spiro essays some general propositions on "culture and personality" (51-162, 51-171). Wallace has an important paper on some "psychological determinants of culture change" (51-199). Wilbur and Muensterberger edit a general volume honoring Róheim, with the title "psychoanalysis and culture" (51-202).

Dealing more with culture history and process, the Australian National University sponsors a seminar discussion on "social processes in the Pacific" (51-6). Dobyns writes on "diffusion of an agricultural technique," and Dozier on "resistance to acculturation and assimilation" in a Pueblo group (51-47, 51-49). Elkin analyzes "reaction and interaction" in the case of aboriginal-European contacts in Australia, and also reviews the status of studies of culture change in Melanesia (51-55, 51-56). Gillin delineates conservative elements which make "the culture of security" in a Guatemalan community (51-68). Held, in Dutch, discusses the Papuan as a "cultural innovator" (51-76), and Hogbin has a book-length study of the "transformation scene" in a changing New Guinea village (51-83).

Lewis has a significant report on a restudy, with some two decades of newer theory and technique at his service, of the Mexican village of Tepoztlan worked in by Redfield (51-113). Lowie writes on "some problems of geographical distribution" of cultural phenomena (51-117). Both Oakes and Starr analyze aspects of the long-term survival of Maya cultural elements (51-135, 51-173). Olmsted discusses "culture contact at the 38th parallel," in terms of interaction between adjacent Korean villages (51-138).

Quimby and Spoehr present case materials and some hypotheses on "acculturation and material culture," using museum artifacts (51-148). Schmidt writes further on culture-historical perspectives (51-158, 51-159). Suttles documents the "early diffusion of the potato" among an Indian group (51-177). Swadesh attacks some older theoretical problems with a critical essay on "diffusional cumulation and archaic residue as historical explanations" (51-179). Tax edits a volume on "acculturation in the Americas" (51-180). Thurnwald writes broadly on culture history in terms of the "human spirit, waking, growing and erring" (51-185). Voget writes on the "native-modified group" in a situation of Indian acculturation (51-197).

Of more specialized topics, various problems of change in relation to social structure are dealt with by Eggan in relation to the western Pueblo peoples (51-54); Fenton on the Iroquois (51-61); Firth on the setting of general theory (51-64); Günther in Germany on the history of marriage (51-72); and Marcozzi in Italy on "progressive" and "regressive" changes in the family (51-119). Regarding the special dimension of urbanization, Beals presents a highly important analysis of this aspect of change (51-11), and Heymans and others, and also Mitchell, discuss urbanism in Africa (51-80, 51-128). In the religious sphere, Bodrogi discusses "religious movements" in Melanesia (51-23), Dittmer in Germany writes in an older

manner on totemism, and Kock on the evolution of mana (51-46, 51-106).
Verging across to political dimensions, the French anthropologist Guiart
writes on "cargo cults" and political evolution in Melanesia (51-71), and
Ellis on "aggression and the war cult" in the southwestern Pueblos (51-57).
Lévi-Strauss writes on "language and the analysis of social laws" (51-112).
Ruesch and Bateson give an important exposition of their theoretical work
on communication (51-156).

Other works on scattered subjects of theoretical significance may be
especially noted. Belshaw gives a case study of extreme cultural shock
represented by a devastating volcanic outbreak in Papua, and also on the
methodological side discusses the training and use of indigenous assistants
in field work in a culture-contact situation (51-14, 51-15). Keesing surveys
existing and needed studies in fields of cultural dynamics for central and
eastern Oceania (51-103). Linton examines critically the "concept of national character" (51-114). Mead reports some of the hypothetical propositions of an interdisciplinary group working at Columbia University on
Soviet culture and society (51-123). Potekhin edits a Soviet symposium
attacking "Anglo-American" ethnography as "imperialistic" (51-146).
Radcliffe-Brown restates his views on "the comparative method" (51-149).
Roberts writes on "small group culture" as represented by three modern
Navaho households (51-154). Vogt shows changing values as relating to
returning Navaho war veterans (51-198).

Again selected studies with a more applied emphasis will be mentioned
to show the range of interest involved: Beals on "applied anthropological
research" (51-10); Belshaw's Papuan studies, including a report on a village
which has industrialized itself (51-14 to 51-17); Busia on government on
the Gold Coast (51-28, 51-29); Comhaire reviewing African problems (51-
36); Demeerseman on the new Tunisia (51-44); Estermann on education in
Portuguese Africa (51-59); Fuchs on anthropology in relation to missions
(51-66); Garcia on Latin American "indigenismo" (51-67); Honigmann on
an aspect of administration relating to an Eskimo group (51-86); Hunt on
a resettlement experiment in Nigeria (51-88); Florence Kluckhohn on
"cultural factors in social work practice and education" (51-105); Mayer
on "two studies in applied anthropology in Kenya" (51-122); Métraux on
"technical assistance and anthropology" (51-125, 51-126); Ashley Montagu
on "new frontiers in education: developing an harmonic human being"
(51-129); Mukerjee and others on intercaste tensions in India (51-131);
Oliver on "planning Micronesia's future," being a review of a series of
applied studies (51-137); Pederson on "cultural differences in the acceptance of recommended practices" (51-141); Sohier on "political integration"
(51-166); a South Pacific Commission report on a "community development"
experiment in Papua (51-167); Spoehr on postwar Tinian (51-172); Thompson
reviewing a series of studies of "personality and government" relating to
Indian tribes (51-184); and Van der Kroef on "foreign aid and social tradition" in Indonesia (51-193).

Dominantly historical and descriptive studies are too numerous to list.

Of archaeological works, Brainerd writes on "chronological ordering in archaeological analysis" (51-24), and Robinson on "a method for chronologically ordering archaeological deposits" (51-155). There are also significant works on aspects of linguistic change by Bright (51-26), Harris (51-74), Hoenigswald (51-85), Martinet (51-121), Snoxall (51-164), Trager (51-190), and Voegelin (51-196).

1952

A sharp growth in the number of sources, both theoretical and descriptive, occurs, indicating how the subject of change is becoming a central interest in cultural anthropology. But the work continues to proliferate in many different directions: a fertile disorder of ideas and case materials.

At the level of more general theory, Beals writes on "acculturation, economics, and social change," with case data from an Ecuador village (52-12). Bock goes critically over old and new ground in discussing "evolution and historical process" (52-25). Coulborn writes on "causes in culture" (52-41). Eaton introduces a concept of "controlled acculturation" in a study of Hutterites (52-53). Erasmus discusses "changing folk beliefs and the relativity of empirical knowledge," and "the leader versus tradition" (52-56, 52-57). Hori in Japan writes on "diffusion and change of culture" (52-92). Lesser has a critical essay on "evolution in social anthropology" (52-116). Price-Mars reviews "culture processes" (52-158). Bernard Siegel writes on "suggested factors of culture change" with reference to Taos case materials (52-180). Spindler and Goldschmidt have an important methodological paper on "experimental design in the study of culture change" (52-189).

Oriented more to the individual, Caudill documents "personality and acculturation" among Japanese Americans (52-33). Hallowell reviews the important work of his group in relation to the same topic among the Ojibwa (52-79). Henry and Bogg write on "child rearing, culture, and the natural world" (52-84). Herskovits discusses "some psychological implications" of Afro-American studies (52-86). Jewell adds another case study to the small but growing list of individual histories of "psychotic" persons, in this instance a modern Navaho Indian (52-98). Kerr writes on "personality and conflict" in Jamaica (52-104). Slotkin and McAllester discuss "individual variation in a primary group" in relation to Menomini Indian peyotism (52-183), and Spindler writes on "personality and peyotism in Menomini Indian acculturation" (52-188). Anthony Wallace tests the usefulness of the Rorschach method for defining the "modal personality" of an Iroquois group (52-221), and E. Wallace and Hoebel present another unit in the Indian personality series, on the Plains Indian Comanche (52-222).

Among studies emphasizing theoretical aspects of culture history and process, the Berndts document aborigine-white contacts in South Australia (52-21). De Laguna discusses "some dynamic forces" in a Northwest Coast Indian society (52-46). Gillin writes on "modern cultural development and synthesis" in Latin America (52-66). Goldfrank compares the "different patterns of adaptation to white authority" of Plains and Pueblo tribes (52-69). Hodgen has a meticulous study of "change and history" with case data primarily from settlement and cultural development in Britain (52-89). Honigmann examines "intercultural relations" with reference to Eskimo-Indian-white contacts in a Canadian frontier zone (52-91).

Keesing presents case materials on the response of a New Guinea group to the extreme cultural shock of a destructive volcanic outbreak (52-102). Opler and Singh discuss various aspects of change in village life in India (52-149 to 52-151). Stern discusses problems of reconstructing change in a Virginia Indian group (52-192). The archaeologist Strong analyzes "cultural resemblances in nuclear America: parallelism or diffusion" (52-196). Sun presents the "results of culture contact in two Mongol-Chinese communities" (52-197). Tax edits two symposia, one on "acculturation in the Americas" and the other on general ethnology of Middle America (52-201, 52-202). Watson has an important study on "acculturation and methodology" with reference to a Brazilian group (52-225). Zborowski and Herzog delineate the modern situation of a Jewish community of eastern Europe (52-227).

Reflecting various European traditions, Hocart in England writes on "the life-giving myth" and other kindred essays (52-88). In Germany, Grahmann discusses early cultural history, and Mühlmann "evolution and history" (52-74, 52-144). Schmidt writes on further aspects of the "culture-historical" method (52-172, 52-173), and also issues in this year the tenth volume of his monumental study of the "origin of the idea of God" (see 26-30). Thurnwald writes on "the role of political organization in the development of man" (52-205). Trends in Soviet ideas on cultural history are reviewed by Tolstoy (52-208).

The most striking development at this time, reflecting both governmental and scholarly interests, is the sudden expansion of works specifically focused on technological development and other aspects of economic change. Besides a work by Beals above (52-12), Dobyns gives case studies of the introduction of new technology to an Indian group living in an arid region (52-48, 52-49). Elkin analyzes the effects of modern technology on Australian aborigines (52-54). Erasmus examines "patterns of resistance and acceptance" as regards agricultural development in Haiti (52-55). Fried writes on "land tenure, geography and ecology in the contact of cultures" (52-62). Hoyt discusses "social and cultural aspects of technological development" in Africa (52-94). Lewis writes on "the effects of technical progress on mental health" in a rural population, using Mexican case materials (52-120), and Mandelbaum on "technology, credit and culture" in a village in India (52-128). Richardson discusses the effects of "technological change" in three Canadian fishing villages, and Sayles has a "case study of union participation and technological change" in the American setting (52-161, 52-168). Shimkin writes of "industrialization, a challenging problem for cultural anthropology" (52-179). Streib documents an attempt

to unionize a semiliterate Navaho group (52-195). Tax reports on the
"penny capitalism" of a Guatemala Indian economy (52-203). Wagner interprets "conservatism and adaptation" in the economic life of an African
group (52-220). UNESCO has a bulletin on "social implications of technological change," with anthropological and other contributors, and Hoselitz
edits the report of an interdisciplinary symposium on "the progress of
underdeveloped areas" in which anthropologists are participants (52-93,
52-211). A relevant volume edited by Spicer, with applied emphasis, is
mentioned below.

A collateral growing interest in urbanization tends also to link back to
the older studies of the "folk society" pioneered in anthropology by Redfield.
Caplow, from a sociological orientation, writes on the "modern Latin
American city" (52-30). Dumas and also Parker document urban situations
in Negro Africa (52-52, 52-154). Lewis discusses "urbanization without
breakdown" in a Mexican setting (52-119). Miner has an important paper
on "the folk-urban continuum" (52-140).

Again some studies emphasize change in relation to social structure:
Barnes on "marriage in a changing society" (52-8); Cheng on kinship in
New York Chinatown (52-34); Collins on "intragroup conflict during acculturation," with reference to an Indian society (52-37); Donahue and Humphrey
on "changing bureaucracy and social power" in a Chicago Ukrainian parish
(52-50); Gough on "changing kinship usages" among the Nayars of Malabar,
India (52-70); Grader on "rural organization and village revival" in Indonesia (52-73); Levy more generally on "the structure of society" (52-118);
Métraux on "hierarchical structure" in Haiti (52-138); Schmitt and Osanai
on old and modern kinship among the Wichita (52-174). Tumin reports on
"the dynamics of caste" in a peasant society (52-210). In a social structure
context, Mandelbaum writes on "soldier groups and Negro soldiers" in the
American setting (52-126).

Relating to stability and change in ideological aspects of culture, Bascom
writes on two forms of Afro-Cuban divination (52-10), and Casagrande on
the persistence of "a ritual attitude" among an Ojibwa group (52-32). Berndt
analyzes a "cargo cult" in the New Guinea highlands (52-20), and Guiart
also discusses dynamic postwar movements in Melanesia, especially the
"John Frum cult" in the New Hebrides area, and an indigenous co-operative
company in the latter territory which combines modern economic with
"cargo cult" characteristics (52-76 to 52-78). Hawthorn and associates
make a definitive study of the Doukhobor religious sect in western Canada
(52-81). Le Grip writes on the Mahdi movement in Africa (52-112). Morioka
discusses Christianity in a Japanese village (52-143). Spencer writes on
"native myth and modern religion" among the Klamath Indians (52-186),
and Louise Spindler on persistence of Menomini witchcraft (52-190). Vogt
interprets "water witching" as a persisting element in a rural American
community (52-218). More broadly, Mitchell has a paper on "the African
conception of causality" (52-141). Burrows discusses "covert" dimensions
of culture with reference to an isolated Micronesian group (52-29). King
writes on "changing cultural goals and patterns" in Guatemala (52-105).

Of more general works on culture theory several may be mentioned as highly relevant. Kluckhohn and co-workers try out a definitive statement on "value" theory, though with emphasis on the dimensions relating to stability rather than change (52-106). Kluckhohn also teams with Kroeber in an inventory analysis of concepts relevant to the study of culture (52-107). Kroeber also issues a series of his essays on "the nature of culture" (52-108). Lévi-Strauss summarizes the studies sponsored by UNESCO on "race and history" (52-117). Manners reviews critically Bidney's paper on "culture in crisis" (52-129). Ashley Montagu writes on "being human" (52-142). Radcliffe-Brown rounds out further his concepts of "structure and function" (52-160). Wallis writes on "values in a world of cultures" (52-223).

Regarding applied problems, a number of the works listed above have relevance, especially those demonstrating the strong contemporary interest in technological change, urbanization, modification in goals and values, and neurosis and psychosis under dynamic conditions. An important volume edited by Spicer deals with "human problems in technological change," with case studies contributed by the editor and also by Apodaca, Bliss, Dobyns, Holmberg, Lantis, Macmillan and Leighton, Morris Opler, Sasaki, Sharp, Singh, and Useem as listed in the bibliography (52-187). Among other studies are various works on Africa by Comhaire (52-38), Cornell (52-40), Decary (52-45), Herskovits (52-85), Hoyt (52-95), Mair (52-123 to 52-125), Phillips (52-156), Schapera (52-169), Smith (52-184, 52-185), and Xabregas (52-226); on Pacific zones by Belshaw (52-15), Haring (52-80), Piddington (52-157), and Van der Kroef (52-214, 52-215); and on American Indian groups by Euler and Naylor (52-58), and Stewart (52-193, 52-194). Of more general works, Murdock writes on anthropology and public health (52-145); Schapera on "anthropology for the administrator" (52-170), and Teicher on anthropology and social work (52-204).

In the archaeological field, Slotkin offers a critique of methods relating to prehistory (52-182), and Daifuku, Goggin, Heizer and Mills, Orr, Spoehr, and Strong demonstrate analysis of change in varied regional settings (52-42, 52-68, 52-82, 52-152, 52-191, 52-196). Studies of linguistic change are by Bartlett, Bittle, Gower, Gross, and Swadesh (52-9, 52-22, 52-72, 52-75, 52-199). Of collateral studies, Bogue analyzes "quantitative study of social dynamics and social change" (52-26), and Gardiner "the nature of historical explanation" (52-65). This last section of the bibliography could have been built out much further than is done, not least of all to take account of the growing interest of economists in the study of economic development and change in other cultural contexts than those of "modern civilization."

5. PRESENT AND FUTURE — AN ASSESSMENT

The works of the recent period show a great expansion of interest in culture change studies, particularly in their theoretical aspects, and at the same time a kind of undisciplined striking out in many experimental directions. Different terminologies, different conceptual approaches, like competing makes and models of a processing machine, have scattered data fed into them relating to different ethnic groups and situations all over the world. Each new worker tends even yet to start more or less freshly, with at most a small number of definite guideposts from the literature, e.g., the standard definition of "acculturation," such concepts as the "folk society" and "nativistic movement."

As noted at the beginning of this analytical survey, the great bulk of modern cultural theory has been developed on the basis of more or less static "models" or constructs relating to behavior, e.g., functional integration, configurational phenomena, modal personality (character structure), social structure, equilibria of interaction. Though earlier cultural anthropology tended to rest its main theoretical case on evolutionary or historical dynamics, these older approaches in themselves fall short of offering a comprehensive enough frame of reference within which the modern studies can be fitted. The first problem, therefore, in assessing the present situation is to ask how far the theoretical work revealed in this bibliography provides an adequate systematics of "universe of discourse" relating to culture in dynamic or time-dimension aspects.

A few works of the recent period have attempted to set out such a general rationale or frame of reference, using modern dimensions of cultural, societal, and personality theory. But all are of relatively brief length, being sections of more general texts or else papers, and each represents a markedly different approach. Most notable seem to be those by Gillin (48-41), Herskovits (48-54), Kroeber (48-64), and Keesing (49-51). A signal advance here, though not falling within the time period covered, is the publication early in 1953, of the first modern book-length study of culture change theory by Barnett.[1] Less systematized, though also very important, are somewhat scattered and incomplete materials on cultural dynamics in two volumes covering the proceedings of the Wenner-Gren Foundation International Symposium on Anthropology.[2] There is clearly a need for more attention to be given to developing the total frame of reference, so that studies of narrower scope can be properly placed within it and gaps and priorities for further research brought to light.

In the sections which follow, the writer's own suggestions as to what a

---

[1]Barnett, H. G., Innovation. New York.
[2]Kroeber, A. L. (ed.), Anthropology Today: An Encyclopaedic Inventory. Chicago Univ. Press (especially a paper by Beals, R. "Acculturation": 621-41). Tax, S. and others (eds.), An Appraisal of Anthropology Today. Chicago Univ. Press.

systematic coverage of the field entails in terms of topics or problem area
will be set out briefly. This analytical scheme, though developed in broad
outline before the bibliography was started (see 49-51), has taken its specific form from the preceding review of the literature. A brief assessment
will be given, in relation to each topic, of the adequacy of coverage to date
and need for further research. The first category will deal with the broad
problem just discussed of an adequate total frame of reference or organization of the field.

A General Frame of Reference

A first obvious need is for greater agreement on, and operational definition of, the body of theoretical concepts with which this facet of cultural
anthropology is manipulated. The disconcerting fact has shown from the
beginning of this inventory that standardization and operational clarity does
not exist even in the basic general labels applied to this field: dynamics,
change, process, acculturation, etc. "Dynamics," though considerably
used by anthropologists, has differing connotations in the various behaviora
sciences, e.g., as covering motivational or interactional phenomena as
well as time-dimensional phenomena. "Change," though perhaps the best
general term in sight, tends to push into the background the equally significant dimensions of nonchange, or deliberate resistance to change. "Acculturation," from the very rigidity of its historical mode of definition since
the time of the 1936 memorandum (36-54) has been in danger of confining
creative work, as will be seen below: this in spite of various later revisions
of the concept, e.g., as by Herskovits (48-54), Kroeber (48-64), and Beals
(footnote, p. 69).

This difficulty of establishing a basic terminology tends to pervade the
whole field, as with the varied and sometimes overlapping and competitive
concepts relating to processes of cultural transfer (below). Even the term
"culture" itself, though valid enough when the focus of constructs is on
single ethnic systems of behavior, may become operationally less useful
than some other "significant system" of reference in situations of great
ethnic heterogeneity, or of extensive change and interpenetration of behavioral elements.

Another basic problem which, though referred to in passing by several
recent writers on theory, has been very little attacked is how far the study
of culture change involves behavioral phenomena genuinely distinctive from
those present in a so-called stable society. For purposes of scientific
analysis, a culture may be looked at as a synchronic construct. Nevertheless, at the behavioral level, individuals and groups are variously learning
and interacting, accepting and rejecting old and new experience, undergoing
conflict and readjustment. Many scholars both in and outside anthropology
have emphasized the pervasiveness of change, e.g., Boas (27-4, 28-6),
Linton (36-35, 40-41), Herskovits (48-53), Kroeber (48-64). To quote
Linton (40-41: 467, 517):

Cultures are infinitely perfectible and everything indicates that all cultures are in a constant state of change. The rate of this change will, of course, differ from one culture to another and even at different points in the same cultural continuum, but some modifications are always under way . . . Cultures are the most flexible of adaptive mechanisms.

The whole picture, as shown perhaps most discerningly by Ruesch and Bateson (49-97), is one of dynamic "open systems," whether the results over time approximate to an equilibrium (or "steady state") or involve "irreversible changes" in the form of historically recognizable additions to, or subtractions from, an existing culture. The question is relevant, therefore, as to how far theoretical models or constructs relating to the diachronic dimensions of cultural dynamics can justifiably be separated out. To the extent that this can be done the way will be open for collateral delineation of models or constructs more realistically appropriate for documenting conditions relating to stability.

Together with this significant problem may be linked the related question as to how far dynamic phenomena usually subsumed under such terms as "diffusion" and "acculturation," which imply "culture contact," involve processes essentially different in any way from those occurring within a single cultural unit under conditions of change. In each case, at the behavioral level, individuals and groups are interacting, standing in hierarchical and other interrelation systems, encountering new experiences, selecting, assimilating, ranging from euphoric to dysphoric responses, and so on. Several theorists (e.g., Gillin, 48-41; Beals, 51-11) have recently noted this general sameness of the processes involved, even though the model or construct systems relating to interaction between two or more separate cultures now have such long-standing definition in cultural anthropology. Here, however, the point comes to mind that situations of contact among individuals and groups within the same cultural tradition involves, in terms of modern theory, a common unifying groundwork of experience to the extent that basic configurations of culture and personality are shared; by contrast, interaction between persons from different ethnic traditions may involve the competition of more or less incongruent systems of covert culture and personality structure. To the extent that the latter is true, separate constructs appear to have their special justification.

Much more satisfactorily treated in the literature than the above questions are those relating to the establishment of cultural "processes" underlying the historic stream of events in time and place. This is a problem, of course, of far wider concern than the purely anthropological frame of reference, being particularly a focus for analysis (and controversy) in the discipline of history. In anthropology the historicalists of the earlier twentieth century were generally content enough to deal with the "unique event" and especially to deal with completed event sequences of invention, diffusion, accumulation, and so on. But the modern emphasis includes the

search for scientifically demonstrable regularities in the dynamic behavior
and motivation of groups and individuals, opening the way so far as possible
to prediction. This involves the difficult question of selectivity of data,
either in terms of evaluating what limited data may be available from past
or present to the observer, or of deliberate selection and sampling of case
materials in terms of their significance to a given hypothesis. Especially
during the 1940's considerable writing in anthropology was devoted to definition of this problem of generalizing events into formal patterns and
"explanatory" processes ("order," "laws," "forces," "causes," etc.) as
by Barnett (40-5), Linton (40-41, 45-75), Kluckhohn (41-48, 45-66), Bidney (44-12, 46-13), Kroeber (44-54, 48-65, 48-64, 51-109), Hallowell
(45-43), Herskovits (45-46, 47-57, 48-54), Gillin (48-41), Taylor (48-101)
and Steward (49-112). Gillin is prepared to state confidently that (48-41:
568—69):

> If we know the conditions under which a culture operates and the
> lines of its internal integration and coordination, we are able to
> predict within certain limits what form and direction cultural
> changes will take. As we perfect our knowledge and our techniques
> for specifying the conditions of compatibility and consistency, our
> predictions become more accurate. As prediction becomes pos-
> sible, so control and manipulation of changes are possible.

One still very recalcitrant aspect of this analysis is the problem of
"cause and effect" relationships in dynamic processes. This basic question
has recently received attention from a number of anthropological scholars,
including Bidney (47-17 to 47-19), Herskovits (48-54), Kroeber (48-64,
48-65, 51-109), Steward (49-112), Coulborn (52-41), and Watson (52-225).
Neither the short-cut thinking of being satisfied to treat the stream of
events as "historical accidents," nor simple attribution of one-way cause-
effect relationships to functionally integrated sequences are adequate in
scientific analysis. What the physicist Nils Bohr called the multidirectional
relations of "complementarity" are likely to show in all time-dimensional
phenomena. Furthermore, studies by Whorf and other scholars have revealed the extent to which concepts such as those involved in one-way
cause-effect expectations pertain to special linguistic modes of organizing
experience, e.g., as in the English language. The problem of causation
has engaged, of course, the attention of philosophers, historians, and perhaps other groups of scholars much more than it has of anthropologists.

A large portion of the task of defining a general frame of reference
concerns delineation of various dimensions and type situations of change.
The folk-urban nexus, for example, has been an important point of reference for more than two decades, but only recently has it been getting
fitted adequately into the total organization of dynamic studies (see below).
As regards culture contact studies, a few classifications have been tried
of the possible levels or degrees of acculturation from initial interaction
to complete assimilation, e.g., by Thurnwald (32-51), Bateson (36-3),
Mair (38-55), Linton (40-41), Hallowell (42-37), Malinowski (45-79),

Gillin (48-41), and Steward (51-174). Scattered references are also found to variable dimensions inherent in different types of contact situations, such as relative size of group, mobility, momentum (aggressive-passive, etc)., hierarchical position (superior-equal-inferior), degree of effective contact, adaptability and compatibility of the cultures involved. One type situation, for example, might approximate to a large passive-superior, etc., group vis-à-vis a small aggressive-inferior, etc., group, and so through the different combinations of variables. The most comprehensive attempts to define such factors appear to be in works by Keesing (39-48), Linton (40-41), Herskovits (48-54), and Kroeber (48-64). The most controlled attempts to bring actual research results to bear on measurement of acculturation types and levels appear to be the work of the Hallowell group and of the Spindlers on Great Lakes Indian tribes, e.g., 42-38, 45-42, 51-73, 52-188, 52-189.

The sections which follow represent other more specific problem areas which the writer sees as lying within an adequate frame of reference of culture change. They represent one possible method of organizing the totality of data and concepts involved, and at the same time a challenge to continuing formulation of other types of approach.

Long-Term Cultural Development and Change

This field of study, as old as cultural anthropology itself, continues to be legitimate so far as valid hypotheses can be established on the basis of the necessarily very limited body of archaeological and other data available from the past.

As seen in the survey, the inadequacies of so much theory and method within and outside anthropology purporting to interpret total culture history, culture origins, early and primitive man, growth and diffusion of culture elements, and processes or laws of development led to critical truncation or rejection of system after system, model after model. A few "early moderns," as with Malinowski, went to the extreme of ruling long-term reconstruction outside the pale of scientific theory relating to culture. But science cannot legitimately by-pass questions so fundamental to human curiosity, and the problems involved continue to challenge thought.

Persistence of various earlier lines of attack have been noted here and there in the recent years, particularly (a) culture-historical and other traditions in Europe, (b) White's neoevolutionism, and (c) American historical and distributional studies. At the same time world-wide archaeology has yielded accumulating data on early cultural sequences and correlations which are being effectively put to work, e.g., as by Linton (45-76), Childe (though with evolutionary holdovers in vocabulary, 46-18, 51-32), Braidwood (48-13), Kroeber (48-64), and Steward (49-112). Newer concepts of early cultural diversification, the "food producing revolution," "era of incipient agriculture," "formative era of basic technologies and peasant cultures," and other broad cultural sequences, afford a framework within which hypotheses of total culture growth can be placed.

With narrower temporal and regional perspectives, culture history is also being delineated with increasing precision for many parts of the world. On the conceptual side the formulations of the historicalists with their stress on cumulative culture processes (invention, diffusion, culture area, age-area, etc.) still have operational validity in the hands of careful workers, though the trait units on which their systems are based are now recognized as having a construct character of varying degrees of generality as being abstracted from the realities of actual behavior. Also of narrower scope, longer-term development and change in particular aspects of culture, economic, social, political, religious, and so on, merit continued critical study.

From the methodological point of view, it seems fair to say that no series of problems in cultural dynamics has been covered more fully and critically than those concerned with these larger perspectives of historical and distributional reconstruction. The modern anthropologist aware of the considerations covered in previous sections may, of course, use or avoid the term "evolution" according to his taste, e.g., Radcliffe-Brown (47-109), and Lesser (52-116). But if he has gone through the mill of modern theory, he will be fully aware of the cautions and limitations that must apply to diffusionist studies, and to using distributional data as a basis for historical reconstruction. It will be noted that broad hypotheses of diffusionist character still fascinate some scholars especially in Europe, e.g., possible relationships between Asia and America, India and Oceania, e.g., Heine-Geldern (50-64). It will also be noted that in addition to critical work of Sapir (16-28) and others in earlier decades, a number of recent writers, including archaeological and linguistic specialists as well as ethnologists, have continued to feel the need to examine critically the methods and assumptions involved in historical and distributional studies, and the implications of such concepts as parallelism, the age-area hypothesis, diffusional cumulation, archaic residue, e.g., Lowie (51-117), Strong (52-196) Swadesh (51-179), Taylor (48-101), Wallis (45-105).

At more general levels Bateson, Gillin, Herskovits, Kroeber, Linton, and others have tried out formulations of longer-term processes such as cultural "drift," cultural "lag," self-reinforcing "circular" change, retardation, sudden "efflorescences," cyclic phenomena, crises and "tipover" points such as revolutions, and what Kroeber has called by analogy "cultural death," or dissolution. These merit continued examination. Again, the dynamic interrelations between cultural development and habitat factors (climate, topography, soil, etc.), biological-psychological factors (the life cycle, nutritional needs, etc.), and demographic-social factors (aggregation, hierarchy, etc.), in general old in anthropological theory, are on the whole well formulated by now. For example, Boas and his followers were particularly influential in building up resistance in professional anthropology to oversimplified nostrums and determinisms, geographic, racial, psychological, psychoanalytic, economic, or sociological. In turn, the later moderns undermined tendencies in the work of the Boas school to reach the dead end of a kind of cultural determinism far apart from the realities of observed behavior. A recent paper by Hallowell on personality structure considered in the total perspectives of human development (50-61) shows that scope exists for further creative formulations here. Further- more, the detailed texture of habitat-psychosomatic-social-cultural inter- relations still offers much to challenge further study, e. g. , reconciliation of rival systems of learning theory, or again personality theory. These dimensions assume particular importance in the study of shorter term phenomena of change which will provide the focus for the further categories of analysis below.

Innovation

This vital aspect of cultural process is represented in the literature back at least to an early paper on "anthropology and social innovation" (66-4). Mostly it has been treated in terms of the much discussed concept of "invention." Earlier scholars such as Seeley and Mason, and somewhat later Harrison in England and the American historicalists such as Boas, Wissler and Dixon, were perhaps most instrumental in giving substance to this concept, and its main corollary, "discovery." But the strong modern tendency has been to speak of this initial point of reference for change in terms of the broader concept of "innovation," as in Barnett's recent definitive work on this topic.

The writer has an impression that the older discussions of innovation, which concentrated on its cultural dimensions, forced this aspect of theory into very limited channels of thought, or, to put it more strongly, a kind of intellectual strait jacket from which even the modern work has not en- tirely freed it. An invention, by definition, occurred at the point in time and place where a more or less new element is added to an ongoing cultural tradition. Furthermore, it was not merely a cultural element produced by an act of individual or group creativity. It had also to gain enough ac- ceptance to become a recognizable part of the culture. From here, to con- tinue the conceptual model, it might be subject to "diffusion" to other ethnic groups, and so continue its cultural adventures.

The newer concept of innovation, particularly in the work of Barnett, takes account of the fact that a "diffusion" process also involves comparable acts of creativity by the individuals and groups who accept a new cultural element brought within the scope of their experience from an outside cul- tural source. In both case situations a significant rearrangement or re- definition occurs of elements within the focus of individual attention: what Linton has referred to as a kind of cultural "mutation" (45-76). How far this process involves something actually "new," or merely a kind of recog- nition of a culmination "juxtaposition" and synthesis in a series of converg- ing elements within the total flux of events, has been discussed by a number of anthropologists besides Barnett, e. g. , as by Harrison (25-11, etc.) Dix- on (28-9), Linton (36-35, 40-41), Greenman (45-38), Gillin (48-41), Hersko- vits (48-54), Kroeber (48-64), Hoebel (49-45). It has, of course, been also a topic of much wider discussion in recent literature on the history of science and in the humanities as regards artistic and other creativity.

The problems involved, however, cannot yet be considered adequately

solved. Of particular promise here is the recent development of various
experimental research programs concentrating on innovative phenomena
in controlled contexts from various social science viewpoints, especially
to date from that of psychology. [1] For anthropologists there is wide scope
for detailed observation of such phenomena, especially in cross-cultural
contexts, including experimentally created situations in which the variable
factors can be held under control to the maximum extent possible. So far
nearly all reporting on innovation has been retrospective only, that is,
dealing with completed action series, usually indeed far back in time. Only
a handful of studies to date have really focused prime attention on an innovative act or the innovator in action, e.g., Voget (50-155); case materials
in Spicer's edited volume on technological change (52-187).

The type of innovation which will lend itself most easily to experimental
work is the presentation by an investigator of an already existing cultural
element (tool, technique, idea, etc.) to individuals for whom it is totally
unfamiliar until brought within their experience, whether in an ongoing
culture or in a cross-cultural situation (a potential "diffusion" experiment).
But ways might also be tried to document original creative acts in process,
as in the work of a dramatist or scientific inventor. Though not in the
recognized vocabulary the writer suggests that a terminological distinction
be made, even if more important as regards historical events and contexts
than of differential processes, between "primary" (or "original") innovation
and "secondary" (or "derivative") innovation of the kind involved in cultural
transfer.

Attention may be pointed finally to an aspect of innovation which has been
generally neglected by anthropologists, namely, individual variability in
experience. This has received some recent treatment, e.g., Herskovits,
48-54, Slotkin and McAllester, 52-183. But the stress in cultural theory
has been almost wholly upon patterning (though sometimes including pattern
variability), group participation, and continuity in behavioral phenomena.
At the level of individual experience, however, each person from before
birth obviously carries on a continuous series of more or less idiosyncratic
innovative acts, especially in waking hours in setting up speech sequences,
handling tools, carrying out his toilet, handling of clothes, behaving as
kinsman or marital partner, and so on through the time-stream of activity.
In a sense the individual innovative act might be looked on as the minimal
"atom" of behavior. Such acts tend, of course, to approximate to a cus-
tomary or acceptable range or response, that is, to the "modes" and "norms"
which are the basis of cultural constructs. They reassemble the cultural
and personal experience into ever varying rearrangements. As has long
been recognized in the literature on invention, an infinitesimal number of
these minor innovative acts, even when falling at an extreme enough point

---

[1] A useful source here is the Clearinghouse Bulletin of Research in
Human Organization, published quarterly by the Society for Applied Anthropology, and reporting current research of this nature.

in relation to the acceptable behavior gradient to attract attention and be considered "novel," make the individual an "innovator" in the narrower sense of providing the beginnings of a new mode or norm, e.g., a bon mot, a makeshift tool, a deviant cooking recipe, a fresh religious interpretation. But they appear to deserve more observational and experimental study in their own right, and proper theoretical placement, than they have received to date in the literature on cultural dynamics.

Processes of Cultural Transfer

To be successfully established in a cultural tradition, a primary or secondary innovation must, on entering the attention of new individuals or groups, undergo a test of acceptance rather than rejection. The earlier schools of theory paid little attention to the processes involved in such an act of transfer, limiting their attention to the elements of culture involved and the historical fact (or supposition) that "diffusion" of the elements occurred. Among later theorists, however, these processes have received extensive attention, even to the point of becoming the major focus of study. They may be counted as perhaps the most fully documented aspect of culture-change studies.

As early as 1920, Boas pointed to the "inner forces . . . [by] which foreign elements are remodelled according to the [prevalent] pattern" (20-2). Somewhat later, Lowie pointed to what he called the seemingly "capricious" nature of selection in the diffusion process, and to the tendency for "contact metamorphosis" to occur.[1] Both scholars, though concentrating their main attention on the historical events of diffusion, were well aware that an element, in passing from one cultural context to another, tends to have its character made over to fit the new setting. By the 1930's a number of other scholars were experimenting with theoretical formulations relating to diffusion or acculturation phenomena of these kinds, as shown in the analysis for that decade. The most important initial attempt to state the problems concerned in a comprehensive way is the "memorandum on acculturation" prepared by Redfield, Linton, and Herskovits (36-54). This offers a tabulated framework on processes and results of acculturation which can still prove most helpful to the field worker and theorist. It may profitably be read along with fuller expositions of the materials involved by two of the authors, Linton (36-35, 40-41), and Herskovits (37-22, 38-38).

From that period forward theory has proliferated, even to the point of considerable overlapping and competition of concepts. Various types of diffusion process have been distinguished by particular scholars: "natural" diffusion, "organized" diffusion, "stimulus" diffusion, "antagonistic" diffusion, "controlled" acculturation (e.g., Wissler, 23-29; Kroeber, 40-38; Devereux and Loeb, 43-16; Eaton, 52-53). Several students have attempted to analyze components of a potential cultural "transaction": the heightened awareness of persons faced with alternatives, perhaps the bringing to con-

---

[1]See especially 37-35; also in Boas (ed.), General Anthropology (38-10).

sciousness of premises or assumptions hitherto in the main covert or implicit; probably some experimental testing by a few individuals; rejection
or acceptance of the new in the light of what are considered gains and
losses involved; fitting of new elements into the context of the recipient
cultural system; repercussions of such adoption, including possible modifications of old elements to the extent they are retained.

The "selectivity" processes here (accepting or rejecting new elements,
conserving or discarding old elements) have evoked such general concepts
or principles as "utility" (including prestige or status enhancement),
"adaptability," "congruence," "compatibility"; the last two obviously refer
to the degree to which the "donor" and "receptor" cultures are alike or
different. The contextualization processes within a recipient group also
have been variously generalized in such terms as "reorientation," "readaptation," "reinterpretation," "indigenization," "syncretization," "recon-
stellation," "synthesis," and, as regards reduction processes, "truncation." It has been noted that in a potential transfer situation, a new element
may be in direct competition with an old element, or it may not, involving
different type dimensions of response. Some theorists have suggested that
every process of cultural elaboration has its own "peculiar" limits which
confine patterns of growth, but this proposition has not been adequately
tested by focused research. A number of students have postulated the more
obvious hypothesis that simplicity in a cultural element tends to facilitate
transfer, and complexity retard it; furthermore, that "nonsymbolic" elements are more nimble than "symbolic" elements, and that "form" is
likely to be transferred more easily than "function." Case studies of the
adoption of artifacts show how separately mobile the differential elements
may be: basic form, materials, decoration, immediate use, meaning,
wider functional context. Watson has recently distinguished "primary"
from "secondary" effects of such acculturation processes (52-225). A
category of analysis pervading all of these factors, namely, that of "value,"
as underlying judgment and choice, is dealt with in a separate section below. Notable examples of recent studies emphasizing analysis of selectivity
processes are works by Beals (52-12), Eaton (52-53), Erasmus (52-55),
Quimby and Spoehr (51-148), Siegel (52-180), and Tax (on "selective cultural change," 51-181).

As with innovation, of which such culture transfer situations form an
extension, the work done to date is prolific on theory but weak in specific
and controlled case material. Practically all the constructs relating to
process, if not built up "off the cuff" from general impressions in field
work, are based on observation of already completed acts of acceptance
or rejection, in fact, on examination of museum specimens or else verbal
and other records from the past. Here, too, there is wide room for controlled observation and experiment in contemporary settings, with this
problem as the direct focus of research attention. A series of carefully
planned experiments in presenting a group with new cultural elements,
familiar to completely exotic, competing and not competing, simple to

complex, and so on through other variable dimensions would yield case materials of great importance. In addition to its value for theoretical clarification, more controlled knowledge of culture transfer processes has vital "applied" significance in the world setting, where economic and other development depend so much on successful "diffusion" of new ideas and practices.

"Values" and Culture Change

A critical category of analysis, as suggested above, is that of choice determination based on "value" or "value-judgments." Groups and individuals, faced by new experience, respond positively or negatively in terms of affectively charged preferences, that is, "values." Those in turn link into the total system of what have variously been called interests, premises, orientations, themes, ideals, purposes, goals, and other terms variously expressing cognitive, affective, or conative aspects of so-called "configurations."

The analysis of value theory in cultural anthropology dates almost wholly from 1940 on, and is based primarily on static cultural models or constructs. It is becoming increasingly realized, however, that the "value" concept (or some equivalent if another conceptual system is used) is crucial to the interpretation of choice behavior in culturally dynamic situations, and that the further development of theory on values can be enriched by the addition of dynamic models.[1] Refinement for scientific purposes of the concept of value, indeed, seems currently to be left mainly to the anthropologists and philosophers, working increasingly in co-operation, by default of other behavioral disciplines. Among the very limited number of specific discussions of values and change to date, most of them quite brief, are those by Aberle (50-1), Bidney (49-10), Firth (51-63), Hallowell (50-61), Kardiner (45-56), Keesing (49-51), Kluckhohn and associates (52-106), LaBarre (49-59), Malinowski (44-59), Mead (42-67), Ruesch and Bateson (51-156), Siegel (48-93), Thompson (46-95, 48-103), Vogt (51-198).

A number of students have pointed out that the basic value system of a group or individual stands as a kind of watchdog or censor, consciously or otherwise, to govern responses in the face of novel stimuli. A new element in experience, whatever its immediate promise of usefulness or pleasure, undergoes a selective screening in terms of established affects, sanctions, and other determinants of value. Correspondingly, to the extent that the latter are evoked in relation to an existing cultural item, it is likely to be persistently adhered to. Deviation in terms of the core of values tends in either case to bring about more or less violent psychosomatic disturbances

---

[1] Another Stanford research project, carried on since 1951, has been the collection and analysis of all discoverable anthropological materials on value theory, using a financial grant from a Stanford interdisciplinary Committee on Contemporary Values; the files of materials concerned have been integrated with those of the culture change project.

in the individual concerned, as well as group revulsions. Contextualization of a newly adopted cultural element tends to be shaped in terms of the currently accepted value system.

But values may themselves undergo change. The very fact that intrusion of new value dimensions, whether by contact between two different ethnic groups or otherwise, tends to make the individuals concerned aware of alternatives in behavior, and may bring to consciousness hitherto "unstated premises" or other implicit dimensions of their own traditions, seems to imply in itself a degree of modification. This has been postulated, for example, by Thurnwald (32-51), as well as others in discussing "initial acculturative" contacts. Again, changes in the total definition of situation, as the shifting of a group or individual to a new habitat, or external authoritarian suppression, may bring modifications at the value level. Voluntary changes may be made as a result of access to what are considered better value-judgments regarding power, truth, goodness, and other basic dimensions of the culture concerned, as, say, among religious converts. One of the most difficult aspects of applied anthropology is that it is likely to involve an "evaluation of values."

In a given dynamic situation, the value system of the culture concerned, with other related configurational dimensions, may be little if at all impaired; or again it may be modified, but with progressive substitution of new values which the people judge as adequate; or it may be seriously interfered with, impaired, or more or less invalidated, without adequate substitution. Several theorists have suggested that, so long as the basic value system stands reasonably firm, selective change can proceed with minimum strain and stress. At the other extreme, some groups and individuals have undergone, or are in process of undergoing, the experience of having their value systems in jeopardy or shattered, catastrophically or through a prolonged series of crisis episodes. The resulting problems of disorganization and reorganization will be discussed under special heads below.

The collection and organization of increasingly controlled case data relating to situations and propositions such as these is particularly challenging. Most of the materials available refer to retrospective conditions, and are rather incidental to more general frames of reference on acculturation. Here, too, careful research planning should be able to sharpen up what to date are very sketchy hypothetical outlines relating to these important value dimensions of change. It may be noted that value dynamics are of special significance to humanistic scholars, as where change and resistance to change in value systems provide some of the main motifs in literature and drama. Collaborative research may profitably be developed here, and a beginning has already been made on a few university campuses, including Stanford.

Voluntary and Involuntary Change

Numbers of field workers have been intrigued by the intrusion into a dynamic situation of some variable of arbitrary control and manipulation, involving real or potential compulsion by an external authority. Such an action pattern interferes with voluntary self-motivated choice by the groups and individuals concerned. It may operate in the direction either of demanding change against a people's will, or of obstructing or inhibiting desired change. It may also occur within a single cultural system, or in a cross-cultural setting.

This problem is particularly acute for the anthropologist who is called upon to handle "applied" problems, as any program with which he is concerned is likely by its very nature to involve originating action from outside rather than by the people on whom it is focused. For the same reason, the record of applied anthropology can be particularly significant for theory to the extent that action problems are documented adequately.

Relevant materials in this category go all the way back to papers on mission and government activities among aborigines starting in the bibliography as early as 1865 (65-2, 65-5, etc.). Yet for all the extensive work done to date, very few if any minute and careful accounts are available which include the whole range from plans to action processes and on to results. The experiment of having a theoretician looking over the shoulder of an applied anthropologist (and of those who act on his recommendations) has never been tried, and any close co-ordination of action and theory is rare enough. The field worker, intent on scientific observation for its own sake, is likely also to encounter numerous case examples of arbitrary manipulation in terms of governmental, missionary, or other outsiders or by internal elites or other authorities: the process is doubtless as old as human history.

Studies of the contrasts between voluntary and forced responses have the special significance of presenting an approximation to experimental "laboratory" conditions as regards control and direction of culture process. But so far the problem has been merely treated incidentally to some larger culture-change study, so that data is scattered through many sources and is very general. Only a small number of studies to date have focused upon it, with a view to bringing it under greater theoretical and methodological control, e.g., Embree (43-21), Goldfrank (52-69), Keesing (45-57, 49-51), Kluckhohn (43-43), Leighton (45-73), Mead (43-55, Schapera (47-122), Thompson (50-139, 51-184), the Wilsons (45-114).

Complex responses may occur in situations involving arbitrary manipulation. Most obvious are various types of accommodation or external conformity in behavior, as where, say, the women of an indigenous group, legally required to wear clothing to meet the moral standards of a ruling society, may wear an upper garment when whites are present, but not otherwise. Useem pointed to the pervasiveness of such a dual standard of behavior in the face of outside administrative control in a Micronesian society (45-103, 46-100). In some situations, a kind of entrepreneur group emerges to mediate between the people concerned and the external authority, in official or nonofficial capacities, and may include individuals of mixed ancestry.

Compulsion may produce negligible resistance and tension under certain conditions, as with suppressing or imposing an element of culture regarded as unessential. But if a measure threatens or undermines basic cultural elements violent reactions may be generated, even to the point where a group or individual may be willing to die rather than conform. The literature of applied anthropology tends to stress the principle that, if an outside authority counts it essential to suppress an old element in an ongoing culture, especially one regarded by the people concerned as vital, some reasonably equivalent substitute should be introduced it at all possible, e.g., active sports for warfare. A related principle, too, is that new elements, in being imposed, should be "indigenized" as far as possible in relation to the existing cultural context. The total stance of relationships between the two interacting groups is of course relevant here, possibly ranging from warm friendliness and general cultural congruence to hostile antagonism and cultural incompatibility.

Rates of Change; Loci of Stability and Change

One of the most tenuous yet potentially important fields of study concerns how far significant regularities may be established as regards rates of change, or to put it another way, the loci or focal points of persistence, conservatism and stability, on the one hand, in culture and personality, and change and mobility, on the other. The literature contains numerous scattered assertions or hypotheses which imply such regularities of "lag" and acceleration in relation to technological, economic, social, religious, and other behavior, either within particular cultural systems or as regards "culture" in the broad sense. Besides being grist to the mill of scientific generalization, any ability to discern and predict tendencies to stability and change would be most important in applied fields. Leonard Broom, stressing this problem from the viewpoint of methodology, says (45-10: 631):

> We must strive to put our findings in such form that we can isolate elements from a given segment of the cultural space, and measure their rates of change. Next we might be able to establish with some precision differential rates of change of phenomena from various segments of a culture. Perhaps finally we shall be in a position to discover [and account for] the differential rates of change in analogous or homologous segments of two or more cultures.

The very general concept of "cultural lag," long familiar in social science studies, has been discussed recently from the viewpoint of anthropology by Gillin (48-41), Herskovits (48-54), and others. Another general approach to this problem of speed of change has been tried out by Herskovits by way of a concept of cultural "focus," namely, those ideas and activities which are in the center of attention and interest, and tend to proliferate into rich variability (see especially 48-54). This zone of a people's cultural experience, he postulates, is particularly amenable to change, provided advantages are anticipated. This line of thought is not incompatible, though it might seem so on the surface, with another general proposition, often stated or implied in theoretical writings, namely, that the basic "configurations" or "integrating factors" of a culture (more or less implicit and unconscious) tend to provide the dead weight of stability and conservatism in behavior.

Several theorists have discussed the even more general point that different cultures appear to be aligned as wholes, at least at given times in their history, in directions that emphasize stability and rigidity, or else mobility and responsiveness to change. Adair and Vogt, for example, have discussed recently the differential "adaptability" of Navaho and Zuni cultures in terms of the markedly contrasting response to returned war veterans (49-2, 51-198). The particular loci of such pervasive sets, to the extent they are valid in determining rates of change, would seem to lie in basic ideological and value dimensions of the culture. Where stability is the dominant note, it may relate variously to long identity and exclusiveness, adaptation to a highly specialized habitat, rigidly institutionalized social structure favorable to homeostasis, the unifying stamp of a single religion, or similar determinants. By contrast, mobility may be basic in a society where populations and ethnic traditions have been diversified and on the move, and frequent adjustment has been historically occurring in the face of technological, political, or other factors of mobility. Change in the sense of "progress" and "advancement" can even become a pervasive value for a group during a given period, as in the contemporary American milieu.

Passing from these very broad approaches to consideration of more specific zones of stability and change, perhaps the most ambitious attempt to collect and systematize the data involved is by Keesing (49-51). By tabulating loci of persistence and of mobility as shown in a number of acculturation studies, he develops a broad framework of hypotheses in relation to each of these facets of dynamics. First are set out those zones in culture which appear to show a high frequency of persistence, as pertaining to basic survival, security, integrity, value, problem solving, for the group concerned, and in which, if change or interference occurs, the greatest disturbance and tension is likely to be generated. Categories cover essentials of psychosomatic conditioning, communication, organic maintenance, primary group relations, prestige status maintenance, territorial security, and ideological (including religious) security. By contrast, zones in which mobility or ready change tend to appear with high frequency are nonaffectively charged techniques summarized as "instrumentalities" (e. g., tools, etiquette, military tactics); voluntary elements of taste and self-expression, achieved status systems, and other elective or competitive types of behavior, and more impersonal or mass social structures. It is recognized, of course, that great variability shows as regards group and personal response within these broad tendencies and such variations challenge further propositional analysis.

Exploration along these lines can relate loci of conservatism in some respects to the body of theory spelling out essential relations between cultural behavior and habitat determinants, biological-psychological determinants, and societal determinants. Conservatism as regards a staple food

and its production, for example, may involve interplay of all three classes
of determinants, though particularly the first. Again, the great tenacity of
indigenous witchcraft usages in so many societies, even some near the
final levels of an assimilative process (e.g., Beaglehole, 46-9; Spindler,
52-190), appears to result particularly from a complex psychological-cul-
tural interplay, involving basic beliefs and affects.

An extension of this line of inquiry, so far barely adumbrated in a few
general statements of possibility, is to relate regularities of stability and
change in particular zones of individual development and group participation.
Most obvious and extensively studied, though in other contexts, are the
basic psychosomatic sets pertaining to infant and early childhood conditioning: here the weight is heavily to the side of persistence in personality and
in cultural transmission. Learning of basic communication techniques,
furthermore, relates primarily to early childhood (learning to talk, facial
expressions, etc.)—another zone of persistence.

By contrast, childhood and early youth appear in all cultures to be
marked by extensive play and other elective behavior, as well as authoritarian learning: a lodgment for the duality of potential mobility and alertness
to new experience along with conservatism even to dogmatism. Young adults,
with work and family matters tending to monopolize time, tend perhaps to
be the main loci of economic and social persistence, even while alert to new
instrumentalities. Status, territorial, and ideological persistence, appear
to be especially associated with the mature and old, and often involve
"classified data" and specialized practitioners. But the elders and privileged
are also likely, when it is to their advantage, or pressure from outside
circumstances requires, to respond with great mobility in the face of new
experience. Even the dead, in the contexts of some cultures, may be aligned
heavily on the side of conservatism, along with other supernatural forces.

Such materials on rates and loci of change and their determinants are
cited here as broad leads, having a familiar ring to a point both from every-
day experience and from monograph reading, yet still remaining to be tested
and refined through cross-cultural data. Whatever may come of them, they
illustrate the extent to which cultural studies offer practically virgin ground
in many respects when dynamic problems are posed.

Cultural Disorganization

Under dynamic conditions of change cultural systems tend to become disorganized. In extreme instances they may become shattered and disintegrated
to a degree where identity and existence may be lost. Instead of the more
or less "steady state" of an ongoing culture, there appears what Radcliffe-
Brown calls "dysnomia" (bad integration), the "disequilibria" of the inter-
actionists, the anxiety-ridden breakdown of habit patterns as cited in learning theory, and so on.

This aspect of process has engaged the attention of sociologists extensively
at the theoretical level, as in "social disorganization," or "social pathology,"
but it has not yet had the specialized attention in anthropological theory and

field work which it appears to deserve. Emphasis on pattern and integration, on norms and modes, even in studies of change, has tended to relegate the phenomena involved to an incidental place.

A search of the literature would, however, turn up a great amount of relevant material. Anthropological works on depopulation in acculturative situations, for example, especially from the time of Rivers' pioneer hypothetical statement in 1922 on social and psychological factors involved (e.g., loss of joie de vivre, "decay of the will to live"), include much discussion of cultural disorganization and its supposed demographic consequences. Again, the weakening of traditional sanction systems under conditions of dynamic change has often been referred to. Keesing has documented the disorganizing effects of dual codes of conduct in acculturative situations, in which an individual is forced as regards some zones of behavior into the situation of being a delinquent in terms of indigenous rules if he obeys those imposed by the outside authority, and vice versa (41-46). Recent work on "factionalism," as in field studies by Collins and French (52-37, 48-35), and on the usually disorganizing effects of urbanization as discussed in a later section, are among the many other ramifications of this process. Indeed, almost any field report on culture change, contains relevant case materials. In the "applied" literature examples of accumulating data are those relating to policy pressures in "colonial" administration, and to the mental health field.

It will be noted by anyone exploring this field that the vocabulary so far available for operating studies of this character is poor. There is nothing comparable with the now considerable precision of categories represented by such terms of stability as trait, function, pattern, configuration. Concepts of "discontinuity" and "dysfunction" have some currency. But they perhaps need to be supplemented by further concepts, or at least standardized modes of reference, to subsume what might awkwardly be called "dyspattern" and "dysconfiguration," to express other dimensions of the increasing inconsistencies involved, and trends toward what might be termed "deculturation." The widening of hitherto narrower behavior "gradients" in relation to norms and modes makes, so to speak, for a greater range of intergradation in individual and group behavior, and is likely to be marked by new or exaggerated discontinuities.

Many of the more specific aspects of dysnomic phenomena are discussed or implied under various other headings of this analytical outline. In relation to ideological and value systems, for example, the thesis seems inherent in recent work by a number of students that if, under conditions of change, the basic cultural rationale retains its validity, even extensive behavioral changes can take place without threat to group or individual integrity and morale, e.g., Linton (36-35), Hallowell (45-43), Kroeber (48-64). But if these basic elements are threatened or undermined, the group or individual concerned is likely to lapse into states of disorganization, insecurity, anxiety, self-depreciation, and low morale, though usually accompanied by attempts to establish a new rationale (see "Reorganization" below). The latter part of this proposition is particularly open to testing in extreme cases where forest pigmies, Australian aborigines, or similar groups with cultural systems in extreme contrast to those of the West now pressing in on them, may be manifesting extreme dysnomic conditions perhaps to the point of depopulation and extinction. Here further testing is needed of the disputed thesis as to how far there is psychosomatic validity to the thesis of the "decay of the will to live" on the part of whole groups, as in the medically recognized individual phenomenon of thanatomania. Other manifestations of disorganization, such as those relating to the effects of change on personality, social structure, and population dynamics, as discussed below, also present challenging opportunities for further stud

Cultural Reorganization

Groups and individuals, under conditions of cultural and personal disorganization, are apparently always likely to strive toward some new and satisfying reorganization or readjustment of experience as a basis for survival and integrity. The "adaptive" processes involved have both theoretica and applied importance, the latter aspect being obvious because the problems of "applied" anthropology relate normally to eunomic goals of order, equilibrium, continuity, high morale, and so on.[1]

Here is encountered one of the most studied aspects of cultural dynamic what are often summed up as "nativistic" movements, with military, religious (including so-called "messianic"), political, economic, or other goals, singly or in combination. Works relating to such phenomena are found from the earliest sections of the bibliography, and of the various attempts at definitive conceptualization that of Linton is probably the best known (43-47). Such movements may be "perpetuative" of old sociocultural elements in the face of a new order, or may move toward institutional and ideological redefinition. The latter tend to arise wherever traditional assumptions and values become demonstrably inadequate, or are impaired through outside manipulation. Their prophets and panaceas can usually evol fervent and dynamic action patterns so long as they promise to yield new and satisfying solutions; and they can lapse as quickly as they may rise. The movements involved may range from mystical or otherwise exotic sect or pseudopractical cults (e.g., the present-day Melanesian "cargo" cults) to intelligent movements of political nationalism or cultural renaissance. Techniques of forceful suppression, so often intruded by outside authority particularly when any movement becomes aggressive or threatening, appea

---

[1]This is not to say that applications of anthropological data and techniqu could not be used, and may not have been used at times, deliberately for dysnomic ends. Consciousness of this possibility led the Society for Applied Anthropology from 1947 on to study and formulate a "Code of Ethics" for professional workers engaged in projects of a practical or utilitarian nature: see in Human Organization, 10, 2: 32 (1951).

to do no more than eliminate overt expression and redirect the tensions and strivings involved into other channels.

Less studied, or even classified, by anthropologists, have been various other types of response aimed at reinforcing group or personal integrity. Some of them at least are well conceptualized and documented in psychological and psychoanalytic contexts, and may show incipiently in infrahuman laboratory experiments with animals. They have also received considerable discussion in the sociological literature on collective behavior and social change. They include various escapist, compensatory, or other behaviors, well structured or otherwise, such as reversion to the past, devotion to novelties, fads and fashions, shows of bravado and "sophistication," acts of romantic supererogation, covert or overt aggression, revolts, conversions, the practice of double standards for in-group and out-group relationships, and on to various extremes of neurosis and psychosis. In culture contact situations involving a superior and an inferior status group, the directions of impulse among the latter may vary from so-called "contra-acculturative" reactions to attempts to become fully assimilated to the dominant society. A quotation from Gillin, couched largely in Yale learning theory terms, will reinforce these points (48-41: 562 – 63):

> For every society undergoing acculturation there would seem to be an inevitable period characterized by some confusion and lack of stability in behavior, a period during which (1) old customs un-adapted to new conditions are being extinguished and new customs are being tried out and developed with corresponding patterns, (2) new patterns, once worked out, are being integrated, and (3) the new patterns in the new integration are being learned and practised as activity. "Will a new culture, exhibited in adapted and predictable behavior result?" This depends on whether or not the situation, once changed, remains relatively stable. Rapidly recurring, capricious, and disorderly alterations of conditions will result in random behavior, social and cultural disorganization, apathy, or withdrawal. It is quite possible for the dominant society in an acculturative situation to manipulate factors, either by accident or intent, in such ways that the foreign cultural component never remains stable.

In these various categories relating to cultural reorganization, the needs and opportunities for further formulation are clearly very great. Case materials available for orderly study range from groups on some cultural frontiers still supposedly "hopeless" and "without the will to live," to groups among whom former known conditions of disorganization have given place to dynamic processes of reorganization or to established newer patterns approximating to stability and equilibrium. The field worker called upon to deal with such phenomena from the applied viewpoint, as has been occurring in Melanesia, Africa, and elsewhere, has the assurance that his data can be important in relation to theoretical levels of analysis.

Not least of all, more examination seems to be needed of the relationships between group phenomena of these types and comparable manifestations in individuals as documented and conceptualized by psychologists,
psychiatrists, and others. The situation, for example, as regards a nativistic movement which involves mass aggressive behavior is not just a
mathematical one of an $\underline{X}$ number of psychotically or otherwise aggressive
individuals juxtaposed in an aggregation, and the question can be posed as
to how it can fairly be conceptualized in terms from individual psychology.
Again the anthropologist may find some nexus of behavior which resembles
what at the individual level is considered to be a manifestation of instabilit`
such as violence of temper, or "paranoid" tendencies, stabilized so to
speak in the culture patterns of an ethnic group and so having great persistence. These problems are, of course, only one phase of the larger
question which continues to engage modern "psychologically" oriented
theorists as to the relations between culture and personality, between
group and individual behavior.

Tensions and Change

Both the theoretically minded anthropologist, and the worker with "applied" problems may profitably take note of the type, locus, and extent of
emotional tensions as indicators in dynamic change. As regards both specific behavioral situations and general "tone," what Radcliffe-Brown has
called "euphoria," or feelings of well-being, may show in manifestations
of security, integrity, self-respect, self-confidence, high morale, and so
on. Alternatively, "dysphoria" is signaled by insecurity, anxiety, unrest,
malaise, low morale, bewilderment, frustration, disillusionment, and so
on, possibly even hopelessness. In relation to others, groups and individua
may, for example, feel superior, equal or inferior, free or suppressed;
the attitudes and sentiments may be those of respect, affection, friendliness, aggressiveness or passivity, resentment, grievance, blame, evasio
hate, or fear.

No working culture, even when counted most stable, is so well integrate
that its practitioners are without insecurity and other strains; every cultural shoe pinches in some places, as can be seen by examining, say, crit
cal points in its religion or those phases in which sharp competition is per
mitted. In dynamic situations, however, the incidence of anxiety and other
indicators of stress appear always to rise, and particularly so to the degre
that basic values are threatened or undermined.

Before World War II the Yale learning experiments and other psycholog
cal leads had already given a number of anthropologists a sense of the significance of tension systems, so that they were beginning to give attention
to good and bad morale, uneasiness, hostility, face-saving mechanisms,
aggression, suicide, and other related factors in cross-cultural contexts,
e. g., Benedict (38-8), Fenton (41-26), Hallowell (38-33, 40-25, etc.),
Henry (40-27), Sapir (38-68). Benedict had a seminar relevant to this seri
of problems at Columbia University, following up some of the ideas adum-

brated in her "patterns of culture" case materials (34-4). The war period suddenly brought such subjects to the forefront as regards studies of "morale," "vulnerabilities" in psychological warfare, military government, control of occupied populations and similar "applied" problems (though mostly the documentation is still "classified" and so not publicly available). Subsequently, topics in this category have had a definite place in case studies of culture change, with a notable recent addition of an emphasis on "mental health." They have also become an increasing focus for theory, as in works by Barnouw, Bateson, Devereux, DuBois, Erickson, Hallowell, Henry, Honigmann, Hsu, Keesing, Kluckhohn, LaBarre, the Leightons, Lewis, Mead, the Oplers, Spiro, and Thompson.

As an example of the types of hypothesis which have been set up for testing in this field, one which gives a very broad frame of reference might be compounded on the basis of leads in a number of recent works. Its propositional frame could run something like this. So far as groups and individuals in a dynamic situation have their self-esteem little impaired, retain confidence that they are keeping in touch with the best sources of security, power and prestige, and so maintain a high level of morale, they will tend to remain "well integrated"; cultural fundamentals are likely to be highly persistent, and voluntary cultural change may occur with a minimum of tension and disorganization. So far as they feel superior, in relation to groups and individuals with whom they are in contact, their culture may be held to the more firmly, or change may go further with little tension. By contrast, to the extent that groups and individuals come to feel themselves inferior, lose confidence in their basic sources of security, power and prestige, and so lapse in morale, the way is opened for extensive and even drastic change. Unless reasonably satisfying cultural substitutes can be found, extreme disorganization and emotional stress will occur. This may persist over considerable periods of time, or may under extreme circumstances threaten the continued existence of the group.

The Individual and Change

The earlier theoretical models or sets, such as historicalism and functionalism, disregarded almost entirely the individual component. Supposedly the anthropologist, concentrating on "culture," could leave the study of the individual to the psychologist. But with a developing interest in a life-history approach (e.g., Parsons, 20-20; Radin, 20-21), and especially the emergence of the so-called "psychological" approaches in anthropology from the 1930's on, this long-standing division of labor broke down. Theoretical systems were initiated within anthropology which took the individual into account from various points of view: for example, personality (character structure) studies, the psychoanalytic emphasis, the Yale learning theory, the interpersonal relations and interaction systems of Chapple and others.

From 1940 on, a growing series of works appeared, year by year, in this category. The fields particularly emphasized, in addition to more general definition of the relations between the individual and culture, have

been personality formation under dynamic conditions, the learning situation
in childhood, with or without psychoanalytic slants, normality and deviation, and life-history data, including case materials on psychotic manifestations. Notable among the contributors have been Aberle, Barnouw, Bateson,
the Beagleholes, Caudill, Devereux, DuBois, Gillin, Goldfrank, Gorer,
Green, Hallowell, Henry, Herskovits, Hsu, Kluckhohn, Kroeber, LaBarre,
the Leightons, Mead, the Spindlers, Spiro, the Oplers, Thompson, Voget,
and Anthony Wallace.

Regardless of the conceptual system used, the problems at the level of
individual behavior remain broadly the same. How, for example, does an
individual learn, unlearn, relearn? To what extent do "enculturation" and
"socialization" of the child under conditions of change, including various
types of culture contact situation where two culture-personality systems
may be in conflict, involve variables different from such pre-adult conditioning in a stable system? How far, and with what strains and stresses, can
an adult take over effectively a cultural tradition markedly different from
his own childhood tradition? Under what conditions does a person tend to
"revert," as in crises, dreams, old age? Are there dimensions of culture
change, concerned with basic personality (character structure) conditioning, which can only be achieved over generations rather than in individual
lifetimes? What, to go back in part to an earlier topic, of the individual
as innovator, or resisting innovation? How far do dynamic situations foster
special personality types? Do any regularities show, for example, as regards "radicals," "progressives," "conservatives," "diehards," "fanatics,"
or, again, the range from the well-integrated to the highly disorganized
person under conditions of choice and change? How far, in sum, do personality "models" or constructs have to be set up differently in dynamic
and stable cultural systems?

Such broad problems are of concern, and are being worked on, in all
social science disciplines; they also have both theoretical and applied dimensions. But the comprehensiveness of the anthropological approach,
with its total culture-personality scope and its cross-cultural perspectives,
gives the anthropologist a major stake in analyzing them. For example,
the question, crucial in the modern world situation of contact, as to how
far persons conditioned from infancy in one culture can shift in basic matters
to another milieu, has already been delineated in general terms by several
anthropological workers. Anthony Wallace, in a recent study of Iroquois
acculturation, states a now perhaps widely held view that "no cultural form
can be successfully introduced, within the space of one generation," which
"requires behavior which is uncongenial to [the modal] personality structure"
(51-199). Hallowell goes further in saying that it is "hard to imagine" how
basic sets of personality structure could be changed fundamentally in "less
than three generations" (52-79). Keesing, however, has suggested that if
the crucial cultural surrogates (e. g. , the mother or foster parents in an
entirely outside setting) are sufficiently in the new tradition, the essentials
of such a shift might be made in two generations—though this is quite ex-

ceptional (49-51). A theoretical model might even be set up for a more or less complete shift within one generation, if personality deviations by the individual concerned from his own cultural system happened to be congruent with normality in a new cultural system. Posing such a question is in itself an illustration of how little is yet understood of the individual dimensions of change, even granting the considerable attention they have received in recent years as shown in the bibliography.

Other Special Problems

The categories above have all dealt with the dynamics of change in whole culture systems, and in relation to the individual within those systems. Additionally there are valid problems of study which have as their focus particular aspects of culture: material culture, economics, social organization, government, law, knowledge, religion, art, leisure activities, language. Particular facets of the ecological and social process can also be taken into account such as population dynamics, patterns of settlement, migration, and urbanization. The following are some of the categories of special interest in recent literature:

a) Culture change and social structure. This theme goes back historically to the extensive evolutionary literature of the nineteenth century on marriage, family, and other topics. It is particularly stressed in modern literature by scholars stimulated by the Radcliffe-Brown "social structure" tradition, including the work of the Chicago group (Eggan, Embree, and others), the Warner surveys, and the writings of British social anthropologists. Firth suggests a distinction between "organizational change and that massive form of it which is structural change . . . [in which] the observer can recognize that a former basic relation has lost its magnitude, its force, its frequency" (51-63: 84). Examples of recent theoretical and field studies focused on social-structure dynamics are by the Aginskys (49-3), Eggan (51-54), Fenton (51-61), Fortes (49-33), Gluckman (51-69), Lévi-Strauss (49-64), Métraux (52-138), Ruesch and Bateson (49-97), Tumin (52-210), and Warner (49-124), etc.

b) Technological development and economic change. Apart from the more general literature purporting to trace longer sequences of economic growth, and also on invention processes, only scattered data appear until recently. Some of the earlier work is within contexts of applied anthropology, or leans toward that emphasis, as in works by Williams in Papua (28-42, 28-43, etc.), and Mair, Reid, Schapera, Thurnwald, and others in Africa (28-34, 34-34, 35-36, 38-66, etc.) The bibliography shows, however, an upsurge of interest in the postwar period, coincident with the emphasis placed by the international agencies and the United States government on world-wide economic development, and by other "metropolitan" governments in their overseas territories. Studies of technological change are especially featured in bibliographic lists for 1951 and 1952. Much closer relations are adumbrated in these studies between anthropologists and economists.

c) The folk-urban nexus; urbanization. The concept of the "folk society,"

though rooted in sociology, was made over for purposes of anthropological
field work and theory by Redfield from 1930 on. It has now tended to con-
join with growing studies of urbanism, urbanization, and relevant migration
and mobility problems. These latter had received only scattered attention
in the earlier literature of anthropology; but now as another sign of the
times they have come quite suddenly to the forefront among dynamic problems, with both theoretical and applied facets. To date most work has been
done in Africa, where movement to the cities is a spectacular trend and
problems of urbanization are in places acute (e.g., 51-80, 51-122, 52-52,
52-154), and in Latin America where the older work on the "folk society"
links to the newer urban literature (50-120, 51-113, 52-30, 52-118). Of
theoretical statements, those by Beals (51-11) and Miner (52-140) appear
to spell out the problems most adequately. [1]

d) Language change and cultural dynamics. Technical analysis of processes of growth and change in linguistic structure and phonology represents an old tradition in anthropological linguistics. But in terms of spelling out the relation between language change and other aspects of culture
change, the literature still seems weak from the theoretical viewpoint.
Mostly it deals with specific semantic shifts in particular languages through
word "borrowing" and other conceptual adaptation to meet new experience,
in contact situations or otherwise. Bilingual or multilingual adjustments,
and especially the rise of makeshift languages such as "trade jargons" and
"creole" speech involved in frontier social stratification, also have a place.
Of modern work, Thompson has been particularly active in applying the
important theoretical work of Whorf to culture contact situations, showing
the problems involved in the meeting of different systems of organizing
the world of experience in terms of linguistic form and content (see especially 50-139). Among other recent studies particularly emphasizing theoretical considerations are those of Bittle (52-22), Bonfante and Sebeok (44-
13), Bright (51-26), Gower (52-72), Herzog (41-38), Hoijer (48-50), Hoenigswald (51-85), Jesperson (41-44), Kroeber (48-64), Lee (43-46), Lévi-Strauss
(51-112), Martinet (51-121), Spencer (50-133), Spicer (43-83), Swadesh
(52-199), and Voegelin (51-196).

Methodology

In general, the conceptual and field work tools and problems involved
in dynamic studies are those common to cultural anthropology as a whole:
use of informants, "participant-observation" over periods that permit
depth-analysis, accumulation of life histories, use of more structured projective and other techniques, the newer problems of sampling and other
statistical validation, techniques of historical and distributional reconstruction, and so on.

---

[1]See also Foster, G.M., "What Is Folk Culture?" AA, 55, 2: 159—73
(1953).

Nevertheless, the literature at both the theoretical and applied levels
contains a number of works on method relating to situations of change.
In general, they deal with the special dimensions involved in culture contact situations, such as types and levels in the acculturation process.
Redfield has given particular attention to the effectiveness of inferring
historical sequences of change from observing communities at different
stages of a common acculturation process (41-65, 50-120, etc.). He and
several other writers have recently stressed the usefulness of periodic
revisiting, or as Elkin has called it "delayed return," so as to make successive synchronic observations over a longer time period as an alternative to a continuing diachronic record. Among useful discussions focused
on the special methods involved in dynamic studies are those by Hallowell
(42-37, 42-38, etc.), Herskovits (45-45, 45-46, etc.), Hunter (34-23),
Lesser (39-54), Mair (34-35), Malinowski (45-79), Mead (43-54), Richards
(35-46), Schapera (35-48), Spindler and Goldschmidt (52-189), Thompson
(50-140, 50-141), and Watson (52-225); to these might be added important
papers related to archaeological reconstruction as discussed earlier.

On the side of "applied" anthropology, a special emphasis in research
has been advocated, called "action" (or "operational") research. This
concept was developed particularly during World War II in England, in
connection with various branches of applied science, and has been introduced to American anthropology particularly by Thompson (50-140). Here
progressive formulation of the data in the laboratory by the research specialist is checked in action or operation with the practical specialist in
the field. Somewhat related to method is a further problem which has
troubled anthropologists from the beginning of applied or utilitarian studies,
namely how far the anthropological researcher should limit himself to
providing "technical information" to the man of action so as to give him
"anthropological sophistication" in dealing with the problems concerned,
or should proceed further to make recommendations or take stands on
policy matters, involving judgments of value and prediction. Keesing, for
example, writes of this (45-57: 384):

> What has to be clarified here is that if the anthropologist makes
> judgments beyond the strictly scientific confines of his work, he is
> committing only himself, not anthropology. At most, in the scien-
> tific mood, he might apply general principles and hypotheses so
> far as they will carry him. In some situations he might venture
> to predict that, if a certain line of action is tried, such and such
> is likely to be the result, and if another, then something else.
> Again, if a definite goal or policy is set, he might try to antici-
> pate what would or would not contribute toward its fulfillment.
> Here he would speak only of probabilities, and even this might
> be the acme of scientific foolhardiness because of the exceedingly
> limited ability of such a human science to predict as yet with any
> exactness.

Nevertheless the fact remains that evaluations have to be made, and factual knowledge translated into action. It seems justifiable, therefore, that if the anthropologist is asked for advice, or is moved to volunteer his judgments, he should feel free to do so provided he makes it clear how far his comments are personal only.

For examples of recent further views on this problem, see discussions by Beals (51-10), Chapple (43-12), Embree (45-21), Evans-Pritchard (46-33), Foster (52-60), Herskovits (48-54), Kluckhohn (49-54), Ashley Montagu (46-76), Schapera (52-170), Shapiro (49-104), Tax (45-100), Thompson (44-71), and Wagner (50-156).

Summary

The classification presented here, as emphasized at the beginning, is inevitably a personalized one drawn from the writer's own studies and synthesis of the literature. But it is illustrative of what was referred to in the first category as a needed frame of reference.

From this point on the bibliography can be left to speak for itself. The Stanford group expects to issue additional materials of this inventory and analysis type which can be used as tools for research (e.g., analyses of important fields of work, tabulations and codifications of significant hypotheses, compilation of critical case materials), and also to undertake further creative and experimental studies in which the tools can be put to work.

Part Two

CHRONOLOGICAL BIBLIOGRAPHY

Abbreviations

A

AA	American Anthropologist. Menasha, etc.
AAAM	American Anthropological Association, Memoirs. Menasha, etc.
AASP	American Association for the Advancement of Science, Proceedings. Washington, D. C.
AAASR	Australian Association for the Advancement of Science, Reports. Australia.
AAn	American Antiquarian and Oriental Journal in Chicago. Chicago.
AAq	American Antiquity. Menasha.
AAy	Art and Archaeology. Baltimore, Washington.
Ac	The Academy. London.
AcA	Acta Americana. Los Angeles.
Ae	L'Anthropologie. Paris.
AEO	Annales de l'Extrême-Orient. Paris.
AESM	American Ethnological Society, Monographs. New York.
Af	Africa. London.
Afa	Afroamerica. Mexico, D. F.
AfS	African Studies. London.
AI	America Indígena. Mexico, D. F.
AIEA	Anales del Instituto de Etnografia Americana, Universidad de Cuyo. Argentina.
AIEBA	Anales del Instituto Etnico Nacional. Buenos Aires.
AIm	American Imago. Boston.
AJO	American Journal of Orthopsychiatry. New York.
AJP	American Journal of Psychiatry. New York.
AJPs	American Journal of Psychology. Ithaca, N. Y.
AJS	American Journal of Sociology. Chicago.
AMo	Atlantic Monthly. New York.
AMNHP	American Museum of Natural History, Anthropological Papers. New York.
An	Anthropos. Salzburg, Vienna.
ANa	American Naturalist. Lancaster, Pa.
AnR	Anthropological Review and Journal of the Anthropological Society of London (JAS). See also Memoirs, Anthropological Society of London.
AnS	L'Année Sociologique. Paris.
ANZAASR	Australian and New Zealand Association for the Advancement of Science, Reports. Australia, New Zealand.
ApA	Applied Anthropology (see also Human Organization). New York.
APSM	American Philosophical Society, Memoirs. Philadelphia.
APSP	American Philosophical Society, Proceedings. Philadelphia.
AR	Asiatic Review. London.
ArA	Archiv für Anthropologie. Braunschweig.
ARLB	Archiv für Religionswissenschaft. Leipzig, Berlin.
As	Asia. New York.
ASAF	Archives de la société Américaine de France. Paris.
ASc	American Scholar. New York.

ASGH   Anales de la Sociedad de Geografía e Historia. Guatemala.
ASJT   Asiatic Society of Japan, Transactions. Tokyo.
ASR   American Sociological Review. College Park, Maryland.
ASSP   American Sociological Society, Publications. College Park, Maryland.
ASWT   Anthropological Society of Washington, Transactions. Washington, D.C.
Au   Ausland, Stuttgart.

B

BA   Baessler Archiv. Berlin, Leipzig.
BAASP   British Association for the Advancement of Science, Proceedings.
            London.
BAASR   British Association for the Advancement of Science, Reports. London.
BAEB   Bureau of American Ethnology, Bulletins. Washington, D.C.
BAER   Bureau of American Ethnology, Reports. Washington, D.C.
BAP   British Academy, Proceedings. London.
BFMSA   Bulletin of the Free Museum of Science and Art. Philadelphia.
BI   Boletin Indigenista. Mexico, D.F.
BIRCB   Bulletin de l'Institut Royal Colonial Belge. Brussels.
BMB   British Museum, Bulletins. London.
BPBMB   Bernice P. Bishop Museum, Bulletins. Honolulu.
BPBMOP   Bernice P. Bishop Museum, Occasional Papers. Honolulu.
BS   Bantu Studies. Johannesburg.
BSAL   Bulletin de la Société d'Anthropologie de Lyon. Lyon.
BSAP   Bulletin de la Société d'Anthropologie de Paris. Lyon.
BSG   Bulletin de la Société de Géographie. Paris.
BSNG   Bulletin de la Société Neuchâtel de Géographie. Neuchâtel.
BSRBG   Bulletin de la Société Royale Belge de Géographie. Brussels.
BTLVI   Bijdragen tot de Taal-, Land- en Volkenkunde van Nederlandsch-Indie.
            The Hague.

C

CES   Comparative Ethnographical Studies. Göteborg, Sweden.
CIP   Canadian Institute, Proceedings. Toronto.
CISB   Cranbrook Institute of Science, Bulletin. Bloomfield Hills, Mich.
CISNL   Cranbrook Institute of Science, News Letter. Bloomfield Hills, Mich.
CISP   Carnegie Institute of Washington, Supplementary Publications. Wash-
            ington, D.C.
CIWP   Carnegie Institute of Washington, Publications. Washington, D.C.
CMNHB   Chicago Museum of Natural History Bulletins. Chicago.
CN   Canadian Naturalist. Ottawa.
CP   Character and Personality. Durham, N.C.
CR   Contemporary Review. London.
CUAS   Catholic University of America, Anthropological Series. Washington, D.
CUCA   Columbia University Contributions to Anthropology. New York.

E

EA   Eastern Anthropologist. Lucknow, India.
Ed   Edoth. Palestine.
EFEOB   École Francaise d'Extrême Orient, Bulletin. Hanoi.

Eg	Ethnologica. Leipzig.
Ep	Ethnographia. Budapest.
EP	El Palacio. Santa Fe.
ER	Ethnological Records. New York.
ESJ	Ethnological Society of London, Journal (1848–1856; new series 1869–1870). New York.
ESS	Encyclopaedea of the Social Sciences.
EST	Ethnological Society of London, Transactions. London.
Et	Ethnos. Mexico, D. F. (to 1925), Stockholm.
EtS	Etnologiska Studier. Göteborg.

F

FA	Fieldiana: Anthropology. Chicago.
FEQ	Far Eastern Quarterly. Menasha.
FES	Far Eastern Survey. New York.
FJ	The Folk-Lore Journal. London.
FMAS	Field Museum of Natural History, Anthropological Series. Chicago.
Fo	Folk-Lore. London.
Fr	Forum. New York.
FR	Fortnightly Review. London.

G

Gl	Globus. Braunschweig.
GM	Geographical Magazine. London.
GR	Geographical Review. New York.
GS	General Series in Anthropology. Menasha, Wis.

H

HB	Human Biology. Baltimore, Md.
Hm	L'Homme. Paris.
HO	Human Organization (formerly Applied Anthropology). New York.
HR	Human Relations. London.

I

IA	Indian Antiquary. Bombay.
IAE	Internationales Archiv für Ethnographie. Leiden.
IAL	Indian Art and Letters. London.
IbA	Ibero-Americana. Berkeley, Cal.
ICAP	International Congress of Americanists, Proceedings.
IFAN	Institut Français d'Afrique Noire. Dakar.
IG	De Indische Gids. Amsterdam.
IIALC	International Institute of African Languages and Cultures. London.
IJAL	International Journal of American Linguistics. Baltimore.
Il	Institut des Belles Lettres Arabes. Tunis.
Im	Imago. Leipzig, Vienna.
IPRH	Institute of Pacific Relations, Honolulu.
IPRNY	Institute of Pacific Relations, New York.
IQ	International Quarterly. Burlington, Vermont.

| IRCBM | Institut Royal Colonial Belge, Section des Sciences Morales et Politiques, Mémoires. Bruxelles. |
| ISAP | Institute of Social Anthropology, Publications. Smithsonian Institute, Washington, D. C. |

J

JAA	Journal of African Administration. London.
JAF	Journal of American Folklore. Boston, Lancaster, etc.
JAfS	Journal of the African Society. London.
JAP	Journal of Abnormal and Social Psychology. Washington, D. C.
JASB	Journal of the Anthropological Society of Bombay. Bombay.
JBORS	Journal of the Bihar and Orissa Research Society. Patna.
JES	Journal of Educational Sociology. New York.
JGP	Journal of General Psychology. Provincetown, Mass.
JIAEA	Journal of the Indian Archipelago and Eastern Asia. Singapore.
JNH	Journal of Negro History. Washington, D. C.
JP	Journal of Psychology. Provincetown, Mass.
JPe	Journal of Personality. Durham, N. C.
JPS	Journal of the Polynesian Society. Wellington, N. Z.
JPT	Journal of Projective Techniques (Rorschach Research Exchange and). New York.
JRAI	Journal of the Royal Anthropological Institute. (Journal of the Anthropological Institute 1865–1906). London.
JRAS	Journal of the Royal Asiatic Society of Great Britain and Ireland. London.
JRASMB	Journal of the Royal Asiatic Society, Malayan Branch. Singapore.
JRASSB	Journal of the Royal Asiatic Society, Straits Branch. Singapore.
JRP	Journal of Religious Psychology. Worcester, Mass.
JRSA	Journal of the Royal Society of Arts. London.
JSAP	Journal de la Société des Americanistes. Paris.
JSAQ	Journal of Studies on Alcohol, Quarterly. New Haven, Conn.
JSP	Journal of Social Psychology. Worcester, Mass.
JSS	Journal of the Siam Society. Bangkok.
JWAS	Journal of the Washington Academy of Science. Washington, D. C.

K

KBDGA	Korrespondenz- Blatt der Deutschen Gessellschaft für Anthropologie, Ethnologie und Urgeschichte. Braunschweig, München.
Kv	Kiva. Tucson, Ariz.
KZ	Kokogaku Zasshi (Journal of the Archaeological Society of Japan). Tokyo.

L

| La | Language. Baltimore, Md. |
| LSMSA | London School of Economics and Political Science, Monographs on Social Anthropology. London. |

M

| Ma | Mankind. Sydney, Australia. |
| MAGW | Mitteilungen der Anthropologischen Gesellschaft in Wien. Wien. |

MAH	Magazine of American History. New York.
MAS	Memoirs, Anthropological Society of London. (1865–1870). London.
MASB	Massachusetts Archaeological Society, Bulletins. Boston.
MH	Mental Hygiene. New York.
MIA	Man in India. Ranchi.
Mk	The Masterkey. Los Angeles.
MKe	Minzokugaku-Kenkyu (Japanese Journal of Ethnology). Tokyo.
Mn	Man. London.
MNMA	Museo Nacional de Mexico, Anales. Mexico, D. F.
Mo	The Monist. Chicago.
MPA	Man in the Pageant of the Ages. U. of New Mexico Press, Albuquerque.
Mu	Le Muséon. Bruxelles.

N

Na	Nature. London.
NAR	North American Review. Boston.
NASP	National Academy of Sciences, Proceedings, Washington, D. C.
NC	Nineteenth Century. London.
NH	Natural History. New York.
NMQR	New Mexico Quarterly Review. Albuquerque.
NRCB	National Research Council, Bulletins. Washington, D. C.
NYAST	New York Academy of Sciences, Transactions. New York.
NZIT	New Zealand Institute, Transactions. Wellington, N. Z.

O

Oc	Oceania. Sydney.
OC	Open Court. Chicago.
Ol	Outlook. New York.

P

PA	Pacific Affairs. New York.
PIM	Pacific Islands Monthly. Sydney.
PM	Primitive Man. Washington, D. C.
PMAEP	Peabody Museum of American Archaeology and Ethnology, Papers. Cambridge, Mass.
PR	Psychoanalytic Review. New York.
Ps	Psychiatry. Baltimore, Md.
PSB	Pacific Science Board, National Research Council. Washington, D. C.
PSc	Philosophy of Science. Baltimore, Md.
PSCP	Pacific Science Congress, Proceedings.
PSM	Polynesian Society Memoirs. Wellington, N. Z.
PSMo	Popular Science Monthly. Garrison, New York.
PSP	Prehistoric Society, Proceedings. Cambridge University Museum of Archaeology and Ethnology. Cambridge, England.
PSQ	Pacific Science Quarterly. Honolulu.

Q

QJSAI	Quarterly Journal of the Society of American Indians. Washington, D. C.

QR   Quarterly Review. London.

R

RA   Revue Anthropologique. Paris.
RAE   Revista de Arqueologia y Etnologia. Habana, Cuba.
RAP   Revue d'Anthropologie de Paris. Paris.
RdA   Rivista di Antropologia. Rome.
RE   Revue d'Ethnographie. Paris.
RHR   Revue de l'Histoire des Religions. Paris.
RIENB   Revista des Instituto Etnologico Nacional Bogotá. Columbia.
RIEUNT   Revista del Instituto do Etnologia de la Universidad Nacional de Tucumán
              Argentina.
RIGBP   Royal Institute of Great Britain, Proceedings. London.
RIS   Rivista Italia di Sociologia. Rome.
RLIC   Rhodes-Livingstone Institute, Communications. Livingstone, North
              Rhodesia.
RLIJ   Rhodes-Livingstone Institute, Journal. Livingstone, North Rhodesia.
RLP   Rhodes-Livingstone Papers. Capetown.
RM   The Red Man. Carlisle, Pa.
RMNL   Revista des Museo Nacional. Lima.
RP   Records of the Past. Washington, D.C.
RS   Rural Sociology. Raleigh, N.C.
RSCT   Royal Society of Canada, Transactions.
RSP   Revue Scientifique. Paris.
RSSAT   Royal Society of South Africa, Transactions. Capetown.

S

SAJS   South African Journal of Science, Johannesburg.
SARP   School of American Research, Papers. San Diego, Cal.
SARR   School of American Research, Reports. San Diego, Cal.
SASC   School of African Studies, Communications. Capetown.
Sc   Science. Washington, D.C.
ScA   Scientific American. Washington, D.C.
SDMB   San Diego Museum Bulletin. San Diego.
SF   Social Forces. Baltimore, Md.
Sg   Sociologia. Saõ Paulo.
SIR   Smithsonian Institute, Reports. Washington, D.C.
SJA   Southwestern Journal of Anthropology. Albuquerque.
Sl   Sociologus. Berlin.
SM   Scientific Monthly. Washington, D.C.
SN   Sudan Notes. Sudan.
So   Sociometry. Beacon, N.Y.
SP   South Pacific. Sydney.
SR   Social Research. New York.
SSR   Sociology and Social Research.
SSRCB   Social Science Research Council Bulletin. Washington, D.C.
SW   Southern Workman. Hampton, Va.
SWL   Southwestern Lore. Gunnison, Colo.
SX   Sigma Xi Quarterly. Burlington, Vt.

T

TITLV	Tijdschrift voor Indische Taal-, Land-, en Volkenskunde. Batavia.
TMIE	Travaux et Memoirs de l'Institut d'Ethnologie. Paris.
TPAR	Territory of Papua, Anthropological Reports. Port Moresby.

U

UCAR	University of California Anthropological Records. Berkeley.
UCPAAE	University of California Publications in American Archaeology and Ethnology. Berkeley and Los Angeles.
UHRP	University of Hawaii Research Publications. Honolulu.
UNMASB	University of New Mexico Bulletin, Anthropological Series. Albuquerque.
UPMB	University of Pennsylvania Museum Bulletin. Philadelphia.
USNMP	United States National Museum, Proceedings. Washington, D.C.
USNMR	United States National Museum, Reports. Washington, D.C.
UWPA	University of Washington Publications in Anthropology. Seattle.

V

VAGW	Verhandlungen der Anthropologie Gesellschaft in Wien. Wien.
VBGA	Verhandlungen der Berliner Gesellschaft für Anthropologie, Ethnologie und Urgeschichte, Berlin.
VNGB	Verhandlungen der Naturforschenden Gesellschaft in Basel. Basel.
VFPA	Viking Fund Publications in Anthropology. New York.

W

WA	Wisconsin Archaeologist. Madison.
WR	Westminster Review. London.

Y

Yr	Ymer. Stockholm.
YUPA	Yale University Publications in Anthropology. New Haven.

Z

ZE	Zeitschrift für Ethnologie. Berlin.
ZFS	Zeitschrift für Sozialwissenschaft. Berlin, Leipzig.
ZGEB	Zeitschrift der Gesellschaft für Erdkunde zu Berlin. Berlin.
ZS	Zeitschrift für Sozialforschung. Frankfort.
ZVR	Zeitschrift für Vergleichende Rechtswissenschaft. Stuttgart, Berlin.

1820-1 Crawfurd, J. History of the Indian Archipelago. 3 vols. Edinburgh.

1821-1 Henderson, J. History of Brazil. London.

1843-1 Klemm, G. Allgemeine Kulturgeschichte der Menschheit. Leipzig. 1843 – 1852.

1854-1 Bollaert, W. Observations on the history of the Incas of Peru, ESJ, 3: 132 – 64.

1854-2 Cull, R. Remarks on the nature, objects, and evidences of ethnological science, ESJ, 3: 103 – 11.

1855-1 Lubbock, J. Prehistoric times, as illustrated by ancient remains, and the manners and customs of modern savages. London.

1856-1 Wilson, J. L. Western Africa: its history, condition, and prospects. New York.

1857-1 Buckle, H. T. History of civilization in England. 2 vols. London. 1857 – 1861.

1858-1 Waitz, T. Anthropologie der Naturvölker. 6 vols. Leipzig.

1860-1 Bastian, A. Der Mensch in der Geschichte. Leipzig.

1861-1 Bachofen, J. J. Das Mutterrecht. Stuttgart.

1861-2 Crawfurd, J. Conditions which favor, retard, or obstruct civilisation, EST, 1: 154 – 77.

1861-3 Maine, H. Ancient law. London.

1862-1 Fergusson, J. History of modern architecture; with an appendix on ethnology from an architectural point of view. London.

1862-2 Jackson, J. W. Ethnology and phrenology as an aid to the historian. London.

1862-3 Wilson, D. Prehistoric man: researches into the origin of civilisation in the Old and New World. London.

1863-1 Knox, R. Influence of climate and of hybridity over man, AnR, 1: 246 – 55

1864-1 Bellecombe, A. de. The importance of methodological classification in American researches, AnR, 2: 191 – 202.

1864-2 Bouverie-Pusey, S. E. B. The Negro in relation to civilised society, AnR, 2, JAS: 274 – 90.

1864-3 Draper, J. W. History of the intellectual development of Europe. London.

1865

65-1 Crawfurd, J. On the commixture of races of man as affecting the progress of civilisation (Africa, Asia, America), EST, 3: 98 – 122, 143 – 45.

65-2 Colenso, J. W. On the efforts of missionaries among savages, AnR, 3, JAS: 248 – 79.

65-3 Galton, F. The first steps toward the domestication of animals, EST, 3: 122 – 38.

65-4 McLennan, J. F. Primitive marriage. London.

65-5 Owen, H. B. Missionary successes and Negro converts, AnR, 3, JAS: 234 – 46, 290 – 94.

65-6 Reade, W. W. Efforts of missionaries among savages, AnR, 3, JAS: 163 – 83.

65-7 Schmidt, K. Die Anthropologie: die Wissenschaft von Menschen in ihrer geschichtlichen Entwicklung und auf ihrem gegenwartigen Handpunkte. Leipzig.

65-8   Tylor, E. B. Researches into the early history of mankind and the develop-
        ment of civilisation. London.

1866

66-1   Andree, R. Anthropologische Beiträge: Il die Ausrottung wilder Völker
        durch die civilisirten Leute. II. Fernere Betrachtungen daruber, Gl, 17.
66-2   Armas y Céspecles, Fr. de. De la esclavidud en Cuba. Madrid.
66-3   Anthropology a practical science, AnR, 4, The Popular Magazine of Anth.,
        1: 6—9. London.
66-4   Anthropology and social innovation, AnR, 4, Pop. Mag. of Anth., 3: 93—97.
66-5   Bial. P. Histoire de la civilisation celtique. Paris.
66-6   Brinton, D. G. The Shawnees and their migrations, Historical Magazine,
        New York, Jan.
66-7   Brodie, J. Observations on the peculiarities of national pronunciation as
        a means of tracing the origin and history of nations, EST, 4: 339—47.
66-8   Fletcher, J., and Kidder, D. P. Brazil and Brazilians; portrayed in his-
        torical and descriptive sketches. Boston.
66-9   Hellwald, J. V. Die amerikanische Völkerwanderung. Wien.
66-10   La Mesle, G. Les Cambogiens, Bull. de la Soc. de Géogr. de Paris, Août:
        113—39.
66-11   Mortillet, G. Le signe de la croix avant le christianisme. Paris.
66-12   Negro revolt in Jamaica, AnR, 4, Pop. Mag. of Anth., 1: 14—20.
66-13   The wilful extinction of aboriginal tribes, AnR, 4, Pop. Mag. of Anth.,
        1: 10—14.
66-14   Travers, W. On the destruction of the aborigines of Chatham Island, EST,
        4: 352—60.
66-15   Vetromile, E. The Abnakis and their history. New York.

1867

67-1   Crawfurd, J. On the origin and history of written language, EST, 5: 96—104.
67-2   Fraas, O. Beiträge zur Culturgeschichte des Menschen während der Eiszeit,
        ArA, 2: 29—50.
67-3   Heyat-i-Afgani, -. History of Afghanistan, by Mohammed Heyat Khan (in
        Hindustani). Lahore.
67-4   Jackson, J. W. The theory of development, and its bearing on science and
        religion, AnR, 5: 257—76.
67-5   Phayre, A. P. On the history of the Burmah race, EST, 5: 13—39.
67-6   Riecke, C. F. Ueber den Ursprung der Sprachen, Sagen und Mythen. Nord-
        hausen, Büchting.
67-7   Tylor, E. B. Phenomena of the higher civilisation traceable to a rudimentary
        origin among savage tribes, AnR, 5: 303—14.
67-8   Westropp, H. M. On the sequence of the phases of civilisation, and con-
        temporaneous implements, AnR, 5, JAS: 192—200.
67-9   Wright, T. E. On the intercourse of the Romans with Ireland, TES, 5: 168—73.

1868

68-1   Bastian, A. Beiträge zur vergleichenden Psychologie. Die Seel und ihre
        Erscheinungsweisen in der Ethnographie. Berlin.

68-2   Brinton, D. G. The myths of the New World; a treatise on the symbolism
       and mythology of the red race of America. New York.
68-3   Burton, R. F. The extinction of slavery in Brazil, AnR, 6: 56−63.
68-4   Cherbonneau, − . Observations sur l'origine et la formation du langage a
       cain, Rêvue Africaine, 67: 69−78.
68-5   Gerland, G. Ueber das Aussterben der Naturvölker. Leipzig.
68-6   Kindere, L. van der, De la race et de sa part d'influence dans les divers
       manifestations de l'activité des peuples. Bruxelles.
68-7   Kremer, −. Geschichte der herrschenden Ideen im Islam. Leipzig.
68-8   Lubbock, J. The early condition of man, AnR, 6: 1-21.
68-9   Schüetz, D. von. Zur Ethnographie von Peru, Gl, 15: 141−45.
68-10 Strodl, M. A. Die Entstehung der Völker. Studie aus einer Philosophie de
       Geschichte in drei Vorlesungen. Schaffhausen.
68-11 Wake, C. S. On the psychological unity of mankind, AnR, 6, JAS: 168−76

1869

69-1   Avery, J. G. Civilisation; with especial reference to the so-called Celtic
       inhabitants of Ireland, AnR, 7: 221−37.
69-2   Baring-Gould, S. Origin and development of religious belief. London.
69-3   Harris, B. The theory of the arts; or, art in relation to nature, civilisa-
       tion, and man . . . the origin, rise, province, principles, and applica
       tion of each of the arts. 2 vols. London.
69-4   Howorth, H. H. The westerly drifting of the nomads from the fifth to the
       nineteenth century, ESJ, (n. s.), 1: 12−34, 378−87; 2: 83−95; 182−92
       469−76; JRAI, 1: 226−53; 2: 114−27, 205−27; 3: 145−73, 277−99,
       452−74. 1869−1874.
69-5   Hunt, S. B. The Negro as a soldier, AnR, 7: 40−54.
69-6   Rosny, L. de. De l'origine du langage. Paris.
69-7   Ule, O. Das Hinsterben der Naturvölker in Berührung mit der Civilisatio
       Salon, 3, 1: 54−61.
69-8   Whitney, W. D. On the present condition of the question as to the origin o
       language, Am. Philolog. Assoc., Trans.
69-9   Wiegelingen Civilisationsbestrebungen bei einem wilden Volke? Holländer
       und Alfurus in Minahassa auf Celebes, Gl, 15: 170ff.

1870

70-1   Bernuzzi, J. Dell' origine e del fine dell' uomo second. l'etnografia. Par
70-2   Bonwick, J. The last of the Tasmanians; or the black war of Van Diemen'
       Land. London.
70-3   Garnier, J. Les migrations polynésiennes, leur origine, leur itinéraire,
       leur étendue, leur influence sur les Australiens de la Nouvelle-Calédo
       BSG, 5, 19: 5ff.
70-4   Green, N. M. Mormonism: its rise, progress and present condition. Har
       ford.
70-5   Herzfeld, L. Geschichte des Volkes Israel. Leipzig.
70-6   Hunt, J. On the acclimatisation of Europeans in the United States of Amer
       AnR, 29: 109−37.

70-7   Kirchhoff, T. Die inianischen "civilisirten Nationen" nördlich vom Red River, Gl, 18: 9ff.
70-8   Krebs, W. Ein besuch bei den halbcivilisirten Indianern Nebraska's, Gl, 17: 14ff.
70-9   Lubbock, J. On the origin of civilisation and the primitive condition of man. Mental and social condition of man. New York.
70-10   Meade, H. A ride through the disturbed districts of New Zealand, together with some account of the South Sea Islands. London.
70-11   Nicholas, T. The influence of the Norman Conquest on the ethnology of Britain, EST (n. s.), 2: 384—400.
70-12   Pike, L. O. On the methods of anthropological research, AnR, 28: 3—13.
70-13   Saisset, A. L'origine des cultes et des mystères. Saint-Germain.
70-14   Spencer, H. Illustrations of early progress; a series of discussions. New York.
70-15   Stülpnagel, C. Rebsch, the Sikhs, an historical sketch. Lahore.
70-16   Wake, C. S. The aim and scope of anthropology, AnR, 29: 1—18.

1871

71-1   Andree, C. Die Aufhebung der Sklaverei in Brasilien, Gl, 20: 13. 1871—1872.
71-2   Badger, G. P. History of the Imâms and Seyyids of 'Omân (transl. from Arabic work by Salîl-ibn-Razîk). London.
71-3   Cramer, C. Eine Revolution in Zacatecas, G. , 19: 56.
71-4   Die halbcivilisirten Indianer, Gl, 19: 79.
71-5   Geiger, A. Das Judenthum und seine Geschichte, Allg. Zeit. , 275.
71-6   Gill, W. Gems from the coral islands or incidents of contrast between Christian and savage life in the south seas. London.
71-7   Heinemann, W. Religion und Naturwissenschaft. Wien.
71-8   Heywood, J. On the aptitude of North American Indians for agriculture, J. Statistical Soc. of London: 456ff.
71-9   Hughes, A. W. Outlines of Indian history, comprising the Hindu, Mohamme- dan, and Christian periods. London.
71-10   Jäger, G. Ueber die Entwickelung der Seele, Au, 41, 42.
71-11   Meade, Adventures in New Zealand during a ride through the disturbed districts, London.
71-12   Müller, F. Ueber den Ursprung der Cultur der amerikanischen Rasse, MGAW, 1: 259—66.
71-13   Nachtigal, - Uebersicht über die Geschichte Wadaïs, ZGE, 345.
71-14   Peabody, A. P. The Chinese in San Francisco, ANa, 4. January.
71-15   Radloff, W. Sibirische Alterthümer, ZE, 3: 83—90.
71-16   Radloff, W. Zur Geschichte der Hausthiere der Kirgisen, ZE, 3: 285—313.
71-17   Spiegel, F. Zur vergleichenden Religionsgeschichte, Au.
71-18   Tylor, E. B. Primitive culture. 2 vols. London.
71-19   Victor, F. F. The Oregon Indians, Overland Mo. , Oct. , Nov.

1872

72-1   Bastian, A. Die Stellung des Kaukasus innerhalb der geschichtlichen Völker- bewegungen, ZE, 4: 1—21.

72-2   Bell, E. The Bengal reversion, another "exceptional case." London.

72-3   Bello y Espinosa Geschichtliche, geographische und statistische Bemerkungen über Puerto Rico. Aus dem spanischen Ms. übers von E. v. Martens, ZE, 4: 36—41.

72-4   Clarke, H. On the prehistoric and protohistoric relations of the populations of Asia and Europe, JRAI, 1: 52—59.

72-5   Dabry de Thiersant, P. Le massacre de Tien-Tsin . . . Paris.

72-6   Dancing Parsons: a treatise on dancing as a religious exercise, showing its rise, progress, and ultimate development in their latter days. London.

72-7   Dudgeon, J. Historical sketch of the ecclesiastical, political and commercial relations of Russia with China. Peking.

72-8   Geiger, L. Ursprung und Entwicklung der menschlichen Sprache und Vernunft. Stuttgart.

72-9   Kaines, J. The anthropology of Auguste Comte, JRAI, 1: 349—62.

72-10 Lanman, C. The Japanese in America. London.

72-11 Lindenschmidt, L. Zur Culturgeschichte der Vorzeit, Gl, 22: 39—55.

72-12 Lubbock, J. On the development of relationships, JRAI, 1: 1—29.

72-13 Martens, E. von. Geschichtliche, geographische und statistische Bemerkungen über Puerto Rico, ZE, 4: 36—42.

72-14 Millett, E. An Australian personage; or the settler and the savage in Western Australia. London.

72-15 Müller, H. G. Oregon und seine Zukunft. Ein Beitrag zur Eintwicklungeschichte des fernen Westens. Leipzig, Cöln.

72-16 Quinemant, J. Du peuplement et de la vraie colonisation de l'Algérie. Constantine.

72-17 Schaaffhausen, H. von. Ueber die Methode de vorgeschichtlichen Forschung ArA, 5: 113—28.

72-18 Schmidt, Dr. Zur Urgeschichte Nordamerikas, Ara, 5: 233—59.

72-19 Spiegel, —. Zur vergleichenden Religionsgeschichte, Au, 1, 2, 10.

72-20 Squier, E. G. The arch in America, JRAI, 1: 78—81.

72-21 Vambéry, H. War between the Atalik Ghazi and the Tungans, Ocean Highways, December: 278—79.

72-22 Vere, S. de. Americanisms; the English of the New World. New York, London.

72-23 Westropp, H. W. On the analogies and coincidences among unconnected nations, JRAI, 1: 221—26.

1873

73-1   Baer, W. Der vorgeschichtliche Mensch. Leipzig. 1873—74.

73-2   Beaton, A. C. The Ashantees: their country, history, wars, government, customs, climate, religion, and present position. London.

73-3   Brulfert, —. Sur l'origine et la disparition de la race polynésienne, BSAP, 7: 817ff.

73-4   Chinesische Sitten in Californien, Gl, 23, 17.

73-5   Chwolson, C. Die fanatischen Völker. Berlin.

73-6   Eitel, E. J. Buddhism: its historical, theoretical and popular aspects. London.

73-7   Evans, J. L'alphabet et son origine, Rev. Scient., 28.

73-8   Gardner, W. J. A history of Jamaica. London.
73-9   Gerlach, A. J. A. Atjih en de Atjinezen. Arnhem.
73-10   Jagor, F. Reisen in den Philippinen. Berlin.
73-11   Leborgne, —. Sur la dépopulation des îles Gambier, BSAP, 7: 682 ff.
73-12   Liebrecht, F. Zur Culturgeschichte, ZE, 5: 77—105.
73-13   Miller, J. Life among the Modocs; unwritten history. London.
73-14   Schleiden, —. Die Rose. Geschichte und Symbolik in ethnographische und
          culturhistorische Beziehung. Leipzig.
73-15   Sherring, M. A. Relation of the native aristocracy to the British govern-
          ment, Indian Evangelical Review, July.
73-16   Travers, W. T. L. On the life and times of Te Rauparaha, NZIT, 5.
73-17   von Meyer, —. Ueber den Ursprung von Rechts und Links, ZE, 5.
73-18   Zehme, H. Der Wahabismus in Arabien seit 1819 und die Staatenbildungen
          auf der Arabischen Halbinsel im 19 Jahrhundert, G. , 23: 344—46, 360—
          63, 379—81.

1874

74-1   Bancroft, H. H. The native races of the Pacific states of North America.
          New York. 1874—76.
74-2   Brackenburg, H. The Ashantee war . . . 2 vols. London.
74-3   Calder, J. E. Some account of the wars of extirpation . . . Tasmania,
          JRAI, 3: 7—28.
74-4   Girard, J. La colonisation anglo-saxonne aux iles Fidji, BSG, 6, 7: 148ff.
74-5   Girard-Teulon, A. Les origines de la famille. Questions sur les antécédents
          des sociétés patriarcales. Genève, Paris.
74-6   Henry, G. A. Future of the Fantis and Ashantis, GM, 4: 148ff.
74-7   Host, F. Die Missionen und die Matacos-Indianer in Gran Chaco, Gl, 25:
          74—76.
74-8   Key, T. H. Language, its origin and development. London.
74-9   Kirchhoff, T. Die Chinesen in San Francisco, Gl, 24, 15, 16.
74-10   Kohn, A. Die Russen in Sibirien, Gl, 26: 91ff. , 103ff.
74-11   Lumby, J. R. The history of the creeds. Cambridge.
74-12   Sachau, E. Zur Geschichte und Chronologie von Khwârizm. Wien.
74-13   von Hellwald, F. Culturgeschichte in ihrer natürlichen Entwickelung bis zur
          Gengenwart. Augsburg.
74-14   Wilson, H. A history of the rise and fall of the slave power in America.
          Boston.
74-15   Winkler, E. T. The Negroes in the Gulf-States, Intern. Rev. : 577ff.
74-16   Wylie, A. History of the Heung-Noo in their relations with China, JRAI,
          3: 401—52.

1875

75-1   Bancroft, H. H. The native races of the Pacific States, NAR, 123.
75-2   Broun, J. A. The origin of our numerals, Na: 316ff.
75-3   d'Estrey, M. Les Hollandais en Afrique. Les Achantis, les Fantis, et les
          Elminois, l'Explorateur Geogr. , 2: 41ff.
75-4   Dunn, R. Some remarks on ethnic psychology, JRAI, 4: 255—65.

75-5   Heath, D. J. Origin and development of the mental function in man, JRAI,
        4: 66–78.
75-6   Jackson, J. W. Ethnology and phrenology as an aid to the historian. London.
75-7   Jacolliot, L. Fétichisme, polythéisme, monothéisme. Le genèse de
        l'humanité. La terre et l'homme. Traditions indoues et chaldéenes. La
        légende de la genèse dans l'Inde. Paris.
75-8   Kirchliche, —. Die Revolution in Venezuela und Mexiko, Deutscher Mercur,
        7, 27.
75-9   Lenormant, F. Die Anfänge der Cultur. Geschichtliche und archeologische
        Studien. Jena, Costenoble.
75-10   Maine, H. J. Early history of institutions. London.
75-11   Notes and queries on anthropology, for the use of travellers and residents
        in uncivilised lands. BAAS. London.
75-12   Pitt-Rivers, A. L.-F. On the evolution of culture, RIGBP, 12.
75-13   Reid, A. P. The mixed or "half-breed" races of northwestern Canada,
        JRAI, 4: 45–52.
75-14   Rosny, L. de. Introduction à une histoire de la céramique chez les Indiens
        du Nouveau Monde, ASAF, 1: 147ff.
75-15   Satow, E. M. The revival of pure Shintô, ASJT, 3, 1: 94ff.
75-16   Sayce, A. H. The origin of the Phoenician cosmogony and the Babylonian
        Garden of Eden, Ac: 299ff.
75-17   Taplin, G. Further notes on the mixed races of Australia, and their migra-
        tions and language, JRAI, 4: 52–57.

1876

76-1   Barber, E. A. Bead ornaments employed by the Indian tribes of Utah and
        Arizona, Bull. U.S. Geol. and Geog. Survey, 2, 1: 67ff.
76-2   Barber, E. A. Language and utensils of the modern Utes, Bull. U.S. Geol.
        and Geog. Survey, 2, 1: 72–76.
76-3   Borde, P. G. L. Histoire de l'île de Trinidad sous le gouvernement espagnol.
        Paris.
76-4   Brackett, A. G. The Sioux or Dakota Indians, SIR: 466–72.
76-5   Brand, J. Observations on popular antiquities, chiefly illustrating the
        origin of our vulgar customs, etc. London.
76-6   Buss, E. Die christliche Mission, ihre principielle Berechtigung und
        praktische Durchführung. Leiden.
76-7   Chil, G. y Naranjo. Estudios historicos, climatologicos y patologicos de
        las islas Ganarias. I: Historia. Las Palmas.
76-8   Christie, J. Cholera epidemics in East Africa . . . London.
76-9   Ecker, A. Zur urgeschichtlichen und culturgeschishtlichen Terminologie,
        ArA, 9: 97.
76-10   Funck-Brentano, —. La civilisation et ses lois. Morale sociale. Paris.
76-11   Grandidier, A. Histoire physique, naturelle, et politique de Madagascar.
        3 vols. Paris.
76-12   Hovelacque, A. Ethnologie et ethnographie, BSAP, 2nd. series, 11: 298ff.
76-13   Kleinpaul, R. Der Ursprung der Sprache, Au, 49.
76-14   Luchs, —. Culturhistorische Wandtafeln. Breslau.
76-15   Malan, C. H. South African missions. London.
76-16   Marty, A. Kritik der Theorien über den Sprachursprung. Göttingen.

76-17   Mercier, E. Histoire de l'établissement des Arabes dans l'Afrique septentrionale . . . Paris.

76-18   Post, A. H. Die Ursprung des Rechts. Oldenburg.

76-19   Powers, S. Centennial mission to the Indians of western Nevada and California, SIR: 449−65.

76-20   Religiöser Fanatismus in Saõ Paulo, Gl, 30, 16.

76-21   Reuleaux, —. Coup d'oeuil sur l'histoire du developement des machines dans l'humanité. Paris.

76-22   Routledge, J. Chapters on the history of popular progress (1660−1820). London.

76-23   Rückschlage aus Civilisation, Gl, 27.

76-24   Zerffi, G. G. A manual of the historic development of art. London.

1877

77-1   Barber, E. A. On the ancient and modern Pueblo tribes of the Pacific slope of the United States, ANa, 11, October.

77-2   Clark, S. N. Are the Indians dying out? Preliminary observations relating to Indian civilization and education. Washington.

77-3   Clough, J. C. On the existence of mixed languages. London.

77-4   d'Abbadie, A. Sur l'origine des Oromo ou Ylmorna de l'Afrique orientale . . . BSAP, 11: 320−25.

77-5   d'Abbadie, A. Les causes actuelles de l'esclavage en Ethiopie. Louvain.

77-6   Davin, N. F. The Irishman in Canada. London.

77-7   Elliott, C. W. Pottery and porcelain from early times . . . New York.

77-8   Henne-Am-Rhyn, O. Allegemeine Culturgeschichte. 2 vols. Leipzig.

77-9   Karsch, —. Die Naturgeschichte des Teufels. Münster.

77-10   MacMahon, R. R. The Anglo Saxon and the North American Indians. Richmond, Va.

77-11   Morgan, L. G. Ancient society. New York.

77-12   Mortillet, G. de. Sur les origines du fer, BSAP, 11: 338−41.

77-13   Noiré, L. Ursprung der Sprache. 8 vols. Mainz.

77-14   Paira Manso, — de. Historia do Congo . . . Lisbonne.

77-15   Quatrefages, A. de. Les migrations et l'acclimatation en Polynésie, RSP, June.

77-16   Rawlinson, G. Origin of nations. 1. On early civilisation. 2. On ethnic affinities. London.

77-17   Regnaud, A. Materiaux pour servir a l'histoire de la philosophie de l'Inde. Paris.

77-18   Spencer, H. On the evolution of the family, PSMo, June.

77-19   Steinthal, H. Der Ursprung der Sprache. Berlin.

77-20   Tylor, A. The origin of numerals; or the object-origin of prehistoric thoughts and ideas illustrated by the history of the invention of the art of calculation and some other useful arts, JRAI, 6: 125−36.

77-21   Van Soest, G. H. Sir James Brooke, Raja van Serawak, Tijdschr. Nederl. Indië, 2: 170−215.

1878

78-1   Andree, R. Ethnographische Parallelen und Vergleiche. Stuttgart.

78-2   Ancona, E. Historia du Yucatan des de la época mas remota hasta nuestros dias. Merida.

78-3   Beck, S. Die Geschichte des jüdischen Volkes und seiner Litteratur. Lissa (Posen).

78-4   Bevölkerung von Tasmanien in 1876, Gl, 33, 16.

78-5   Blanchard, E. Blancs et métis aux iles Fidji ou Viti, RAP, 378.

78-6   Buller, J. Forty years in New Zealand: including . . . the Christianisation and colonisation of the country. London.

78-7   Dabry, P. La mahometisme en Chine et dans le Turkestan oriental. 2 vols. Paris.

78-8   Doerkens, H. Grundlinien einer Wissenschaft der Geschichte. 2 vols. Leipzig.

78-9   Eggleston, G. C. Red Eagle, and the wars with the Creek Indians of Alabama. New York.

78-10 Gaffarel, P. Histoire du Brésil francais au XVIe siècle. Paris.

78-11 Janssen, J. Geschichte des deutschen Volkes. Freibourg en Brisgau. 1878-79.

78-12 Leutemann, H. Die Eskimos in Paris, Die Natur, 9.

78-13 Malleson, B. G. History of the Indian mutiny. London.

78-14 Müller, M. On the origin of reason, CR, February.

78-15 Müller, M. On the origin and growth of religion, CR, May.

78-16 Poesche, T. Die Aries. Ein Beitrag zur historischen Anthropologie. Jena.

78-17 Rey, H. Etude sur la colonie de Guadaloupe. Paris.

78-18 Ridpath, J. C. A popular history of the United States of America, from the aboriginal times to the present day. Cincinnati.

78-19 Wake, C. S. The evolution of morality; being a history of the development of moral culture. 2 vols. London.

1879

79-1   Baldwin, C. C. Early Indian migrations in Ohio, AAn, 1, 4ff.

79-2   Barrett, H. J. Fifteen years among the Zulus and Boers. London.

79-3   Campbell, J. On the origin of some American Indian tribes, CN, 9: 4ff.

79-4   Clint, W. The aborigines of Canada under the British crown: glances at their customs, characteristics, and history. Trans. Lit. and Hist. Soc. Quebec.

79-5   Dawson, G. M. The past and present condition of the Indians of Canada, CN, 4: 3ff.

79-6   Denis, H. Des origines et de l'évolution du droit économique. Phil. Positive Rev., Decembre.

79-7   Dennys, N. B. Pidgin English, JRASSB, 2.

79-8   Farber, J. A. Zululand and the Zulus . . . London.

79-9   Fowle, T. W. The place of the will in evolution, NC, March.

79-10 Lefèvre, A. L'homme à travers les âges, essays de critique historique. Paris.

79-11 Losker, E. Ursprung, Zweck, und Entwickelung der Sprache, Deutsche Rundschau, Nov.

79-12 Müller, F. M. Lectures on the origin and growth of religion . . . Scribner and Welford.

79-13   Proctor, R. A. The origin of the week, CR, 35: 404-21.
79-14   Tylor, E. B. A history of games, Eclectic, July. Century, June 7-14.
        Living Age, May 31. PSMo, June.
79-15   Tylor, E. B. On the game of patolli in ancient Mexico and its probably
        Asiatic origin, JRAI, 8: 116-29.
79-16   Wainwright, A. The origin and practice of polo, Scribner's Monthly, 18.

1880

80-1   Avery, J. Influence of the aboriginal tribes upon Aryan speech in India,
        Oriental and Biblical Journ., 3.
80-2   Beck, L. Das Meteoreisen in technischer und culturgeschichtlicher Bezie-
        hung, ArA, 12: 293-314.
80-3   Conder, J. The history of Japanese costume, ASJT, 8, 3: 369-415.
80-4   Cox, G. W. The migration of popular stories, Eclectic, Sept.
80-5   d'Abertis, L. M. New Guinea: what I did and what I saw. 2 vols. London.
80-6   Dunbar, J. B. The Pawnee Indians; their history and ethnology, MAH, 8,
        April.
80-7   Dunbar, J. B. Sketch of Pitalesharu, head chief of the Pawnees, MAH,
        8, November.
80-8   Dunbar, J. B. The decrease of the North American Indians, Kansas City
        Rev., Sept.
80-9   Gore, J. H. The development of deliberative government among the North
        American Indians, ASWT, 1: 58ff.
80-10   Guyan, M. De l'origine des religions, Rev. Philosophique, Dec.
80-11   Havard, V. French and Indian half-breeds, ASWT, 1: 12ff.
80-12   Hough, M. B. W. A Question of classification, ASWT, 1: 88-92.
80-13   Hough, MBV. Civilization, ASWT, 1: By title; summary in Abstract of
        AWST, Powell, J. W. (ed.): 100ff. Washington, D.C. 1881.
80-14   Howorth, H. H. History of the Mongols from the ninth to the sixteenth
        century. The so-called Tartars of Russia and central Asia. Divisions
        1 and 2. London.
80-15   Icazbalceta, J. G. Historia de los Mexicanos por sus pinturas, MNMA,
        2: 85-106.
80-16   Jackson, S. Alaska and the missions in the North Pacific coast. New York.
80-17   Keane, A. H. On the relations of the Indo-Chinese and inter-oceanic races
        and languages, JRAI, 9, 3: 254-90.
80-18   Lemly, H. R. Among the Arrapahoes, Harper's Mag., March.
80-19   Lesson, A. Les Polynésiens, leur origine, leurs migrations, leur langage;
        ouvrage rédigé, d'après le manuscrit de l'auteur, par Ludovic Martinet.
        Paris.
80-20   Powell, J. W. On the evolution of language, as exhibited in the specializa-
        tion of the grammatic processes, the differentiation of the parts of
        speech, and the integration of the sentence, from a study of Indian
        languages, ASWT, 1: By title: Summary in Abstract AWST, Powell, J.W.
        (ed.): 35ff. Washington, 1881.
80-21   Putnam, F. W. The Indians of California, Bull. Essex Inst., 12.
80-22   Renouf, P. leP. The origin and growth of religion as illustrated by the re-
        ligion of ancient Egypt. Hibbert Lectures for 1874. New York.
80-23   Royce, C. C. An inquiry into the history and identity of the Shawnee Indians,

AWST, 1: By title; summary in Abstract ASWT, Powell, J. W. (ed.): 94ff. Washington, 1881.

80-24 Wylie, A. History of the south-western barbarians and Chaou-Sëen . . . JRAI, 9: 53–96.

1881

81-1   Bastian, A. Die Vorgeschichte der Ethnologie. Berlin.

81-2   Beauchamp, W. M. Indian missions of the colonial period. New York.

81-3   Carrington, H. B. The Dacotah tribes; their beliefs and our duty to them outlined. Salem, Mass.

81-4   Dally, E. Causes of human degeneracy, BSAP, 4: 339ff.

81-5   Dorman, R. M. The origin of primitive superstitions, and their development into the worship of spirits and the doctrine of spiritual agency among the aborigines of America. Philadelphia and London.

81-6   Hovelacque, A. Les debuts de l'humanité. Paris.

81-7   Lippert, J. Der Seelencult in seinen Beziehungen zur althebräischen Religion. Berlin.

81-8   Mason, O. T. The uncivilized mind in the presence of higher phases of civilization. Am. Assoc., Cincinnati.

81-9   Mitchell, A. The past in the present: what is civilization? New York.

81-10 Powell, J. W. On the evolution of language, BAER, 1: 3–16.

81-11 Rawlinson, G. The origin of nations. New York.

81-12 Rawlinson, G. The prospective civilization of Africa, Princeton Rev., Sept.

81-13 Rowbotham, J. F. Certain reasons for believing that the art of music in prehistoric times, passed through three stages of development . . . (that) invariably succeed one another in the same order in various parts of the world, JRAI, 10: 380–89.

81-14 Schurz, C. Present aspect of the Indian problem, NAR, 129.

81-15 Thébaud, A. J. Native tribes of North America and the Catholic missions. 11. Process of conversion among the Hurons, etc. Month., July.

81-16 Tylor, A. The laws of ornament in the organic world, and on the origin of the human form, JRAI, 10: 108.

81-17 Tylor, E. B. Anthropology. London.

81-18 Tylor, E. B. On the origin of the plough and wheel carriages, JRAI, 10: 74–80.

81-19 Yarrow, H. C. Medical facts relating to the Zuñi Indians of New Mexico, Rocky Mt. Med. Rev.: 192–94. Colorado Springs.

1882

82-1   Allen, N. The law of human increase, PSMo, 22: 39–48.

82-2   Caverly, R. B. Indian wars of New England. Boston.

82-3   David, P. R. Origin and growth of religion. New York.

82-4   de Harlez, C. Du rôle des mythes dans le formation des religions antiques, Mu, 1.

82-5   Ellis, G. E. The red man and the white man in North America from its discovery to the present time. Boston.

82-6   Ferguson, J. The history of architecture in all countries. New York.
82-7   Frere, H. B. On the laws affecting the relations between civilised and sav-
        age life, as bearing on the dealings of colonists with aborigines, JRAI,
        11: 313–52.
82-8   Frost, J. The history of Mexico and its wars . . . New Orleans.
82-9   King, A. F. A. The evolution of marriage ceremonies and its import,
        ASWT, 1–2: 36ff.
82-10   Mason, O. T. The savage mind in the presence of civilization, ASWT, 1–2:
        44ff.
82-11   Peet, S. D. The origin of architectural orders, AAn, 4: 4ff.
82-12   Proctor, R. A. The influence of food on civilization, NAR: 547–63.
82-13   Robins, E. The evolution of magic, AMo, 49: 685–95.
82-14   Tylor, E. B. Notes on the Asiatic relations of Polynesian culture, JRAI,
        11: 401–05.
82-15   Williams, G. W. The history of the negro race in America from 1619 to
        1881. New York.
82-16   Wilson, G. S. How shall the American savage be civilized? AMo, 50: 596–607.
82-17   Wilson, J. D. The origin of government, CR, 42: 413–27.
82-18   Wood, C. E. S. Among the Thlinkits in Alaska, The Century, July.

1883

83-1   Allen, G. Idiosyncrasy, PSMo, 24: 387–403.
83-2   Azam, — . Les altérations de la personnalité, RSP, 32: 610–18.
83-3   Beauchamp, W. M. Contributions to aboriginal history in Skaneateles,
        Syracuse, and Baldwinsville. New York Papers. New York.
83-4   Belrghaus, A. Das Aussterben der Naturvölker. Europa.
83-5   Bennett, G. An account of Elau, a Malayan Papuan child, Austral. M. Gaz.,
        2: 255–58. Sydney.
83-6   Büchner, M. African psychology, PSMo, 13: 399–404.
83-7   Deniker, J. Les Ghiliaks d'après les derniers renseignements, RE, 2: 289–
        310.
83-8   Fuentes y Guzman, F. A. Historia de Guatemala o recordación florida
        escrita en le Siglo 17, 2.
83-9   Gilliam, E. W. The African in the United States, PSMo, 22: 433–44.
83-10   Guss, A. L. Early Indian history of the Susquehanna, Historical Register,
        Harrisburg, Penn.
83-11   Hale, H. Indian migrations, as evidenced by language, Proc., Am. Assoc.,
        Montreal (also AAn, Jan., April).
83-12   Howitt, A. W. and Fison, L. From mother-right to father-right, JRAI,
        12: 30–46.
83-13   Ingersoll, E. Wampum and its history, ANa, 17: 467ff.
83-14   Lagneau, G. La décroissance de la population, BSAP, 6: 571–78.
83-15   Lang, A. The early history of the family, CR, 44: 406–22.
83-16   Leftschik, K. Evolutsia semyi. Moscow.
83-17   Lippert, J. Allgemeine Geschichte des Priestertums. 2 vols. Berlin,
        1883–1884.
83-18   Maine, H. S. Dissertations on early law and custom. London.
83-19   Melendez, L. Monomanía religiosa; ideas impulsivas; suicidio, Rev. Méd. —
        Quir., 10: 173–75. Buenos Aires.

83-20   Pagliani, L. Etude sur le développement de la famille, Ann. de Démog.
        Internat. , 6: 197–204.
83-21   Parker, G. W. On the new code of laws for the Hova Kingdom of Madagascar
        JRAI, 12: 306–18.
83-22   Routledge, R. Discoveries and inventions of the 19th Century. London.
83-23   Scherzer, K. von. Die Anfänge menschlicher Industrie. Berlin.
83-24   Schneider, O. Naturwissenschaftliche Beiträge zur Geographie und Cultur-
        geschichte. Dresden.
83-25   Seely, F. A. An inquiry into the origin of inventions, ASWT, 2: 70–90.
83-26   Taylor, I. The alphabet, an account of the origin and development of letters.
        London.

                                    <u>1884</u>

84-1   Andree, R. Besessene und Geisteskranke, ethnographisch betachtet, MAGW,
        14: 60–62.
84-2   Atkinson, E. T. Notes on the history of religion in the Himalaya of the
        N. W. Provinces, JASB, 53: 1ff.
84-3   Bastian, A. Grundzüge der Ethnologie. Berlin.
84-4   Beck, L. Die Geschichte deo Eisens in technischer und kulturgeschichtlicher
        Beziehung. Braunschweig.
84-5   Bonwick, J. The lost Tasmanian race. London.
84-6   Carr, L. The mounds of the Mississippi valley historically considered.
        Cincinnati.
84-7   Clavel, M. La dépopulation aux îles Marquises, BSAP, 7: 490–500.
84-8   Cook, F. C. The origins of religion and language. London.
84-9   Cushing, F. H. On the development of industrial and ornamental art among
        the Zuñis of New Mexico, Brit. Assoc. , Montreal, Na, 34.
84-10   Day, S. The Indian census, ANa 18: 215–16.
84-11   Ell, M. Dokibati, or the god of the Puget Sound Indians, AAn, 6: 389–92.
84-12   Flower, W. H. On the aims and prospects of the study of anthropology,
        JRAI, 13: 488–501.
84-13   Giraud-Teulon, A. Les origines du mariage et de la famille. Paris.
84-14   Hale, H. On the origin of wampum, Brit. Assoc. , Montreal, Na 30.
84-15   Hirth, G. Kulturgeschichtlisches Bilderbuch aus drei Jahrhunderten, 17–24
        Lfg. München, 20: 515–768.
84-16   Jacolliot, L. Histoire naturelle et sociale de l'humanité. Le monde primitif,
        les lois naturelles, et les lois sociales. Paris.
84-17   Letourneau, C. L'évolution de la morale, RSP, 33: 673–84
84-18   Lippert, S. Die Geschichte der Familie. Stuttgart.
84-19   Löher, F. von. Beiträge zur Geschichte und Völkerkunde. Frankfort.
84-20   Mackenzie, A. History of the relations of the government with the hill tribes
        of the north-eastern frontier of Bengal. Calcutta.
84-21   Matthews, W. Navajo silversmiths, BAER, 2: 167–78.
84-22   Meyer, E. Geschichte des Alterthums. Erster Band. Geschichte des Orients
        bis zur Begründung des Kaiserreichts. Stuttgart.
84-23   Penck, A. Mensch und Eisziet, ArA, 15: 211–28.
84-24   Petitot, E. F. S. Sur l'habitat et les fluctuations de la population peau rouge
        en Canada, BSAP, 7.
84-25   Piètrement, C. A. Sur les origines der fer, BSAP, 7.

84-26 Pitt-Rivers, B. H. L. — F. On the development of primitive locks and keys. London.
84-27 Post, A. H. Zur Entwicklungsgeschichte der Familie, Deutsche Geogr. Blätter.
84-28 Renan, E. Nouvelles études d'histoire religieuse. Paris.
84-29 Reville, A. Lectures on the origin and growth of religion. The Hibbert Lectures for 1884. London.
84-30 Schmidt, R. A. Geschichte de Erziehung. 2 vols., 1884.
84-31 Wake, C. S. The nature and origin of group-marriage, JRAI, 13: 151—61.
84-32 Weeden, W. B. Indian money as a factor in New England civilization, 8—9, 2, Johns Hopkins Univ. Studies. Baltimore.
84-33 Wilkie, F. B. The great inventions; their history from the earliest period to the present; their influence on civilization. Chicago.
84-34 Withington, C. F. The perils of rapid civilization, PSMo, 26: 224—39.
84-35 Woodward, — . The Nez Perces on the Indian reservation being destroyed by malaria, Gaillard's Med. Journ., 37: 225ff. New York.

1885

85-1   Bates, H. H. Discontinuities in nature's methods, ASWT, 3: 51—55.
85-2   Baur, T. A. Ueber Fetischdienst und Seelenkult als Urform der Religion. KBDGA, 16: 9—13, 19—21.
85-3   Beauchamp, W. M. Permanence of early Iroquois clans and sachemships, AAASP, also AAn, 8: 91ff., 1886.
85-4   Beauregard, O. Ceylan et ses habitants aux temps anciens, moyens et modernes, BSAP, 18: 86—128.
85-5   Buckland, A. W. Facts suggestive of prehistoric intercourse between East and West, JRAI, 14: 222—32.
85-6   Carneri, B. Zur Geschichte der Moral, Kosmos, 1, 81; 321ff.
85-7   Clavel, A. Les Marquisiens, Arch. d. Med. Nav., Paris, 42, 194ff; 43, 209ff, 353ff.
85-8   Dall, W. H. Masks, labrets, and certain aboriginal customs, with an inquiry into the bearing of their geographical distribution, BAER, 3: 67—202.
85-9   Dareste, M. Hypothèse sur l'origine des droitiers et des gauchers, BSAP, 43: 415—18.
85-10 Darmesteter, J. The Mahdi, past and present, London.
85-11 Darmesteter, J. Le Mahdi depuis les origines de l'Islam jusqu'à nos jours. Paris.
85-12 Dorsey, J. O. A visit to the Siletz agency. AAASP.
85-13 Fabart, F. Histoire philosophique et politique de l'occulte, magie, sorcellerie, spiritisme, etc. Paris.
85-14 Fletcher, A. C. Historical sketch of the Omaha tribe of Indians in Nebraska. Washington.
85-15 Gannett, H. Are we to become Africanized? PSMo, 27: 145—50.
85-16 Gatschet, A. S. The Aruba language and the Papiamento jargon, Kansas City Rev., Nov.
85-17 Gregory, J. M. Elements of modern civilization, ASWT, 3: 57—64.
85-18 Hale, H. Chief George H. M. Johnson. His life and work among the Six Nations, MAH, 19. Feb.

85-19 Hale, H. The obsequies of Red Jacket at Buffalo. Trans. Buffalo Hist. Soc., 3.

85-20 Hovelacque, A. L'évolution du langage. Conférence Transformiste. Paris.

85-21 Holmes, W. H. Examples of iconoclasm by the conquerors of Mexico, ANa, 19: 1031−37.

85-22 Letourneau, C. L'évolution de l'esclavage dans les diverses races humaines. Paris.

85-23 McLennan, J. F. The patriarchal theory. London.

85-24 Meyer, G. Essays und Studien zur Völker. Kassel.

85-25 Mongeolle, P. Origines et évolution de la parure, RAP, 8: 79−98.

85-26 Oviedo y Banos, J. Historia de la conquista y población de la provincia de Venezuela. Madrid.

85-27 Peet, S. D. The growth of symbolism, AAn, 7.

85-28 Ploss, H. H. Geschichtliches und Ethnologisches über Knabenbeschneidung. Leipzig.

85-29 Powell, J. W. From savagery to barbarism, ASWT, 3: 173−96.

85-30 Ratzel, F. Völkerkunde. 3 vols. Berlin, 1885−1888.

85-31 Réclus, E. Les primitifs. Études d'ethnologie comparée. Paris.

85-32 Seely, F. A. The genesis of inventions, ASWT, 3: 147−68.

85-33 Seignobos, C. Histoire de la civilisation. Paris.

85-34 Smith, E. A. Artificial wampum, Sc, Jan. 2.

85-35 Swank, J. M. History of the manufacture of iron in all ages. Philadelphia.

85-36 Tiele, C. P. Manuel de l'histoire des religions. Paris.

85-37 Véron, E. Histoire naturelle des religions. Paris.

85-38 Ward, L. F. Mind as a social factor, ASWT, 3: 31−38.

85-39 Ward, L. F. Moral and material progress contrasted, ASWT, 3: 121−36.

85-40 Warren, W. W. History of the Ojibways, based upon traditions and oral statements. Minnesota Historical Society, 5.

1886

86-1 Alsberg, M. Die Anfänge der Eisenkultur. Berlin.

86-2 Baker, F. Evolution in architecture, PSMo, 28: 642−49.

86-3 Bancroft, H. H. History of the Pacific States of North America. San Francisco. 1886−89.

86-4 Beauvois, E. Deux sources de l'histoire des Quetzalcoatl, Mu, 427, 597.

86-5 Berlin, A. F. Fraudulent stone objects, AAn, 8: 228−30.

86-6 Bosch-Reitz, G. J. A. History of the origin, customs, religion, wars, and travels of the Caribs, savages of the Antilles in America. Temehri-Demerara, Br. Guiana.

86-7 Cardus, J. Las misiones franciscanas entre los infieles de Bolivia. Barcelona.

86-8 Clarke, J. C. C. The origin and varieties of the Semitic alphabet. Am. Pub. Soc. of Hebrew. Chicago.

86-9 Colin, —. La population du Bambouck, Senegal-Niger, RAP, 3, 1: 432−47.

86-10 Crombie, J. W. History of the game of hop-scotch, JRAI, 15: 403−08.

86-11 Danvers, F. C. Historical and recent famines in India, J. Soc. of Arts, 34: 317−49.

86-12 Dorsey, J. O. On the migrations of Siouan tribes, ANa, 20: 121−222.

86-13 Douglass, F. The future of the colored race, NAR, 142: 436−40.

86-14 Grimm, — . Abriss der Kulturgeschichte Ostafrikas, Verhandl., Badisch.
       Geog. Gesellsch., Karlsruhe: 1–56.
86-15 Hale, H. H. Origin of primitive money, PSMo, 28: 296–306.
86-16 Higginson, T. W. English sources of American dialect, Am. Antiq. Soc.,
       Proc., 4: 159–66.
86-17 Holmes, W. H. Origin and development of form and ornament in ceramic
       art, BAER, 4: 437–65.
86-18 Hovelacque, A. The evolution of language, PSMo, 98–106.
86-19. Huxley, T. H. The evolution of theology, NC, April; PSMo, 28: 449–59.
86-20 Keane, A. H. The Lapps, their origin . . . present state, future prospects,
       JRAI, 15: 213–34.
86-21 La Borde, S. de. History of the origin, customs, religion, wars, and
       travels of the Caribs . . ., Timehri-Demerara, Br. Guiana, 5: 224–54.
86-22 Lippert, J. Kulturgeschichte der Menschheit in ihrem organischen Aufbau.
       Stuttgart, 1886–87. (Trans. by Murdock, G. P. The evolution of culture.
       New York, 1931.)
86-23 Maine, H. S. The age of progress, in Popular government: four essays.
       New York.
86-24 Maxwell, W. E. The history of Perak from native sources, JRASSB, 14:
       305–21.
86-25 McLennan, J. F. Studies in ancient history. London.
86-26 Moncelon,—. Métis de Français et de Néo-Calédonien, BSAP, 3, 9: 10–19.
86-27 Morgan, C. L. The springs of conduct: an essay in evolution. London.
86-28 Morse, E. S. Ancient and modern methods of arrow release, Bull. Essex
       Inst., 18.
86-29 Petri, E. Unser Verhältnis zu den Völkern niederer Kultur, Gl, 47.
86-30 Sabatier, — . Du progrès indéfini dans l'humanité, Hm, 3: 97–103.
86-31 Shaw, G. A. Madagascar of today. Rel. Tract Soc., London.
86-32 Smith, C. The influence of invention on civilization, PSMo, 28: 474–84,
       656–67.
86-33 Stuart-Glennie, J. S. Folklore as the complement of culture-lore in the
       study of history, FJ, 4: 213–21.
86-34 Tsakny, N. Les sectes religieuses en Russie, RSP, Series 3, 5.
86-35 Wake, S. Les Cambodgiens et leur origine, RAP, 1: 204–25.
36-36 Wood, J. G. Man and his handiwork. London.

1887

87-1   Anutchine, D. N. Bows and arrows. Archaeological and ethnological study.
       (in Russian). Moscow.
87-2   Beauchamp, W. M. Changes in the languages of Indians, Sc, 10: 251ff.
87-3   Best, G. Morality and utility. London.
87-4   Brinton, D. G. The rate of change in American languages, Sc, 10: 274ff.
87-5   Conder, C. R. The present condition of the native tribes in Bechuanaland,
       JRAI, 16: 76–96.
87-6   d'Alviella, G. Histoire religieuse du feu. Biblioth. Gilon, 173. Verviers.
87-7   Eicken, H. von. Geschichte und System der mittelalterlichen Weltanschauung.
       Stuttgart.
87-8   Featherman, A. Social history of the races of mankind. 4 vols. 1887–1889.

87-9 Féré, C. Contribution to the pathology of dreams and of hysterical paralysis. Paris.

87-10 Haberlandt, M. Zum Ursprung des Bogens, MAGW, 17: 116.

87-11 Kappler, A. Surinam, sein Land, sein Natur, Bevölkerung und seine Kulturverhältnisse mit bezug auf Kolonisation. Stuttgart.

87-12 Letourneau, C. L'évolution de la morale. Paris.

87-13 Rawlinson, G. Ancient history. New York.

87-14 Roth, H. L. On the origin of agriculture, JRAI, 16: 102−36.

87-15 Royce, C. C. The Cherokee nation of Indians, BAER, 4: 121−378.

87-16 Ten Kate, H. Ueber mohammedanische Bruderschaften in Algerien, VBGA: 372−75.

1888

88-1 Armstrong, S. C. The future of the American Negro, Proc. Nat. Conf. Char., 14: 167−70. Boston.

88-2 Backhouse, T. W. The natural history of the Roman numerals, Na, 36: 555ff

88-3 Balfour, H. On the evolution of a characteristic pattern on the shafts of arrows from the Solomon Islands, JRAI, 17: 328−32.

88-4 Barrows, W. Indian's side of the Indian question. New York.

88-5 Bates, H. H. Discontinuities in nature's methods, AA, 1: 135−48.

88-6 Benton, G. Mahommedism in Africa, NAR, Feb.: 222ff.

88-7 Boas, F. Census and reservations of the Kwakiutl Nation, Bull. Am. Geog. Soc., 19: 225−32.

88-8 Boas, F. The occurrence of similar inventions in areas widely apart, Sc, 9: 485ff.

88-9 Browning, O. Aspects of education; a study in the history of pedagogy, Mon. Ind. Ed. Ass., New York, 1: 131−76.

88-10 Chalmers, J. Pioneering in New Guinea, Na, 36: 255ff.

88-11 Cowles, E. Insistent and fixed ideas, AJPs: 222−70.

88-12 Crane, T. F. Diffusion of the popular tales, JAF, 1: 8−14.

88-13 Elliott, A. M. Speech mixture in French Canada, Am. Journ. Philol., 8: 133−57.

88-14 Féré, C. Dégénerescence et criminalité, Rev. Philos., 24: 337−77. Paris.

88-15 Frothingham, A. L. The development and character of Mohammedan education, Proc. Am. Orient. Soc., Oct.: 114−16.

88-16 Grove, W. R. Antagonism, PSMo, 33: 608−24.

88-17 Hale, H. H. The development of language, CIP, 3rd Series, 6: 92−134.

88-18 Hill, S. A. The life statistics of an Indian province, Na, 38.

88-19 Holmes, W. H. A study of the textile art in its relation to the development of form and ornament, BAER, 5.

88-20 Iljinski, A. Feasibility of preserving condition of women for an indefinite time. (in Russian). Moscow.

88-21 La Borde, P. de. History of the origin, customs, religion, etc. of the Caribs of Antilles, Timehri, Br. Guiana, Na, 36: 309ff.

88-22 Lapouge, G. de. La dépopulation de la France, RAP, 3rd series, 3: 69−80.

88-23 Letourneau, C. L'évolution du mariage et de la famille. Paris.

88-24 Maine, H. J. S. Lectures on the early history of institutions. London, New York.

88-25   Mason, O. T. The occurrence of similar inventions in areas widely apart, Sc, 9: 534ff.

88-26   Matthews, W. Further contributions to the study of consumption among the Indians, Trans. Am. Climatological Assoc., Phila.: 1–20.

88-27   Morgan, E. D. The customs of the Ossetes and the light they throw on the evolution of law, JRAS, 54.

88-28   Powell, J. W. Competition as a factor in human evolution, AA, 1: 297–324.

88-29   Powell, J. W. From barbarism to civilization, AA, 1: 97–124.

88-30   Ranke, J. Der Menschheit die Heutigen und die vorgeschichtlichen Menschen-rassen. Leipzig.

88-31   Reynolds, H. L. Algonkin metal smiths, AA, 1: 341–52.

88-32   Rink, H. The migrations of the Eskimo indicated by their progress in com-pleting the kayak implements, JRAI, 17: 68–75.

88-33   Sabatier, —. De l'éducation des peuples conquis; de l'action du peuple educateur étudiée dans ses conditions d'efficacité et dans ses effets, Hm, 4: 33–46.

88-34   Smith, de C. Witchcraft and demonism of the modern Iroquois, JAF, 1: 184–93.

88-35   Ujfalvy, C. E. de. L'influence du milieu sur les peuples de l'Asie centrale, BSAP, 3rd series, 10: 459–60.

88-36   Vinson, J. Les religions actuelles, leurs doctrines, leur évolution, leur histoire, Paris.

1889

89-1   Bacon, T. S. The beginnings of religion. London.

89-2   Baker, S. W. African development: the Soudan, FR, 46: 551–72.

89-3   Barron, G. B. Town life as a cause of degeneracy, PSMo, 34: 324–30.

89-4   Bataillard, P. Les debuts de l' immigration des Tsiganes dans l'Europe occidentale, BSAP, 12: 255–65.

89-5   Beauchamp, W. M. Silver brooches and crosses and iron axes, AAn, 21: 248–49.

89-6   Boyle, D. Modern Indian dress, etc. Archaeol. Rep., Council of the Ca-nadian Institute, Sessional Papers, 21, 5, 42: 42. Toronto.

89-7   Chulow, G. The origin and manufacture of playing cards, Jnl. Soc. Arts, 37: 571–79.

89-8   Croffut, W. A. The peons of Mexico, AA, 2: 80ff.

89-9   Daly, D. The Mexican messiah, AAn, 11: 14–30.

89-10   Dareste, R. Etudes d'histoire du droit. Paris.

89-11   Ducoudray, G. History of ancient civilization. New York.

89-12   Edwards, C. L. Folk-lore of the Bahama Negroes, AJPs, 2: 519–42.

89-13   Fishback, W. M. Statehood for the Indians, NAR, 148: 648ff.

89-14   Friedrichs, K. Ueber den Ursprung des Matriarchats, ZVR, 8.

89-15   Fry, Lord Justice Imitation as a factor in human progress, CR, May.

89-16   Gale, H. The origin of holidays, PSMo, 34: 516–24.

89-17   Gomme, G. L. The conditions for the survival of archaic customs, Archaeol. Rev., London, 4: 422–38.

89-18   Jagem, B. Ein Fall von "Amoklaufen" eines Malayen, MAGW, 9: 32ff.

89-19   Holmes, W. H. Debasement of Pueblo art, AA, 2: 320ff.

89-20   Howarth, O. H. The survival of corporal penance, JRAI, 18: 275–81.

89-21 Letourneau, C. L'évolution de la propriété. Paris.
89-22 Mason, O. T. The beginnings of the carrying industry, AA, 2: 21–46.
89-23 Peet, S. D. The history of the knife, AAn, 11: 122–28.
89-24 Peet, S. D. Autochthonous origin of the American civilization, AAn, 11: 314–20.
89-25 Roth, H. L. An account of the aborigines of Tasmania . . . from the time of their first contact with Europeans until their final extermination. London.
89-26 Savage, M. J. The effects of evolution on the coming civilization. Boston.
89-27 Shufeldt, R. W. The drawings of a Navajo artist, MAH, 23: 463–68.
89-28 Smith, V. A. Graeco-Roman influence on the civilisation of ancient India, JASB, 58: 107–97.
89-29 Starcke, C. N. The primitive family in its origin and development. New York.
89-30 Tylor, E. B. On a method for investigating the development of institutions; applied to laws of marriage and descent, JRAI, 18: 245–75.
89-31 Wake, C. S. The development of marriage and kinship. London.
89-32 Ward, C. O. A history of the ancient working people from the earliest known period to the adoption of Christianity by Constantine. Washington, D. C.

1890

90-1   Achelis, T. Die Geschlechtsgenossenschaft und die Entwicklung der Ehe, ZGEB, 25: 302–16.
90-2   Achelis, T. Ethnologie und Geschichte, Au 63: 548–52.
90-3   Balfour, H. On the structure and affinities of the composite bow, JRAI, 19: 220–57.
90-4   Basu, K. Some relics of primitive fashions, JASB, 2: 92–95.
90-5   Bellamy, E. What nationalism means, CR, 57: 1–18.
90-6   Bolton, H. C. Gombay, a festival rite of Bermuda Negroes, JAF, 3: 222–26
90-7   Bourke, J. G. The Indian messiah, Nation, 51: 439ff.
90-8   Bourke, J. G. Vesper hours of the stone age, AA, 3: 55–63.
90-9   Brinton, D. G. The African race in America. Chambers' Cyclopedia. Edinburgh.
90-10 Brinton, D. G. Races and peoples. New York.
90-11 Chadwick, J. W. Evolution and social reform, in The theological method, West, J. H. (ed.): 256–74. Boston.
90-12 Chamberlain, A. F. Origin and development of grammatical gender, CIP, 3, 7: 216–17.
90-13 Cherry, R. R. Lectures on the growth of criminal law in ancient communities. London.
90-14 Cope, E. D. The evolution of mind, ANa, 24: 899–913.
90-15 Cordier, H. Les juifs en Chine, Ae, 1: 547–51.
90-16 Culin, S. Chinese secret societies in the United States, JAF, 3: 39–43.
90-17 Culin, S. Customs of the Chinese in America, JAF, 3: 191–200.
90-18 Culin, S. The I Hing or "patriotic rising." A secret society among the Chinese in America. Rep. Proc. Numismat. and Antiq. Soc., Philadelphia, 1887–9.

90-19 Durfee, W. F. The development of American industries since Columbus. I. Early steps in ironmaking, PSMo, 38: 145−72.
90-20 Espinas, A. Les origines de la technologie, Rev. Phil., 30: 113ff., 295ff. Paris.
90-21 Ferree, B. Climatic influences in primitive architecture, AA, 3: 147−58.
90-22 Fouillee, A. L'evolutionnisme des idées-forces, Rev. Phil., 29: 267ff., 337ff., 113ff., Paris.
90-23 Hale, H. The Oregon trade language or "Chinook Jargon." London.
90-24 Hamilton, J. C. The African in Canada, AAASP, 38: 364−40.
90-25 Holmes, W. H. On the evolution of ornament-an American lesson, AA, 3: 137−46.
90-26 Kerr, J. History of curling. Edinburgh.
90-27 Kielstra, E. B. Sumatra's westkust van 1836−1840, BTLVI, 5, 5: 127−221; 248−63.
90-28 Kovalewsky, M. Tableau des origines de l'évolution de la famille et de la propriété. Stockholm.
90-29 Lefevre, A. L'évolution religieuse, BSAP, 4th series, 1.
90-30 Letourneau, C. L'évolution juridique dans les diverses races humaines. Paris.
90-31 Letourneau, C. L'évolution mythologique, REAP, 1.
90-32 Letourneau, C. L'évolution politique dans les diverses races humaines. Paris.
90-33 Mallery, G. Israelite and Indian. A parallel in planes of culture, AAASP, 38: 287−331.
90-34 McGee, A. N. The evolution of a sect, AAASP, 38.
90-35 McGee, W. J. Some principles of evidence relating to the antiquity of man, AAASP, 38: 333.
90-36 Milanese, G. Origine prima della famiglia umana, Giorn. degli Econom., 5. Padua.
90-37 Modi, J. J. On the funeral ceremonies of the Parsees, their origin and explanation, JASB, 2: 405−40. 1890−92.
90-38 Monroe, K. A forgotten remnant. Scribner's Mag., 7: 303−17.
90-39 Mortillet, G. de. Origines de la chasse, de la pêche, et de l'agriculture. Paris.
90-40 Murphy, J. J. The factors of evolution in language, Journ. Transactns, Victoria Institute, 23: 237−48.
90-41 Pendleton, L. Notes on Negro folk-lore and witchcraft in the south, JAF, 3: 201−07.
90-42 Pierson, H. Evolution of the gondola, Cosmopolitan, 8: 529−36. New York.
90-43 Popoff, L. L'origine de la peinture, RSP, 46: 399−403.
90-44 Rand, S. T. The coming of the white man revealed, AAn, 12: 155−56.
90-45 Rees, J. D. Meddling with Hindu marriages, NC, 28.
90-46 Renan, E. Histoire du peuple d'Israël. Paris.
90-47 Risley, H. H. The race basis of Indian political movements, CR, 57: 742−59.
90-48 Robinson, J. Der Ursprung der Blutrache, Gl, 51.
90-49 Salmoné, H. A. The main cause of the rise and fall of the Arab dominion, AR, 10: 434−47.
90-50 Smirnoff, J. N. Les Votjaks; aperçu historique et ethnographique. Kazan.
90-51 Smith, W. W. Who first made maple sugar? AAn, 12: 176−77.

90-52   Spencer, H. The origin of music, Mind, 15: 449–68. London, Edinburgh.
90-53   Stolpe, H. Utvecklingsföreteelser i naturfolkens ornamentik, Yr, 10.
90-54   Stuart-Merritt, C. La Russie dans le passé, le present, l'avenir, Bull.
          Soc. d. Géog. d. Lyon, 8: 569–99.
90-55   Taylor, I. The origin of the Aryans: an account of the prehistoric ethnology
          and civilization of Europe. New York.
90-56   Thomson, J. The results of European intercourse with Africa, CR, 57:
          339–52.
90-57   Wake, C. S. The growth of the marriage relation, in The Modern Science
          Essayist, 21: 67–87. Boston.
90-58   Westermarck, E. Der Ursprung der Strafe, ZFS.
90-59   White, A. Recent experiments in colonisation, CR, 57: 655–72.
90-60   Wilser, L. Anthropologie und Geschichte, Au, Stuttgart, 63: 913–18, 928–
          34.
90-61   Wilser, L. Der Ursprung der Bronze, Au, 63: 386–92.
90-62   Zmigrodzki, M. Zur Geschichte der Suastika, ArA, 19: 173–81.

<u>1891</u>

91-1   Boas, F. Dissemination of tales among the natives of North America, JAF,
          4: 13–20.
91-2   Culin, S. Social organization of the Chinese in America, AA, 4: 347–52.
91-3   Deschamps, E. Les Vaddas de Ceylon et leur rapports, avec les peuples
          environnants . . . Ae, 2: 297–337.
91-4   Ellis, A. B. Survivals from marriage by capture, PSMo, 39: 207–22.
91-5   Ferree, B. Comparative art. The historical origin of art, AAn, 8: 225–28.
91-6   Fletcher, R. The new school of criminal anthropology, AA, 4: 201–36.
91-7   Friedrichs, K. Mensch und Person, Au, 64.
91-8   Fromm, E. Urgeschichte und Archäologie, ArA, 9, Suppl. 1–164.
91-9   Grinnell, G. B. Account of the north Cheyennes concerning the Messiah
          superstition, JAF, 4: 61–69.
91-10   Hubbard, G. G. The evolution of commerce, BAER, 8: 647–60.
91-11   Laborde, J. V. Introduction à l'étude de la fonction du langage, REAP, 1:
          353–69.
91-12   Laurent, E. L'anthropologie criminelle et les nouvelles théories du crime.
          Paris.
91-13   Lefèvre, A. La religion. Paris.
91-14   McGee, A. N. An experiment in human stirpiculture, AA, 4: 319–26.
91-15   McGee, W. J. Some principles of evidence relating to the antiquity of man,
          AAn, 13: 69–79.
91-16   Manouvrier, L. L'atavisme et le crime, REAP, 1: 225–40.
91-17   Mason, O. T. The natural history of folk-lore, JAF, 4: 97–105.
91-18   Mateer, S. On social reforms among the Nayars of Malabar, JASB, 2: 317–
          20.
91-19   Mooney, J. The growth of a myth, AA, 4: 393–94.
91-20   Nisbet, N. The Papuan and his master, FR, 49: 413–26.
91-21   Phister, N. P. The Indian messiah, AA, 4: 105–09.
91-22   Reclus, E. Primitive folk: studies in comparative ethnology. New York.
91-23   Regnault, F. Le costume, son origine et ses transformations, RSP. 47.
91-24   Remondino, P. C. History of circumcision from the earliest times to the
          present. Philadelphia, London.

91-25 Rubbens, C. Evolution religieuse au Congo, BSAP, 4th series, 2: 257–73.
91-26 Ryder, J. A. An attempt to illustrate some of the primary laws of mechanical evolutions, Proc. Acad. Nat. Sci., Phila.: 62–70.
91-27 Tendall, G. F. A short history of vocal music from its earliest times . . AAASR, 3: 366–94.
91-28 Tylor, E. B. The history of human marriage, Ac, 22.
91-29 Ward, L. F. The transmission of culture, Fr, 11: 312–19.
91-30 Westermarck, E. History of human marriage. London.
91-31 Winternitz, M. Zur Geschichte der Ehe, Gl, 52.

1892

92-1   Bandelier, A. F. An outline of the documentary history of the Zuñi tribe, Jnl. Am. Eth. and Arch., 3: 1–115.
92-2   Baring-Gould, S. The origin and development of religious belief. 2 vols. London.
92-3   Barnum, C. K. Totemism in the evolution of theology, PSMo, 42: 395–404.
92-4   Barrows, S. J. The evolution of the Afro-American, Evolution series, 28: 315–45. New York.
92-5   Batchelor, J. The Ainu of Japan. New York.
92-6   Bordier, A. Le milieu social, REAP, 2: 1–11.
92-7   Chapin, H. D. The survival of the unfit, PSMo, 41: 182–87.
92-8   Chapman, M. Notes on the Chinese in Boston, JAF, 5: 291ff.
92-9   Colenso, H. E. and Werner, A. White and black in Natal, CR, 61: 205–13.
92-10 Conway, W. M. Dawn of art in the ancient world. New York.
92-11 Dargun, L. Mutterrecht und Vaterrecht. Leipzig.
92-12 Donovan, J. The festal origin of human speech, Mind, 1 (n. s.): 325–39.
92-13 Garnier, C. and Armann, A. L'histoire de l'habitation humaine. Paris.
92-14 Grinnell, G. B. Development of a Pawnee myth, JAF, 5: 127–34.
92-15 Grinnell, G. B. Early Blackfoot history, AA, 5: 153–64.
92-16 Hill, D. J. The festal development of art, PSMo, 42: 734–49.
92-17 Holmes, W. H. Evolution of the aesthetic, AAASP, 40.
92-18 Jadrinzeff, N. M. The nomadic life of nations and its relation to history of human culture, Protok. zasaid, Russk. Antrop. Obsb., St. Petersburg, 3: 64–69.
92-19 Lang, H. R. The Portugese element in New England, JAF, 5: 9–18.
92-20 Lea, H. C. Superstition and force. Philadelphia.
92-21 Letourneau, C. L'origine de la littérature, REAP, 2.
92-22 Letourneau, C. L'évolution religieuse dans les diverses races humaines. Paris.
92-23 Lombroso, C. Les applications de l'anthropologie criminelle. Paris.
92-24 Mason, O. T. The birth of invention, SIR: 603–11.
92-25 Mooney, J. Improved Cherokee alphabets, AA, 5: 63–64.
92-26 Morse, E. S. Natural selection and crime, PSMo, 41: 433–46.
92-27 Mortillet, A. de. Evolution de la hache en bronze en Italie, REAP, 2: 313–29.
92-28 Read, C. H. On the origin and sacred character of certain ornaments of the S. E. Pacific, JRAI, 21: 3–13.
92-29 Reuleaux, F. Technology and civilization. Washington, D. C.
92-30 Ridgeway, W. Origin of currency and weight standard. London.

92-31　Stolpe, H. Entwicklungerscheinungen in der Ornamentik der Naturvolker,
　　　　MAGW, 12: 19–62 (Trans. from Ymer, Stockholm).
92-32　Vance, L. J. The evolution of dancing, PSMo, 41: 739–56.
92-33　Vinson, J. L'évolution du Bouddhisme, BSAP, 3: 398–426.
92-34　Walmsley, F. H. Outlines of insanity . . . the salient features of mental
　　　　disorder. London.
92-35　Welling, J. C. The law of torture: a study in the evolution of law, AA, 5:
　　　　193–215.
92-36　Wells, D. D. Evolution in folk-lore. An old story in a new form, PSMo,
　　　　41: 45–54.
92-37　Winternitz, M. On a comparative study of Indo-European customs, with
　　　　special reference to the marriage customs. Trans., International Folk-
　　　　lore Congress. London.

1893

93-1　Achelis, T. Die Entwicklung der Ehe. Berlin.
93-2　Alvares, L. F. The Hawaiians. Why are they dying out? Pacific M. J.,
　　　　San Francisco, 36: 407–09.
93-3　Balfour, H. The evolution of decorative art. London.
93-4　Bandelier, A. F. A. The gilded man (El Dorado) and other pictures of the
　　　　Spanish occupancy of America. New York.
93-5　Borden, W. C. The vital statistics of an Apache Indian community, Boston
　　　　M. and S. Journ., 129: 5–10.
93-6　Bordier, A. Naissance et évolution des idées et des pratiques médicales,
　　　　REAP, 3: 41–59.
93-7　Brinton, D. B. The beginning of man and the age of the race, Fr, 16: 452–
　　　　58.
93-8　Cruikshank, E. Early traders and trade-routes in Ontario and the West,
　　　　1760–83, AAn, 15: 327–47.
93-9　Cushing, F. H. Habitations affected by environment, Great Divide, Denver,
　　　　9: 78ff.
93-10　Ellis, W. G. The Amok of the Malays, J. Ment. Sc., London, 39: 325–38.
93-11　Fletcher, R. The poet—is he born, not made? AA, 6: 117–35.
93-12　Gatschet, A. S. Report of an Indian visit to Jack Wilson, the Payute Messiah,
　　　　JAF, 6: 108–11.
93-13　Grinnell, G. B. The Pawnees. New York.
93-14　Harris, W. R. History of the early missions in western Canada. Toronto.
93-15　Laurent, E. L'anthropologie criminelle et les nouvelles théories du crime.
　　　　Paris. (This is one of a large number of late nineteenth century refer-
　　　　ences on "criminal anthropology.")
93-16　Legrand, —. Une colonie pénitentiaire; la Nouvelle-Calédonie, Arch. de
　　　　l'Anth. Crim., Paris, 8: 93–104.
93-17　MacDonald, A. Abnormal man; being essays on education, crime and re-
　　　　lated subjects. Washington, D.C.
93-18　Macgowan, D. J. The artifical making of wild men in China, China M. Miss.
　　　　Journ., Shanghai, 7: 79–81.
93-19　MacRichie, D. The Aïnos (primitive inhabitants of northern Japan). London.
93-20　Manouvrier, L. La genèse normale du crime, BSAP, 4: 405–58.
93-21　Marques, A. The population of the Hawaiian islands, JPS, 2.

93-22 Peal, S. E. On the morong, as possibly a relic of pre-marriage communism, JRAI, 42: 244−61.

93-23 Powell, J. W. Are our Indians becoming extinct? Fr, 15: 343−54.

93-24 Richard, G. Essai sur l'origine de l'idée de droit. Paris.

93-25 Ryder, J. A. Energy as a factor in organic evolution, APSP, 31: 192−203.

93-26 Schrader, F. De l'influence des formes terrestres sur le développenent humain, REAP, 3: 205−19.

93-27 Stolpe, H. Evolution in the ornamental art of savage peoples, Trans. , R. H. A. Sc. Soc.

93-28 Treon, F. The effect of education on the American Indian, Med. Rec. , New York, 43: 389−92.

1894

94-1   Allen, G. The origin of cultivation, FR, 61: 578−92.

94-2   Arganceli, F. Le evoluziona della proprietà. Rome.

94-3   Balfour, H. Evolution in decorative art, JRSA, 43.

94-4   Bastian, A. Controversen in der Ethnologie. Berlin.

94-5   Beauchamp, W. H. The origin of the Iroquois, AAn, 16: 61−69.

94-6   Black, J. W. Savagery and survivals, PSMo, 45: 388−401.

94-7   Boas, F. The half-blood Indian, PSMo, 45: 761−70.

94-8   Brinton, D. B. The origin of sacred numbers, AA, 7: 168−73.

94-9   Caillard, E. M. Personality as the outcome of evolution, CR, 65: 713−21.

94-10 d'Alviella, B. The migrations of symbols. London.

94-11 Dorsey, J. B. A study of Siouan cults, BAER, 11: 351−544.

94-12 Eells, M. The Chinook jargon, AA, 7: 300−12.

94-13 Grosse, E. Anfänge der Kunst. Berlin.

94-14 Holmes, W. H. Order of development of the primal shaping arts, AAASP, 42: 289−300.

94-15 Holmes, W. H. Natural history of flake stone implements, Mem. Int. Cong. of Anth. , 1893, Chicago: 120−39.

94-16 Holmes, W. H. Caribbean influence in the prehistoric art of southern states, AA, 7: 71−79.

94-17 Jarvis, S. The ascent of life; or psychic laws and forces in nature, Arena, Boston: 1−25.

94-18 Keller, O. Geschichte de Musik. Leipzig.

94-19 Kovalewsky, M. Les origines du devoir. Rev. Int. de Sociologie, Paris, 2.

94-20 Letourneau, C. L'évolution littéraire dans les diverses races humaines. Paris.

94-21 Letourneau, C. Passé, présent et avenir du travail, REAP, 4.

94-22 McGuire, J. D. The development of sculpture, AA, 7: 358−66.

94-23 Mason, O. T. Technogeography, or the relation of the earth to the industries of mankind, AA, 7: 137−61

94-24 Mason, O. T. Migration and the food quest, AA, 7: 275−92.

94-25 Moorehead, W. K. The Sioux messiah, Archaeologist, Waterloo, Indiana, 2: 146, 168.

94-26 Müller, F. Ethnologie und Weltgeschichte, Gl, 55: 15−17.

94-27 Powell, J. W. The course of human progress, Sc, 11: 220ff.

94-28 Reed, C. H. On the evolution of the art of working in stone, ANa, 27.

94-29 Steinmetz, S. R. Suicide among primitive peoples, AA, 7: 53−60.

1895

95-1   Balfour, A. J. The foundations of belief. London.
95-2   Barré, P. Les peuples que disparaissent: les Todas de l'Inde, RSP, 4: 124—26.
95-3   Bordeau, L. The beginnings of agriculture, PSMo, 45: 678—88.
95-4   Chatelain, H. Some causes of the retardation of African progress, JAF, 8.
95-5   Durkheim, E. Règles de la méthode sociologique. Paris.
95-6   Fewkes, J. W. The Tusayan ritual: a study of the influence of environment on aboriginal cults, SIR: 683—700.
95-7   Fraser, J. The Malayo-Polynesian theory, JPS, 4: 240—54; 5: 92—100; 7: 1—14. 1895—1898.
95-8   Haddon, A. C. Evolution in art. London.
95-9   Hodge, F. W. The early Navaho and Apache, AA, 8: 223—40.
95-10   Hoffman, W. J. The beginnings of writing, PSMo, 48: 274ff.
95-11   Hubbard, J. M. Russia as a civilizing force in Asia, Atlantic, 75: 197—205.
95-12   Hubbard, J. M. Transformation of Africa, Nation, 61: 306ff.
95-13   Ingram, J. K. A history of slavery and serfdom. London.
95-14   Jacoby, A. Ueber das Erlöschen der Naturvölker des hohen Nordens, ArA, 23: 1—20.
95-15   Letourneau, C. La guerre dans les diverses races humaines. Paris.
95-16   Lombroso, C. The savage origin of tattooing, PSMo, 48: 793—803.
95-17   McGee, W. J. The beginning of agriculture, AA, 8: 350—75.
95-18   McGee, W. J. The relation of institutions to environment, BAER, 12: 701—11.
95-19   Mason, O. T. Similarities in culture, AA, 8: 101—17.
95-20   Mason, O. T. The origins of invention. London.
95-21   Newell, W. W. Theories of diffusion of folk-tales, JAF, 8: 7—18.
95-22   Peet, S. D. The beginnings of history, AAn, 17.
95-23   Powell, J. W. Proper training and the future of the Indians, Fr, 18: 622—29.
95-24   Powell, J. W. Relation of primitive peoples to environment, illustrated by American examples, BAER, 12: 625—37.
95-25   Reindorf, C. C. History of the Gold Coast and Ashanti. Basel.
95-26   Wilutzky, P. Vorgeschichte des Rechts. 3 vols. Leipzig.

1896

96-1   Alexander, S. Moral order and progress. London.
96-2   Boas, F. The limitations of the comparative method of anthropology, Sc (n. s.), 4: 901—08.
96-3   Boas, F. The growth of Indian mythologies, JAF, 9: 1—11.
96-4   Brinton, D. G. An ethnologist's view of history. Philadelphia.
96-5   Conant, L. L. The number concept, its origin and development. New York, London.
96-6   Fellows, G. E. The relation of anthropology to the study of history, AJS, 1: 41—49.
96-7   Ferrero, B. Les formes primitives du travail, RSP, series 5, 2.
96-8   Grosse, E. Die Formen der Familie und die Formen der Wirtschaft. Freiburg.
96-9   Haddon, A. C. Magic and fetishishm. London.

96-10 Hahn, E. Die Haustiere und ihre Beziehung zur Wirtschaft des Menschen. Leipzig.
96-11 Keane, A. H. Ethnology. Cambridge.
96-12 McGee, W. J. The beginning of marriage, AA, 9: 371–90.
96-13 McLennan, J. F. Studies in ancient history. The second series . . . London.
96-14 Mason, O. T. Introduction of the iron age into America, AA, 9: 191–217.
96-15 Mauss, M. La religion et les origines du droit pénal, RHR, 16.
96-16 Mercer, H. C. An inquiry into the origin of games, ANa, 29.
96-17 Mooney, J. The ghost dance religion. BAER, 14, 2.
96-18 Nathubai, T. M. On conversion to Hinduism, JASB, 4: 272–310.
96-19 Posada, A. Théories modernes sur les origines de la famille, de la société, et de l'état. Paris.
96-20 Powell, J. Seven venerable ghosts, AA, 9: 67–91.
96-21 Ray, S. H. The common origin of Oceanic languages, JPS, 5: 58–68.
96-22 Regnault, F. Essai sur les débuts de l'art ornemental géometrique chez les peuples primitifs, BSAP, 7: 532–49.
96-23 Regnault, F. Origines de l'art ornemental, Na, 27.
96-24 Starr, F. Popular celebrations in Mexico, JAF, 9: 161–69.
96-25 Tautain, L. F. Sur la couvade, Ae, 7: 118–19.
96-26 Tylor, E. B. Introduction to Ratzel, F. The history of mankind (trans. from German). London.
96-27 Tylor, E. B. On American lot-games as evidence of Asiatic intercourse before the time of Columbus, IAE, 9: 55–67.
96-28 Vierkandt, A. Naturvölker und Kulturvölker, Leipzig.
96-29 Vierkandt, A. Der Ursprung der Haustierzucht und die Wirtschaftsformen, Gl, 57.
96-30 Zaborowski, —. La circoncision, ses origines et sa répartition en Afrique et à Madagascar, Ae, 7: 653–75.

1897

97-1   Allen, G. The evolution of the idea of God. London.
97-2   Allen, J. R. The evolution of the textile industries. Reliquary and Illustr. Archaeol., London, 3: 165–74.
97-3   Baldwin, S. M. Social and ethical interpretations in mental development. New York.
97-4   Beauchamp, W. M. The new religion of the Iroquois, JAF, 10: 169–80.
97-5   Boas, F. Northern elements in the mythology of the Navaho, AA, 10: 371–76.
97-6   Chamberlain, A. F. The mythology and folk-lore of invention, JAF, 10: 89–100.
97-7   Christian, F. W. On the distribution and origin of some plant and tree names in Polynesia and Micronesia, JPS, 6: 123–40.
97-8   Crawley, E. S. The origin and development of number systems, PSMo, 51: 524–34.
97-9   Cunow, H. Zur Urgeschichte de Ehe, Deutsche Worte, 17. Leipzig.
97-10 Currier, C. W. Origine, progrès et caractères de la race caribe, ICAP, 11: 504–11.
97-11 Errera, P. Quelques phases de l'évolution de la propriété. Paris.
97-12 Espinas, A. Les origines de la technologie. Paris.

97-13 Etheridge, R. On modifications in form and ornament of the Australian aboriginal weapon, the Lillil or Woggara, etc., IAE, 10: 7—16.

97-14 Harrigan, D. F. The evolution of slavery, WR, 148.

97-15 Kéreval, P. Le langage écrit: ses origines, son developpement et son mécanisme. Paris.

97-16 Lang, A. The evolution of the idea of God, CR, 72: 768—81.

97-17 Lefébure, E. Les origines du fétichisme, Mélusine. Paris.

97-18 Letourneau, C. L'évolution du commerce dans les diverses races humaines Paris.

97-19 McGee, W. J. The beginnings of zooculture, AA, 10: 215—40.

97-20 Pomare, M. Education among the Maoris, Good Health, Battle Creek, Mich 32: 134—36.

97-21 Réville, A. Origin and growth of religion, as illustrated by native religions of Mexico and Peru. London.

97-22 Rubin, M. A measure of civilisation, Jnl. Royal Statistical Society, London, 60: 148—61.

97-23 Schrader, F. Des conditions d'arrêt ou d'avortement des groupes humains, REAP, 11.

97-24 Smith, S. P. The peopling of the north: notes on the ancient Maori history of the north-peninsula . . . , JPS, 6, supplement: 1—108.

97-25 Starr, F. A study of a census of the pueblo of Cochiti. Proc. Davenport Acad. Nat. Science, 7.

97-26 Stien, L. Origine psychique et charactère sociologique de la religion. Paris.

97-27 Tillier, L. Le mariage. Sa genèse, son évolution. Paris.

97-28 Vierkandt, A. Die Kulturtypen der Menschheit, ArA, 25: 61—75.

1898

98-1 Bastian, A. Die Aufgaben der Ethnologie. Batavia.

98-2 Berlin, J. Neue Gedanken über die Entstehung der Familie und der Religion. Leipzig.

98-3 Curtin, J. Creation myths of primitive America in relation to the religious history and mental development of mankind. Boston.

98-4 Cushing, F. H. The genesis of implement-making, AAASP, 1897, Salem, 46: 337—39.

98-5 Doughty, H. M. Witchcraft and Christianity, Blackwoods Magazine, Edinburgh, 158: 378—97.

98-6 Durkheim, E. La prohibition de l'inceste et ses origines. AnS, 1.

98-7 Ellis, H. Mescal: a new artificial paradise, BAER, 14: 537—48.

98-8 Fewkes, J. W. Growth of the Hopi ritual, JAF, 11: 173—93.

98-9 Frobenius, L. Die Weltanschauung der Naturvölker. Weimar.

98-10 Frobenius, L. Der Ursprung der Kultur. Berlin.

98-11 Frobenius, L. Der Ursprung der afrikanischen Kulturen, ZGEB, 33.

98-12 Guevara Silva, T. Historia de la civilización de Araucanía. Santiago.

98-13 Haddon, A. C. The study of man. New York.

98-14 Hewitt, B. A. The history of the forms and migrations of the signs of the Cross and the Suastika, WR, 149: 385—97.

98-15 Hough, W. The origin and range of the Eskimo lamp, AA, 11: 116—22.

98-16 Lang, A. The making of religion. London.

98-17 Lasch, R. Rache als Selbstmordmotiv, Gl, 75.
98-18 Letourneau, C. La synthèse de l'évolution mentale, REAP, 12: 333ff.
98-19 Letourneau, C. L'évolution de l'éducation dans les diverses races humaines. Paris.
98-20 McGee, W. J. The course of human development, Fr, 26: 56–65.
98-21 McGee, W. J. Piratical acculturation, AA, 11: 243–49.
98-22 Makarewicz, J. Evolution de la peine, Arch. de l'Anthrop. Crim., Paris, 13.
98-23 Mason, O. T. Women's share in primitive culture. New York.
98-24 Mucke, J. R. Urgeschichte des Ackerbaues und der Viehzucht. Greifswald.
98-25 Murray-Aynesley, R. G. M. The development of idol-worship, Fo, 9: 183–85.
98-26 Nyropp, K. Kulturhistoriske Skitser, I Kysset og dits Historie. Copenhagen.
98-27 Powell, J. W. The evolution of religion, Mo, 7.
98-28 Réclus, E. Etude sur l'évolution des religion, Human. Nouv. Brussels.
98-29 Smeaton, O. Tattooing and its history, WR, 149.
98-30 Solotaroff, H. On the origin of the family, AA, 9: 229–42.
98-31 Sutherland, A. The origin and growth of the moral instinct. 2 vols. London.
98-32 Tautain, L. F. Etude sur la dépopulation de l'archipel des Marquises, Ae, 9: 298–318, 418–36.
98-33 Tillier, L. Le mariage: sa genèse, son evolution. Paris.
98-34 Wallaschek, R. Urgeschichte de Saiteninstrumente, MAGW, 28, 1: 1–5.

1899

99-1 Balfour, H. The natural history of the musical bow. Oxford.
99-2 Bouchal, L. Beitrag zur Urgeschichte der Musikinstrumente, MAGW, 29, 1: 11–13.
99-3 Christian, F. M. The Caroline Islands. London.
99-4 Ellis, H. The evolution of modesty; in reply to H. M. Stanley, Sc, 9: 553–54.
99-5 Frazer, J. G. The origins of totemism, FR, 55: 647–65.
99-6 Hahn, E. Zur Theorie der Enstehung des Ackerbaues, Gl, 76.
99-7 Jevons, F. B. The place of totemism in the evolution of religion, Fo, 10.
99-8 Karutz, R. Ursprung und Formen der Wiege, Gl, 76.
99-9 Lang, A. Are savage gods borrowed from missionaries? NC, 43: 132–44.
99-10 McGee, W. J. The trend of human progress, AA (n. s.), 1: 401–47.
99-11 McGee, W. J. The beginning of mathematics, AA, (n. s.) 1: 646–73.
99-12 Melnikow, N. Die Burjäten des irkutskischen Gouvernemente, VBGA, 31: 439–48.
99-13 Mooney, J. The end of the Natchez, AA (n. s.), 1: 510–21.
99-14 Olshausen, —. Beitrag zur Geschichte des Haarkammes, VBGA, 31.
99-15 Peyton, W. W. The resurrection. A study in the evolution of religion, CR, 75: 123–44.
99-16 Pierce, P. B. The origin of the "Book of Mormon," AA (ns.), 1: 675–94.
99-17 Pikler, J., and Somlo, F. Der Ursprung des Totemismus, Jahrb. der intern. Ver. f. vergl. Rechtsw. Berlin.
99-18 Ratzel, F. Anthropogeographie. 2 vols. Stuttgart.
99-19 Schmoller, G. Die Urgeschichte der Familie. Mutterrecht und Gentilverfassung, Jahrb. f. Gesetzgeb. Ver. u. Völksw. Berlin.

99-20 Scott, A. F. Offering and sacrifice. An essay on comparative customs and religious development. London.

99-21 Smith, S. P. Wars of the northern against the southern tribes of New Zealand in the nineteenth century, JPS, 8: 13–164, 201–30; 9: 1–37, 85–120, 145–68; 10: 21–49, 78–88. 1899–1901.

99-22 Stanley, H. M. The evolution of modesty, Sc, 9: 553–54.

99-23 Steinmetz, S. R. Over den oorsprong der slavernij, Ned. Tijdschr, v. Geneeskunde. Amsterdam.

99-24 Temple, R. C. Beginnings of currency, JRAI, 29: 99–122.

99-25 Thomas, H. Social evolution, WR, 152: 577–78.

99-26 Thulié, H. Origine du mysticisme, REAP, 9: 323–27.

1900

00-1 Boyle, D. On the paganism of the civilized Iroquois of Ontario, JRAI, 30: 263–73.

00-2 Culin, S. The origin of ornament, BFMSA, 1.

00-3 Guevara, T. Historia de la civilizacíon de Araucanía. Santiago.

00-4 Hirn, Y. The origins of art. London.

00-5 Hollis, A. C. Notes on the history of the Vumba, East Africa, JRAI, 30: 275–98.

00-6 Hough, W. Oriental influences in Mexico, AA, 2: 66–74.

00-7 Howerth, I. W. Brinton's theory of the origin of religion, Mo, 9.

00-8 Hubbard, J. M. Colonial government in Borneo, Nat. Geog. Mag., 11: 359–63.

00-9 Jenks, A. E. A remarkable counterfeiter, AA, 2: 292–96.

00-10 Letourneau, C. L'évolution de langage, REAP, 9.

00-11 Letourneau, C. Beginnings of currency, Indian Antiquary, 29.

00-12 Levat, L. A. Les origines de la ferrure, RSP, 13: 754–56.

00-13 Marett, R. R. Pre-animistic religion, Fr, 11: 162–82.

00-14 Mason, O. T. Traps of the Amerind-a study in psychology and invention, AA, 2: 657–75.

00-15 Mooney, J. The Cherokee river cult, JAF, 13: 1–10.

00-16 Neef, S. A. Die Passionisten des Südwestens von Nordamerica, Gl, 77: 24–

00-17 Rakestraw, C. D. The Shaker Indian of Puget Sound, SW, 29: 703–09.

00-18 Schurtz, H. Urgeschichte der Kultur. Leipzig. Wein.

00-19 Super, C. W. The evolution of ethics, AAn, 22.

00-20 Wardle, H. N. The Sedna cycle: a study in myth evolution, AA, 2: 568–80.

00-21 Wead, C. K. Contributions to the history of musical scales, USNMR, 17.

1901

01-1 Boas, F. The mind of primitive man, JAF, 14: 1–11.

01-2 Culin, S. A summer trip among the western Indians, BFMSA, 3: 1–22, 88–122, 143–75.

01-3 Edge-Partington, J. The genesis of the Maori scroll-pattern, Mn, 41.

01-4 Folsom, C. M. Guiding the Indian, SW, 30: 605–10.

01-5 Fraser, J. The Polynesian numerals, JPS, 10: 171–77; 11: 1–10; 12: 107–20. 1901–1903.

01-6   Friedmann, M. Ueber Wahnideen im Völkerleben. Berlin.
01-7   Guyot, Y. Les indigènes de l'Afrique du sud, BSAP, 2nd series, 2: 362−68.
01-8   Hahn, E. Ursprungsgebiet und Entstehungsweise des Ackerbaues, ZGEB, 36.
01-9   Hewitt, J. F. History and chronology of the myth-making age. London.
01-10   Hinde, S. L. The last of the Masai. London.
01-11   Hobhouse, L. T. Mind in evolution. London.
01-12   Hollis, A. C. Notes on the history and customs of the people of Taveta,
        East Africa, JAfS, 1.
01-13   Hough, W. The development of illumination, AA, 3: 342−52.
01-14   Lang, A. Magic and religion. London.
01-15   Letourneau, C. La femme à travers les âges, REAP, 10: 273−90.
01-16   Liengme, G. Un potentat Africain: Goungounyane et son règne.
01-17   Mooney, J. Calendar history of the Kiowa Indians, BAER, 17: 129−445.
01-18   Myres, J. L. Collateral survival of successive styles of art in North
        Africa, Mn, 1: 102−03.
01-19   Regnault, F. Le coutume, son origine et ses transformations, RSP, 15:
        103−12.
01-20   Sully, J. The laughter of savages, Intern. Mo., Burlington, Vt., 4: 379ff.
01-21   Vaschide, V. and Pieron, H. Le rêve prophétique dans les croyances et les
        traditions des peuples sauvages, BSAP, 2nd series, 2.

1902

02-1   Achelis, T. Ethnology and the science of religion, IQ, 6: 305−29.
02-2   Achelis, T. Die Ekstase in ihrer kulturellen Bedeutung. Berlin.
02-3   Brinton, D. G. The basis of social relations. New York.
02-4   Chamberlain, A. F. Algonkian Words in American English, JAF, 15: 240−
        67.
02-5   Chamberlain, A. F. The American Indian element in the Philippines, AAn,
        24: 97− 100.
02-6   Chamberlain, A. F. The contact of "higher" and "lower" races, Pedag.
        Sem., Worcester, Mass., 9: 507−20.
02-7   Crawley, A. E. The mystic rose. London.
02-8   Culin, S. The Indians of Cuba, BFMSA, 3: 185−226.
02-9   Goblet d'Alviella, E. Des causes qui ont amené la différentiation des sociétés
        humaines, BSRBG.
02-10   Gudgeon, W. The whence of the Maori, JPS, 11: 170−89, 247−56; 12: 51−61,
        166−79. 1902−1903.
02-11   Guevara, T. Historia de la civilización de Araucania, An. Univ. Santiago
        de Chile, 112: 43−71, 249−68, 367−95. 113: 147−89, 305−65, 561−90.
        1902−1903.
02-12   Haddon, A. C. Evolution in art, BFMSA, 3: 239−48.
02-13   Holland, T. H. The Kaneta of Kulu and Lahoul, Punjab: a study in contact
        metamorphism, JRAI, 32: 96−123.
02-14   Howerth, I. W. Education and social progress, Educ. Rev., 23: 355−70.
02-15   Keane, A. H. Native American culture: its independent evolution, Intern.
        Mo., Burlington, Vt., 5: 338−57.
02-16   Morgan, C. L. The beginnings of mind, IQ, 6.

02-17 Panhuys, L. C. van. Indian words in the Dutch language and in use in Dutch
       Guiana, ICAP, 13: 205–08.
02-18 Smith, S. P. Niue island, and its people, JPS, 11: 80–106; 12: 163–78.
       1902–1902.
02-19 Thomas, N. W. Der Ursprung der Exogamie, ZFS, 4.
02-20 Turquan, V. Contribution a l'étude de la population et de la dépopulation.
       BSAL, 21, 1.
02-21 Vecchio, G. del. L'evoluzione dell' ospitalità, RIS, 5.

1903

03-1   Alford, T. W. The Shawnees of the present, SW, 32: 385–86.
03-2   Amadori-Virgilj, G. L'instituto famigliare nelle società primordiali. Bari.
03-3   Atkinson, J. J. The natives of New Caledonia, Fo, 14.
03-4   Chamberlain, A. F. The contributions of the American Indian to civilization,
       Proc. Amer. Antiq. Soc., Worcester, 16: 91–126.
03-5   Codrington, R. H. On the stability of unwritten languages, Mn, 11: 25–26.
03-6   Dixon, R. B. System and sequence in Maidu mythology, JAF, 16: 32–36.
03-7   Eells, M. The decrease of the Indians, AAn, 25: 145–49.
03-8   Girard-Teulon, P. Communication sur les origines de la famille, BSAL, 20.
03-9   Gleason, R. P. Industrial problems in the Philippines, SW, 32: 529–35.
03-10 Hill, H. The Maoris—today and tomorrow, NZIT, 35.
03-11 Hill-Tout, C. Totemism. A consideration of its origin and import, RSCT.
03-12 Lang, A. and Atkinson, J. T. Social origins and primal law. London.
03-13 Lang, A. The origins of marriage prohibitions, Mn, 3: 179–82.
03-14 Lanz-Liebenfels. Die Urgeschichte der Künste, Pol.-Anth. Rev. Berlin.
03-15 Lockyer, N. The influence of brain power on history (address, President
       British Association), PSMo, 64: 71–86.
03-16 Mason, O. T. The past is in the present, RP, 2: 332–35.
03-17 Millard, T. F. The passing of the American Indian, Fr, 34: 466–80.
03-18 Prince, J. D. and Speck, F. G. The modern Pequots and their language,
       AA, 5: 193–212.
03-19 Ridgeway, W. The origin of jewelry, Brit. Ass. Session, Southport.
03-20 Sebestyen, G. Ursprung der Bustrophedonschrift, ZE, 25: 755–71.
03-21 Shaler, N. S. The natural history of war, IQ, 8: 17–30.
03-22 Stoppord, J. G. B. English governor and African chiefs, JAfs, 2: 308–11.
03-23 Vernes, M. L'histoire des religions et l'anthropologie, REAP, 13: 144–64.
03-24 Wilutzky, P. Vorgeschichte des Rechts. 3 vols. Breslau.

1904

04-1   Armstrong, W. N. Civilization by reindeer, SW, 33: 209–15.
04-2   Boas, F. Some traits of primitive culture, JAF, 17: 243–54.
04-3   Boas, F. What the Negro has done in Africa, ER, 5: 104–09.
04-4   Bourdeau, L. Histoire de l'habillement et de la parure. Paris.
04-5   Bücher, K. Die Entstehung der Volkswirtschaft. Tübingen.
04-6   de la Mazelière, M. L'évolution de la famille japonaise, BSAP, 5: 650–71.
04-7   DuBois, W. E. B. The development of a people (the Negro), Int. Jour. of
       Ethics, Phil., 14: 292–311.

04-8   Farrand, L. The significance of mythology and tradition, JAF, 16: 14–23.
04-9   Frazer, J. G. The origin of circumcision, Indep. Rev., 4: 204ff.
04-10 Friedrich, E. Allgemeine und spezielle Wirtschafts Geographie. Leipzig.
04-11 Guibert, A. Évolution mentale, BSAP, 5: 615–30.
04-12 Gunn, J. M. History of the pueblos of Laguna and Acoma, RP, 3: 291–310, 323–44.
04-13 Hartland, E. S. Folk-lore: what it is and what is the good of it. (2nd ed.) London.
04-14 Hermant, P. Évolution economique et sociale de certaines peuplades de l'Amérique du Nord, BSRBG.
04-15 Howard, G. E. A history of matrimonial institutions. 3 vols. London.
04-16 Kelles-Krauz, C. de. L'origine des interdictions sexuelles, Rev. Intern. de Sociol., 11.
04-17 Laufer, B. Religiöse toleranz in China, Gl, 85: 219–20.
04-18 Lenz, R. Los elementos indios del castellano de Chile. Santiago.
04-19 Marett, R. R. From spell to prayer, Fo, 15: 132–65.
04-20 Mauss, M. Esquisse d'une théorie général de la magie, AnS, 7: 1–146.
04-21 Powell, F. Y. Tradition and its conditions, Fo, 15: 12–23.
04-22 Preuss, T. Der Ursprung der Menschenopfer in Mexico, Gl, 86.
04-23 Preuss, T. Der Ursprung der Religion und Kunst, Gl, 86: 321–27, 355–63, 375–79, 388–92.
04-24 Rostagno, L. R. Sull' origine del totemismo. Rome.
04-25 Rutland, J. On the survival of ancient customs in Oceania, JPS, 13.
04-26 Smith, S. P. The occupation of Wai-rarapa by Ngati Kahu-Ngunu, JPS, 13: 153–65.
04-27 Speck, F. G. A modern Mohegan-Pequot text, AA (n. s.), 6: 469–76.
04-28 Stimson, H. A. The evolution of chastity, Bibl. Sacra. London.
04-29 Thomas, N. W. The origin of marriage prohibitions. A reply to Mr. Lang, Mn, 2.
04-30 Tregear, E. Polynesian origins, JPS, 13: 105–21, 133–52.
04-31 Westermarck, E. The magic origin of Moorish designs, JRAI, 34: 211–22.

1905

05-1   Aimes, H. H. S. African institutions in America, JAF, 18: 16–32.
05-2   Ankermann, B. Kulturkreise und Kulturgeschichten in Africa, ZE, 37.
05-3   Blyden, E. W. The Koran in Africa, JAfS, 4: 157–71.
05-4   Boas, F. Decorative designs of Alaskan needle cases, USNMP, 34: 321–44.
05-5   Bowman, E. Migrations précolombiennes dans le Nord-Ouest de l'Argentine, JSA, 2: 91–108.
05-6   Cowan, J. The last of the Ngati-Mamoe; some incidents of southern Maori history, JPS, 14: 193–99.
05-7   Crawley, E. The tree of life: a study of religion. London.
05-8   Curtis, W. E. Education and morals among the Navajos and Pueblos, AAn, 27: 259–64.
05-9   Farnell, L. R. The evolution of religion. An anthropological study. London.
05-10 Fewkes, J. W. Climate and cult, Rep., 8th Int. Geograph. Congress, 1904: 664–70.
05-11 Fletcher, A. C. Preparation of Indians for citizenship, SW, 34: 425–28.
05-12 Frazer, J. G. Lectures on the early history of the kingship. New York.

05-13 Frazer, J. G. The beginnings of religion and totemism among the Australian aborigines, FR, 84, 162–72, 452–66.

05-14 Gollier, M. T. L'ethnographie et l'expansion civilisatrice, Congrès Int. d'Expans. Econ. Mondiale, Mons.

05-15 Graebner, F. Kulturkreise und Kulturgeschichten in Ozeanien, ZE, 37: 28–53.

05-16 Grant, W. Magato and his tribe, JRAI, 35: 266–70.

05-17 Gusinde, K. Einiges über Rhythmus, Wort und Weise, Mitt. d. Schles. Ges. f. Volksk., Breslau, 4: 9–22.

05-18 Hahn, E. Das Alter der wirtschaftlichen Kultur der Menschheit. Heidelberg.

05-19 Hewett, E. L. Ethnic factors in education, AA, 7: 1–16.

05-20 Junod, H. A. The native language and education, JAfS, 5: 28–37.

05-21 Kohler, J. Ueber die Urgeschichte der Ehe, ZVR, 17.

05-22 Landtman, G. The origin of priesthood. Ekenaes.

05-23 Lang, A. The primitive and the advanced in totemism, JRAI, 35: 315–36.

05-24 Matthews, B. American character, Columbia U. Quarterly, New York, 8: 97–114.

05-25 Petrucci, R. Les origines naturelles de la propriété. Instituts Solvay, Notes et Mémoires.

05-26 Reinach, S. L'origine des sciences et la religion, Ae, 16: 657–63.

05-27 Reinsch, P. The Negro race and the European civilization, AJS, 11: 145–67.

05-28 Smith, S. P. The migration of Kahu-Ngunu, JPS, 14: 81–95.

05-29 Smith, S. P. Some Whanganui historical notes, JPS. 14: 131–60.

05-30 Thomas, N. W. Ueber Kulturkreise in Australien, ZE, 37: 759–67.

05-31 Van Brandt, M. Nach dem Kriege. Japan in politischer und wirtschaftlicher Beziehung, Gl, 88: 213–16.

1906

06-1 Annadale, N. The introduction of the blow gun into southern India, Mn, 15.

06-2 Bailey, W. F. The native and the white in South Africa, NC, 50, 314–30.

06-3 Bushnell, D. I. The origin of wampum, JRAI, 36: 172–77.

06-4 Dadachanji, R. K. The origin of the practices of circumcision and idol-worship . . . and their influence on human civilization and progress, JASB, 17.

06-5 Gennep, A. van. L'idée d'évolution dans les mythes des semi-civilisés, Rev. des Idées, Paris.

06-6 Günther, F. Die Wissenschaft vom Menschen. Leipzig.

06-7 Hall, B. S. The undeveloped races in contact with civilization, Bull. Wash. Univ. Assoc., St. Louis, 4: 145–50.

06-8 Hervé, G. Noirs et blancs, REAP, 16.

06-9 Hobhouse, L. T. Morals in evolution. London.

06-10 Jevons, F. B. An introduction to the history of religion. London.

06-11 Jevons, F. B. Religion in evolution. London.

06-12 Messing, O. Ueber den Gebrauch des Opiums bei den Chinesen, ZE, 38: 205–19.

06-13 Oppert, G. Ueber die indische Parias, ArA, 4: 149–59.

06-14 Petrie, W. M. F. Migrations, JRAI, 36: 189–232.

06-15 Pitt-Rivers, B. H. L-F. The evolution of culture. Oxford.

06-16 Rivers, W. H. R. The Todas. London, New York.

06-17   Rivet, P. Le Christianisme et les Indiens de la République de l'equateur,
        Journ. Social Américain, 2: 81–101.
06-18   Tuhua, T. and Smith, S. P. (trans.) Incidents in the history of Horehore
        pa, . . . Hawkes Bay district, JPS, 15: 69–93.
06-19   Westermarck, E. The origin and development of the moral ideas. London.
06-20   Wissler, C. Ethnic types and isolation, Sc, 23: 147–49.

1907

07-1   Crawley, A. E. The origin and function of religion, Soc, Pap. London.
07-2   DeCora, A. An effort to encourage Indian art, ICAP, 15, 2: 205–09.
07-3   Diguet, L. Le "peyote" et son usage rituel chez les Indiens de Nayarit,
        JSAP, 4: 21–29.
07-4   Durand, R. A. Christian influence on African folklore, An, 2: 976–80.
07-5   Fewkes, J. W. The aborigines of Porto Rico and neighboring islands, BAER,
        25: 1–220.
07-6   Gerard, W. R. Virginia's Indian contributions to English. AA, 9: 87–112.
07-7   Hébert, J. Survivances décoratives au Brésil, JSAP, 4: 185–91.
07-8   Lang, A. The origin and terms of human relationship, BAP, 3: 1–20.
07-9   Laufer, B. A theory of the origin of Chinese writing, AA, 9: 487–92.
07-10   Mooney, J. The Powhatan confederacy, past and present, AA, 9: 129–52.
07-11   Revesz, B. Rassen und Geisteskrankheiten. Einbeitrag zur Rassenpathologie,
        ArA, 6: 180–87.
07-12   Rivers, W. H. R. On the origin of the classificatory system of relationships,
        in Anthropological Essays presented to E. B. Tylor in honour of his 75th
        Birthday. London.
07-13   Rivet, P. Les Indiens Jibaros: étude géographique, historique et ethno-
        graphique, Ae, 18: 333–68, 583–618.
07-14   Rougier, E. Maladies et médicines à Fiji autrefois et aujourd'hui, An, 2:
        994–1007.
07-15   Salone, E. Les sauvages du Canada et les maladies importées . . . au
        XVIIe et XVIIIe siècle: la picote et l'alcoolisme, JSAP, 4: 7–20.
07-16   Scott, H. L. The early history and the names of the Arapaho, AA, 9: 545–60.
07-17   Smith, S. P. History and traditions of the Taranaki coast, JPS, 16: 120–
        219; 17: 1–78, 111–47; 18: 1–83, 154–204; 19: 1–38, 47–136. 1907–1910.
07-18   Thomas, N. W. On the origin of exogamy, in Essays Presented to E. B.
        Tylor in Honour of his 75th Birthday. London.
07-19   Tozzer, A. M. Survivals of ancient forms of culture among the Mayas of
        Yucatan and the Lacandones of Chiapas, ICAP, 15, 2: 283–88.
07-20   Vierkandt, A. Die Anfänge der Religion und Zauberei, Gl, 93.
07-21   Westermarck, E. Le origini del celibato religioso, Riv. di Scienza, 1. Rome.
07-22   Willoughby, C. C. The Virginia Indians in the seventeenth century, AA, 9:
        57–86.
07-23   Wissler, C. The diffusion of culture in the plains of North America, ICAP,
        15, 2.

1908

08-1   Archambault, M. Sur les chances de durée de la race canaque, BSAP, 9:
        492–502.

08-2   Assman, E. Zur Vorgeschichte von Kreta, Philologus, 67. Leipzig.
08-3   Batemen, L. C. The Maine Indians of today, SW, 37: 145–52.
08-4   Buchner, M. Benin und die Portugiesen, ZE, 40, 981–92.
08-5   Dundas, K. R. Notes on the origin and history of the Kikuyu and Dorobo tribes, Mn, 76.
08-6   Emerson, N. B. Hawaii's race problem, SW, 37: 110–13.
08-7   Halbfuss, W. Industrie, Verkehr und Natur, Gl, 94: 270–73.
08-8   Hambruch, P. Das Meer in siener Bedeutung für die Völkerverbreitung, ArA, 7: 75–88.
08-9   Harsha, W. J. Industrial conditions on Indian reservations, SW, 37: 557–66.
08-10 Hellwig, A. Zufall und Aberglaube, Gl, 94: 293–97.
08-11 Hubert, H. and Mauss, M. Introduction à l'analyse de quelques phénomènes religieux, RHR, 28.
08-12 Kroeber, A. L. A mission record of the California Indians, UCPAAE, 8.
08-13 Lasch, R. Das Fortleben geschichtlicher Ereignisse in der Tradition der Naturvölker, Gl, 93: 287–89.
08-14 Lehmann, J. Einiges über Ornamentik, KBDGA, 39: 134–36.
08-15 Modi, J. J. Some Parsee marriage customs, how far are they borrowed from the Hindus? JASB, 8: 425–30.
08-16 Moisel, M. Zur Geschichte von Bali und Bamûm, Gl, 93: 117–20.
08-17 Palmer, H. R. The Kano chronicle, JRAI, 38: 58–98.
08-18 Reitzenstein, F. von. Urgeschichte der Ehe. Ihre Bildung und Entwichlungs gang. Berlin.
08-19 Ridgeway, W. The origin of the guitar and fiddle, Mn, 7.
08-20 Sapir, E. Herder's "Ursprung der Sprache," Modern Philology, 5: 109–42
08-21 Schmidt, W. L'origine de l'idée de Dieu, An, 3: 336–68; 4: 1075–91; 5: 231–45.
08-22 Speck, F. G. The Negroes and the Creek nation, SW, 37: 106–10.
08-23 Stoll, O. D. Geschlechtsleben in der Völkpsychologie. Leipzig.
08-24 Thomson, B. The Fijians, A study of the decay of custom. London.
08-25 Vierkandt, A. Das Problem der Felszeichnungen und der Ursprung des Zeichnens, ArA, 7.
08-26 Vierkandt, A. Führende Individuen bei den Naturvölkern, ZFS, 10.
08-27 Walsh, T. The passing of the Maori, NZIT, 40.
08-28 Webster, H. Primitive secret societies. New York.

1909

09-1   Buxton, T. F. V. Missions and industries in East Africa, JAfS, 8: 279–87.
09-2   Caillot, A. C. E. Les Polynésiens orientaux au contact de la civilisation. Paris.
09-3   Chamberlain, A. F. Note sur l'influence exercée sur les indiens Kitonaqa par les missionaires catholiques, Rev. d. Et. Ethnogr. et Sociol., Paris, 2: 155–58.
09-4   Foucart, G. La méthode comparative dans l'histoire des religions. Paris.
09-5   Foy, W. Zur Geschichte der Eisentechnik, insbesondere des Gebläses, Eg.
09-6   Foy, W. Ethnologica, 2 vols., 1909–1913. Berlin.
09-7   Franke, O. Die Ausbreitung des Buddhismus von Indien nach Turkestan und China, ARLB, 12: 207–20.

09-8   Graebner, F. Die melanesische Bogenkultur und ihre Verwandten, An, 4: 726–80, 998–1032.
09-9   Grignard, F. A. The Oraons and Mundas from the time of their settlement in India; an essay of constructive history, An, 4: 1–19.
09-10   Gulliford, H. Todas and Tibetans. A study in the evolution of religion, QR, 111: 97–110.
09-11   Hallock, C. Loyalty of tradition, AAn, 31: 159–63.
09-12   Harsha, W. J. Social conditions on Indian reservations, SW, 38: 441–45.
09-13   Hartland, E. S. Primitive paternity. The myth of supernatural birth in relation to the history of the family. 2 vols. 1909–1910.
09-14   Hrdlička, A. Tuberculosis among certain Indian tribes of the United States. BAEB, 42.
09-15   Hubert, H. and Mauss, M. Mélanges d'histoire des religions. Paris.
09-16   Lang, A. and Schmidt, E. On the sociological development of the tribes of Australia, etc., An, 4: 1096–99.
09-17   Lowie, R. H. An ethnological trip to Lake Athabasca, Amer. Mus. Journ., New York, 9: 10–15.
09-18   Maliandi, G. Saggio sull'origine dei fenomeni religiosi, RIS, 12.
09-19   Marett, R. R. The threshold of religion. London.
09-20   Merrick, G. Notes on Hausa and pidgin English, JAfS, 8: 303–07.
09-21   Moffett, T. C. Christian Indians in the making, Assembly Herald, Philadelphia, 15: 58–64.
09-22   Moreira, A. P. Zur Kennzeichnung der Farbigen Brasiliens, Gl, 93: 75–78.
09-23   Orsmond, J. M. with notes by Smith, S. P. The genealogy of the Pomare family of Tahiti, JPS, 2: 25–92.
09-24   Pratt, R. H. The Indian no problem, Proc. Del. Co. Inst. Sci., Media, Pa., 5: 1–21.
09-25   Proctor, H. The origin of the art of writing, AAn, 31: 168–69.
09-26   Reitzenstein, F. von. Der Kausalzusammenhang zwischen Geschlechtsverkehr und Empfängis im Glauben und Brauch der Natur- und Kulturvölker, ZE, 41: 644–83.
09-27   Rimini, T. W. The fall of Pukenina, Oreiwhata and Poutuia pas, JPS, 2: 43–50.
09-28   Schmidt, W. Die Mythologie der anstronesischen Völker, MAGW, 39: 240–59.
09-29   Shand, A. The occupation of the Chatham Islands by the Maoris in 1835, JPS, 1: 83–94, 153–63, 202–09; 2: 74–86. 1909–10.
09-30   Shaw, G. C. The Chinook jargon and how to use it, Seattle.
09-31   Singh, S. N. The Americanization of Oriental women, SW, 38: 91–100.
09-32   Stefansson, V. The Eskimo trade jargon of Herschel island, AA, 11: 217–32.
09-33   Stewart, C. T. The origin of the werewolf superstition. Univ. of Missouri Studied, Soc. Sci. Series, 2, 3.
09-34   Taylor, J. D. Native progress in Natal. SW, 38: 27–36.
09-35   Whitley, D. G. The high intellectual character of primeval man, RP, 8: 39–56.

1910

10-1   Abel, A. H. The Indians in the Civil War, Am. Histor. Review, 15: 281–96.
10-2   Adan, E. Las danzas de Coatetelco, MNMA, 2: 133–94.

10-3   Balfour, H. Origin of West African crossbows, BAER, 28: 635–50.

10-4   Boas, F. Psychological problems in anthropology, AJPs, 21: 371–84.

10-5   Brownell, A. Turning savages into citizens, Outlook, 96: 921–31.

10-6   Delafosse, M. Monographie historique et ethnique du cercle de Bamako,
        L'Afrique Française.

10-7   Foy, W. Zur Geschichte des Gebläses und zur Herkunft der Eisentechnik,
        Gl, 97: 142–44.

10-8   Frazer, J. G. Totemism and exogamy. 4 vols. London.

10-9   Gennep, A. van. La formation des légendes, Paris.

10-10   Goldenweiser, A. A. Totemism, an analytical study, JAF, 23: 179–93.

10-11   Graebner, F. Noch einmal P. W. Schmidt und die sudostaustralische Kul-
        turgeschichte, Gl, 97: 362–66.

10-12   Haddon, A. C. Environment versus heredity, Na, 85: 11–12.

10-13   Herrick, S. B. A summer festival in Tahiti, Century, 80: 701–08.

10-14   Jacoby, A. Der Ursprung des judicium Office. ARLB, 13.

10-15   Kluge, F. Zur Geschichte des Brutofens, MAGW, 40: 195–96.

10-16   Lang, A. The "historicity" of Arunta traditions, Mn, 69.

10-17   Laufer, B. Zur kulturhistorischen Stellung der chinesischen Provinz
        Shansi, An, 5: 181–205.

10-18   Lévy-Bruhl, L. Les fonctions mentales dans les sociêtés inférieures. Paris

10-19   Ludwick, L. The Oneidas of today, SW, 39: 34–36.

10-20   Manuel, V. The Pimas: Christian Indian tribe of the Southwest, SW, 39:
        161–62.

10-21   Meyer, R. M. Mythologische studien aus der neuesten Zeit, ARLB, 13:
        270–90.

10-22   Michow, H. Zur Geschichte der Bekanntschaft mit Sibirien vor Jermak,
        MAGW, 40.

10-23   Ober, S. E. A new religion among the west coast Indians, Overland, 56:
        583–94.

10-24   Parker, A. C. The origin of Iroquois silversmithing, AA, 12: 349ff.

10-25   Pastor, W. Die Musik der Naturvölker und die Anfänge der europäischen
        Musik, ZE, 42: 655–75.

10-26   Peacock, M. Religious dancing, Fo, 21: 515.

10-27   Ridgeway, W. The influence of environment on man, JRAI, 40: 10–22.

10-28   Schmidt, W. Grundlinien einer Vergleichung der Religionen und Mythologien
        der Austronesischen Völker, Denkschr. d. K. Akad. d. Wiss. in Wien.,
        Phil.-hist. Kl., 53, 8: 1–142.

10-29   Shakespear, J. Manipur festival, Fo, 21: 79–82.

10-30   Sharpe, A. Recent progress in Nyasaland, JAfS, 9: 337–48.

10-31   Smith, H. I. A visit to the Indian tribes of the Northwest coast, Amer.
        Mus. Jnl., 10: 31–42.

10-32   Smith, S. P. The coconut and the peopling of the Pacific, JPS, 19: 60–62.

10-33   Webster, H. Influence of superstition on the evolution of property. AJS, 15.

10-34   Werner, A. The evolution of agriculture, JAfS, 9: 410–15.

                                  1911

11-1   Ameghino, F. Origen poligenico del lenguaje. Arch. de Pedag., 9: 133–92.
        La Plata.

11-2   Andrews, C. T. Indian education in New York State, RM, 4: 91–98.

11-3   Arrhenius, S. Uber den Ursprung des Gestirnkultus, St, 9, 2: 420−34.
11-4   Barrett, S. A. The dream dance of the Chippewa and Menominee Indians of northern Wisconsin, Bull. of the Public Museum of the City of Milwaukee, 1, 4: 251−406.
11-5   Bell, H. H. Recent progress in northern Nigeria, JAfS, 10: 377−91.
11-6   Boas, F. The mind of primitive man. New York.
11-7   Bullock, D. S. The agricultural conditions and needs of the Araucanian Indians, BAEB.
11-8   Chamberlain, A. F. Some influences of race contact upon the art of primitive peoples, Journ. of Race Devel. , 2: 206−09.
11-9   Chapman, J. W. The Indian of the Yukon: his helps and his hindrances, RM, 3: 446−49.
11-10   Clark, A. B. The Indians of Rosebud, SW, 15: 42−45.
11-11   Dimock, J. A. A despoiled people, Ol, 91: 201−06.
11-12   Eichhorn, A. Beiträge zur Kenntnis der Waschambaa, BA, 1: 155−222.
11-13   Emmons, G. T. Native account of the meeting between La Perouse and the Tlingit, AA, 13: 294−98.
11-14   Emmons, G. T. The Tahltan Indians, Philadelphia.
11-15   Evans, M. S. Black and white in southeast Africa: a study in sociology. London.
11-16   Frazer, J. G. The magic art and the evolution of kings. 2 vols. London.
11-17   Fremantle, J. M. A history of the region comprising the Katagum division of Kano province, JAfS, 10: 298−319, 398−421; 11: 62−74, 187−200.
11-18   Gennep, A van. Les rites de passage. Paris.
11-19   Goddard, P. E. The Indian problem in Canada, RM, 4: 133−36.
11-20   Government of Formosa, Bureau of Aboriginal Affairs. Report on the control of Aboriginal affairs. Taihoku, Formosa.
11-21   Graebner, F. Methode der Ethnologie. Heidelberg.
11-22   Haberlandt, M. Zur Kritik der Kulturkreise, KBDGA, 42: 162−65.
11-23   Hartland, E. S. Totemism and exogamy, Fo, 22: 362−74.
11-24   Henning, P. Apuntes étnograficos sobre los Otomies del Distrito de Lerma, MNMA, 3: 57−85.
11-25   Johnston, H. H. Alcohol in Africa, NC, 415: 476−98.
11-26   Ketkar, S. V. An essay on Hinduism, its formation and future. Second vol. of History of caste in India. London.
11-27   Kinnaman, J. W. Chippewa history as told by themselves and French documents, AAn, 33: 32−40.
11-28   Kroeber, A. L. Incorporation as a linguistic process, AA, 13: 577−84.
11-29   Lang, A. Totemism and exogamy, Fo, 22: 91−93.
11-30   Laufer, B. The introduction of vaccination into the Far East, OC, 25: 525−31.
11-31   Lowie, R. H. A new conception of totemism, AA, 13: 189−207.
11-32   Lowie, R. H. Methods of American ethnologists, Sc, 34: 604−05.
11-33   Mačias, C. and Rodriguez, Gil, A. Los actuales indios tuxpaneca del Estado de Jalisco, MNMA, 2: 195−220.
11-34   Margoliouth, D. S. Language as a consolidating and separating influence, in Papers on inter-racial problems, Spiller, G. (ed.): 57−62. London.
11-35   Meillet, A. Differenciacion et unificacion dans les langues, St, 9, 2: 402.
11-36   Meritt, E. B. The American Indian: his progress and some of his needs, RM, 4: 145−49.
11-37   Mitra, S. M. Analysis of Indian unrest, FR, 95: 144−52, 277−88.

11-38   Nilsson, M. P. Der Ursprung der Tragedie, Neue Jabrb. Klass, Alt., 27, 28.

11-39   Nkonjera, R. History of the Kamanga tribe of Lake Nyasa. A native account, JAfS, 10: 331–41.

11-40   Parker, A. C. Additional notes on Iroquois silversmithing, AA, 13: 283–93.

11-41   Patten, S. N. The laws of environmental influence, PSMo, 79: 396–402.

11-42   Preuss, K. T. Die Opferblutschale der alten Mexikaner erläutert nach den Angaben der Cora-Indianer, ZE, 43: 293–306.

11-43   Reinsch, P. S. Influence of geographic, economic and political conditions, in Papers on inter-racial problems, Spiller, G. (ed.): 49–57. London.

11-44   Rhys Davids, T. W. and Mrs. Religion as a consolidating and separating influence, in Papers on inter-racial problems, Spiller, G. (ed.): 62–67. London.

11-45   Rivers, W. H. R. An ethnological analysis of culture, BAAASP, 480–499.

11-46   Sapir, E. The history and varieties of human speech, PSMo, 79: 45–67.

11-47   Sergi, G. Differences in customs and morals, and their resistance to rapid change, in Papers on inter-racial problems, Spiller, G. (ed.): 67–73. London.

11-48   Seyffert, C. A. Das Messer. Eine Kulturhistorischethnographische Skizze, ArA, 9: 91–150.

11-49   Singh, S. N. India's "untouchables," SW, 9: 279–90.

11-50   Speck, F. G. The Jackson-Whites, SW, 40: 104–07.

11-51   Speck, F. G. Missions in the Creek nation, SW, 40: 206–08.

11-52   Stanford, D. A. Indian topics; or, experiences in Indian missions. New York.

11-53   Stefansson, V. The Indian and civilization, Independent, New York, 71: 1434–38.

11-54   Thiel, H. van. Businza unter der Dynastie der Bahinda, An, 6: 497–520.

11-55   Thompson, E. H. The genesis of the Maya arch, AA, 13, 4: 501–16.

11-56   Thompson, E. H. A kindlier light on early Spanish rule in America, Proc, Amer. Antiq. Soc., 21: 277–83.

11-57   Tozzer, A. M. The value of ancient Mexican manuscripts in the study of the general development of writing, SIR: 493–506.

11-58   Tschöcke, A. Die Entstehung der Unsterblichkeistslehre, Ztsch. f. Relig. Psych., 5: 1–24.

11-59   Weissert, C. Indians and the trading-posts in the northwest of Barry County, Mich. Hastings, Mich.

11-60   Westermarck, E. Totemism and exogamy, Fo, 22: 81–91.

1912

12-1   Abbott, F. H. Agricultural progress among Indians, RM, 4: 313–18.

12-2   Abbott, F. H. Important reforms in Indian administration, RM, 5: 148–52.

12-3   Anckermann, —. Die Lehre von den Kulturkreisen, MAGW, 42.

12-4   Boas, F. Notes on Mexican folk-lore, JAF, 25: 204–60.

12-5   Chakravartti, V. A short note on the Hinduization of aborigines: the swelling of the Chandala caste, IA, 41: 75–76.

12-6   Chamberlain, A. F. How the American Indian named the white man, RM, 4: 177–82.

12-7   Cunow, H. Zur Urgeschichte der Ehe und der Familie. Stuttgart.

12-8   Dixon, R. B. The independence of the culture of the American Indians, Sc, 35: 46–55.

12-9   Donehoo, G. P. The "white plague" of the red man, RM, 5: 3−16.

12-10 Edge, H. T. A Fijian on the decline of his race, Theosophic Path., Pt. Loma, 7: 400−04.

12-11 Ellenberger, D. G. History of the Basuto, ancient and modern. London.

12-12 Evans, M. S. Education among the Bantu of Southeast Africa, SW, 51: 363−68.

12-13 Fauquet, G. Note sur la population de la Martinique. Eléments ethniques et catégories sociales, BSAP, 3: 154−61.

12-14 Friedman, M. How education is solving the Indian problem. Some practical results, RM, 4: 232−41, 271−83.

12-15 Hocart, A. M. On the meaning of Kalou and the origin of Fijian temples, JRAI, 42: 437−49.

12-16 Hocart, A. M. A native Fijian on the decline of his race, Hibbert Jnl., 11: 85−98.

12-17 Jones, S. B. The West Indian immigrant, SW: 169−76.

12-18 Kellogg, G. W. Carlisle's former students who are making good, RM, 4: 183−91.

12-19 Komarov, V. L. O russkom' naselenii Kamtchatki, K. Antr. Zh., 2−3: 100−36. Moscow.

12-20 Kroeber, A. L. Ishi, the last aborigine, World's Work, 24: 304−08.

12-21 Laufer, B. History of the finger-print system. SIR: 631−52.

12-22 Lowie, R. H. On the principle of convergence in ethnology, JAF, 25: 24−42.

12-23 McKenzie, F. A. The Indian and citizenship, RM, 4: 284−95.

12-24 Mitra, S. M. Christianity in Hinduism, NC, 72: 701−17.

12-25 Morel, E. D. The future of tropical Africa, SW, 51: 353−62.

12-26 Münsterberg, O. Early Christian missions in Japan and their influence on its art, OC, 26: 726−43.

12-27 Nicholson, A. The Menominee Indians working their way, RM, 5: 17−23.

12-28 Parker, A. C. Progress for the Indian, SW, 41: 628−35.

12-29 Rivers, W. H. R. The disappearance of useful arts, in Westermarck Anniversary Volume. London.

12-30 Rôheim, G. Survivals of shamanistic cure in a nursery rhyme, Ep, 23: 360−62.

12-31 Sapir, E. Language and environment, AA, 14: 226−41.

12-32 Sapir, E. Review of Goldenweiser's "Totemism, an analytical study," Psychological Bulletin, 9: 454−61.

12-33 Sapir, E. The history and varieties of human speech, SIR, 573−95.

12-34 Sapir, E. Review of Stumpf, C., "Die Anfänge der Musik," Current Anthropological Literature 1: 275−82.

12-35 Schmidt, W. Die Anwendung der kulturhistorischen Methode auf Amerika, An, 7: 505−06.

12-36 Schmidt, W. Kulturhistorischer Zusammenhang oder Elementargedanke, An, 7: 1060−62.

12-37 Schurtz, H. Urgeschichte der Kultur. Leipzig, Wien.

12-38 Scott, D. C. Traditional history of the confederacy of the six nations, RSCT, 3rd series, 52: 195−246.

12-39 Skinner, A. The Menominees of yesterday, RM, 4: 265−68.

12-40 Speck, F. G. Conservation for the Indians, SW, 41: 328−32.

12-41 Taft, G. E. Cayuga notes, AAn, 34: 29−32.

12-42 Takamine, J. The Japanese in America, Journal of Race Development, 2: 236−45.

12-43   Thurnwald, R. Die Siedlungs Kolonie in den Baining-Bergen. Gazelle-Halb-
        insel, Deutsche Kolonialzeit., 35: 579–82.
12-44   Triggs, O. L. The decay of aboriginal races, OC, 26: 584–603.
12-45   Valentine, R. G. The big job of solving the Indian problem, RM, 4: 389–96.
12-46   Vaux, G. Conditions among the five civilized tribes, RM, 5: 135–47.
12-47   Watermulder, G. E. The past and present of the Winnebagoes, SW, 41: 270–
        81.
12-48   Wundt, W. Elemente der Völkerpsychologie. Leipzig.

1913

13-1   Avelot, R. Notice historique sur les Ba-Kalé, Ae, 24: 197–240.
13-2   Beech, W. H. Une espèce de manie de suicide chez les a-Kikuyu, Mn, 13,
        30.
13-3   Carus, P. Evolution of the artistic observation, OC, 27: 17–24.
13-4   Chamberlain, A. F. "New religions" among the North Americans, JRP,
        5: 1–49.
13-5   Chamberlain, A. F. Some interesting phases of the contact of races indi-
        vidually and en masse, OC, 27: 25–38.
13-6   Chamberlain, A. F. The "antagonism" of city and country, JRP, 6: 279–
        93.
13-7   Cook, S. A. The evolution and survival of primitive thought, in Essays and
        Studies presented to William Ridgway, Quiggen, E. C. (ed.). Cambridge.
13-8   Darnand, J. Un sauvage converti, Mataafa, Rev. de Philos., Paris, 8:
        559–74.
13-9   Delafosse, M. Traditions historiques et légendaires du Soudan occidental
        (trans. from Arabic manuscript). Paris.
13-10   Delafosse, M. and Gaden, H. Chroniques du Foûta sénégalais (trans. from
        two Arabic manuscripts). Paris.
13-11   Denys Bray, J. C. S. The life-history of a Brāhūī. Royal Asiatic Soc.,
        London.
13-12   Donehoo, G. P. The real Indian of the past, and the real Indian of the pres-
        ent, RM, 5: 227–32.
13-13   Dupré, J. De l'assimilation des indigènes aux nationaux au point de vue
        repressif en Cochinchina. Thesis, U. of Toulouse.
13-14   Foucart, G. Histoire des religions et méthode comparative. Paris.
13-15   Foy, W. Die Religionen der Südsee, Allgemeines: 1905–1910, ARLB, 15:
        488–512.
13-16   Frazer, J. G. Psyche's task: a discourse concerning the influence of super-
        stition on the growth of institutions. London.
13-17   Gilfillan, J. A. Ne-bun-esk-kunk, the ideal soldier, RM, 5: 194–98.
13-18   Goldenweiser, A. A. The principle of limited possibilities in the develop-
        ment of culture, JAF, 26: 259–90.
13-19   Graebner, F. Zwei Bootmodelle von den nördlichen Salomo-Inseln, Et, 2:
        15–24.
13-20   Graebner, F. Zur Kulturgeschichte der Melville-Insel, Et, 2: 1–13.
13-21   Graebner, F. Krückenruder, BA, 3: 191–204.
13-22   Haberlandt, A. Prähistorisch-ethnographische Parallelen, ArA, 12: 1–25.
13-23   Harrington, M. R. Grievances of the Chitimacha Indians living near Charen-
        ton, St. Mary Parish, La., QJSAI, 1: 61–63.

13-24   Hawkes, E. W. Transforming the Eskimo into a herder. An account of the reindeer industry in Alaska, An, 8: 359-62.

13-25   Herrick, E. P. The Negroes of Cuba, SW, 42: 45-47.

13-26   Hilts, H. M. The California Mission Indians, SW, 42: 336-43.

13-27   Hobhouse, L. T. Development and purpose. London.

13-28   Hobhouse, L. T. Development and purpose: an essay toward a philosophy of evolution, Nation, 97: 163-64.

13-29   Hoernes, M. The earliest forms of human habitation and their relation to the general development of civilization, BAER: 571-78.

13-30   Hunter, L. E. The Nebraska Winnebagos, SW, 42: 217-22.

13-31   Kroeber, A. L. The determination of linguistic relationship, An, 8: 389-401.

13-32   Krüger, F. Über Entwicklungspsychologie, ihre sachliche und geschichtliche Notwendigkeit. Leipzig.

13-33   Meyer, E. Religiöse Wahnideen, ARLB, 16: 1-15.

13-34   Morgan, J. de. Feudalism in Persia: its origin, development and present condition, BAER: 579-606.

13-35   Murray, G. Cult of snakes in New Guinea, ARLB, 15: 628.

13-36   Panhuys, L. C. van. Development of ornament amongst the Bush-Negroes in Suriname, ICAP, 18: 380-81.

13-37   Parker, A. C. The code of Handsome Lake, the Seneca prophet. N. Y. State Museum Bull. 163.

13-38   Radin, P. The influence of the whites on Winnebago culture, Proc. State Histor. Soc. of Wisconsin, 61: 137-45.

13-39   Radin, P. Personal reminiscences of a Winnebago Indian, JAF, 26: 293-318.

13-40   Rivers, W. G. R. Survival in sociology, The Sociological Review, 6: 303ff.

13-41   Rivers, W. H. R. The contact of peoples, in Essays and studies presented to William Ridgway. Quiggen, E. C. (ed.), Cambridge.

13-42   Schanz, J. Geschichte der Dschagga, BA, 4.

13-43   Schmidt, W. Kulturkriese und Kulturgeschichten in Sudamerika, ZE, 14.

13-44   Schmidt, W. "The disappearance of useful arts." Notes on W. H. R. Rivers' paper with this title . . . , An, 8: 558-89.

13-45   Schmidt, W. Verbreitung des Ruders mit Krückengriff, An, 8: 559-62.

13-46   Seefried, F. von. Beiträge zur Geschichte des Manguvolkes in Togo, ZE, 45: 421-35.

13-47   Skinner, A. How I became a dreamer, SW, 42: 110-12.

13-48   Skinner, A. European folk-tales collected among the Menominee Indians, JAF, 26: 64-80.

13-49   Smith, H. I. The Indians of Canada, SW, 42: 478-79.

13-50   Smith, W. R. Australian conditions and problems from the standpoint of present anthropological knowledge, AAASR, 14: 3-24.

13-51   Speck, F. G. Conserving and developing the good in the Indian, RM, 5: 463-65.

13-52   Speck, F. G. European folk-tales among the Penebscot, JAF, 26: 81-84.

13-53   Spinden, H. J. A study of Maya art; its subject matter and historical development. Cambridge, Mass.

13-54   Thorne, M. M. Do educated Indians go back to the blanket? SW, 42: 611-17.

13-55   Thurnwald, R. Ethno-psychologische Studien an Südseevölkern auf dem Bismarck-Archipel und den Salomo-Inseln. Leipzig.

13-56 Watson, C. R. The Moslem of Sumatra as a type, Moslem World, 3: 159–69.

13-57 Weissenberg, S. Die "Klesmer" sprache, MAGW, 43: 127–42.

13-58 Wissler, C. The relation of culture to environment from the standpoint of invention, PSMo, 164–68.

1914

14-1 Beth, K. Religion und Magie bei den Naturvölkern. Leipzig, Berlin.

14-2 Calonne, A. de. Études Bakango (notes de sociologie coloniale). Liège.

14-3 Cook, S. A. The study of religions. London.

14-4 Crooke, W. The stability of caste and tribal groups in India, JRAI, 44: 270–80.

14-5 Fewkes, J. W. Relations of aboriginal culture and environment in the Lesser Antilles, Bull. Am. Geog. Soc., 46: 662–78.

14-6 Gaynor, W. C. The Catholic Negro in Louisiana, An, 9: 539–45.

14-7 Hartland, E. S. On the evidential value of the historical traditions of the Baganda and Bushongo, Fo, 25, 4: 428ff.

14-8 Hartland, E. S. Ritual and belief. London.

14-9 Hocart, A. M. The disappearance of a useful art in Rotuma, Mn, 82.

14-10 Hocart, A. M. The seventh day in Fiji, An, 9: 330.

14-11 Homberger, L. Etude sur la phonétique historique du Bantu. Paris.

14-12 Hooper, L. The loom and spindle: past, present and future, BAER, 629–78.

14-13 Jenks, A. E. Assimilation in the Philippines, as interpreted in terms of assimilation in America, AJS, 19: 773–91.

14-14 Kelsey, D. H. Status and needs of the Five Civilized tribes, SW, 43: 275–79.

14-15 Kroeber, A. L. Eskimos as aboriginal inventors, ScA, 110: 54ff.

14-16 Laufer, B. History of defensive armor. Field Museum, Chicago.

14-17 Marett, R. R. The threshold of religion. London.

14-18 Millar, P. S. Recent developments in the art of illumination, BAER: 611–28.

14-19 Nimuendajú, C. Die Sagen von der Erschaffung und Vernichtung der Welt als Grundlagen der Religion der Apapocuva-Guarani, ZE, 46: 284–403.

14-20 Oskison, J. M. Arizona and forty thousand Indians, SW, 43: 148–56.

14-21 Parsons, E. C. Feminism and conventionality, Ann. Am. Acad., 56: 47–53.

14-22 Preuss, K. T. Die geistige Kultur der Naturvölker. Leipzig.

14-23 Radin, P. A sketch of the peyote cult of the Winnebago, JRP, 3: 1–22.

14-24 Regnault, F. The role of depopulation, deforestation and malaria in the decadence of certain nations, SIR: 593–97.

14-25 Reinach, A. A propos de l'origine de l'alphabet, Revue Epigraphique, Spring: 135–55.

14-26 Rivers, W. H. R. The history of Melanesian society. 3 vols., Cambridge.

14-27 Rivers, W. H. R. Kinship and social organisation. London.

14-28 Róheim, G. The origin of the mana concept. Budapest.

14-29 Seligmann, B. Z. On the origin of the Egyptian zar, Fo, 25, 3: 300–32.

14-30 Skinner, A. The Plains Cree, SW, 43: 344–49.

14-31 Skinner, A. The Plains Ojibway, SW, 43: 91–100.

14-32 Speck, F. G. In Micmac summer camps, SW, 43: 676–81.

14-33 Swanton, J. R. and Dixon, R. B. Primitive American history, AA, 16: 376–412.

14-34   Temple, R. C. Anthropology as a practical science. London.
14-35   Temple, R. C. The value of a training in anthropology for the administra-
        tor, Mn, 19: 34–36.
14-36   Wissler, C. The influence of the horse in the development of Plains cul-
        ture, AA, 16: 1–25.

                                    1915

15-1   Ankermann, B. Ausdrucks- und Spieltätigkeit als Grundlage des Totemismus,
        An, 10–11: 586–92.
15-2   Barbeau, C. M. Wyandot tales, including foreign elements, JAF, 28: 83–95.
15-3   Birket-Smith, K. Foreløbigt bidrag til Kap Farvel-Distrikternes Kultur-
        historie. Copenhagen.
15-4   Cadman, C. W. Idealization of Indian music, Music Quart., 1: 387–96.
15-5   Camboué, P. P. Education et instruction en Madagascar, An, 10–11: 844–
        60.
15-6   Elmore, W. T. Dravidian gods in modern Hinduism. University of Nebraska,
        University Studies, 15, 1.
15-7   Fewkes, J. W. The origin of the unit types of the Pueblo architecture, JWAS,
        5: 543–52.
15-8   Furlong, C. W. The Alaculoofs and the Yahgans, the world's southernmost
        inhabitants, ICAP, 19, 1: 420–31.
15-9   Furlong, C. W. The Haush and Ona, primitive tribes of Tierra del Fuego,
        ICAP, 19, 1: 432–44.
15-10   Goldenweiser, A. A. Atlanta riots and the origin of magic, New Republic,
        3: 225.
15-11   Goldenweiser, A. A. Heuristic value of traditional records, AA, 17: 763–64.
15-12   Goldenweiser, A. A. The method of investigating totemism, An, 10–11:
        256–65.
15-13   Graebner, F. Totemismus als kulturgeschichtliches Problem. An, 10–11:
        248–56.
15-14   Grinnell, G. B. The fighting Cheyennes. New York.
15-15   Hill, G. F. The development of Arabic numerals in Europe. Oxford.
15-16   Hobhouse, L. T. Social effects of the war, Atlantic, 115: 544–50.
15-17   Hobhouse, L. T. Wheeler, G. C., and Ginsberg, M. The material culture
        and social institutions of the simpler peoples. London.
15-18   Hovorka, O. Leitmotive und Elementarmethoden der allgemeinen Heilkund,
        MAGW, 45.
15-19   Kazarow, G. L. Sources et études, Publications of the Balkan Inst. of
        Bosnia and Herzogovina, 5, 2. Serajevo.
15-20   Koppers, W. Die ethnologische Wirtschaftsforschung, An, 11.
15-21   Krueger, F. Entwickelungspsychologie, Bd. I, H. 1. Leipzig.
15-22   Lowie, R. H. The Crow Indians, SW, 44: 605–12.
15-23   Marty, P. L'Islam en Mauritanie et au Sénégal. Paris.
15-24   Nordenskiöld, E. Die religiösen Vorstellungen der Itonama-Indianer in
        Bolivia, ZE, 47: 105–13.
15-25   Parsons, E. C. Social freedom. New York.
15-26   Poech, R. Studien an Eingeborenen von Neu-Südwales und an australischen
        Schädeln, MAGW, 45, 3.
15-27   Reagan, A. B. The Jemez Indians, SW, 44: 343–51.

15-28   Rivers, W. H. R. Sun cults and megaliths in Oceania, AA, 17: 431—45.
15-29   Roy, S. C. The Orāons of Chota Nagpur. Their history, economic life,
        and social organization. Calcutta.
15-30   Skinner, A. The Iowa Indians, SW, 44: 677—84.
15-31   Smith, G. E. The migration of early culture. Manchester.
15-32   Smith, G. E. Pre-Columbian representations of the elephant in America,
        Na, 96: 340—41.
15-33   Sniffen, M. K. Some Alaska Indians, SW, 44: 153—61.
15-34   Speck, F. G. The eastern Algonkian Wabanaki confederacy, AA, 17: 492—
        508.
15-35   Speck, F. G. The Nanticokes of Delaware, SW, 44: 391—97.
15-36   Wallis, W. D. Individual initiative and social compulsion, AA, 17: 647—65.
15-37   Waterman, T. T. The last wild tribes of California, PSMo, 86: 233—44.
15-38   Westermann, W. L. Economic basis of the decline of ancient culture, Am.
        Hist. Rev., 20: 723—43.

1916

16-1   Bertoni, M. S. Influencia de la lengua guaraní en Sud-América y Antillas.
        Asunción.
16-2   Boas, F. Development of folk-tales and myths, SM, 3: 335—43.
16-3   Boas, F. The origin of totemism, AA, 18: 319—26.
16-4   Cuidano, P. Where fashions do not change, World Outlook, 2: 7.
16-5   Goldenweiser, A. A. Culture and environment, AJS, 21: 628—33.
16-6   Goldenweiser, A. A. Diffusion vs. independent origin, a rejoinder to Prof.
        G. Elliot Smith., Sc, 44: 531—33.
16-7   Goldenweiser, A. A. Use inheritance and civilization, AA, 18: 292—94.
16-8   Goldenweiser, A. A. Reconstruction from survivals in Western Australia,
        AA, 18: 466—78.
16-9   Hahn, E. Entwicklung der wirthschaftlichen Kultur, Anzeiger, Geograph.:
        297—300.
16-10   Horwitz, H. T. Beiträge zur aussereuropäischen und vorgeschichtlichen
        Technik. Berlin.
16-11   Hough, W. The distribution of man in relation to the invention of fire-making
        methods, AA, 18: 257—63.
16-12   Jenks, A. E. Indian-white amalgamation. Studies in Social Science, U. of
        Minnesota, 6.
16-13   Karsten, R. Der Ursprung der indianischen Verzierung in Südamerika,
        ZE, 48: 155—216.
16-14   Kazarow, G. J. Beiträge zur Kulturgeschichte der Thraker. Zur Kunde der
        Balkanhalbinsel. Sarajevo.
16-15   Koppers, W. Wirtschaft's Forschung ethnologische, An, 10: 611—51.
16-16   Loewenthal, J. Erfindung des Pfluges, ZE, 48: 11—17.
16-17   Lowie, R. H. Plains Indian age-societies: historical and comparative sum-
        mary. AMNHP, 2, 13.
16-18   Maybon, C. B. Les marchands européans en Cochinchine et au Tonkin. Ed.
        Revue Indochinoise, Hanoi.
16-19   Nelson, N. C. Chronology of the Tano ruins, New Mexico, AA, 18.
16-20   Parker, A. C. Social elements of the Indian problem, AJS, 22: 252—67.
16-21   Parsons, E. C. American society, New Republic, 9: 184—86, 214—16.

16-22 Parsons, E. C. Holding back in crisis ceremonialism, AA, 18: 41ff.

16-23 Radin, P. The native problem in Mexico, New Republic, 9: 90—91.

16-24 Reagan, A. B. The Zia Indians, SW, 45: 25—29.

16-25 Reagan, A. B. The San Felipe and Santa Ana Indians, SW, 45: 625—27.

16-26 Roy, S. N. The conversion of Santals to Hinduism, JBORS, 2: 87—88.

16-27 Sapir, E. Culture in the melting-pot, Nation, 103, suppl. 2.

16-28 Sapir, E. Time perspective in aboriginal American culture. A study in
       method. Canadian Geological Survey, Anth. Series, Mem., 90, 13.
       Ottawa.

16-29 Sapper, K. Die Bedrohung des Bestan des der Naturvölker, Archiv für
       Rassen. und Gesellschafts-Biologie: 268—320, 417—39. 1916—1917.

16-30 Sarfert, E. Leit gedanke über der Entwicklung der Kultur, Jahrb. d. Städt
       Museums f. Völkerkde. z. Leipzig, 6: 29—33.

16-31 Schmidt, W. Totemismus, viehzüchterischer Nomadismus und Mutterrecht,
       An, 10: 593—610.

16-32 Schwiedland, E. Anfänge und Wesen der Wirtschaft, Arbeits nach weis der
       Wien, 10: 257—73.

16-33 Seligman, C. G. Early history of the Anglo-Egyptian Sudan, ScA, 81: 270—
       72.

16-34 Seymour, G. Peyote worship: an Indian cult and a powerful drug, Survey,
       36: 181—84.

16-35 Skinner, A. A. European tales from the Plains Ojibwa, JAF, 29: 330—40.

16-36 Skinner, H. D. Evolution in Maori art, JRAI, 46: 184—96, 309—21.

16-37 Smith, G. E. The influence of ancient Egyptiaic civilization in the East and
       in America. New York.

16-38 Smith, G. E. The origin of the pre-Columbian civilization of America, Sc,
       44: 190—95; 45: 241—46. 1916—1917.

16-39 Speck, F. G. Remnants of the Machapunga Indians of North Carolina, AA,
       18: 271—76.

16-40 Speck, F. G. Manchapunga remnants, SW, 45: 174—76.

16-41 Steensby, H. P. An anthropological study of the origin of Eskimo culture.
       Copenhagen.

16-42 Ten Kate, H. F. C. Psychologie en Ethnologie in de koloniale Politiek, IG,
       Juni-Juli.

16-43 Walter, P. A. F. Santa Fe-Taos art movement, AAy 4: 330—38.

16-44 Wissler, C. The aboriginal maize culture as a typical culture-complex,
       AJS, 21: 656—61.

16-45 Wissler, C. Genetic relations of certain forms in American aboriginal art,
       ScA, 82: 285.

16-46 Wissler, C. Psychological and historical interpretations of culture, Sc, 43:
       193—201.

1917

17-1   Barbeau, C. M. Growth and federation in the Tsimshian phratries, ICAP,
       19: 402—08.

17-2   Bussell, F. W. The persistence of primitive beliefs in theology. A study in
       Syrian syncretism, Fo, 28: 279—94.

17-3   Chinnery, E. W. P., and Haddon, A. C. Five new religious cults in British
       New Guinea, The Hibbert Jnl., 15, 3: 448—63.

17-4   Dominian, L. Some aspects of the land as a factor in Mexican history, ICAP, 19: 515−16.

17-5   Fokken, H. Gottesanschauungen und religiöse Überlieferungen der Masai, ArA, 15: 237−52.

17-6   Funke, E. Der Gottesname in den Togosprachen, ArA, 15: 161−63.

17-7   Hrdlička, A. The vanishing Indian, Sc, 46: 266−67.

17-8   Jenness, D. The Copper Eskimos, GR, 4: 81−91.

17-9   Kroeber, A. L. The superorganic, AA, 19: 41−54.

17-10   Laufer, B. The reindeer and its domestication, AAAM, 4: 91−147.

17-11   Lowie, R. H. Culture and ethnology. New York.

17-12   Lowie, R. H. Oral tradition and history, JAF, 30: 161−67.

17-13   Marty, P. Etudes sur l'Islam au Sénégal. Paris.

17-14   Moses, B. The social revolution of the eighteenth century in South America, ICAP, 19: 521.

17-15   Nordenskiöld, E. The Guarani invasion of the Inca Empire in the 16th century: an historical Indian migration, GR, 4: 103−21.

17-16   Nordenskiöld, E. Das relative Alter eines Kulturelementes, ZE, 49: 10−20.

17-17   Nordenskiöld, E. Bevölkerungsbewegung unter den Indianern in Bolivien, Pet. Metteil., 63: 109−112.

17-18   Prince, L. B. Early Pueblo Indian missions in New Mexico. ICAP, 19: 506−14.

17-19   Sapir, E. Psychoanalysis as a pathfinder, Dial, 63: 267−79.

17-20   Schuchardt, H. Sprachverwandtschaft, Sitzungsber, d. Kgl. Pr. Ak. d. Wiss., philos.-histor. Kl., 37: 518−29.

17-21   Smith, G. E. Origin of the pre-Columbian civilization of America, Sc, 44: 190−95; 45: 241−46. 1916−1917.

17-22   Speck, F. G. Pequot Indian remnants, SW, 46: 100−04.

17-23   Vierkandt, A. Studien zur Ethnologie und Sociologie, Leipzig.

17-24   Wallis, W. D. Similarities in culture, AA, 19: 41−54.

17-25   Wallis, W. D. Psychological and statistical interpretations of culture, AJS, 22: 650−56.

17-26   Wallis, W. D. The influence of anthropology on history, SM, 5: 433−38.

17-27   Waterman, T. T. Ishi, the last Yahi Indian, SW, 46: 528−37.

17-28   Winstedt, R. O. Hindustani loan-words in Malay, JRASSB, 76: 67−68.

17-29   Winstedt, R. O. The advent of Muhammadanism in the Malay peninsula and archipelago. JRASSB, 77: 171−75; 81: 5−6. 1917, 1920.

1918

18-1   Birket-Smith, K. A geographic study of the early history of the Algonquian Indians. IAE, 24.

18-2   Fullerton, A. Passing of the totem-pole, Bellman, 25: 263−65.

18-3   Goldenweiser, A. A. Diffusion of clans in North America, AA, 20: 118−20.

18-4   Goldenweiser, A. A. History, psychology, and culture, Jour. of Philos., Psych., and the Scientific Method, 15: 561−71; 589−607.

18-5   Grinnell, G. B. Early Cheyenne villages, AA, 359−80.

18-6   Harsha, W. J. When the Indian became a person, SW, 47: 393−99.

18-7   Jenness, D. The Eskimos of Northern Alaska: a study in the effect of civilization, GR, 5: 89−101.

18-8   Knabenhaus, A. Die erziehung bei den Naturvölkern, Jahrb. d. Geogr.-Ethn Ges.: 1−41. Zurich.

18-9   Kroeber, A. L. Heredity, environment, and civilization; factors controlling human behavior as illustrated by the natives of the southwestern United States, ScA, 86: 210−12.

18-10   Kruijt, A. C. Beitrag zum Dynamismus der Bareŝ sprechenden Toradja und einiger umwohnender Völker, BTLVI, 74: 233−260; 75: 36−133.

18-11   Landtman, G. Kulturens ursprungsformer. Helsingfors.

18-12   Laufer, B. Review of "culture and ethnology" by R. H. Lowie, AA, 20, 1: 87−91.

18-13   Lehmann, H. Die Vorkultur der Menschheit, ArA, 15: 183−223.

18-14   Lowie, R. H. Anthropology put to work, Dial, 65: 98−100.

18-15   Lowie, R. H. Survivals and the historical method, AJS, 23: 529−35.

18-16   Marett, A. A. The psychology of culture-contact, Fo, 28: 13−35.

18-17   Marty, P. L'Islam en Guinée (Fonta-Diallon), Revue du Monde Musulman, 34: 68−124; 36: 160−228; 38: 102−209. 1918−1920.

18-18   Parsons, E. C. Pueblo-Indian folk-tales, probably of Spanish provenience, JAF, 31: 216−54.

18-19   Perry, W. J. The megalithic culture of Indonesia. Manchester.

18-20   Petrie, W. M. F. History in tools, BAER: 563−72.

18-21   Read, C. H. Primitive art and its modern developments, JRAI, 48: 11−21.

18-22   Rôheim, G. Psychoanalysis and ethnology: I Ambivalence and the law of reversal; II The meaning of symbols and the ontogenesis of the libido, Ep, 29: 49−90, 206−45.

18-23   Speck, F. G. Remnants of the Nehantics, SW, 47: 65−70.

18-24   Swanton, J. R. Some anthropological misconceptions, ScA, 86: 325.

18-25   Wallis, W. D. Messiahs: Christian and pagan. Boston.

1919

19-1   Banergee, G. Hellenism in ancient India. Calcutta.

19-2   Boas, F. Nationalism, Dial, 66: 232−37.

19-3   Breasted, J. H. The origins of civilisation. London, 1919−20.

19-4   Breton, A. C. Relationships in Central America, Mn, 19: 186−92.

19-5   Chinnery, E. W. P. The application of anthropological methods to tribal development in New Guinea, JRAI, 49: 36−41.

19-6   Hrdlička, A. Effects of the war on the American people, SM, 8: 542−45.

19-7   Kreglinger, R. Études sur l'origine et le développement de la vie religieuse. Bruxelles. 1919−22.

19-8   Kroeber, A. L. On the principle of order in civilization as exemplified by changes in fashion, AA, 21: 235−63.

19-9   La Favarie, S. de. La révolution américaine et la révolution français, JSAP, 11: 385−401.

19-10   Laufer, B. Sino-Iranica: Chinese contributions to the history of civilization in ancient Iran, FMNH.

19-11   Lehmann-Haupt, —. Die Herleitung des phönizischen Alphabets, Zeit. d. D. Morgenl. Ges., 78: 51−79.

19-12   Lowie, R. H. Economic interpretation of history: a footnote, Dial, 66: 35−36.

19-13   Marett, R. R. Interpretation of survivals, QR, 231: 445−61.

19-14   Marty, P. L'émirat des Trarzas. Paris.

19-15   Mondanton, G. La généalogie des instruments de musique et les cycles de civilisation. Arch. Suisses d'Anthropol. Gén., 3, 1: 1−120.

19-16 Nordenskiöld, E. Comparative ethnographic studies, 1–6. Gothenburg.
19-17 Nopcsa, F. Die Genese der primitiven Pflugtypen, ZE, 51: 234–42.
19-18 Orozco, E. Persistance du culte fétichiste secret près du Popocatapetl, El Mexico Antiguo, 1: 73–81.
19-19 Rivers, W. H. R. Psychiatry and the war, Sc, 49: 367–69.
19-20 Rivet, P. Les Indiens du Texas et les expéditions françaises de 1720–21 à la "Baie Saint-Bernard," JSAP, 11, 4: 6ff.
19-21 Sapir, E. Civilization and culture, Dial, 67: 233–36.
19-22 Schmidt, W. Die kulturhistorische Methode und die nordamerikanische Ethnologie, An, 14–15: 546–63.
19-23 Spinden, H. J. Origin of American agriculture, ScA, 88: 120–21.
19-24 Teggart, F. J. Anthropology and history, Jour. of Philos., Psychol., and Scientific Method, 26: 691–96.
19-25 Tessman, G. Die Urkulturen der Menschheit und ihre Entwicklung, ZE, 51: 132–62.
19-26 Werner, H. Die Ursprünge der Metaphor. Leipzig.

1920

20-1 Arriaga, P. J. de. La extirpación de la idolatría en el Peru. Lima.
20-2 Boas, F. The methods of ethnology, AA, 22: 311–21.
20-3 Burns, A. History of Nigeria. London.
20-4 Cooke, G. W. The social evolution of religion. Boston.
20-5 Diels, P. Die Slawen. Aus Natur und Geisteswelt. Berlin.
20-6 Genin, A. Notes on the dances, music, and songs of the ancient and modern Mexicans. SIR: 657–78.
20-7 Gennep, A. van. L'État actuel du problème totémique. Paris.
20-8 Goldenweiser, A. A. A new approach to history, AA, 22: 26–47.
20-9 Hadfield, E. Among the natives of the Loyalty Group. London.
20-10 Hamilton, L. Ursprung der französischen Bevölkerung Canadas. Berlin.
20-11 Hewett, E. L. Recent southwestern art, AAy, 9: 30–48.
20-12 Hoernes, M. Urgeschichte der Menschheit. Berlin.
20-13 Hrdlička, A. On the relations of anthropology and psychology, Sc, 51: 199–201.
20-14 Jaekel, O. Das problem der chinesischen Kunst-Entwicklung, ZE, 52–53: 493–518. 1920–21.
20-15 Junod, H. A. Should heathen games be preserved in a Christian community? A Bantu speaks, Int. Rev. Miss., 9: 274–80.
20-16 Lowie, R. H. Primitive society. New York.
20-17 Marett, R. R. Psychology and folk-lore. London.
20-18 Marty, P. Études sur l'Islam et les tribus du Soudan. 2 vols. Paris.
20-19 Nordenskiöld, E. The changes in the material culture of two Indian tribes under the influence of new surroundings. CES, 2.
20-20 Parsons, E. C., and Crow-Wing. A Pueblo Indian journal. AAAM, 32.
20-21 Radin, P. The autobiography of an American Indian. UCPAAE, 16: 381–473.
20-22 Radin, P. The sources and authenticity of the history of the ancient Mexicans, UCPAAE, 17: 1–150.
20-23 Rivers, W. H. R. History and ethnology, History, 5: 65–80.
20-24 Schmidt, M. Grundriss der ethnologische Völkswirtschaftslehre. 2 vols. Stuttgart. 1920–21.

20-25 Shastri, M. H. Contributions of Bengal to Hindu civilisation, JBORS, 6: 54–68.

20-26 Thurnwald, R. Politische Gebilde bei Naturvölkern, ZVR, 37: 376–408.

20-27 Weule, K. Zusammenhänge und Konvergenz. Ein Wort zu F. v. Luschan's Glaubensbekenntnis, Peterm. Geogr. Mitteil., Gotha.

20-28 Winstedt, R. O. The Indian origin of Malay folk-tales, JRASSB, 82: 119–26.

20-29 Wolff, L. Der Missionar als Forscher. Aachen.

1921

21-1 Frazer, J. G. The scope and method of mental anthropology, Science Progress, 16: 582–83.

21-2 Fuller, F. A vanishing dynasty— Ashanti. London.

21-3 Gamio, M. La población del valle de Teotihuacán. 3 vols. México.

21-4 Haddon, A. C. The practical value of ethnology. London.

21-5 Hartland, E. S. Primitive society; the beginning of the family and the reckoning of descent. London.

21-6 Heine-Geldern, R. Mutterrecht und Kopfjagd in westlichen Hinterindien, MAGW, 51: 105–40.

21-7 Jaeger, K. Zur Geschichte und Symbolik des Hakenkreuses. Leipzig.

21-8 Jenks, A. E. Relation of anthropology to Americanization, SM, 12: 240–45.

21-9 Jenks, A. E. The practical value of anthropology to our nation, Sc, 53: 147–56.

21-10 Jenness, D. The cultural transformation of the Copper Eskimo, Ms. in Victoria Memorial Museum, Ottawa, reproduced in Human Relations Area Files, Yale Univ., New Haven.

21-11 Koppers, W. Die Anfänge des menschlichen Gemeinschaftslebens im Spiegel der neuen Völkerkunde. Mödling.

21-12 Langenfelt, G. Origin of tribal names, An, 15: 295–313.

21-13 Rivet, P. Aires de civilisation, aires linguistiques, aires anthropologiques, Ae, 31: 118–19.

21-14 Rôheim, G. Primitive man and environment, Int. Jnl. of Psychoanalysis, 2: 157–78.

21-15 Rôheim, G. Ethnologie und Völkerpsychologie, Zeitschr. intern. f. ärztl. Psychoanalyse, 3: 163–94.

21-16 Roy, S. C. A new religious movement among the Oraons, MIA, 1: 267–324.

21-17 Sapir, E. Language. An introduction to the study of speech. New York.

21-18 Sapir, E. The life of a Nootka Indian, Queens Quarterly, 28: 232–43, 351–67.

21-19 Schmidt, W. Kulturhistorische Methode und der nordamerikaner Ethnologie, An, 15: 540–63.

21-20 Schmidt, W. W. Wundts Völkerpsychologie. VII und VIII Band. Die Gesellschaft, MAGW, 51: 1–24.

21-21 Spat, C. Melanesian influence in the east of Indonesia. Verslagen der Ethnologenbijeenkomsten, Amsterdam. 1921–1924.

21-22 Spier, L. The sun dance of the Plains Indians: its development and diffusion. AMNHP, 16, 7.

21-23 Spier, L. The sun dance of the Plains Indians, AA, 16: 459–527.

21-24 Thurnwald, R. Entstehung von Staat und Familie. Berlin.

21-25 Thurnwald, R. Gemeind der Banaro. Beiträge zur Enstehgeschichte von
       Familie und Staat, ZVR, 38: 362−474; 39: 68−219.
21-26 Valdez de la Torre, C. Evolución de las comunidades de indigénas. Lima.
21-27 Vendryes, J. La langage; introduction linguistique à l'histoire. Paris.
21-28 Villiers du Terrage, M. de. Le massacre de l'expédition espagnole du
       Missouri (11 août 1720), JSAP, 13: 239−55.

1922

22-1   Andrus, C. W. Changing Indian conditions, SW, 51: 25−31.
22-2   Antonius, O. Grundzüge einer Stammesgeschichte der Haustier. Jena.
22-3   Christian, V. Vor- und frühgeschichtliche Völkerwanderungen in vorderen
       Orient, An, 16−17: 577−87.
22-4   Connelley, W. E. Religious conceptions of the modern Hurons, Miss, Vall.
       Hist. Rev., 9: 110−25.
22-5   Cushing, F. H., Fewkes, J. W., and Parsons, E. C. Contributions to
       Hopi history, AA, 24: 253−98.
22-6   Danzel, T. W. Prinzipien und Methoden der Entwicklungspsychologie, in
       Handbuch der biologischen Arbeitmethoden, Abderbalden, E. (ed.),
       6: 45−108.
22-7   Goldenweiser, A. A. Early civilization. New York.
22-8   Hough, W. Evolution of ethnographical objects, USNMP, 60, 9: 1−47.
22-9   Jesperson, O. Language; its nature, development and origin, London.
22-10 Koppers, P. W. Kulturkreislehre und Buddhismus, An, 16−17: 442−58.
22-11 Koppers, W. Methode der Völkerkunde, Düsseld. Missionskursus: 244−58.
22-12 Lévy-Bruhl, L. Les fonctions mentales dans les sociétés inférieurs. Paris.
22-13 Mitra, S. C. On the conversion of tribes into castes in North Bihar, JASB,
       12: 734−43.
22-14 Nordenskiöld, E. Deductions suggested by the geographical distribution of
       some post-Columbian words used by the Indians of South America, CES, 5
22-15 Nordenskiöld, E. Indianer und Weisse in Nordostbelivien. Stuttgart.
22-16 Ogburn, W. F. and Thomas, D. Are inventions inevitable? A note on social
       evolution, Pol. Sci. Quart., 37: 83−99.
22-17 Rivers, W. H. R. (ed.) Essays on the depopulation of Melanesia. Cambridge
22-18 Savolle, C. Histoire de la Nouvelle Calêdonie. Paris.
22-19 Schmidt, P. W. Die Abwendung vom Evolutionismus und die Hinwendung
       zum Historizismus in der Amerikanistik, An, 16−17: 487−519.
22-20 Spier, L. A suggested origin of gentile organization, AA, 24: 487−89.
22-21 Swanton, J. R. Early history of the Creek Indians and their neighbors.
       BAEB, 73.
22-22 Tello, J. Five consecutive civilizations in Peru, Inter-America, 5: 238−50.
22-23 Thurnwald, R. Psychologie des primitiven Mensch, im Handbuch f. angew.
       Psychologie, Kafka, C. (ed.). München.
22-24 Torday, E. Culture and environment: cultural differences among the various
       branches of the Batetela, JRAI, 52: 370−84.
22-25 Villiers du Terrage, M. de. Documents concernant l'histoire des Indiens
       de la région orientale de la Louisiane, JSAP, 14: 127−40.

1923

23-1   Bartlett, F. C. Psychology and primitive culture. New York.

23-2   Benedict, R. The concept of the guardian spirit in North America. AAAM, 29.
23-3   Engert, J. Zur Psychologie von Naturmystik und Spiritismus, An, 18−19: 621−55.
23-4   Frisanchs, J. Problemas nacionales, Inca, 1, 2: 321−28.
23-5   Herskovits, M., and Willey, M. M. The cultural approach to sociology, AJS, 29, 1: 188−99.
23-6   Hocart, A. M. Convergence of customs, Fo, 34: 224−33.
23-7   Hrdlička, A. The origin and ancestry of the primitive population of America, SIR: 481−94.
23-8   Kroeber, A. L. Anthropology. New York.
23-9   Kroeber, A. L. American culture and the Northwest Coast, AA, 25: 1−20.
23-10   Leclerc, J. De l'évolution et du développment des institutions annamites et cambodgiennes sous l'influence française. Thesis, U. de Rennes, Rennes.
23-11   MacLeod, W. C. Natchez political evolution, AA, 26: 201−29.
23-12   Mills, J. P. The lesson of the red man, MIA, 3: 217−23.
23-13   Morgan, J. de. Sur la propagation des éléments culturels, RE, 4.
23-14   Muntsch, A. Evolution and culture. St. Louis.
23-15   Murray, J. H. The population problem in Papua, PSCP, Australia, 1: 236−37.
23-16   Perry, W. J. The children of the sun. London.
23-17   Petazzoni, R. L'origine et l'évolution du monothéisme, Rev. de l'histoire des religions. Paris.
23-18   Preuss, K. T. Der geistige Kultur der Naturvölker. Leipzig.
23-19   Radcliffe-Brown, A. R. The methods of ethnology and social anthropology, SAJS: 124−47.
23-20   Sidaway, E. Les manifestations religieuses de l'Egypte moderne, An, 18−19: 278−96.
23-21   Speck, F. G. Algonkin influence upon Iroquois social organization, AA, 25: 219−27.
23-22   Struck, B. Geschichtliches über die östlichen Tschi- Länder (Goldküste), An, 18−19.
23-23   Swanton, J. R. New light on the early history of the Siouan peoples, JWAS, 13: 33−43.
23-24   Ulrich, H. Logische Studien zur Methode der Ethnologie An, 18−19: 447−64, 733−52.
23-25   Ungad, A. Uber die Ausbreitung des Pferdes, Zeitschr. d. D. Morg. Ges., 77: 81−91.
23-26   Wanger, W. R. The Zulu notion of God, An, 18−19: 659−87.
23-27   Williams, F. E. The Vailala madness and the destruction of native ceremonies in Papua. TPAR, 4.
23-28   Willoughby, W. C. Race problems in the New Africa. Oxford.
23-29   Wissler, C. Man and culture. New York.
23-30   Wit, A. de. Island-India. New Haven.

1924

24-1   Ajisafe, A. K. History of Abeokuta. Burigay.
24-2   Boas, F. Evolution or diffusion? AA, 26: 340−44.
24-3   Buck, P. H. The passing of the Maori. NZIT, 55.

24-4 Buck, P. H. The evolution of Maori clothing, JPS, 33: 25–47, 121–29, 185–97, 293–316; 34: 61–92, 99–123, 223–51, 321–55; 35: 111–49. 1924–1926.

24-5 Castro Pozo, H. Nuestra comunidad indígena. Lima.

24-6 Danzel, T. W. Magie und Geheimwissenschaft in ihrer Bedeutung für Kultur und Kuturgeschichte. Stuttgart.

24-7 Gifford, E. W. Euro-American acculturation in Tonga, JPS, 33: 281–92.

24-8 Goldenweiser, A. A. Anthropological theories of political origins, in History of political theories, Merriam, C. E. and Barnes, H. E. (eds.). New York.

24-9 Graebner, F. Weltbild der Primitiven. München.

24-10 Hewett, E. L. Present status of the Pueblos, EP, 17, 10: 227–241. Letter pub. in SARP, 9, 1925.

24-11 Hobhouse, L. T. Social development. London.

24-12 Jochelson, W. The Yukaghir and the Yukaghirized Tungus, AMNHM, 13, Jessup No. Pac. Expedition, 9: 135–341.

24-13 Lacombe, R. La méthode sociologique de Durkheim. Paris.

24-14 Linton, R. The degeneration of human figures used in Polynesian decorative art, JPS, 33: 321–24.

24-15 Lowie, R. H. Origin and spread of cultures, American Mercury, 1: 463–65.

24-16 Lowie, R. H. Primitive Religion, New York.

24-17 MacLeod, W. C. The origin of the state, reconsidered in the light of the data of aboriginal North America. Philadelphia.

24-18 Perry, W. J. The growth of civilisation. New York.

24-19 Planert, W. Le développement des idées morales, examiné au point de vue linguistique, Le monde oriental, 18: 122–39.

24-20 Sapir, E. Culture, genuine and spurious, AJS, 29: 401–17.

24-21 Savina, F. M. Histoire des Miao. Hong Kong.

24-22 Schmidt, W. and Koppers, W. Völker und Kulturen: Erster T.: Gesellschaft und Wirtschaft der Völker. Regensberg.

24-23 Skinner, H. D. The origin and relationships of Maori material culture and decorative art, JPS, 33: 229–43.

24-24 Slater, G. The Dravidian element in Indian culture. London.

24-25 Smith, G. E. Elephants and ethnologists. London.

24-26 Stegmann, F. P. Die Rassengeschichte der Wirtschaftstiere. Jena.

24-27 Swanton, J. R. Southern contacts of the Indians north of the Gulf of Mexico, ICAP, 20, 1: 53–60.

24-28 Wahle, E. Vorgeschichte des deutschen Volkes. Leipzig.

24-29 Washburn, H. E. Origin and evolution of religion. New Haven, London, Oxford.

24-30 Waterman, T. T. The Shake religion of Puget Sound, SIR: 499–507.

24-31 Weatherford, W. D. The Negro from Africa to America. New York.

1925

25-1 Allier, R. La psychologie de la conversion chez les peuples non-civilisés. 2 vols. Paris.

25-2 André, P. J. L'Islam noir. Paris.

25-3 Browne, G. St. J. O. The vanishing tribes of the Kenya. London.

25-4 Cooper, J. M. Culture diffusion and culture areas in southern South America, ICAP, 21, 1: 406–21.

25-5   Dart, R. A. The historical succession of central impacts upon South Africa, Na, Mar. 21: 425–29.

25-6   Deacon, A. B. The Kakihan society of Ceram and New Guinea initiation cults, Fr, 85: 332–61.

25-7   Dorsey, G. A. Why we behave like human beings. London.

25-8   Goldenweiser, A. A. Diffusion and the American school of historical ethnology, AJS, 31, 1: 19–38.

25-9   Guimarães, A. Os Portuguezes na conquista do novo reino de Granada, JSAP, 17: 77–84.

25-10   Handy, W. C. Kaoha! Marquesan sketches, Yale Rev., Jan. New Haven.

25-11   Harrison, H. S. The evolution of the domestic arts. Handbook of the Horniman Museum, I. (2nd edition). London.

25-12   Hewett, E. L. Letters on the Pueblo Indian situation. SARP, 9.

25-13   Hewett, E. L. Present condition of the Pueblo Indians. SARP, 10.

25-14   Krause, F. E. A. Geschichte Ostasiens. Göttingen.

25-15   Kroeber, A. L. Handbook of the Indians of California. BAEB, 78.

25-16   Kühn, H. Ursprung und Entwicklung der paläolithischen Kunst, Mannus, Zeitschr. f. Vorgeschichte, 17: 271–78.

25-17   Lowie, R. H. On the historical connection between certain Old world and New World beliefs, ICAP 21: 546–49.

25-18   Métraux, A. Méthodes de travail chez les éthnographes, RE, 6: 266–90.

25-19   Michelson, T. The autobiography of a Fox Indian woman. BAER, 40: 291–337.

25-20   Preuss, K. T. Die Gestalt des Morgensterns nach Textaufnahmen bei den Mexicano im Staate Durango, Mexiko, ICAP, 21: 458–71.

25-21   Rivet, P. Les mélanéso-polynésiens et les australiens en Amérique, An, 20: 51–54.

25-22   Rôheim, G. Australian totemism. London. (Published as Social anthropology. New York.)

25-23   Scheidt, W. Die Stellung der Anthropologie zur Völkerkunde, Geschichte und Urgeschichte, ArA, 20: 138–46.

25-24   Schuchardt, H. Der Individualismus in der Sprachforschung, Sitzungsberichte d. Akad. d. Wissensch. in Wien, 204: 3–21.

25-25   Tozzer, A. M. Social origins and social continuities. New York.

25-26   Vogel, J. P. The influences of Indian art. London.

25-27   Wanger, W. R. The Zulu notion of God, An, 20: 558–78.

25-28   White, L. A. Personality and culture, OC, 39: 145–49.

1926

26-1   Arsenjew, W. K. Russen und Chinesen in Ostsibirien. Berlin.

26-2   Bittremieux, L. P. Scheut: Overblijfselen van den Katholieken Godsdienst in Lager Kongoland, An, 21: 797–805.

26-3   Bernard, L. L. Interdependence of factors basic to the evolution of culture, AJS, 32: 177–205.

26-4   D'Ividlla, G. Ce que l'Inde doit à la Grèce. Brussels.

26-5   Evans, I. H. N. Dusuns and the Chinese, JRASMB, 4: 153–155.

26-6   Goldenweiser, A. A. Immigration and national life, in Population problems, Dublin, L. I. (ed.): 195–209. New York.

26-7   Goldfrank, E. S. Isleta variants: a study in flexibility, JAF, 39: 70–78.

26-8   Guimarães, A. Os judeus portuguezes e brazileiros na America Hespanhola, JASP, 18: 297–312.

26-9 Hallowell, A. I. Bear ceremonialism in the northern hemisphere, AA, 28: 1–175.

26-10 Harrison, H. S. Variations and mutations in invention, Mn, 26: 101.

26-11 Harrison, H. S. Inventions: obtrusive, directional and independent, Mn, 26: 154–58.

26-12 Herskovits, M. J. The cattle complex in east Africa, AA, 28: 230–72, 361–88, 494–528, 633–64.

26-13 Hewitt, E. L. On the revival of certain indigenous arts, ICAP, 22. Rome.

26-14 Hilzheimer, M. Natürliche Rassengeschichte der Haussäugetiere. Berlin.

26-15 Jones, H. G. Uganda in transformation. London.

26-16 Kern, F. Kulturenfolge, Archiv f. Kulturgeschichte, 17: 2–19.

26-17 Lahille, R. Materiaux pour servir à l'histoire des Oonas. La Plata, Argentina.

26-18 MacLeod, W. C. On Natchez cultural origins, AA, 28: 409–13.

26-19 Malinowski, B. Anthropology, Encyclopaedia Britannica, 13 edition.

26-20 Malinowski, B. Anthropology and administration, Na, 118: 768.

26-21 Morlet, A. Invention et diffusion de l'alphabet néolithique, Le Mercure de France, Ier avril: 35–50.

26-22 Muntz, E. The influence of civilization upon native character, An, 21: 264–68.

26-23 Plischke, H. Von den Barbaren zu den Primitiven. Leipzig.

26-24 Pinard de la Boullhaye, H. P. La psychologie de la conversion chez les peuples non-civilisés, An, 21: 825–32.

26-25 Radin, P. Crashing Thunder: the autobiography of a Winnebago Indian. New York.

26-26 Rivers, W. H. R. Psychology and ethnology. London.

26-27 Rivet, P. Le rôle des Océaniens dans l'histoire du peuplement du monde et de la civilisation, Annal. Géogr., 35: 385–90. Paris.

26-28 Rôheim, G. Die Völkerpsychologie und die Psychologie der Völker, Im, 12: 273–91.

26-29 Schmidt, M. The primitive races of mankind: a study in evolution, London.

26-30 Schmidt, W. Der Ursprung der Gottesidee. Münster (10 volumes had appeared up to 1952).

26-31 Smith, G. E. Ancient mariners and the spread of early civilization ScA, 134: 293–94.

26-32 Smith, G. E. and Malinowski, B. Is civilization contagious? Fr, 76: 171–85.

26-33 Speiser, R. Isaak Iselin, über die Geschichte der Menschheit. Basel.

26-34 Talbot, P. A. The peoples of southern Nigeria: a sketch of their history, ethnology and languages. London.

26-35 Trimborn, H. Grundsätzliches zur Methode der historischen Rechtsforschung ZVR, 42: 1–7.

26-36 Uhle, M. L'origine de certains éléments de la culture de l'Amérique du Sud, éléments provenu de l'Amérique central, Anales de la Univ. Centr. del Ecuador, 36: 255ff.

26-37 Unkrig, W. A. Ein moderner buddhistischer Katechismus für burjatische Kinder, An, 21: 148–81, 523–45.

26-38 Von Wing, J. Une évolution de la coutume bakongo, Congo, 2: 353–59.

26-39 Wood, Jones F. The claims of the Australian Aborigine, AAASR, 18: 497–519.

26-40 Ziehen, M. L. Der Mysterienkult von Andania, ARLB, 24: 29–60.

1927

27-1   Allier, R. Le non-civilisé et nous. Différence irréductible ou identité
         foncière? Paris.
27-2   Baumann, H. Die Kulturhistorische Stellung der Azande und Mangbetu, BA,
         11: 1–131.
27-3   Best, E. The discovery and settlement of Rarotonga by Polynesians, JPS,
         36: 122–34.
27-4   Boas, F. Primitive Art. Oslo, Cambridge.
27-5   Delmas, S. La religion ou le paganisme des Marquisiens. Braine-le-Comte.
27-6   Descamps, P. Les causes de l'exogamie et l'endogamie, Rev. de l'Inst. de
         Sociologie, Bruxelles, 7: 67–79.
27-7   Dixon, R. B. The building of cultures, Scribners Mag., 82: 347–53.
27-8   Duisburg, A. von. Zur Geschichte der Sultanate Bornu und Wandala (Man-
         dara), An, 22: 187–96.
27-9   Ellwood, C. A. Cultural evolution. New York.
27-10   Ellwood, C. A. Primitive concepts and the origin of cultural patterns, AJS,
         33: 1–13.
27-11   Frank, L. K. Physiological tensions and social structure, ASSP, 22.
27-12   Friedenthal, B. H. Menschheitskunde. Leipzig.
27-13   Goldenweiser, A. A. Anthropology and psychology, in the social sciences
         and their interrelations, Ogburn, F. and Goldenweiser, AA (eds.):
         69–88. New York.
27-14   Gower, C. D. The northern and southern affiliations of Antillean culture.
         AAAM, 35.
27-15   Grubb, K. G. The lowland Indians of Amazonia; a survey of the location and
         religious condition of the Indians of Colombia, Venezuela, the Guianas,
         Ecuador, Peru, Brazil, and Bolivia. London.
27-16   Hambly, W. D. Origins of education among primitive peoples. London.
27-17   Hambly, W. D. Tribal dancing and social development. London.
27-18   Herskovits, M. J. Acculturation and the American Negro, Southwest. Pol.
         and Soc. Sci. Quart., 8: 211–24.
27-19   Hocart, A. M. Kingship. Oxford.
27-20   Izaguirre, B. Historia de las misiones franciscanas en el oriente del Perú.
         Producciones en lenguas indígenas de varios misioneros de la orden,
         publicadas sor el Padre Leay, 13, 14. Lima. 1927–29.
27-21   Leroy, O. La raison primitive. Paris.
27-22   Lindblom, M. K. G. Die technische Erfindung der Stelzen. Riksmus,
         Etnografiska Avdeling, Sm. Meddel., 3. Stockholm.
27-23   Lowie, R. H. Theoretische Ethnologie in Amerika, Jahrbuch für Soziologie,
         3: 111–27.
27-24   Lowie, R. H. The origin of the state. New York.
27-25   Majumdar, R. C. Ancient Indian colonies in the Far East. Lahore.
27-26   Marett, R. R. The diffusion of culture. London.
27-27   Métraux, A. Migrations historiques des Tupi-Guaraní, JSAP, 19: 1–45.
27-28   Mötefindt, H. Studien über Geschichte und Verbreitung der Barttracht, An,
         22: 828–64; 23: 617–55. 1927–1928.
27-29   Muntz, E. E. Christianity and the American Indian, NC, 101: 58–72.
27-30   Muntz, E. E. The effect of contact on the social organization of the American
         Indian, SM, 24: 161–68.

27-31 Nyèssen, D. J. H. The passing of the Frisians. The Hague.

27-32 Pitt-Rivers, G. H. L.-F. The clash of cultures and contact of peoples. London.

27-33 Pitt-Rivers, G. H. L.-F. The effect on native races of contact with European civilisation, Mn, 27: 3−5.

27-34 Radcliffe-Brown, A. R. The Australian Aborigines. IPRH.

27-35 Rôheim, G. Die Urformen und der Ursprung des Eigentums, IAE, 28: 1−28.

27-36 Safford, W. E. Our heritage from the American Indians, SIR: 405−410.

27-37 Sapir, E. The unconscious patterning of behavior in society, in The unconscious; a symposium, Dummer, E. S. (ed.): 114−42. New York.

27-38 Schwientek, J. Shin-butsu-dô-tai: Der Synkretismus von Shintô und Buddhismus in Japan, An, 22: 430−39.

27-39 Smith, G. E., Malinowski, B., Spinden, H. J., and Goldenweiser, A. A. Culture, the diffusion controversy. New York.

27-40 Spier, L. The ghost dance of 1870 among the Klamath of Oregon, UWPA, 2: 39−56.

27-41 Swanton, J. R. The interpretation of aboriginal mounds by means of Creek Indian customs, SIR: 495−506.

27-42 Wissler, C. The culture-area concept in social anthropology, AJS, 32: 881−91.

1928

28-1 Abegg, E. Der Messiasglaube in Indien und Iran. Berlin, Leipzig.

28-2 Adam, T. The spirit of India in Javanese dance-drama, As, 28: 102−05.

28-3 Alba, C. M. M. Etnologia y población histórica de Panamá. Panamá.

28-4 Benedict, R. Psychological types in the cultures of the Southwest, ICAP, 23: 572−81.

28-5 Best, E. Maori and Maruiwi: the arrival of the first Polynesian settlers at Whakatane. Origin of the mixed Toi tribes, JPS, 37: 175−225.

28-6 Boas, F. Anthropology and modern life, New York.

28-7 Carvalho, E. de, Origens da sociedade Brasileira, ICAP, 23, 2: 279−82.

28-8 Chapin, F. S. Cultural change. New York.

28-9 Dixon, R. B. The building of cultures. New York.

28-10 Feige, E. Über wirtschaftliche und natürliche Haustiergebiete, Landwirtschaftliche Jahrbücher. Berlin.

28-11 Folsom, J. K. Culture and social progress, New York.

28-12 Hallowell, A. I. Recent historical changes in the kinship terminology of the St. Francis Abenaki, ICAP, 22: 97−145. Rome.

28-13 Hawley, F. Pueblo social organization as a lead to Pueblo history, AA, 30: 504−22.

28-14 Jacob-Friesen, K. H. Grundfragen der Urgeschichtsforschung. Rassen, Völker und Kulturen. Hanover.

28-15 Keesing, F. M. The changing Maori. New Plymouth.

28-16 Keesing, F. M. The Maoris of New Zealand, PA, 1, Oct: 1−6.

28-17 Kern, F. Die Entwicklungsumrisse des Staates überhaupt, Schmoller's Jahrb., 52, 3: 393−415.

28-18 Kern, F. Kulturhistorische Richtung der Völkerkunde, Arch. f. Kulturgeschichte, 19, 1: 1−9.

28-19 Lips, J. Les origines du théâtre chez les peuples primitifs, Tagungsberichte d. Anthropologen- Kongresses in Köln, 1927: 44–52. Leipzig.

28-20 Lowie, R. H. Individual differences and primitive culture, in Schmidt Festschrift, Koppers, W. (ed.): 495–500. Vienna.

28-21 MacLeod, W. C. The American Indian frontier. New York.

28-22 MacLeod, W. C. Big business and the North American Indian, AJS, 34: 480–91.

28-23 MacLeod, W. C. Suttee in North America: its antecedents and origin. JSAP, 20: 107–20.

28-24 Mead, M. Coming of age in Samoa, esp. appendix III, Samoan civilization as it is today. New York.

28-25 Mead, M. An inquiry into cultural stability in Polynesia. CUCA, 9.

28-26 Mendizabal, M. O. de. Influencia de la sal en la distribución geográfica de los grupos indígenas de México. Mexico.

28-27 Morice, A. G. The fur trader in anthropology, and a few related questions, AA, 30: 60–84.

28-28 Ngata, A. T. Anthropology and the government of native races in the Pacific, Australasian Jnl. of Psychology and Philosophy, 6, 1: 1–14.

28-29 Parsons, E. C. Spanish elements in the kachina cult of the Pueblos, ICAP, 23: 582–603.

28-30 Plischke, H. Expansion, Kultur- und Universalgeschichte: 558–67. Leipzig.

28-31 Preuss, K. Der Ursprung der Gottesidee, An, 23: 464–70.

28-32 Redfield, R. Calpolli-barrio in a present-day Mexican pueblo, AA, 30: 282–94.

28-33 Reichard, G. A. A few instances of cultural resistance in southwest North America, ICAP, 22: 289–96.

28-34 Schapera, I. Economic changes in South African native life, Af, 1: 170–88.

28-35 Schmidt, W. Ein Versuch zur Rettung des Evolutionismus, IAE, 29: 99–126.

28-36 Thomas, H. B. An experiment in African native land settlement, Journ. African Society.

28-37 Torday, G. The influence of the kingdom of Kongo on Central Africa, Af, 1: 157–69.

28-38 Trimborn, H. Die Kulturhistorische Stellung der Lamazucht in der Wirtschaft der peruanischen Erntevölker, An, 23: 656–64.

28-39 Trimborn, H. Kulturhistorische Analyse der Alt peruanischen Soziologie, ICAP, 22: 415–26.

28-40 Wallis, W. D. Probability and the diffusion of culture traits, AA, 30: 94–106.

28-41 Warner, W. L., Radcliffe-Brown, A. R., and Burton, F. W. Some aspects of the Aboriginal problem in Australia, The Australian Geographer, 1, 1: 67–69.

28-42 Williams, F. E. Orokaiva magic. London.

28-43 Williams, F. E. Native education, TPAR, 9. Port Moresby.

28-44 Williams, F. E. The blending of native and European cultures, AAASR, 20.

28-45 Willoughby, S. C. The soul of the Bantu. New York.

28-46 Wissler, C. The culture area concept as a research lead, AJS, 33: 894–900.

1929

29-1 Agüero, M. C. La influencia del "keshua" en la Argentina, Ensayos, 1, 5: 1–3. Tucumán.

29-2   Angulo, J. de and Freeland, L. S. A new religious movement in north-
       central California, AA, 31: 265–70.
29-3   Azikiwe, B. N. Nigerian political institutions, JNH, 14: 328–40.
29-4   Barthold, W. L'étude historique des peuples tures, Zeit. d. D. Morgenl.
       Ges., 83: 121–42.
29-5   Blackmar, F. W. Socialization of the American Indian, AJS, 34: 653–69.
29-6   Boas, F. Migrations of Asiatic races and cultures to North America, SM,
       28: 110–17.
29-7   Bonnerjea, B. Possible origin of the caste system in India, IA, 60: 49–52,
       67–70, 91–95.
29-8   Bunzel, R. The Pueblo potter. New York.
29-9   Cooper, J. M. The origin and the early history of religion, PM, 2: 33–51.
29-10 Cuisinier, J. The Indian influences upon the dances in the Far East, IAL,
       3: 101–05.
29-11 Drewes, G. W. J. The influence of western civilisation on the language of
       the East Indian archipelago, in The effects of western influences . . .
       in the Malay archipelago, Schrieke, B. (ed.): 126–57. Batavia.
29-12 Dubois, H. M. Assimilation or adaptation, Af, 2: 1–22.
29-13 Firth, R. Primitive economics of the New Zealand Maori. London.
29-14 Haga, B. J. Influence of the western administration on the native community
       in the outer provinces, in The effects of western influence . . . in the
       Malay archipelago, Schrieke, B. (ed.): 237–47. Batavia.
29-15 Handy, W. C. Renaissance in Indo-China, PA, 2: 71–72.
29-16 Hough, W. Development of culture in relation to population, SM, 28: 513–17.
29-17 Hough, W. Development of agriculture, SM, 29: 304–16.
29-18 Keesing, F. M. Maori progress on the East Coast (New Zealand). Te
       Wananga, vols. 1, 2. Wellington.
29-19 Kolff, G. H. van der. European influence on native agriculture, in The
       effects of western influence . . . in the Malay archipelago, Schrieke, B.
       (ed.): 103–25. Batavia.
29-20 Krause, F. L'évolution de la civilisation et le caractère ethnologique du
       peuple, MAGW, 59: 247–65.
29-21 Kruyt, A. C. The influence of western civilisation on the inhabitants of
       Poso (Central Celebes), in The effects of western influence . . . in the
       Malay archipelago, Schrieke, B. (ed.): 1–9. Batavia.
29-22 Labouret, H. and Rivet, P. Le royaume d'Arda et son évangélisation au
       XVIIième siècle. Paris.
29-23 Lesser, A. Kinship origins in the light of some distributions, AA, 31: 710–
       30.
29-24 Lothrop, S. K. Christian and pagan in Guatemala, Nation, 128: 74–76.
29-25 Lowie, R. H. Are we civilized? Human culture in perspective. New York.
29-26 Lynd, R. S. and Lynd, H. M. Middletown, a study in contemporary Ameri-
       can culture. New York.
29-27 MacLeod, W. C. Origin of servile labor groups, AA, 31: 89–113.
29-28 MacLeod, W. C. On the diffusion of Central American culture to coastal
       British Columbia and Alaska, An, 24: 231–39.
29-29 Malinowski, B. Practical anthropology, Af, 2: 22–38.
29-30 Maunier, M. R. Les débuts et les formes du contact des races, RE, 10:
       35–60.
29-31 Mead, M. Americanization in Samoa, American Mercury, 16: 264–70.

29-32 Middendorp. W. The administration of the outer provinces of the Netherlands Indies, in The effects of western influence . . . in the Malay archipelago, Schrieke, B. (ed.): 34—70. Batavia.

29-33 Nieuwenhuis, A. W. Ten years of hygiene and ethnography in primitive
Borneo (1891—1901), in The effects of western influence . . . in the
Malay archipelago, Schrieke, B. (ed.): 10—33. Batavia.

29-34 Nordenskiöld, E. The American Indian as an inventor, JRAI, 59: 273—309.

29-35 Parsons, E. C. Ritual parallels in Pueblo and Plains cultures, AA, 31:
642—54.

29-36 Redfield, R. The material culture of Spanish-Indian Mexico, AA, 31: 602—18.

29-37 Róheim, G. La psychologie raciale et les origines du capitalisme chez les
primitifs, Rev. Française Psychoanal., 3: 122—49.

29-38 Schrieke, B. (ed.) The effect of western influence on native civilisations
in the Malay archipelago. Batavia.

29-39 Schrieke, B. Native society in the transformation period, in The effect of
western influence . . . in the Malay archipelago, Schrieke, B. (ed.).
Batavia.

29-40 Seligman, C. G. Temperament, conflict, and psychosis in a stone-age
population, Brit. Jnl. of Medical Psychology, 9: 187—202.

29-41 Smith, G. E. The migrations of early culture. Manchester.

29-42 Smith, R. G. Concept of the culture-area, SF, 7: 421—32.

29-43 Spier, L. Problems arising from the cultural position of the Havasupai,
AA, 31: 13—22.

29-44 Spranger, E. Kulturzyklentheorie und der Problem der Kulturzerfalls,
Geisteskultur, 38: 65—90.

29-45 Sternberg, L. The Ainu problem, An, 24: 755—99.

29-46 Steward, J. H. Diffusion and independent invention: a critique of logic, AA,
31: 491—95.

29-47 Stutterheim, W. F. A Javanese period in Sumatran history. Surakarta.

29-48 Taft, D. R. Cultural opportunities through race contacts, JNH, 14: 12—20.

29-49 Ten Haar, B. Western influence on the law for the native population, in The
effects of western influence . . . in the Malay archipelago, Schrieke,
B., (ed.): 158—70. Batavia.

29-50 Thurnwald, R. Direction et séthisation comme problème socio-psychologique,
Congr. internat. de Psychologie appliquée. Paris.

29-51 Thurnwald, R. Social problems of Africa, Af, 2: 130—36.

29-52 Thurnwald, R. Grund probleme der vergleichenden Völkerpsychologie,
Zeitsch. f. d. ges. Staatswissensch., 87, 2. Tübingen.

29-53 Thurnwald, R. Psychische Einwirkungen in Leben und Erleben von Naturvölkern, All. Arztl. Zentralblatt. f. Psychother., 2: 537—58.

29-54 Thurnwald, R. Modern volkenkunde, war haar drijft en wat zij wil, Mensch
en Maatschappij, 5: 1—16.

29-55 Wallis, W. D. Magnitude of distribution, centrifugal spread, and centripetal
elaboration of culture traits, AA, 31: 755—71.

29-56 Wallis, W. D. Contemporary society as a culture phenomenon, SSR, 14:
17—24.

29-57 Whitehead, G. O. Social change among the Bari, Sudan Notes and Records,
12: 91—97. London.

29-58 Wissler, C. An introduction to social anthropology. New York.

29-59 Wissler, C. The influence of aboriginal Indian culture on American life with references to traces of origins, in Some Oriental influences on western culture. IPRNY.

<u>1930</u>

30-1   Abel, T. Is a cultural sociology possible? AJS, 35: 739–52.
30-2   Azikiwe, B. N. Fragments of Onitsha history, JNH, 15: 474–97.
30-3   Barbeau, M. Totem poles, a recent native art of the Northwest Coast of America, GR, 20: 258–72.
30-4   Basauri, C. Los indios Otomies y la mision cultural de Actopan, Quetzalcoatl, 1: 16–19. Mexico.
30-5   Benoit, F. Survivance des civilisations méditerranéennes chez les Berbères, RA, 40: 278–93.
30-6   Birket-Smith, K. Folk wanderings and culture drifts in northern North America, JSAP, 22: 1–12.
30-7   Bleakley, J. W. Can our aborigines be preserved? ANZAASR, Brisbane.
30-8   Cooper, J. M. The early history of the family, PM, 3: 56–68.
30-9   Darlington, H. S. The probable origin of some North American dice games, An, 25: 303–10.
30-10 Descamps, P. État social des peuples sauvages. Paris.
30-11 Driberg, J. H. The East African problem. London.
30-12 Fletcher, H. J. The use of genealogies for the purpose of dating Polynesian history, JPS, 39: 189–94.
30-13 Goldenweiser, A. A. Evolution, social, ESS.
30-14 Goldenweiser, A. A. Man and woman as creators, in Our changing morality, Kirchway, F. (ed.). New York.
30-15 Handy, E. S. C. The renaissance of East Indian culture, PA, 3: 362–69.
30-16 Harrington, J. P. Reaction of the American Indian to his European conquerors, Pan-American Magazine, 43: 220–34.
30-17 Harrison, H. S. Evolution in material culture, BAASR, 98: 139–59.
30-18 Harrison, H. S. Opportunism and the factors of invention, AA, 32: 106–25.
30-19 Herskovits, M. J. The Negro in the New World: the statement of a problem, AA, 32: 145–55.
30-20 Hoffman, F. L. The Navaho population problem, ICAP, 23: 620–32.
30-21 Hogbin, H. I. The problem of depopulation . . . as applied to Ontong Java (Solomon Islands), JPS, 39: 43–66.
30-22 Hough, W. The bison as a factor in ancient American culture history, SM, 30: 315–19.
30-23 Hough, W. How did we come by art? SM, 31: 434–41.
30-24 Keesing, F. M. Government of Pacific dependencies, PA, 3: 448–59.
30-25 Koppers, W. Die Frage des Mutterrechts und des Totemismus in alten China, An, 25: 981–1002.
30-26 Kroeber, A. L. Diffusion, ESS.
30-27 Kroeber, A. L. Cultural relations between North and South America, ICAP, 23: 5–22.
30-28 Laufer, B. The early history of felt, AA, 32: 1–18.
30-29 Mackay, E. Painted pottery in modern Sind: a survival of an ancient industry JRAI, 60: 127–36.
30-30 Malinowski, B. The rationalization of anthropology and administration, Af, 3: 405–29.

30-31 Malinowski, B. Culture, ESS: 621—45.
30-32 Mendizabal, M. O. de. La Evolucion des Noroeste de Mexico, Mexico, D. F.
30-33 Ner, M. Au pays du droit maternel; compte rendu de missions, EFEOB, 30: 533—76.
30-34 Nordenskiöld, E. Modifications in Indian culture through inventions and loans. Göteborg.
30-35 Parsons, E. C. Spanish elements in the katchina cult of the Pueblos, ICAP, 23: 582—603.
30-36 Parsons, E. C. Zapotecan prayers at New Year; with Spanish trans., Mexican Folkways, 6, 1: 38—46.
30-37 Price, M. T. The concept "culture conflict": in what sense valid? SF, 9: 164—67.
30-38 Radcliffe-Brown, A. R. Review of "The chronological aspects of certain Australian social institutions as inferred from geographical distribution," by Davidson, D. S., Oc, 1: 367—70.
30-39 Radcliffe-Brown, A. R. Applied anthropology, ANZAASR: 1—14. Brisbane.
30-40 Radcliffe-Brown, A. R. The social organization of Australian tribes, Oc, 1—4. 1930—31.
30-41 Redfield, R. Tepoztlan. Chicago.
30-42 Röck, F. Die kulturhistorische Bedeutung von Ortungsrechen und Ortungsbildern, An, 25: 255—302.
30-43 Röheim, G. Animism, magic, and the divine king. London.
30-44 Sapir, W. Communication. Custom. Fashion. ESS.
30-45 Spinden, H. J. The population of ancient America, SIR: 451—71.
30-46 Swanton, J. R. Some neglected data bearing on Cheyenne, Chippewa and Dakota history, AA, 32: 156—60.
30-47 Swanton, J. R. An Indian social experiment and some of its lessons, SM, 31: 368—76.
30-48 Whorf, B. L. An Aztec account of the period of Toltec decline, ICAP, 23: 122—29.
30-49 Williams, F. E. Orokaiva society. Oxford.

1931

31-1   Barbeau, M. Our Indians, their disappearance, Queen's Quarterly, 38: 691—707. Kingston, Canada.
31-2   Benedict, R. The science of custom, in The making of man, Calverton, V. F. (ed.). New York.
31-3   Buck, P. H. The evolution of Maori clothing. PSM, 7. Wellington, New Zealand.
31-4   Calverton, V. F. Modern anthropology and the theory of cultural compulsives, in The making of modern man, Calverton, V. F. (ed.). New York.
31-5   Chattopadhay, K. P. Contact of peoples as affecting marriage rules, 18th Indian Science Congress. Nagpur.
31-6   Clerq, A. de. L'attitude des Baluba vis-à-vis de la pénétration des idées européennes, BIRCB, 2: 46—51.
31-7   Gann, T., and Thompson, E. The history of the Maya. New York.
31-8   Handy, E. S. C. Cultural revolution in Hawaii. IPRH.
31-9   Handy, E. S. C. History and culture in the Society Islands, BPBMB, 79.
31-10 Hirschberg, W. Die arabisch-persisch-indische Kultur an der Östküste

Afrikas: ihre beziehungen nach den Inneren des Kontinents, MAGW, 61, 5: 269—84.

31-11 Hodgen, M. T. Doctrine of survivals: the history of an idea, AA, 33, 2: 307—24.

31-12 Hogbin, H. I. Education at Ongtong Java, Solomon Islands, AA, 33, 4: 601-14.

31-13 Hough, W. Material culture and the racial matrix, SM, 33: 164—67.

31-14 Johnson, G. B. The Negro spiritual: a problem in anthropology, AA, 33, 2: 157—71.

31-15 Keesing, F. M. A memorandum on the mandated territory of Western Samoa and American Samoa. IPRH.

31-16 Keesing, F. M. Dependencies and native peoples of the Pacific. IPRH.

31-17 Kidder, A. V. The future of man in the light of the past: the viewpoint of an archaeologist, SM, 22: 289—93.

31-18 Knak, D. S. Einflüsse der europäischen Zivilisation auf das Familienleben der Bantu, Af, 4: 178—201.

31-19 Koppers, W. Familie, in Handwörterbuch der Soziologie: 112—22. Stuttgart

31-20 Kroeber, A. L. The culture-area and age-area concepts of Clark Wissler, in Methods in social science, a case book, Rice, S. A. (ed.): 248—65.

31-21 Kroeber, A. L. Historical reconstruction of culture growths and organic evolution, AA, 33, 2: 149—56.

31-22 LaPiere, R. T. and Wang, C. Incidence and sequence of social change, AJS, 37: 399—409.

31-23 Laufer, B. Columbus and Cathay, and the meaning of America to the Orientalist, Journ. of Am. Oriental Soc., 51: 87—103.

31-24 Lippert, J. Evolution of culture. New York. Trans. and ed. by Murdock, G. P., from the 1886—87 Kulturgeschichte der Menschheit in ihrem organischen Aufbau.

31-25 Lowie, R. H. Inventeness of the American Indian, American Mercury, 24: 90—93.

31-26 MacLeod, W. C. Origin and history of politics. New York.

31-27 MacLeod, W. C. Hook-swinging in the Old World and in America: a problem in cultural integration and disintegration, An, 26: 551—62.

31-28 Manchen-Helfen, O. Reise ins asiatische Tuwa. Berlin.

31-29 Mead, M. Stevenson's Samoa today, World Today, 58: 343—50.

31-30 Merrill, E. D. The phytogeography of cultivated plants in relation to assum pre-Columbian Eurasian-American contacts, AA, 33, 3: 375—82.

31-31 Métraux, A. Les hommes-dieux chez les chiriguano et dans l'Amérique du Sud, RIEUNT, 2: 61—91.

31-32 Mills, J. P. The effect on the tribes of the Naga Hill District of contacts with civilization in 1931. Extract from Census of India, 1931.

31-33 Moeller, M. L'adaptation des sociétés indigènes de la province orientale à la situation créé par la colonisation, BIRCB, 2: 52—66.

31-34 Noble, W. J. The black trek; from village to mine in Africa. London.

31-35 Read, M. The Indian peasant uprooted. London, New York.

31-36 Ricard, R. L' "incorporation" de l'Indien par l'école au Mexique, JSAP, 23: 47—70, 441—57.

31-37 Sapper, K. T. Die Indianer und ihre Kultur einst und jetzt, Geopolitik, 8: 235—39, 306—13, 383—87.

31-38 Schmidt, W. The origin and growth of religion, Rose, H. J. (trans.). New York.

31-39 Snouk Hurgronje, C. Mekka in the latter part of the nineteenth century. Daily life, customs and learning, the Moslims of the East Indian Archipelago. Leiden.

31-40 Speck, F. G. Birch-bark in the ancestry of pottery forms, An, 26: 407–12.

31-41 Steward, J. H. A Uintah Ute bear dance, March, 1931, AA, 34, 2: 263–73.

31-42 Suslov, I. M. Shamanism and the fight against it. Leningrad.

31-43 Thurnwald, R. Die menschliche Gesellschaft in ihren ethnosoziologischen Grundlagen. I. Repräsentative Lebensbilder von Naturvölkern. Berlin, Leipzig.

31-44 Thurnwald, R. Soziologische Forschungen über Veränderungen in Leben des Afrikaners unter den Einwirkungen der europäischen Zivilisation, Forschungen und Forschritte, 7.

31-45 Thurnwald, R. Die menschliche Gesellhaft in ihren ethnosoziologischen Grundlagen. Berlin.

31-46 Thurnwald, R. The missionary's concern in sociology and psychology, Af, 4: 418–33.

31-47 Webster, H. Ancient civilization. Boston.

1932

32-1 Adler, B. Der gegenwärtige Stand der Menschenkunde in der U. d. S. S. R. (Russland), ArA, 22: 29–43.

32-2 Beals, R. The comparative anatomy of northern Mexico before 1750, IbA, 2: 104ff.

32-3 Beals, R. Aboriginal survivals in Mayo culture, AA, 34: 28–39.

32-4 Benedict, R. Configurations of culture in North America, AA, 34: 1–27.

32-5 Berg, C. C. Hindu literature in Java, IAL, 6: 122–41.

32-6 Bertrand, A. La structure des sociétés indigènes et quelque problèmes de politique indigène, BIRCB, 3: 326–33.

32-7 Boas, F. Anthropology and modern life. New York.

32-8 Boas, F. Current beliefs of the Kwakiutl Indians, JAF, 45: 177–260.

32-9 Boas, F. The aims of anthropological research, Sc, 76: 605–13.

32-10 Chinnery, E. M. P. Studies of the native population of the East Coast of New Ireland, ANZAASP.

32-11 De Jonghe, E. La structure des sociétés indigènes et quelque problèmes de politique indigène, BIRCB, 3: 315–25.

32-12 Dempwolff, O. Pater Schmidts Anwendung seiner Kulturkreislehre auf die Sprachwissenschaft, ArA, 22: 72–77.

32-13 Dixon, R. B. The problem of the sweet potato in Polynesia, AA, 34: 40–66.

32-14 Driver, H. E., and Kroeber, A. L. Quantitative expression of cultural relationships, UCPAAE, 31: 211–56.

32-15 Elkin, A. P. Five year plan of research, Af, 5: 1–13.

32-16 Foreman, G. Indian removal, the emigration of the five civilized tribes of Indians. Norman.

32-17 Fox, C. The personality of Britain. London.

32-18 Ghurye, G. S. Caste and race in India. London.

32-19 Greenman, E. F. Origin and development of the burial mound, AA, 34: 286–95.

32-20 Henderson, R. The African negro and white civilization, SW, 61: 367–72.

32-21 Herskovits, M. J. An African game in the New World, JRAI, 62: 23–38.

32-22 Hough, W. Human postures and the beginnings of seating furniture, SM, 35: 328−32.

32-23 Jensen, A. E. Die staatliche Organisation und die historischen Überlieferungen der Barostse am oberen Zambesi. Württemburg Vereins fur Handelsgeographie, 50: 71−115. Linden Museum, Stuttgart.

32-24 Keesing, F. M. Language change in relation to native education in Samoa, Mid-Pacific Magazine, 44: 303−13.

32-25 Keesing, F. M. Education and native peoples: a study in objectives, PA, 5: 675−88.

32-26 Krause, F. Ethnology and the study of culture change, Af, 5: 383−92.

32-27 Krout, M. H. Culture and culture change, AJS, 38: 253−63.

32-28 Kruijt, A. C. The influence of western civilization on the inhabitants of Poso. Batavia.

32-29 Lowrie, S. H. Culture conflict in Texas. New York.

32-30 MacLeod, W. C. Aspects of the earlier development of law and punishment, J. Crim. Law, 23: 169−90.

32-31 Marett, R. R. The beginnings of morals and culture: an introduction to social anthropology, in An outline of modern knowledge, Rose, W. (ed.). London.

32-32 Mead, M. The changing culture of an Indian tribe. New York.

32-33 Means, P. A. Fall of the Inca empire and the Spanish rule in Peru, 1530−1780. New York.

32-34 Mekeel, S. A modern American Indian community in the light of its past: a study in cultural change. New Haven.

32-35 Mekeel, S. A discussion of culture change as illustrated by material from a Teton-Dakota community, AA, 34: 274−85.

32-36 Monteil, C. Djênnê; metropole du delta central du Niger. Paris.

32-37 Murray, H. Depopulation in Papua, Oc, 3: 207−13.

32-38 Nelson, N. C. The origin and development of material culture, SX, 20: 102−23.

32-39 Parsons, E. C. Zapoteca and Spanish tales of Mitla, Oaxaca, JAF, 45: 277−317.

32-40 Parsons, E. C. Folklore from Santa Ana Xalmimilulco, Puebla, Mexico, JAF, 45: 318−62.

32-41 Piddington, R. Psychological aspects of culture-contact, Oc, 3: 312−24.

32-42 Plischke, H. Das Zeitalter der Weltumsegelungsfahrten und die Naturvölker Ein Beitrag zur Geschichte der Völkerkunde, ArA, 22: 56−65.

32-43 Price, M. T. Social science materials in Far Eastern culture, AJS, 37: 748−59.

32-44 Radcliffe-Brown, A. R. The present position of anthropological studies, BAASR: 141−71.

32-45 Repa, T. Wi, Depopulation in New Zealand, Oc, 3: 227−34.

32-46 Roberts, H. H. The reason for the departure of the Pecos Indians for Jemez pueblo, AA, 34: 359−60.

32-47 Rôheim, G. Psychoanalysis of primitive cultural types, Int. Journ. of Psycho-Analysis, 13: 1−224. London.

32-48 Sapir, E. Cultural anthropology and psychiatry, JASP, 27: 229−42.

32-49 Solomons, E. V. The Arabs in Java, LM, 2: 266−67.

32-50 Stokes, J. F. G. Spaniards and the sweet potato in Hawaii and Hawaiian-American contacts, AA, 34: 594−600.

32-51 Thurnwald, R. The psychology of acculturation, AA, 34: 557−69.

32-52   Thurnwald, R. Social transformations in East Africa, AJS, 38: 175–84.
32-53   Tyagaraju, A. S. Sumero-Dravidian affinities, MS, 23: 222–28.
32-54   Wagner, G. Entwicklung und Verbreitung der Peyote-Kultur, BA, 15: 59ff.
32-55   Warner, W. L. Malay influence on the aboriginal cultures of north-eastern
        Arnheim Land, Oc, 2: 476–95.
32-56   Watt, K. S. Applied anthropology in Africa, SR, 24: 287–302.
32-57   Weinert, H. Ursprung der Menschheit. Stuttgart.
32-58   Westermarck, E. A. Early beliefs and their social influence. London.

1933

33-1   Adams, R. C. The peoples of Hawaii. IPRH.
33-2   Anderson, J. C. Maori music with its Polynesian background, JPS, 42,
        supplement: 141–88.
33-3   Archey, G. Evolution of certain Maori carving patterns, JPS, 42: 171–90.
33-4   Barbeau, M. Disappearance of the red man's culture, ScA, 148: 22–24.
33-5   Becker, H. Early generalizations concerning population movement and cul-
        ture contact: prolegomena to a study of mental mobility, SR, 25: 45–55,
        137–52, 218–32.
33-6   Cole, F.-C. The long road from savagery to civilization. Baltimore.
33-7   Cooper, J. M. The Cree Witiko psychosis, PM, 6: 20–24.
33-8   Durward, E. W. The Maori population of Otago, JPS, 42: 49–82.
33-9   Elkin, A. P. A policy for the aborigines. Morpeth, Australia.
33-10   Frobenius, L. Kulturgeschichte Afrikas. Zürich.
33-11   Garth, T. A. The intelligence and achievement of mixed blood Indians, JSP,
        4, 1: 134–37.
33-12   Goldenweiser, A. A. History, psychology, and culture. New York.
33-13   Gorodzov, V. A. The typological method in archaeology, AA, 35: 95–102.
33-14   Handy, E. S. C. Culture and education: what is the cultural destiny of
        Pacific peoples? PA, 6: 267–80.
33-15   Herskovits, M. J. On the provenience of New World Negroes, SF, 12: 247–
        62.
33-16   Hewitt, J. N. B. Status of women in Iroquois polity before 1784, SIR: 475–
        88.
33-17   Hodgen, M. T. Survivals and social origins: the pioneers, AJS, 38: 583–94.
33-18   Hunter, M. The effects of contact with Europeans on the status of the Pondo
        women, Af, 6: 259ff.
33-19   Izikowitz, K. G. L'origine probable de la technique du simili-velours
        péruvien, JSAP, 25: 9–16.
33-20   Jochelson, W. History, ethnology and anthropology of the Aleut. CIWP.
33-21   Jones, J. R. R. and Saffery, A. L. Social and economic conditions of native
        life in the Union, BS, 7: 235–55, 317–40; 8: 61–94, 193–211. 1933–34.
33-22   Keesing, F. M. Education and native peoples, PA, 5: 675–88.
33-23   Lesser, A. Cultural significance of the ghost dance, AA, 35: 108–15.
33-24   Lesser, A. The Pawnee ghost dance hand game; a study of cultural change,
        CUCA, 16.
33-25   MacLeod, W. C. Mortuary and sacrificial anthropophagy on the Northwest
        Coast of North America and its culture-historical sources, JSAP, 25,
        2: 335–66.
33-26   Marett, R. R. The growth and tendency of anthropological and ethnological

studies, Compte rendu, Congrès international des sciences anthropologique et ethnologiques, 1: 39—53, London.

33-27 Mendonça, R. A influencia africana no português do Brasil. Rio de Janeiro.

33-28 Mus, P. Cultes indiens et indigènes au champs, EFEOB, 33: 367—410.

33-29 Parsons, E. C. Some Aztec and pueblo parallels, AA, 35: 611—31.

33-30 Redfield, R. The Maya and modern civilization, SM, 37: 110—23.

33-31 Redfield, R. , and Villa Rojas, A. Chan Kom, a Maya village. CIWP, 448.

33-32 Rogers, H. Native administration in the Union of South Africa. BS, supp. 6. Johannesburg.

33-33 Róheim, G. The study of character development and the ontogenetic theory of culture, in Essays presented to C. G. Seligman: 281—93. London.

33-34 Sayce, R. U. Primitive arts and crafts. Cambridge.

33-35 Solanke, L. Yoruba constitutional law and its historical developments, Wasu, 2: 28—38.

33-36 Speck, F. G. Notes on the life of John Wilson, the revealer of peyote, as recalled by his nephew, George Anderson, General Magazine and Historical Chronicle, 36: 13—18.

33-37 Taylor, P. S. A Spanish-Mexican peasant community: Arandas in Jalisco, Mexico. IbA, 4.

33-38 Vanoverbergh, M. Philippine Negrito culture: independent or borrowed? PM, 6, 2: 25—35. Catholic Anthropological Conf. , Washington.

33-39 von Gasenapp, H. Die Inder in Guayana und Westindien, Ibero-Amerikenisches Archiv, 7: 295—305.

33-40 Westermarck, E. Pagan survivals in Mohammedan civilization. London.

33-41 Williams, F. E. Depopulation of Suau District, TPAR. 13.

33-42 Williams, F. E. Practical education: the reform of native horticulture. TPAR, 14.

33-43 Williams, J. J. Voodoos and obeahs, phases of West India Witchcraft. London.

1934

34-1 Ashton, J. W. Jack a Kent: the evolution of a folk figure, JAF, 47: 362—68.

34-2 Baker, A. G. , and Sarvis, G. W. Missions, culture and social change; review of Christian missions and a new world culture, Jnl. of Relig. , 14: 330—52.

34-3 Bartlett, K. Spanish contacts with the Hopi, Museum notes of the Museum of Northern Arizona, 6: 55—59.

34-4 Benedict, R. Patterns of culture. New York.

34-5 Benedict, R. Anthropology and the abnormal, JGP, 10: 59—82.

34-6 Bergmann, G. Eine papuanische Schwämerei. Neuendettelsauer Missionsblatt, 15, 4, S. 28.

34-7 Cooper, J. M. Mental disease situations in certain cultures; a new field for research, JAP, 29: 10—17.

34-8 Deacon, A. B. Malekula: a vanishing people in the New Hebrides. London.

34-9 Dollard, J. The psychotic person seen culturally, AJS, 39: 1—9.

34-10 Elkin, A. P. Anthropology and the future of the Australian aborigines, Oc, 5, 1: 1—18.

34-11 Embree, E. R. Objectives of colonial education, Political Quarterly, 5: 221—35.

34-12 Forde, C. D. Habitat, economy and society. London.

34-13   Goreaud, J. Les derniers Indiens guyanais, Reg. sur le monde, 25: 15–17.
34-14   Groves, W. C. Tabar today, Oc, 5: 221–41, 346–61; 6: 147–58. 1934–35.
34-15   Hallowell, A. I. Culture and mental disorder, JASP, 29: 1– 9.
34-16   Hellman. E. The native in the towns, in Schapera, I., Western civilization
        and the natives of South Africa. London.
34-17   Henzler, J. O. Culture contact and institutional change, in Reuter, E. B.
        (ed.), Race and culture contact: 48–56. New York.
34-18   Herskovits, M. J. and F. S. Rebel destiny: among the Bush Negroes of
        Dutch Guiana. New York.
34-19   Hewett, E. L. Quiriga revisited, SARR: 18–21.
34-20   Hogbin, H. I. Culture change in the Solomon Islands, Oc, 4: 233–67.
34-21   Hornell, J. Indonesian influence on East African culture, JRAI, 64: 305–32.
34-22   Hough, W. Domestication of animals, SM, 39: 144–50.
34-23   Hunter, M. Methods of study of culture contact, Af, 7: 335–50.
34-24   Jacobs, M. Notes on the structure of Chinook jargon, ICAP, 24: 257–58.
34-25   Keesing, F. M. Modern Samoa: its government and changing life. London
        and Stanford.
34-26   Keesing, F. M. The changing life of native peoples in the Pacific area,
        AJS, 39, 4: 443–58.
34-27   Keesing, F. M. Samoa: islands of conflict. Foreign Policy Association
        Report, 9, 26.
34-28   Keesing, F. M. and M. Taming Philippine headhunters: a study of govern-
        ment and culture change in North Luzon. London, Stanford.
34-29   Kennedy, R. Bark-cloth in Indonesia, JPS, 43: 229–43.
34-30   Klineberg, C. Notes on the Huichol, AA, 36: 446–60.
34-31   Lehmann, M. R. R. Prophetismus in Ozeanien, Christentum und Wissen-
        schaft, 10: 56–68.
34-32   MacLeod, W. C. The nature, origin and linkages of the rite of hookswing-
        ing: with special reference to North America, An, 29: 1–38.
34-33   MacLeod, W. C. Law, procedure, and punishment in early bureaucracies,
        J. Crim. Law, 25: 225–44.
34-34   Mair, L. P. An African people in the twentieth century. London.
34-35   Mair, L. P. The study of culture contact as a practical problem, Af, 7,
        4: 415–22.
34-36   Malinowski, B. Whither Africa? Review of Ntara, S. Y., Man of Africa,
        and Schapera, I. Western civilisation and the natives of South Africa,
        Intern. Rev. of Missions, 25: 401–07.
34-37   Métraux, A. L'organisation sociale et les survivances religiuses des
        Indiens Uru-Cipaya de Caraigas, ICAP, 25, 1: 191–213.
34-38   Moeller, A. Les grandes lignes des migrations des Bantous de la province
        orientale, BIRCB, 5: 63–111.
34-39   Montauban, P. Schwarmgeister auf den Salomonen, Kreuz und Karitas,
        Mai: 137ff.
34-40   Mühlmann, W. E. Die Begriffe 'Ati und Mataeinaa: ein Beitrag zur poli-
        tischen Entwicklung und Besiedlungsgeschichte Polynesiens, An, 29:
        739–56.
34-41   Nettelton, G. E. History of the Ngamiland tribes up to 1926, BS, 8: 343–60.
34-42   Opler, M. E. Anthropology and the abnormal, JGP, 10.
34-43   Petrullo, V. The diabolic root. Philadelphia.
34-44   Redfield, R. M. Culture change in Yucatan, AA, 36: 57–69.
34-45   Rôheim, G. The evolution of culture, Int. Jnl. of Psycho-Anal., 15: 381–
        418.

34-46   Sapir, E. Tne emergence of the concept of personality in a study of cultures, JSP, 5: 408—15.
34-47   Sarkar, H. B. Indian influences on the literature of Java and Bali. Calcutta.
34-48   Schapera, I. Labour migration from a Bechuanaland Reserve, Royal African Society, 1934.
34-49   Schapera, I. (ed.) Western civilization and the natives of South Africa. London.
34-50   Seligman, C. G. Egypt and Negro Africa; a study in divine kingship. London.
34-51   Steward, J. H. Two Paiute autobiographies, UCPAAE, 33: 423—28.
34-52   Westermann, D. The African today. London.
34-53   Williams, F. E. The Vailala madness in retrospect, in Essays in Honour of C. G. Seligman: 369—79. London.
34-54   Wissler, C. Rebirth of the vanishing American, NH, 34: 415—30.
34-55   Zunser, H. A New Mexican village, JAF, 48: 125—78.

1935

35-1   Bateson, G. Culture contact and schismogenesis, Mn, 199.
35-2   Baker, G. C. An experiment in applied anthropology, Af, 8: 304—14.
35-3   Beaglehole, E. and P. Hopi of the second mesa. AAAM, 44.
35-4   Bennett, W. C., and Zingg, R. M. The Tarahumara. Chicago.
35-5   Boas, F. The tempo of growth of fraternities, NASP, 21, 7.
35-6   Bodin, H. Migrations of mankind (trans. from Sociêtê des Etudes Ocêaniennes), JPS, 44: 124—29.
35-7   Bonnerjea, B. Reminiscences of a Cheyenne Indian, JSAP, 27: 129—43.
35-8   Brelsford, U. History and customs of the Basala, JRAI, 65: 205—15.
35-9   Brown, G. G., and Hutt, A. Anthropology in action. London.
35-10   Camavitto, D. La decadenza della popolazione messicane al tempo conquista. Rome.
35-11   Cantril, H. Psychological reason for the lag of non-material culture traits, SF, 13: 376—79.
35-12   Carriaga, R. R. The Filipinos in Honolulu, Social Science, 10, 1: 39—46.
35-13   Childe, V. G. Changing methods and aims in prehistory, PSP.
35-14   Childe, V. G. Man makes himself. London.
35-15   Coulter, C. W. Problems arising from industrialization of native life in Central Africa, AJS, 40: 582—92.
35-16   Culwick, A. T. and G. M. A method of studying changes in primitive marriage, JRAI, 65: 185—95.
35-17   Culwick, A. T. and G. M. Culture change on the fringe of civilisation in Africa, Af, 8: 163—70.
35-18   Davidson, D. S. The chronology of Australian watercraft, JPS, 44: 192—207.
35-19   Drapkin, I. Contribution to the demographic study of Easter Island, BPBMOP 11, 12.
35-20   Duff, R. Tribal Maori and the great society. Thesis, Canterbury University College, Christchurch.
35-21   Elkin, A. P. Civilized aborigines and native culture, Oc, 6: 117—46.
35-22   Elkin, A. P. A mission policy for primitive peoples, The Morpeth Review, 27.
35-23   Evans-Pritchard, E. E. Witchcraft, Af, 8: 417—42.
35-24   Gilfillan, S. C. The sociology of invention. Chicago.

35-25   Gonda, J. Indian influences on the literature of Java and Bali, IG, 57: 637–43.

35-26   Gray, I. M. Early history of Baganda, Uganda Journal, 2: 259–71.

35-27   Ganke, L. The first social experiments in America; a study in the development of Spanish Indian policy in the sixteenth century. Cambridge.

35-28   Hanson, E. P. Social regression in the Orinoco and Amazon basins, GR, 23: 578–98.

35-29   Hellman, E. Native life in a Johannesburg slum yard, AF, 8: 34–62.

35-30   Herskovits, M. J. Social history of the Negro, in A handbook of social psychology, Murchison, C. (ed.). Worcester.

35-31   Karsten, R. The head-hunters of Western Amazona: the life and culture of the Jibaro Indians . . . Societas Scientiarum Fennica: Commentationes Humanarum Litterarum, 7, 1. Helsingfors.

35-32   Keesing, F. M. Standards of living among native peoples of the Pacific, PA, 8, 3.

35-33   Klimek, S. Culture element distributions, I: the structure of California Indian culture, UCPAAE, 37, 1: 1–70.

35-34   Kroeber, A. L. History and science in anthropology, AA, 37: 539–69.

35-35   Lasswell, H. D. Collective autism as a consequence of culture contact, ZS, 4: 232–47.

35-36   Lewis, C. B. The part of the folk in the making of folklore, Fo, 46: 11137–75.

35-37   Lovén, S. Origins of the Tainan culture, West Indies. Göteborg.

35-38   Mead, M. Sex and temperament in three primitive societies. New York.

35-39   Mead, M. Review of Róheim, G., The riddle of the sphinx, CP, 3.

35-40   Mekeel, H. S. Clinic and culture, JAP, 30: 292–300.

35-41   Opler, M. E. The psychoanalytic treatment of culture, PR, 22: 138–57.

35-42   Parodi, L. R. Relaciaones de la agricultura prehispánica con la agricultura argentina actual, Anales de la Academia Nacional de Agronomía y Veterinaria, 1: 115–67. Buenos Aires.

35-43   Quaritch Wales, H. G. A newly-explored route of ancient Indian cultural expansion, IAL, 9: 1–31.

35-44   Radcliffe-Brown, A. R. On the concept of function in social science, AA, 37: 394–402.

35-45   Richards, A. I. A modern movement of witch finders, Af, 8: 448–62.

35-46   Richards, A. I. The village census in the study of culture contact, Af, 8, 20.

35-47   Sastri, K. A. N. L'origine de alphabet du Champa, EFEOB, 35: 233–41.

35-48   Schapera, I. Field methods in the study of modern culture contacts, Af, 8: 315–28.

35-49   Spier, L. The prophet dance of the Northwest and its derivatives. GS, 1.

35-50   Spiller, G. The origin and nature of man. London.

35-51   Stutterheim, W. F. Indian influences in old Balinese art. London.

35-52   Sutherland, I. L. G. The Maori situation. Wellington.

35-53   Taylor, D. The island Caribs of Dominica, AA, 37: 265–72.

35-54   Thompson, D. F. Notes on a hero cult from the Gulf of Carpenteria, JRAI, 64: 217–36.

35-55   Thurnwald, H. Die schwarze Frau im Wandel Afrikas, Stuttgart.

35-56   Thurnwald, R. T. Black and white in East Africa. London.

35-57   Thurnwald, R. T. Werden, Wandel und Gestaltung von Staat und Kultur. Berlin, Leipzig.

35-58 Thurnwald, R. T. Entwicklung und Kultur, Forsch, u. Fortschr., 11: 94–96.
35-59 Todd, J. A. Native offences and European law in southwest New Britain, Oc, 5: 437–60.
35-60 Turney-High, H. The diffusion of the horse to the Flatheads, Mn, 35: 183–85.
35-61 Williams, F. E. The blending of cultures: an essay on the aims of native education. TPAR, 16. (Republished as Papua and New Guinea Official Research Pub. 1. Port Moresby, 1951.)
35-62 Williams, H. W. The reaction of the Maori to the impact of civilization, JPS, 45: 216–43.
35-63 Wilkinson, R. J. Early Indian influences in Malaysia, JRASMB, 13, 2: 1–16.
35-64 Woodard, J. W. Intellectual realism and culture change. Hanover.
35-65 Závala, S. A. La encomienda indiana. Madrid.
35-66 Zipf, G. K. The psycho-biology of language, an introduction to dynamic philology. Boston.

1936

36-1 Alford, T. W. Civilization. Norman, Okla. (Shawnee autobiography).
36-2 Barbeau, M. The modern growth of the totem pole on the North-West coast, in Essays presented to R. R. Marett, Custom is King: 87–96.
36-3 Bateson, G. Naven. London.
36-4 Boas, F. History and science in anthropology: a reply, AA, 38: 137–41.
36-5 Brooke, F. A. The science of social development. London.
36-6 Buck, P. H. Regional diversity in the elaboration of sorcery in Polynesia. YUPA, 2.
36-7 Camavitto, D. Le leggi dell'evoluzione dei popoli e il Messico precortesiano. RdA, 31.
36-8 Cator, W. J. The economic position of the Chinese in the Netherlands Indies. Chicago.
36-9 De Jonghe, E. Formations récentes de sociétés secrètes au Congo Belge, Af, 9: 56–63.
36-10 De Laytono, D. Os africanismos do dialecto guacho. Porto Alegre.
36-11 Elkin, A. P. The reaction of primitive races to the white man's culture: a study in culture contact, The Hibbert Journal, 35: 537–45.
36-12 Firth, R. We the Tikopia. London.
36-13 Fitzgerald, W. Impact of western civilization on Negro Africa, GR, 26: 77–87.
36-14 Fortes, M. Culture contact as a dynamic process, Af, 9: 24–55.
36-15 Gillin, J. The configuration problem in culture, ASR, 1: 373–86.
36-16 Goldenweiser, A. A. Loose ends of a theory on the individual, pattern, and involution in primitive society, in Essays in anthropology presented to A. L. Kroeber, Lowie, R. H. (ed.): 99–104. Berkeley.
36-17 Groves, W. C. Native education and culture-contact in New Guinea. Melbourne.
36-18 Hallowell, A. I. The passing of the Midewiwin in the Lake Winnipeg region, AA, 38: 32–51.
36-19 Hallowell, A. I. Psychic stresses and culture patterns, AJP, 92: 1291–1310.
36-20 Harrisson, T. H. Savage civilization. London.

36-21 Herskovits, M. J. Applied anthropology and the American anthropologist, Sc, 83: 215—22.

36-22 Herskovits, M. J. Significance of West Africa for Negro research, JNH, 21: 15—30.

36-23 Herskovits, M. J. and F. S. Surinam folk-lore. New York.

36-24 Hestermann, F. Die Schmidtsche Kulturkreistheorie und Sprach-wissenschaft in Südamerika, Actes du Congrès international de linguistes: 199—203, Copenhagen.

36-25 Hilger, M. I. In the early days of Wisconsin, an amalgamation of Chippewa and European cultures, WA, 16: 32—49.

36-26 Hodgen, M. T. The doctrine of survivals. London.

36-27 Holden, W. C. Studies of the Yaqui Indians of Sonora, Mexico. Texas Tech. Bull. of Science, Series 2. Lubbock.

36-28 Hunter, M. Reaction to conquest: effects of conflict on the Pondo of South Africa. Oxford.

36-29 Keesing, F. M. Hawaiian homesteading on Molokai, UHRP, 12.

36-30 Kluckhohn, C. Some reflections on the method and theory of the Kulturkreislehre, AA, 38, 2: 157—96.

36-31 Koppers, W. Der Totemismus als menschheitsgeschichtliches Problem, An, 31: 159—76.

36-32 Kroeber, A. L. Culture element distributions, III: area and climax, UCPAAE, 37, 3: 101—16.

36-33 Lévy-Bruhl, L. The Cartesian spirit and history, in Philosophy and history, Klibanksy, R. and Paton, H. J. (eds.): 11—25. London.

36-34 Lighthall, W. D. Is the end of the diffusion-of-culture controversy in sight? RSCT, 30, 2: 49—55.

36-35 Linton, R. The study of man. New York.

36-36 Linton, R. Errors in anthropology, in The story of human error, Jastrow, J. (ed.): 292—321. New York.

36-37 Mair, L. P. Native policies in Africa. London.

36-38 Malinowski, B. Native education and culture contact, Int. Rev. of Missions, 25: 480—515.

36-39 Malinowski, B. Culture as a determinant of behavior, SM, 43: 440—49.

36-40 Marett, R. R. Tylor. London.

36-41 Maude, H. E. Culture change and education in the Gilbert and Ellice islands, Seminar-Conference on education in Pacific countries, Proceedings (mimeographed). Honolulu.

36-42 Mekeel, H. S. An anthropologist's observations on Indian education, Progressive Education, 13, 3: 151—59.

36-43 Mekeel, H. S. The economy of a modern Teton Dakota community. YUPA, 6.

36-44 Meyers, M. and Cushing, H. Types and incidence of behavior problems in relation to cultural background, AJO, 6: 110ff.

36-45 Mühlmann, W. Rassen- und Völkerkunde. Lebensprobleme der Rassen, Gesellschaften und Völker. Braunschweig.

36-46 Mukerjee, R. Migrant Asia. Rome.

36-47 Opler, M. E. The influence of aboriginal pattern and white contact on a recently introduced ceremony, the Mescalero peyote rite, JAF, 49: 143—66.

36-48 Parsons, E. C. Mitla: town of the souls. Chicago.

36-49 Parsons, E. C. Early relations between Hopi and Keres, AA, 38: 554—60.

36-50 Pellegrin, A. Culture arabe et culture française en Afrique du Nord, R. Pol. et Litt., 74: 843—46.

36-51 Pemberton, H. E. A curve of culture diffusion rate, ASR, 1: 547—56.

36-52 Perham, M. F. (ed.) Ten Africans. London.

36-53 Ray, V. F. The Kolaskin cult: a prophet movement of 1870 in Northeastern Washington, AA, 38: 67—75.

36-54 Redfield, R., Linton, R., and Herskovits, M. J. A memorandum on acculturation, AA, 38: 149—52.

36-55 Rentse, A. Majapahit amulets in Kelantan, JRASMB, 14, 3: 302—04.

36-56 Sands, W. F. Mexico in evolution, ASc, 5: 199—211.

36-57 Schapera, I. The contributions of western civilisation to modern Ba Kxatla culture, RSSAT, 24, 3: 221—52.

36-58 Schwidetzky, J. Anthropologie und Geschichtswissenschaft, Zeit. für Rassenkunde, 4: 268—84.

36-59 Shapiro, H. Heritage of the "Bounty." New York.

36-60 Spier, O. Die Geschichte von Dschewri Tschelebi, An, 31: 800—20.

36-61 Stephen, A. M. Hopi journal, Parsons, E. C. (ed.). CUCA, 23.

36-62 Strong, W. D. Anthropological theory and archaeological fact, in Essays in anthropology presented to A. L. Kroeber. Berkeley.

36-63 Taylor, D. Additional notes on the island Carib of Dominica, AA, 38: 462—68.

36-64 Thurnwald, R. C. The crisis of imperialism in East Africa and elsewhere, SF, 15: 84—91.

36-65 Thurnwald, R. C. The price of the white man's peace, PA, 9: 347—52.

36-66 Thurnwald, R. C. Contributions toward analysis of the mechanism of culture. I: Civilization and culture. II: Progress viewed as a component in the configuration of culture, ASR, 1: 387—95, 604—13.

36-67 Trimborn, H. Fuentes de la historia cultural de la América precolumbina. Stuttgart (with German translation).

36-68 Van der Noot, A. Quelques éléments historiques sur l'empire luba, son organisation et sa direction, Bull. des Juridictions Indigènes et du Droit Coutumier Congolais, 4: 141—49.

36-69 Vroklage, B. Kulturströmungen an der Nordküste Neuguineas, Tropisch Nederland, 9: 103—08.

36-70 Wedgwood, C. H. Report on research work in Nauru island, Central Pacific, Oc, 6: 359—91; 7: 1—33.

36-71 Westermarck, E. The future of marriage in western civilization. New York.

36-72 Whitehead, G. O. A note on Bari history, Sudan Notes and Records, 19: 152—57.

36-73 Wilbur, C. M. The history of the crossbow, SIR: 427—38.

36-74 Williams, F. E. Bull-roarers in the Papuan Gulf. TPAR, 17.

36-75 Wissler, C. Population changes among the northern plains Indians. YUPA, 1.

36-76 Wissler, C. Changes in population profiles among the northern Plains Indians, AMNHP, 36, 1: 1—67.

1937

37-1 Arensberg, C. M. The Irish countryman: an anthropological study. New York

37-2   Bateson, G. An old temple and a new myth, Overdruk uit Djawa, 5, 6: 1–18.
37-3   Beaglehole, E. Emotional release in a Polynesian community, JAP, 32: 319–28.
37-4   Beaglehole, E. Some Modern Hawaiians. UHRP, 19.
37-5   Bowers, R. V. The direction of intra-societal diffusion, ASR, 2: 826–36.
37-6   Childe, V. G. A prehistorian's interpretation of diffusion, in Independence, convergence, and borrowing in institutions, thought, and art: 3–21. Cambridge.
37-7   Collins, H. B. Culture migrations and contacts in the Bering Sea region, AA, 39: 375–84.
37-8   Cunow, H. Geschichte und Kultur des Inkareiches. Amsterdam.
37-9   Danckert, W. Musikethnologische Erschliessung der Kulturkreise, MAGW, 67, 1–2: 53–57.
37-10   DuBois, C. Some psychological objectives and techniques in ethnography, JSP, 8: 285–300.
37-11   DuBois, C. Some anthropological perspectives on psychoanalysis, PR, 24: 254ff.
37-12   Eckert, A. Prophetentum in Melanesien, ZE, 69: 135–40.
37-13   Eggan, F. Historical changes in the Choctaw kinship system, AA, 39: 34–52.
37-14   Erickson, E. H. Observations on Sioux education, JP, 7: 101–56.
37-15   Fettweis, E. Ueber die Entwicklung des räumlichen Vorstellungsvermögens bei Völkern nichteuropider Rasse und in der europäischen Vorzeit, St, 62: 13–21.
37-16   Forde, C. D. Social change in a West African community, Mn, 5.
37-17   Frazer, J. G. Aftermath. A supplement to the Golden Bough. New York.
37-18   Goldenweiser, A. A. Anthropology. New York.
37-19   Hallowell, A. I. Temporal orientation in western civilization and in a preliterate society, AA, 39: 647–70.
37-20   Hawley, F. M. Pueblo social organization as a lead to Pueblo history, AA, 39: 504–22.
37-21   Heine-Geldern, R. von. L'art prebouddhique de la Chine et l'Asie du Sud-Est et son influence on Océanie, Revue des arts asiatiques, 11: 177–206.
37-22   Herskovits, M. J. The significance of the study of acculturation for anthropology, AA, 39: 259–64.
37-23   Herskovits, M. J. African gods and Catholic saints in New World Negro belief, AA, 39: 635–43.
37-24   Herskovits, M. J. Life in a Haitian valley. New York.
37-25   Hutton, J. H. Assam origins in relation to Oceania, Na, 140: 487–89.
37-26   Hyde, G. E. Red Cloud's folk. U. of Oklahoma.
37-27   Keesing, F. M. Education in Pacific Countries. Report of seminar-conference of educators, anthropologists, and others, Yale U. and U. of Hawaii. Honolulu and Shanghai.
37-28   Keesing, F. M. The taupo system of Samoa—a study of institutional change, Oc, 8, 1–14.
37-29   Kennard, E. A. Hopi reactions to death, AA, 39: 491–96.
37-30   Landes, R. The Ojibwa of Canada, in Cooperation and competition among primitive peoples, Mead, M. (ed.) New York.
37-31   Lastres, J. B. Las causas de la enfermedades nerviosas en el antiguo Peru, RMN, 6, 1,: 25–42.
37-32   Leenhardt, M. Gens de la grande terre. Paris.

37-33   Leenhardt, M. Le temps et la personnalité chez les Canaques de la Nouvelle Calédonie, Rev. Philos., 124: 43–58.

37-34   Leighton, A. H. Twilight of the Indian porpoise hunters, NH, 40: 410–16.

37-35   Lowie, R. H. The history of ethnological theory. New York.

37-36   Lynd, R. S. and Lynd, H. M. Middletown in transition; a study in cultural conflicts. New York.

37-37   Majumdar, D. N. A tribe in transition: a study in culture pattern. London.

37-38   Mandelbaum, D. G. Boom periods in the history of an Indian tribe, SF, 16: 117–119.

37-39   Markley, M. C. Archaeology as a tool for use in predicting the permanency of agriculture, Sc, 86: 492–93.

37-40   Mead, M. and others. Cooperation and competition among primitive peoples. New York.

37-41   Mekeel, S. The social science approach to case work with the American Indian, Family, 18: 204–07.

37-42   Mirsky, J. The Dakota, in Cooperation and competition among primitive peoples, Mead M. (ed.). New York.

37-43   Murphy, G. Personality and social adjustments, SF, 15: 472ff.

37-44   Nash, P. The role of religious revivalism in the formation of an intercultural community on Klamath Reservation, in Social anthropology of North American tribes, Eggan, F. (ed.). Chicago.

37-45   Nevermann, H. Altes und Neues in der heutigen Kultur der Gesellschaftsinseln, Ethnologischer Anzeiger 4: 99–105.

37-46   Pemberton, H. E. The effect of a social crisis on the curve of diffusion, ASR, 2: 55–61.

37-47   Perham, M. F. Native administration in Nigeria. London.

37-48   Radin, P. Primitive religion: its nature and origin. New York.

37-49   Redfield, R. The second epilogue to Maya history, CISP, 28. (Also Hispan. Am. Hist. Rev., 17: 170–81.)

37-50   Sapir, E. The contribution of psychiatry to an understanding of behavior in society, AJS, 42: 862–70.

37-51   Sarasin, F. Uber die Geschichte des Ankers, VNGB, 49: 9–53.

37-52   Schaeffer, C. The first Jesuit mission to the Flathead, 1840–1850: a study in culture conflicts, Pac. Northwest Quart., 28: 227–50.

37-53   Schapera, I. Cultural changes in tribal life, in The Bantu-speaking tribes of South Africa: 368ff. London.

37-54   Schrieke, B. The American Negro and the colonial native: education and equality, PA, 10: 289–304.

37-55   Schmidt, W. Handbuch der Methode der kulturhistorischen Ethnologie, Münster.

37-56   Schultes, R. E. Peyote and the American Indian, Nature Magazine, 30: 155–57.

37-57   Shirokogoroff, S. M. Ethnographie und Ethnologie; zur Lage der modernen Völkerkunde; ausschnitt aus dem Vorwork zu dem Werk "Psychomental complex of the Tungus," Mühlmann, W. (trans.), ArA, 52: 1–7.

37-58   Sorokin, P. Social and cultural dynamics. New York.

37-59   Tax, S. Municipios of the midwestern highlands of Guatemala, AA, 39: 423–44.

37-60   Thurnwald, H. Menschen der Südsee. Charaktere und Schicksale. Stuttgart.

37-61   Thurnwald, R. Entwicklung und Fortschritt im Lichte der Völkerforschung, Trav. du IXe Congr. Intern. d. Philos., Paris: 175–81.
37-62   Thurnwald, R. Contributions toward analysis of the mechanism of culture. III Cultural rotation, its propulsion and rhythm. IV The spell of limited possibilities, ASR, 2: 26–42, 195–203.
37-63   Tommasini, G. La civilización cristiana del Chaco. Buenos Aires.
37-64   Voegelin, E. W. Suicide in northeastern California, AA, 39: 445–56.
37-65   Williams, F. E. Native art and education, ANZAASR, 23.
37-66   Wilson, G. H. Native government in South Africa, ER, 148: 582–87.
37-67   Wissler, C. Twilight of the old West, NH, 39: 307–17.
37-68   Wissler, C. The Indian and the white man's buffalo, NH, 40: 625–30.
37-69   White, L. A. Some suggestions for a program in anthropology in China, Chin. Soc. Pol. Sci. Rev., 21: 120–34.

1938

38-1   Alvarez, W. C. The emergence of modern medicine from ancient folk ways, SIAR: 409–30.
38-2   Ayrosa, P. M. S. Subsidios para o estudo da influencia do tupí na fonologia portugesa. Analo do primeiro Congresso de lingua nacional cantada. Prefeitura do municipio de São Paulo: 679–90. São Paulo.
38-3   Anderson, J. M. Change and personality, J. Philos., 35: 505–17.
38-4   Barbeau, C. M. Modern growth of the totem pole on the Northwest coast, JWAS, 28: 385–93.
38-5   Barrett, J. W. Australian aborigines, Na, 141: 476ff.
38-6   Beaglehole, E. Note on cultural compensation, JAP, 33: 121–23.
38-7   Beals, R. L. Reply to Hawley's "Pueblo social organization," AA, 40: 340–41.
38-8   Benedict, R. Continuities and discontinuities in cultural conditioning, Ps, 1: 161–67.
38-9   Blumenthal, A. The relations between culture, human social interaction, personality and history. Marietta, Ohio.
38-10   Boas, F. "Invention," in General anthropology, Boas, F. (ed.). Boston.
38-11   Bowers, R. V. Differential intensity of intra-societal diffusion, ASR, 3: 21–31.
38-12   Bruens, A. Catholic study of the pygmy, Cath. World, 147: 220–23.
38-13   Buck, P. H. My people, the Maoris, As, 38: 581–86.
38-14   Burrows, E. G. Western Polynesia, a study in cultural differentiation, EtS, 17: 1–192. Göteborg.
38-15   Childe, V. G. The Orient and Europe, Na, 142: 557–59, 600–603.
38-16   Coolidge, D. and M. R. The last of the Seris. New York.
38-17   Davis, E. C. See the funny white man! How we look to savages, summarized in a collection of 700 pictures of natives' portrayals of Europeans, Science News Letter, 34: 102–03.
38-18   Davidson, D. S. Northwestern Australia and the question of influences from the East Indies, Am. Orient. Soc. Journ., 58: 61–80.
38-19   De Klerck, E. S. History of the Netherlands East Indies. 2 vols. Rotterdam.
38-20   Delawarde, J. B. Les Derniers Caraibes. Leur vie dans une réserve de la Dominique, JSAP, 30: 167–204.

38-21   Densmore, F. The influence of hymns on the form of Indian songs, AA, 40: 175–77.

38-22   Dyk, W. Son of Old Man Hat. New York.

38-23   Emeneau, M. B. Toda culture thirty-five years after: an acculturation study, Annals of the Bhandarkar Oriental Research Institute, 19: 101–31.

38-24   Fêng Han-Yi and Shryrock, J. K. The historical origins of the Lolo, Harvard J. of Oriental Studies, 3, 2: 103–27.

38-25   Fortes, M. Culture contact as a dynamic process, in Methods of study of culture contact in Africa. Memorandum 15, IIALC.

38-26   Fortes, M. Social and psychological aspects of education in Taleland. London.

38-27   Fox, W. S. How the melting pot melts, RSCT, 32, 2: 1–14.

38-28   Frobenius, L. Denkformen vergangener Menschheit, St, 64: 135–44.

38-29   Goldenweiser, A. A. The concept of causality in the physical and social sciences, ASR, 3: 624–36.

38-30   Gorer, G. Himalayan village. London.

38-31   Haines, F. Where did the Plains Indians get their horses? AA, 40: 112–17.

38-32   Haines, F. The northward spread of horses among the Plains Indians, AA, 40: 429–37.

38-33   Hallowell, A. I. Fear and anxiety as cultural and individual variables in a primitive society, JSP, 9: 25–47.

38-34   Hallowell, A. I. Shabwan: a dissocial Indian girl, AJO, 8: 329–40.

38-35   Hallowell, A. I. The incidence, character and decline of polygamy among the Lake Winnipeg Cree and Salteaux, AA, 40: 235–56.

38-36   Heine-Geldern, R. Kunststile und Kulturwanderungen in Südostasien und Ozeanien, ZE, 70: 310–30.

38-37   Henríquez Ureña, P. Para la historia de los indigenismos. Facultad de filosofia y letras de la Universidad de Buenos Aires, Instituto de filología, Buenos Aires.

38-38   Herskovits, M. J. Acculturation: the study of culture contact. New York.

38-39   Hewett, E. L. Conservation of culture, EP, 44, 3–4: 30–37.

38-40   Holden, W. H. Civilization and sudden death, NH, 42, 5: 328–37.

38-41   Hutton, J. H. Anthropology as an imperial study; abstract, Na, 141: 699–700.

38-42   Junod, H. P. Bantu heritage. Johannesburg.

38-43   Keesing, F. M. Population and land utilization among the Lepanto, Northern Philippines, Proceedings, International Congress of Geographers, Amsterdam, 3C, 2: 458–64.

38-44   La Barre, W. The peyote cult. YUPA, 19.

38-45   Landes, R. The abnormal among the Ojibwa Indians, JAP, 33: 14–33.

38-46   Landes, R. The personality of the Ojibwa, CP, 6: 51–60.

38-47   Landes, R. The Ojibwa woman. New York.

38-48   Landtman, G. The origin of the inequality of the social classes. Chicago.

38-49   Lehmann, W. Die Geschichte der Königreiche von Colhuacan und Mexico. Stuttgart.

38-50   Lindgren, E. J. An example of culture contact without conflict: Reindeer Tungus and Cossacks of Northeastern Manchuria, AA, 40: 605–62.

38-51   Linton, R. Culture, society, and the individual, JASP, 33: 425–36.

38-52   Linton, R. The present status of anthropology, Sc, 87: 241–48.

38-53   Luomala, K. Navaho life of yesterday and today. Nat'l. Park Service,
        Berkeley.
38-54   Mair, L. P. (ed.) Methods of study of culture contact in Africa. Memoran-
        dum 15, IIALC. London, New York.
38-55   Mair, L. P. The place of history in the study of culture contact, in Methods
        of study of culture contact in Africa. Memorandum 15, IIALC.
38-56   Malinowski, B. Anthropology of changing African cultures, in Methods of
        study of culture contact in Africa. Memorandum 15, IIALC.
38-57   Malinowski, B. Modern anthropology and European rule in Africa. Rome.
38-58   Mühlmann, W. Methodikder Völkerkunde. Stuttgart.
38-59   Mühlmann, W. Biologie und Geisteswissenchaften; zur uberwindung der
        Antithetik von Natur und Geschichte, ArA, 52: 89–95.
38-60   Nevermann, H. Indonesische Einflüsse auf Neuguinea, Mitt. der Gesell.
        f. Völkerkunde, 8: 17–24.
38-61   Nordenskiöld, E. An historical and ethnological survey of the Cuna Indians.
        Comparative Ethnl. Studies, 10, Göteborg Museum Ethnografisk a
        Avdelningen. Göteborg, Sweden.
38-62   Opler, M. E. Use of peyote by the Carrizo and Lipan Apache tribes, AA,
        40: 271–85.
38-63   Opler, M. E. Dirty Boy: A Jicarilla tale of raid and war, AAAM, 52.
38-64   Pemberton, H. E. Spatial order of cultural diffusion, ASR, 22: 246–51.
38-65   Phillips, R. E. The Bantu in the city; a study of cultural adjustment in
        Witwatersrand. Lovedale.
38-66   Read, M. Native standards of living and African culture change. Memoran-
        dum 16, IIALC.
38-67   Reinecke, J. E. "Pidgin English" in Hawaii, AJS, 43: 778–89.
38-68   Sapir, E. Why cultural anthropology needs the psychiatrist, Ps, 1: 7–12.
38-69   Sayce, R. U. The ecological study of culture, St, 63: 279–85.
38-70   Schapera, I. Contact between European and native in South Africa, in
        Methods of study of culture contact in Africa. Memorandum 15, IIALC.
38-71   Schultze-Jena, L. Indiana: Band III. Bei den Azteken, Mixteken und
        Tlapaneken der Sierra Madre del Sur van Mexico. Jena.
38-72   Sellin, J. T. Culture conflict and crime. SSRCB, 41.
38-73   Steward, J. H., and Setzler, F. M. Function and configuration in archae-
        ology, AAq, 4: 4–10.
38-74   Sydow, E. von. Ancient and modern art in Benin city, Af, 11: 55–62.
38-75   Taylor, D. The Caribs of Dominica, BAEP, 3, 119: 103–60.
38-76   Thompson, L. M. The culture history of the Lau islands, Fiji, AA, 40:
        181–98.
38-77   Thomson, D. F. Policy and the aborigines of Australia; abstract, Na, 141:
        68; 142: 106.
38-78   Thurnwald, R. C. The African in transition: some comparisons with Mela-
        nesia, Af, 11.
38-79   Thurnwald, R. C. Africa and Melanesia in transition; abstract, Na, 141:
        1061.
38-80   Thurnwald, R. C. Europaër und Eingeborene in Ostafrika, Reale Accademia
        d'Italia, Fondazione Alessandro Volta, 8: 1–14. Roma.
38-81   Thurnwald, R. C. Zur Völkerpsychologie ungarisher Bauern . . . ArA,
        24: 281–83.
38-82   Tomori, V. Zur Psychologie der ungarischen Volksbrauche, Ungarische
        Jahrbücher, 17, 4.

38-83 Townsend, J. G. Disease and the Indian, SMo, 47: 479—95.

38-84 Tschopik, H. Taboo as a possible factor involved in the obsolescence of Navaho pottery and basketry, AA, 40: 257—62.

38-85 Tüting, L. (Thompson, L.) Kulturgeschichte der Lauinseln (Fidschigruppe), ArA, 24: 140—51.

38-86 Wauchope, R. Modern Maya houses. A study of their archaeological significance. CIWP, 502.

38-87 Westermann, D. Die Völker Africas Heute und Morgen, St, 64: 221—28.

38-88 Wissler, C. Depression and revolt; the story of the last Indian uprising and its youth movement, NH, 41: 108—12.

38-89 Wissler, C. Sitting with the Indian judges, NH, 41: 271—74.

38-90 Woodward, A. A brief history of Navaho silversmithing. Museum of Norther Arizona, Bull. 14. Flagstaff.

38-91 Zelenin, D. Les peuples de l'extrême nord après la grande révolution socialiste d'Octobre. Sovetskaia Arkheologiia, Moscow, 1: 15—52.

1939

39-1 Aginsky, B. W. Time levels in societal analysis; role of the family in aboriginal society, AA, 41: 416—32.

39-2 Aginsky, B. W. Psychopathic trends in culture, CP, 7: 331—43.

39-3 Barbeau, C. M. Deux cents ans d'orfèvrerie chez nous, RSCT, 33, 1: 183—91.

39-4 Barbeau, C. M. Indian silversmiths on the Pacific coast, RSCT, 33, 2: 23—28.

39-5 Basadre, J. El estado de los Incas, ICAP, 27, 2: 385—89.

39-6 Bates, D. Passing of the aborigines. New York.

39-7 Beaglehole, E. Culture and psychosis in New Zealand. JPS, 48: 144—55.

39-8 Beaglehole, E. Some modern Hawaiians. UHRP, 19.

32-9 Bloom, L. A Cherokee clan: a study in acculturation, AA, 41: 266—68.

39-10 Brockelmann, C. Geschichte der islamischen Völker und Staaten. München, Berlin.

39-11 Buck, P. H. Anthropology and Religion. New Haven.

39-12 Burrows, E. G. Relations between Chinese and Japanese in Hawaii during the Sino-Japanese conflict. IPRHB.

39-13 Carpenter, T. M., and Steggerda, M. The food of the present-day Navaho Indians of New Mexico and Arizona, Journal of Nutrition, 18: 297—305. Springfield, Ill.

39-14 Chapple, E. D. Quantitative analysis of the interaction of individuals, NASP, 25: 58—67.

39-15 Cooper, J. M. Is the Algonquian family hunting ground system pre-Columbian? AA, 41: 66—90.

39-16 Cooper, J. M. A note on adjustment and culture, PM, 12: 57—59.

39-17 Culwick, G. M. New ways for old in the treatment of adolescent African girls, Af, 12, 4: 425—32.

39-18 Devereux, G. Maladjustment and social neurosis, ASR, 4: 844—51.

39-19 Dmitrievsky, I. Kingdom of the reindeer: the Evenks, As, 39: 328—31.

39-20 Dollard, J. Culture, society, impulse, and socialization, AJS, 45: 50—63.

39-21 DuBois, C. The 1870 ghost dance. UCAR, 3.

39-22 Du Bois, W. E. B. Black folk then and now. New York.

39-23 East, R. (ed. and trans.) Akiga's story: the Tiv tribe as seen by one of its members. IIALC. London, New York.

39-24 Ekvall, R. B. Cultural relations on the Kansu-Tibetan border. Chicago Univ. Press.

39-25 Ellenberger, V. History of the Batlokwa of Guberones, BS 13, 3: 165–98.

39-26 Embree, J. F. New local and kin groups among the Japanese farmers of Kona, Hawaii, AA, 41, 3: 400–07.

39-27 Emeneau, M. B. Christian Todas, APSP, 81, 1: 93–106.

39-28 Erickson, E. H. Observations on Sioux education, JP, 7: 101–156.

39-29 Fleure, H. J. Folk-lore and culture-contacts, John Rylands Library Bulletin, 23: 403–16.

39-30 Ford, C. S. Society, culture, and the human organism, JGP, 20: 135–79.

39-31 Forde, C. D. Human geography, history and sociology, The Scottish Geographical Magazine, 45: 217–35.

39-32 Fortune, R. F. (ed.) Yao society: a study of a group of primitives in China, Lingnan Science Journal, 19: 324, 341–455. Canton.

39-33 Gifford, E. W. Typology for archaeology, ICAP, 27, 2: 7–11.

39-34 Gillin, J. Some unfinished business in cultural anthropology, Ohio Archaeological and Historical Quarterly, 48: 44–52.

39-35 Gusinde, M. Der Peyote-Kult, St. Gabriel Festschrift, Wien-Mödling: 401–99.

39-36 Hallowell, A. I. Some European folktales of the Berens River Salteaux, JAF, 52: 155–79.

39-37 Hallowell, A. I. The child, the savage, and human experience, Proceedings, Sixth Institute on the Exceptional Child, Child Research Clinic of the Woods School: 8–34.

39-38 Halpern, L. Un mariage chez les tarasques, ICAP, 27, 2: 493–500.

39-39 Hart, H. The culture-complex concept as a research tool, SF, 18: 10–17.

39-40 Haekel, J. Uber Wesen und Ursprung des Totemismus, MAGW, 69, 3: 243–60.

39-41 Herskovits, M. J. The ancestry of the American Negro, ASc, 8, 1: 84–94.

39-42 Hill, W. W. Stability in culture and pattern: the Night Way chant of the Navaho, AA, 41: 258–60.

39-43 Hogbin, H. I. Experiments in civilization. London.

39-44 Janowsky, L. B. Conversion of a pagan American, Mission Review, 62: 77–79.

39-45 Jansen, H. J. Ethnographische bi bijzonderheden van enkele Ambonsche negorijen, BTLVI, 98, 3: 325–68.

39-46 Kardiner, A., and Linton, R. The individual and his society. New York.

39-47 Keesing, F. M. The Menomini Indians of Wisconsin, a study of three centuries of cultural change. APSM, 11.

39-48 Keesing, F. M. Some notes on acculturation study, PSCP, 4.

39-49 Kirk, W. Social change among the highland Indians of Guatemala, SSR, 23: 321–33.

39-50 Kluckhohn, C. Theoretical basis for an empirical method of studying the acquisition of culture by individuals, Mn, 38, 89.

39-51 Kluckhohn, C. On certain recent applications of association coefficients to ethnological data, AA, 41: 345–77.

39-52 Kroeber, A. L. Cultural and natural areas of native North America. Berkeley.

39-53 Ledón, L. C. Estado de Castellanización de México, ICAP, 27, 2: 563–67.

39-54   Lesser, A. Research procedure and laws of culture, PSc, 6: 345—55.

39-55   Linton, R. The effects of culture on mental and emotional processes, Res. Pub. Assoc. Nerv. Ment. Diseases, 19: 293—304.

39-56   Lips, J. E. Naskapi trade—a study in legal acculturation, JSAP, 31: 129—95.

39-57   Majumdar, D. N. Tribal cultures and acculturation, MIA, 19: 99—173.

39-58   Malinowski, B. The present state of studies in culture contact, Af, 12: 27—47.

39-59   Malinowski, B. The dynamics of contemporary diffusion, Congrès International des Sciences Anthropologiques et Ethnologiques: 357—60. Copenhagen.

39-60   Manê, J. I. R. Sistemas de gobierno y organización de las provincias de la Nueva Espana en la Colonia, ICAP, 27, 2: 598—602.

39-61   Meinhard, H. The Javanese wayang and its Indian prototype, Mn, 39, 109—11

39-62   Mengin, E. Unos annales históricos de la nacion mexicana. BA, 22, 2—3; 23, 4. 1939—1940.

39-63   Mera, H. P. Style trends of Pueblo pottery in the Rio Grande and Little Colorado cultural areas from the sixteenth to the nineteenth century. Santa Fe.

39-64   Miner, H. St. Denis: a French-Canadian parish. Chicago.

39-65   Nandris, G. Earliest contacts between Slavs and Romanians, Slavonic Review, 18: 142—54.

39-66   Newcomb, F. J. How the Navaho adopt rites, EP, 46: 25—27.

39-67   Noone, H. D. Chinchem: a study of the role of dream-experience in culture-contact amongst the Temiar Senoir of Malaya, Mn, 39: 57.

39-68   Opler, M. E. Description of a Tonkawa peyote meeting held in 1902, AA, 41: 433—39.

39-69   Parsons, E. C. The Franciscans return to Zuni, AA, 41: 337—38.

39-70   Powdermaker, H. After freedom, a cultural study of the Deep South. New York.

39-71   Radin, P. The mind of primitive man, New Republic, 98: 300—03.

39-72   Raglan, Lord. How came civilization. London.

39-73   Redfield, R. Culture contact without conflict: the Ladinos and the Indians of Guatemala, AA, 41: 514—17.

39-74   Reichard, G. Dezba: woman of the desert. New York.

39-75   Roe, F. G. From dogs to horses among the western Indian tribes, RSCT, 33: 209—75.

39-76   Rôheim, G. Racial differences in the neurosis and psychosis, Ps, 2: 375—90.

39-77   Rouse, B. I. Prehistory in Haiti, a study in method. YUPA, 21.

39-78   Sanielevici, H. Une loi de l'évolution sociale, RA, 49, 4—6: 116—23.

39-79   Schmidt, W. The culture historical method of ethnology, Sieber, S. A. (trans.). New York.

39-80   Schmidt, W. Ursprung und Entwicklung des Eigentums, Sc, 65: 47—58.

39-81   Shapiro, H. L. Migration and environment. London.

39-82   Shyrock, R. H. Cultural factors in the history of the South, Journal of Southern History, 5, 3: 333—46.

39-83   Sims, N. LeR. The problem of social change. New York.

39-84   Stern, B. J. The family and cultural change, ASR, 4: 199—208.

39-85   Steward, J. H. Changes in Shoshonean Indian culture, SM, 49: 524—37.

39-86 Stutterheim, W. F. Note on cultural relations between South-India and Java, TITLV, 79: 73–84.

39-87 Swanton, J. R. Survival of horses brought to North America by de Soto, AA, 41: 170–71.

39-88 Swanton, J. R. Some thoughts on the problem of progress and decline. Sc, 89: 253–58.

39-89 Tax, S. Culture and civilization in Guatemalan societies, SM, 48: 463–67.

39-90 Thurnwald, R. Kolonial Gestaltung. Methode und Probleme überseeischer Ausdehnung. Hamburg.

39-91 Vaillant, G. C. Twilight of the Aztec civilization; ancient Mexican painting . . . sheds new light on Spain's 16th century colonial enterprise, NH, 43: 38–46.

39-92 Vu-Van-Quang. Le problème des Eurasiens en Indochine. Dans Viet Nam, le Peuple Vietnamien, 112. Hanoi.

39-93 Wagner, G. Die traditionelle und die moderne Familie bei den Bantu-Kavirondo, ArA, 53, 1: 1–35.

39-94 Wagner, G. The changing family among the Bantu Kavirondo, Af, 12, 1, supplement.

39-95 Wallis, W. D. Religion in primitive society. New York.

39-96 Westermann, D. The African today and tomorrow. New York. (revised from 1933 edition).

39-97 Whitman, W. Xube, a Ponca autobiography, JAF, 52: 180–93.

39-98 Woodward, J. W. Culture evolution and the social order, Jnl. Social Philosophy, 4, 4: 313–26.

39-99 Zingg, R. M. A reconstruction of Uto-Aztecan history. U. of Denver Contributions to Ethnology, 2. New York.

1940

40-1   Aginsky, B. W. and Buck, P. H. Interacting forces in the Maori family, AA, 42, 2: 195–210.

40-2   Arensberg, C. M. and Kimball, S. T. Family and community in Ireland. Cambridge, Mass.

40-3   Barbeau, M. Indian trade silver, RSCT, 36, 2: 27–41.

40-4   Barbeau, M. The modern growth of the totem pole on the Northwest Coast, SIR: 491–98.

40-5   Barnett, H. G. Culture processes; the Yurok, the Hupa, and the Karok of northwestern California, AA, 42, 1: 21–48.

40-6   Beaglehole, E. Notes on interpersonal theory, Ps, 3: 511–26.

40-7   Beaglehole, E. Psychic stress in a Tongan village, PSCP, 6, 4: 43–52.

40-8   Blumenthal, A. A new definition of culture, AA, 42, 4: 571–86.

40-9   Bunzel, R. The role of alcoholism in two central American cultures, Ps, 3, 3: 361–87.

40-10 Carneiro, E. The structure of African cults in Bahia, JAF, 53: 271–78.

40-11 Chapple, E. D. "Personality" differences as described by invariant properties of individuals in interaction, NASP, 26: 10–16.

40-12 Chapple, E. D. and Arensberg, C. M. Measuring human relations. Genetic Psychology Monographs, 22.

40-13 Chapple, E. D. and Harding, C. F. Simultaneous measures of human relations and emotional activity, NASP, 26: 319–26.

40-14 Cooper, J. M. Andamanese-Semang-Eta cultural relations, PM, 13, 2: 29-47.

40-15 Count, E. W. Red and black, a survey and a query, An, 35-36: 68-77.

40-16 Devereux, G. Social negativism and criminal psychopathology, J. Crim. Psychopath., 1: 323-38.

40-17 Eckert, G. von. Prophetentum und Kulturwandel in Melanesien, BA, 23, 1: 26-41.

40-18 Elkin, A. P. Society, the individual and change, with special reference to the war and other present day problems. Livingstone Lectures, Sydney.

40-19 Elkin, H. The northern Arapaho of Wyoming, in Acculturation in seven American Indian tribes, Linton, R. (ed.) New York.

40-20 Evans-Pritchard, E. E. Social anthropology: past and present, Mn, 50, 198.

40-21 Flannery, R. The cultural position of the Spanish River Indians, PM, 13, 1: 26-41.

40-22 Gillin, J. and Raimy, V. Acculturation and personality, ASR, 5, 3: 371-81.

40-23 Goldman, I. The Alkatcho Carrier of British Columbia, in Acculturation in seven American Indian tribes, Linton, R. (ed.) New York.

40-24 Gluckman, M. Analysis of a social situation in modern Zululand, BS, 14, 2: 91-146.

40-25 Hallowell, A. I. Aggression in Salteaux society, PS, 3: 395-407.

40-26 Harris, J. S. The White Knife Shoshoni of Nevada, in Acculturation in seven American Indian tribes, Linton, R. (ed.). New York.

40-27 Henry, J. Some cultural determinants of hostility in Pilagá children, AJO, 10: 111-19.

40-28 Henry, J. and Z. Speech disturbances in Pilagá Indian children, AJO, 10: 362-69.

40-29 Hill, W. W. Some Navaho cultural changes during two centuries, in Essays in historical anthropology of North America, SIMC, C: 395-415.

40-30 Hogbin, H. I. "Polynesian" colonies in Melanesia, JPS, 49: 199-220.

40-31 Huard, P. Les Portugais et l'Indochine, Institut Indochinois pour l'Étude de l'Homme, 3: 47-65.

40-32 Hunt, G. T. The wars of the Iroquois: a study in intertribal trade relations. U. of Wisconsin Press, Madison.

40-33 Joffe, N. F. The Fox of Iowa, in Acculturation in seven American Indian tribes, Linton, R. (ed.). New York.

40-34 Jones, C. L. Guatemala past and present. U. of Minn. Press, Minneapolis.

40-35 Kinietz, V. European civilization as a determinant of native Indian customs: the Delaware Indian big house ceremony, AA, 42: 116-21.

40-36 Koppers, W. Probleme der indischen Religionsgeschichte, An, 35-36: 761-814.

40-37 Kroeber, A. L. Psychosis or social sanction, CP, 8: 204-15.

40-38 Kroeber, A. L. Stimulus diffusion, AA, 42, 1: 1-20.

40-39 Kroeber, A. L. and Richardson, J. Three centuries of women's dress fashions, UCAR, 5.

40-40 Linton, R. Psychology and anthropology, J. Soc. Philos., 5: 115-26.

40-41 Linton, R. (ed.) Acculturation in seven American Indian tribes. New York. (Chapters 8-10 by Linton reprinted under title "Acculturation")

40-42 Lowie, R. H. American culture history, AA, 42, 3: 409-28.

40-43 Luomala, K. Notes on the development of Polynesian hero-cycles, JPS, 49: 367-74.

40-44 Malinowski, B. La "transculturación," su vocablo y su concepto, Revista Bimestre Cubana, 46: 220−28.

40-45 Malouf, L. Prehistoric exchange in the northern periphery of the Southwest, AAq, 6: 115−22.

40-46 Mandelbaum, D. G. The Plains Cree. AMNHP, 37.

40-47 Mead, M. Education and cultural surrogates, JES, 14, 2: 92−109.

40-48 Mead, M. Character formation in two South Sea societies, Trans., Am. Neurolog. Assn., 66: 99−103.

40-49 Mera, H. P. Population changes in the Rio Grande Glaze-paint area. Lab. of Anth. Tech. Series, 9. Santa Fe.

40-50 Milling, C. J. Red Carolinians. Chapel Hill, North Carolina.

40-51 Opler, M. K. The southern Ute of Colorado, in Acculturation in seven American Indian tribes, Linton, R. (ed.) New York.

40-52 Opler, M. K. Character and history of the southern Ute peyote rite, AA, 42: 463−78; 44: 151−59. 1940, 1942.

40-53 Ortiz, F. Contrapunteo del tobaco y el azucar. Havana (with Introduction by Malinowski, B.). Cuban counterpoint: tobacco and sugar. New York, 1947.

40-54 Radcliffe-Brown, A. R. On social structure, JRAI, 70: 1−12.

40-55 Redfield, R. The folk society and culture, AJS, 45: 731−42.

40-56 Richards, A. I. Bemba marriage and present economic conditions. RLP, 4.

40-57 Sachs, C. The history of musical instruments. New York.

40-58 Savannah Unit, Georgia Writers Project of WPA, Drums and shadows: survival studies among the Georgia coastal Negroes. Athens, Ga.

40-59 Schmitt, A. Untersuchungen zur Geschichte der Schrift. Leipzig.

40-60 Senior, C. Democracy comes to a cotton kingdom: the story of Mexico's La Laguna. Mexico, D. F.

40-61 Smith, M. W. The Puyallup of Washington, in Acculturation in seven American Indian tribes, Linton, R. (ed.). New York.

40-62 Steward, J. H. Culture change among Shoshoni Indians; abstract, Na, 145: 192.

40-63 Strong, W. D. From history to prehistory in the northern Great Plains, SIMC, 100: 353−94.

40-64 Sutherland, I. L. G. (ed.) The Maori people today. Wellington.

40-65 Thompson, L. Fijian frontier. New York.

40-66 Thurnwald, R. Funktion und Entwicklung . . . , ArA, 24: 40−45.

40-67 Tindale, N. B. Survey of the half-caste problem in South Australia, Royal Geog. Soc., South Australian Br., Proc,: 66−151.

40-68 Tschopik, H. Navaho basketry: a study of culture change, AA, 42, 3: 444−62.

40-69 Vasquez, G. V. Doctrinas y realidades en la legislacion para los indios. Depto. de Asuntos Indigenas. Mexico, D. F.

40-70 Velasco, A. La escuela indigeral de Warisata, Bolivia. Depto. de Asuntos Indigenas. Mexico, D. F.

40-71 Wagley, C. The effects of depopulation upon social organization as illustrated by the Tapirapé Indians, NYAST, 3, 1: 12−16.

40-72 Ware, C. F. (ed.) The cultural approach to history. Columbia U. Press, New York.

40-73 White, L. The symbol: the origin and basis of human behavior, PSc, 7: 451−63.

40-74 Whitman, W. The San Ildefonso of New Mexico, in Acculturation in seven American Indian tribes, Linton, R. (ed.). New York.

40-75   Wilbur, G. B. The reciprocal relationship of man and his ideological milieu, AIm, 3, 4: 3–48.

40-76   Zolotariev, A. M. and Levin, M. G. On the antiquity and origin of reindeer breeding, Academy of Sciences, 1: 171–89. Moscow.

1941

41-1   Anduze, O. B. Los mayas: fin de una cultura. Imprenta de la Camara de Diputados, Mexico, D. F.

41-2   Barber, B. Acculturation and messianic movements, ASR, 6, 5: 663–69.

41-3   Barnett, H. G. Personal conflicts and cultural changes, SF, 20: 160–71.

41-4   Bascom, W. R. Acculturation among the Gullah Negroes, AA, 43, 1: 43–50.

41-5   Bateson, G. The frustration-aggression hypothesis and culture, Psycholog. Rev., 48: 350–55.

41-6   Bateson, G. and Mead, M. Principles of morale building, JES, 15, 4: 206–20.

41-7   Beaglehole, E. and P. Pangai, a village in Tonga. PSM, 18.

41-8   Beaglehole, E. The Polynesian Maori, Polyn. Anthr. Studies: 39 –70. Wellington.

41-9   Beynon, W. The Tsimshians of Metlakatla, Alaska, AA, 43, 1: 83–88.

41-10   Bourrin, C. Le vieux Tonkin. Le théâtre, le sport, la vie mondaine. Dans Viet Nam, le Peuple Vietnamien. 2 vols. Hanoi.

41-11   Byers, D. S. The taxonomic approach redefined, MASB, 2: 21–25.

41-12   Canals, S. Los aborígenes de la pampa en la epoca colonial, AIEA, 2: 207–38.

41-13   Capell, A. and Lester, R. H. Local divisions and movements in Fiji, Oc, 11, 4: 313–41.

41-14   Childe, V. G. Man makes himself. London.

41-15   Cooper, J. M. Temporal sequences and the marginal cultures, CUAS, 10.

41-16   Davis, A., Gardner, B. B. and Gardner, M. R. Deep South: a social anthropological study of caste and class. Chicago.

41-17   Debo, A. The road to disappearance: a history of the Creek Indians. U. of Okla. Press, Norman.

41-18   Densmore, F. Native songs of two hybrid ceremonies among the American Indians, AA, 43, 1: 77–82.

41-19   Dollard, J. and Miller, N. E. Social learning and imitation. New Haven.

41-20   Eggan, F. Some aspects of culture change in the northern Philippines, AA, 43, 1: 11–18.

41-21   Embree, J. F. Nisei, today and tomorrow, Nippu Jiji, Jan. 3, Honolulu.

41-22   Embree, J. F. Acculturation among the Japanese of Kona, Hawaii. AAAM, 59.

41-23   Farmer, M. F. The growth of Navaho culture, SDMB, 4, 1: 8–16.

41-24   Feeney, B. C. Arch-isolationists. San Blas Indians, Nat. Geographic, 79: 193–220.

41-25   Fenton, W. N. Contacts between Iroquois herbalism and colonial medicine, SIR: 503–26.

41-26   Fenton, W. N. Iroquois suicide: a study in the stability of a culture pattern, BAEB, 128, 14: 80–137.

41-27   Fenton, W. N. Tonowanda longhouse ceremonies: ninety years after Lewis Henry Morgan, BAEB, 128, 15: 140–66.

41-28 Ford, C. S. Smoke from their fires: the life of a Kwakiutl chief. New Haven.
41-29 Gillin, J. Emergent races and cultures in South America, SM, 52: 268–73.
41-30 Goldman, I. Alkatcho Carrier: historical background of crest prerogatives, AA, 43, 3: 396–418.
41-31 Greenberg, J. H. Some aspects of Negro-Mohammedan culture-contact among the Hausa, AA, 43, 1: 51–61.
41-32 Grigson, W. V. The aboriginal problem in the Central Provinces and Berar. Oxford.
41-33 Hallowell, A. I. The Rorschach method as an aid in the study of personalities in primitive societies, CP, 9, 3: 235–45.
41-34 Heizer, R. F. A Californian messianic movement of 1801 among the Chumash, AA, 43, 1: 128–29.
41-35 Henry, J. Jungle people. A Kaingáng tribe of the Highlands of Brazil. New York.
41-36 Herskovits, M. J. The myth of the Negro past. New York.
41-37 Herskovits, M. J. Some comments on the study of cultural contact, AA, 43, 1: 1–10.
41-38 Herzog, G. Culture and language: shifts in the Pima vocabulary, in Language, culture and personality, Essays in memory of Edward Sapir, Spier. L., Hallowell, A. I., and Newman, S. S. (eds.): 66–74. Menasha.
41-39 Honigmann, J. J. Ethnography and acculturation of the Fort Nelson slave. New Haven.
41-40 Humphrey, N. D. Concept of culture in social case work, SSR, 26: 53–60.
41-41 Humphrey, N. D. Social insight, nuance, and mind-types: a polar hypothesis. Philosophy of Science, 8: 580–84.
41-42 Humphrey, N. D. Mexican repatriation from Michigan, Social Service Review, 15: 495–513.
41-43 Jenness, D. Prehistoric culture waves from Asia to America, SIR: 383–96.
41-44 Jesperson, O. Efficiency in language change. Copenhagen.
41-45 Kardiner, A. and Spiegel, H. The traumatic neuroses of war. National Research Council. Washington, D.C.
41-46 Keesing, F. M. The South Seas in the modern world. New York.
41-47 Keur, D. L. Big Bead Mesa: an archaeological study of Navaho acculturation, 1745–1812. Soc. for Am. Arch. Mem., 1.
41-48 Kluckhohn, C. Patterning as exemplified in Navaho culture, in Language, culture and personality, Essays in memory of Edward Sapir, Spier, L., Hallowell, A. I., and Newman, S. S. (eds.): 109–30. Menasha.
41-49 Kluckhohn, C. The Navahos in the machine age. The Technology Review, 44, 4: 2–6.
41-50 Kluckhohn, C. The way of life, The Kenyon Review, 160–179.
41-51 Koppers, W. Meine Völkerkundliche Forschungsreise zu den Primitivstämmen Zentral-Indiens, 1938– 1939, IAE, 41: 141–52.
41-52 La Barre, W. A cultish drug addiction in an Indian alcoholic, Bul. of Menninger Clinic, 5, 2: 40–46.
41-53 Leighton, A. H. and D. C. Elements of psychotherapy in Navaho religion, Ps, 4: 515–23.
41-54 Linton, A., Fisher, M. S., and Ryan, W. C. Culture and personality. American Council on Education. Washington, D. C.
41-55 Macgregor, R. C. Twentieth century Indians. New York.
41-56 Mandelbaum, D. G. Culture change among the Nilgiri tribes, AA, 43, 1: 19–26.

41-57 Mead, M. On methods of implementing a national morale program, ApA, 1: 20—24.

41-58 Murphy, J. Racial crossing and cultural efflorescence, Mn, 41, 1—14, 6—10.

41-59 Nevermann, H. von. Zauberei und Geisterglaube auf Martinique, BA, 24, 2: 47—59.

41-60 Olen, L. and Loomis, G. P. Culture of a contemporary rural community, El Cerrito, Mexico. Rural Life Studies 1— US Dept. of Agric. Washington, D. C.

41-61 Overton, A. Trade goods, WA, 21: 71—73.

41-62 Perham, M. F. Africans and British rule. London.

41-63 Rainey, F. A new form of culture on the Arctic coast, NASP, 27, 3: 141—44.

41-64 Ramos, A. Acculturation among the Brazilian Negroes, JNH, 26: 244—50.

41-65 Redfield, R. The folk culture of Yucatan. Chicago.

41-66 Rogers, M. J. Aboriginal culture relations between southern California and the Southwest, SDMB, 5, 3: 1—6.

41-67 Rôheim, G. The psycho-analytic interpretation of culture, Int. Jnl. of Psycho-An., 22: 147—69.

41-68 Sanchez, G. I. New Mexicans and acculturation, NMQR, 11, 1.

41-69 Sieber, S. A. and Meuller, F. H. The social life of primitive man. St. Louis.

41-70 Siegel, M. Problems of education in Indian Guatemala, Jour. of Experimental Education, 9, 4: 285—95.

41-71 Siegel, M. Religion in western Guatemala: a product of acculturation, AA, 43, 1: 62—76.

41-72 Siegel, M. Resistances to culture change in western Guatemala, SSR, 15, 5.

41-73 Speck, F. G. Indian apostates, General Magazine and Historical Chronicle, 44: 24—27.

41-74 Steward, J. H. Recording culture changes among the Carrier Indians of British Columbia, SIR, explorations and field work, 83—90.

41-75 Tax, S. World view and social relations in Guatemala, AA, 43, 1: 27—42.

41-76 Vaillant, G. C. Aztecs of Mexico. Garden City.

41-77 Warner, W. L. and Lunt, P. S. The social life of a modern community. Yale U. Press, New Haven.

41-78 Warner, W. L., Junker, B. H., and Adams, W. A. Color and human nature; Negro personality development in a northern city, Washington, D. C.

41-79 Whiting, J. Becoming a Kwoma. New Haven.

41-80 Whorf, B. L. The relation of habitual thought and behavior to language, in: Language, Culture and personality, essays in memory of Edward Sapir, Spier, L. and others (eds.). Menasha.

41-81 Wieschoff, H. A. Divorce laws and practices in modern Ibo culture, JNH, 26, 3: 299—324.

41-82 Wilson, A. An essay on the economics of detribalization in Northern Rhodesia. RLP, 1941—42.

1942

42-1 Aginsky, B. Acculturation, Pr. 8th Am. Sci. Congress, 2: 211—16.

42-2 Arensberg, C. Report on a developing community, Poston, Arizona, ApA, 2, 1: 1—21.

42-3   Arensberg, C. The nature of world equilibrium, Proc. Amer. Acad. of
         Arts and Sci., 75: 29–32.
42-4   Arensberg, C. and Macgregor, D. Determination of morale in an industrial
         company, ApA, 1, 2: 12–34.
42-5   Bailey, A. G. The Indian problem in early Canada, AI, 2, 3: 35–39.
42-6   Barnett, H. G. Applied anthropology in 1860, ApA, 1, 3: 19–32.
42-7   Barnett, H. G. Cultural growth by substitution, Research Studies of State
         Coll. of Wash. 10, 1: 26–30.
42-8   Barnett, H. G. Invention and cultural change, AA, 44, 1: 14–30.
42-9   Bateson, G. Social planning and the concept of deutero-learning, Report
         of the Conference on Science, Philosophy and Religion, New York.
42-10   Bateson, G. Some systematic approaches to the study of culture and per-
         sonality, CP, 11: 76–82.
42-11   Bateson, G. Morale and national character, in Civilian Morale, Watson,
         G. (ed.): 71–91. Boston.
42-12   Benedict, R. Anthropology and cultural change, ASc, 11: 243–48.
42-13   Buck, P. H. The disappearance of canoes in Polynesia, JPS, 51: 191–99.
42-14   Burgess, E. W., Warner, W. L., Mead, M. and others, Environment and
         education. Chicago.
42-15   Chapple, E. D. and Coon, C. S. Principles of anthropology. New York.
42-16   Chapple, E. D. How a world equilibrium can be organized and administered,
         Proc. Amer. Acad. of Arts and Sci., 75: 33–37.
42-17   Chapple, E. D. The measurement of interpersonal behavior, NYAST, 4:
         222–33.
42-18   Colton, H. S. Archaeology and the reconstruction of history, AAq, 8: 33–40.
42-19   Cooper, J. M. Areal and temporal aspects of aboriginal South American
         culture, PM, 15: 1–38.
42-20   Cooper, J. M. The South American marginal cultures, Proceedings 8th
         Amer. Science Congress, 2: 147–60.
42-21   Cordry, D. B. The first Indian state fair of Mexico in Oaxaca City, Mk,
         14, 4: 133–38.
42-22   Coulter, J. W. Fiji, little India of the Pacific. U. of Chicago Press, Chi-
         cago.
42-23   Davis, H. E. The village of Chinchero, AI, 2, 2: 42–50.
42-24   Devereaux, G. The mental hygiene of the American Indian, MH, 26: 71ff.
42-25   Dietschy, H. Mensch und Gott bei mexikanishen Indianern, An, 35–36:
         326–40.
42-26   Elkin, A. P. The reaction of primitive peoples to the white man's culture,
         in When peoples meet, Locke, A. and Stern, B. J. (eds.): 551–57.
42-27   Emory, K. P. Oceanian influence on American Indian culture. Norden-
         skiöld's view, JPS, 51: 126–35.
42-28   Fettweis, E. Amerikanistik und Geschichte der Mathematik, An, 37–40:
         896–900.
42-29   Firth, R. The effects of western culture upon primitive peoples, in When
         peoples meet, Locke, A. and Stern, B. J. (eds.): 107–11.
42-30   Ford, C. S. Culture and human behavior, SM, 55: 546–57.
42-31   Frazier, E. F. Negro family life in Bahia, Brazil: influence of African
         culture patterns, ASR, 7: 465–78.
42-32   Friederici, G. The business of scalping, in When peoples meet, 165–70.
42-33   Ghurye, G. S. The British and the Indian caste system, in When peoples
         meet, Locke, A. and Stern, B. J. (eds.): 618–21.

42-34 Gillin, J. Acquired drives in culture contact, AA, 44, 4: 545–54.

42-35 Gillin, J. Emergent races and cultures: a new field for anthropological research in South America, in When peoples meet, Locke, A. and Stern, B. J. (eds.): 217–25.

42-36 Gusinde, M. Die Kongo-Pygmäen in Geschichte und Gegenwart. Nova Acta Leopoldina, 11, 76. Halle.

42-37 Hallowell, A. I. Acculturation processes and personality changes as indicated by the Rorschach technique, Rorschach Research Exchange, 6, 2: 42–50.

42-38 Hallowell, A. I. Some psychological aspects of measurement among the Salteaux, AA, 44, 1: 62–77.

42-39 Hallowell, A. I. The role of conjuring in Salteaux society. Philadelphia.

42-40 Herskovits, M. J. Africa lives on, in When peoples meet, Locke, A. and Stern, B. J. (eds.): 74–80.

42-41 Herskovits, M. J. On the values of culture, SM, 54: 557–60.

42-42 Herskovits, M. J. and F. S. Negroes of Brazil, Yale Review, 32, 2: 263–79.

42-43 Hirsch, W. Assimilation as concept and as process, SF, 21: 35–39.

42-44 Hobbs, C. C. Christian education and the Burmese family, Unpublished thesis, Dept. of Education, Colgate-Rochester Divinity School, Rochester New York.

42-45 Hodgen, M. T. Geographical distribution as a criterion of age, AA, 44, 3: 345–68.

42-46 Honigsheim, P. The philosophical background of European anthropology, AA, 44, 3: 376–87.

42-47 Hunter, M. Contemporary European-Bantu relations in South Africa, in When peoples meet, Locke, A. and Stern, B. J. (eds.): 198–207.

42-48 Hunter, M. The beginnings of Bantu nationalism, in When peoples meet, Locke, A. and Stern, B. J. (eds.): 516–20.

42-49 Kennedy, R. Contours of culture in Indonesia, FEQ, 2: 5–14.

42-50 Kluckhohn, C. Navaho witchcraft. PMAEP, 22.

42-51 Kluckhohn, C. Myths and rituals: a general theory, Harvard Theological Review, 35: 45–79.

42-52 LaFarge, O. (ed.) The changing Indian. U. of Okla, Press, Norman.

42-53 Landero, F. M. Aspectos del indigenismo en Honduras, AI, 2, 1: 4–44.

42-54 Lanyon-Orgill, P. A. A Polynesian settlement in New Britain, JPS, 51, 87–114.

42-55 Leighton, A. H. and Leighton, D. C. Some types of uneasiness and fear in a Navaho community, AA, 44, 2: 194–209.

42-56 Lewis, O. The effects of white contact upon Blackfoot culture with special reference to the role of the fur trade. AESM, 6.

42-57 Linton, R. Acculturation in seven Indian tribes, In When peoples meet, Locke, A. and Stern, B. J. (eds.): 558–66.

42-58 Locke, A. and Stern, B. J. The universality of cultural interchange, in When peoples meet, Locke, A. and Stern, B. J. (eds.): 30–38.

42-59 Locke, A. and Stern, B. J. (eds.) When peoples meet. Progressive Educ. Assn., New York.

42-60 Londoño, C. M. El problema de despoblación en Colombia, Universidad Catolica Bolivariana, 8, 25–26: 237–75, Medellín.

42-61 Lowie, R. H. Transition of civilizations in primitive society, AJS, 47: 527–43.

42-62 Malouf, C. Gosiute peyotism, AA, 44, 1: 93–103.
42-63 Marchant, A. From barter to slavery: the economic relations of Portuguese and Indians in the settlement of Brazil 1500–1580. Johns Hopkins Press, Baltimore.
42-64 McGillicuddy, V. T. The significance of the Indian ghost dance religion, in When peoples meet, Locke, A. and Stern, B. J. (eds.): 514–15.
42-65 McKern, W. C. Taxonomy and the direct historical approach, AAq, 8: 170–72.
42-66 Mead, M. The family in the future, in Beyond victory, Anshen, R. M. (ed.), New York.
42-67 Mead, M. The comparative study of culture and the purposive cultivation of democratic values. Comments by Benedict, Kluckhohn, Lee, Gorer, and Bateson, Science, Philos. and Religion; Second Symposium: 56–69. New York.
42-68 Means, P. A. The fall of the Incas, in When peoples meet, Locke, A. and Stern, B. J. (eds.): 148–150.
42-69 Métraux, A. A Quechua messiah in eastern Peru, AA, 44, 4: 721–25.
42-70 Nadel, S. F. A black Byzantium. Oxford Univ. Press.
42-71 Ogburn, W. F. Inventions, population and history, in Studies in the history of culture. Council of Learned Societies: 232–45.
42-72 Oliver, D. A case of a change in food habits in Bougainville, British Solomon Islands, ApA, 1, 2: 34–36.
42-73 Opler, M. K. Psychoanalytic techniques in social analysis. JSP, 15: 91–127.
42-74 Opler, M. K. Fact and fancy in Ute peyotism, AA, 44, 1: 151–59.
42-75 Parsons, E. C. Anthropology and prediction, AA, 44, 2: 337–44.
42-76 Passin, H. Culture change in southern Illinois, RS, 7, 3: 303–17.
42-77 Philipps, T. The continental-European ethnic and cultural composition of the Canadian nation, An, 37–40: 887–89.
42-78 Pierson, D. Negroes in Brazil. Univ. of Chicago Press, Chicago.
42-79 Pitt-Rivers, G. The detribalization of the natives of the Pacific Islands, in: When peoples meet, Locke, A. and Stern, B. J. (eds.): 206–09.
42-80 Pitt-Rivers, G. Types of culture contact, in When peoples meet, Locke, A. and Stern, B. J. (eds.): 104–06.
42-81 Read, M. Migrant labor in Africa and its effects on tribal life, Internatl. Labour Review, 45: 605–31.
42-82 Redfield, R. Culture contact in Central America, in When peoples meet, Locke, A. and Stern, B. J. (eds.): 112–22.
42-83 Redfield, R. Españoles e Indios, RMN, 11: 97–116.
42-84 Redfield, R. Comment on the changing Mexican family, ASR, 7: 497.
42-85 Redfield, R. El indio en Mexico, Revista Mexicana de la Sociologia, 4, 3: 75–80.
42-86 Richards, E. S. Culture change due to migration; study of Negro migration to California, SSR, 26: 334–45.
42-87 Russell, W. E. Rotuma, its history, conditions and customs, JPS, 51: 229–55.
42-88 Sandoz, M. Crazy horse (the strange man of the Oglalas). New York.
42-89 Sapir, E. Language and national antagonisms, in When peoples meet, Locke, A. and Stern, B. J. (eds.): 659–61.
42-90 Schader, E. Acuturacão, linguistica numa communidade rural, So, 4, 3: 268–84.

42-91 Schapera, I. The outcome of European domination of Africa, in When peoples meet, Locke, A. and Stern, B. J. (eds.): 637—49.

42-92 Scholes, F. V. Spanish policy and the Yucatan, in When peoples meet, Lock A. and Stern, B. J. (eds.): 179—83.

42-93 Schwab, F. Fritz Graebner y el método Etnológico, RMN, 11, 1: 40—45.

42-94 Shapiro, H. L. The instability of the human organism, in When peoples meet, Locke, A. and Stern, B. J. (eds): 454—64.

42-95 Shapiro, H. L. The world in motion, in When peoples meet, Locke, A. and Stern, B. J. (eds.): 97—98.

42-96 Shimkin, D. B. Dynamics of recent Wind River Shoshone history, AA, 44, 3: 451—61.

42-97 Shreve, M. Modern Papago basketry, Kv, 8, 2: 10—16.

42-98 Simmons, L. (ed.) Sun chief: the autobiography of a Hopi Indian. New Haven

42-99 Speck, F. G. The historical approach to art in archaeology in the northern woodlands, AAq, 8: 73—75.

42-100 Stern, B. J. The status of women, in When peoples meet, Locke, A. and Stern, B. J. (eds.): 280—86.

42-101 Steward, J. H. The direct historical approach to archaeology, AAq, 7: 337—44.

42-102 Stout, D. B. San Blas Cuña acculturation, SF, 21 October.

42-103 Suáner, P. La situación real del indio en el Ecuador, AI, 2, 1: 59—62.

42-104 Tannous, A. Emigration, a force of social change in an Arab village, RS, 7, 1: 62—74.

42-105 Thompson, L. Guam and its people. IPRNY. New York.

42-106 Wagley, C. Os efeitos dos despovoamento sobre organização social os indios Tapirapé, So, 4, 4: 407—12.

42-107 Warner, W. L. and Lunt, P. S. The status system of a modern community. New Haven.

42-108 Webster, H. Taboo, a sociological study. Stanford, Cal.

42-109 Westermann, D. Islam in Africa, in When peoples meet, Locke, A. and Stern, B. J. (eds.): 70—73.

42-110 Willems, E. and Baldus, H. Culture change among Japanese immigrants in Brazil, SSR, 26: 525—37.

42-111 Wissler, C. Our culture debt to the Indians, in When peoples meet, Locke, A. and Stern, B. J. (eds.): 81—85.

42-112 Yount, G. C. A sketch of the Hopi in 1942, Mk, 16, 6: 193—99.

42-113 Zingg, R. M. The genuine and spurious values in Tarahumara culture, AA, 44, 1: 78—92.

1943

43-1 Beals, R., Redfield, R. and Tax, S. Anthropological research problems with reference to the contemporary peoples of Mexico and Guatemala, AA, 45: 1—21.

43-2 Benedict, R. Recognition of cultural diversities in the postwar world, Ann. Am. Acad. Pol. Soc. Sci., 228: 101—07.

43-3 Benedict, R. Two patterns of Indian acculturation, AA, 45: 207—12.

43-4 Bennett, J. W. A history of the Mississippi cultures, WA, 24: 34—42.

43-5 Bennett, J. W. Recent developments in the functional interpretation of archaeological data, AAq, 9: 208—19.

43-6   Bennett, J. W. Some comments on Colton's "principle of analogous types,"
        AA, 45: 637—41.
43-7   Birket-Smith, K. The origin of maize cultivation. Det. Kgl. danske viden-
        skabernes selskab historiskfilogogiske meddelesser, Copenhagen, 29, 3.
43-8   Bogardus, E. S. Culture conflicts in relocation centers, SSR, 27: 381—90.
43-9   Botelho de Magalhães, A. O problema de civilação dos indios no Brazil,
        AI, 3, 2: 153—60.
43-10   Bühler, A. Materialen zur Kenntnis der Ikattechnik. IAE, 43, supplement.
43-11   Cahnman, W. J. Mediterranean and Caribbean regions— a comparison in
        race and culture contacts, SF, 22: 209—14.
43-12   Chapple, E. D. Anthropological engineering: its use to administrators, ApA,
        2, 2: 23—32.
43-13   Coghlan, H. H. The evolution of the axe from prehistoric to Roman times,
        JRAI, 73, 1: 27—56.
43-14   Colton, H. S. The principle of analogous pottery types, AA, 45: 316—20.
43-15   Devereux, G. and Loeb, E. M. Some notes on Apache criminality, Jour.
        of Criminal Psychopathology, 4: 424—30.
43-16   Devereux, G. and Loeb, E. M. Antagonistic acculturation, ASR, 8: 133—48.
43-17   Eggan, D. The general problem of Hopi adjustment, AA, 45: 357—73.
43-18   Elkin, A. P. Anthropology and the peoples of the Southwest Pacific: the
        past, present and future, Oc, 14, 1: 1—19.
43-19   Embree, J. F. Dealing with Japanese-Americans, ApA, 2, 2: 37—41.
43-20   Embree, J. F. The relocation of persons of Japanese ancestry in the United
        States: some causes and effects, JWAS, 33, 8: 238—42.
43-21   Embree, J. F. Resistance to freedom: an administrative problem, ApA,
        2, 4: 10—14.
43-22   Fenton, W. N. and Deardorff, M. H. The last passenger pigeon hunts of
        the cornplanter Senecas, JWAS, 33: 289—315.
43-23   Furnivall, J. S. Educational progress in Southeast Asia. IPRNY.
43-24   Goldfrank, E. S. Historic change and social character: a study of the Teton
        Dakota, AA, 45, 1: 67—83.
43-25   Handy, E. S. C. Two unique petroglyphs in the Marquesas which point to
        Easter Island and Malaysia, in Studies in the anthropology of Oceania and
        Asia presented in memory of R. B. Dixon, Coon, C. S. and Andrews,
        J M. (eds.) PMAAE, 14: 22—31.
43-26   Haring, D. Blood on the rising sun. Philadelphia.
43-27   Hatch, D. S. Rural reconstruction in Mexico, ApA, 2, 4: 17—21.
43-28   Hayner, N. and U. Three generations of Pacific Northwest Indians, ASR,
        8: 650—56.
43-29   Heizer, R. F. A Pacific Eskimo invention in whale hunting in historic
        times, AA, 45: 120—22.
43-30   Herskovits, M. J. Education and cultural dynamics, AJS, 48: 737—49, and
        in Education and the Cultural Process, Johnson, C. S. (ed.) New York.
43-31   Herskovits, M. J. The Negro in Bahia, Brazil: a problem in method, ASR,
        8.
43-32   Herskovits, M. J. The southernmost outposts of New World Africanisms,
        AA, 45: 495—510.
43-33   Herskovits, M. J. Some next steps in the study of Negro folklore, JAF,
        56: 1—7.
43-34   Hewett, E. L. From cave dwelling to Mount Olympus, MPA.
43-35   Honigmann, J. J. White man's new burden, what anthropology indicates as
        the best colonial policy, Commonweal, 37: 511—14.

43-36   Hooper, O. Possibilities for improvement among rural Panamanians, ApA, 2, 4: 4–10.

43-37   Hsu, F. L. K. Magic and science in western Yunnan. IPRNY.

43-38   Humphrey, N. D. A generic folk culture of Mexico, RS, 8, 4: 364–77.

43-39   Humphrey, N. D. On assimilation and acculturation, Ps, 6, 4: 343–45.

43-40   Johnson, J. B. A clear case of linguistic acculturation, AA, 45: 427–34.

43-41   Kennedy, R. Acculturation and administration in Indonesia, AA, 45, 2: 185–92.

43-42   Kennedy, R. Islands and peoples of the Indies. Smithsonian Institution War Background Studies 14. Washington, D. C.

43-43   Kluckhohn, C. Covert culture and administrative problems, AA, 45: 213–27

43-44   Kraus, W. W. The Portuguese and Spanish in Hawaii, AcA, 2: 252–60.

43-45   Krieger, K. Studien über Afrikanische Kunstperlen Besprechungen. BA, 25, 2.

43-46   Lee, D. D. The linguistic aspect of Wintu acculturation, AA, 45: 435–40.

43-47   Linton, R. Nativistic movements, AA, 45; 230–40.

43-48   Loomis, C. and Grisham, G. The New Mexican experiment in village rehabilitation, ApA, 2, 3: 12–37.

43-49   Loram, C. T. and McIlwraith, T. F. (eds.) The North American Indian today. Toronto.

43-50   Loyo, G. La redistríbución de grupos indigenas en Mexico, AI, 3, 1: 39–48.

43-51   Malinowski, B. The Pan-African problem of culture contact, AJS, 48, 6.

43-52   Malouf, C. and Arline, A. The Gosuite Indians—from bows to bombers, Mk, 17, 3: 96–99.

43-53   Mayer, J. R. Flintlocks of the Iroquois, 1620–1687. Research Records 6, Museum of Arts and Sciences, Rochester.

43-54   Mead, M. News of developing research methods, ApA, 2: 35.

43-55   Mead, M. The role of small South Sea cultures in the post war world, AA, 45: 193–95.

43-56   Mead, M. And keep your powder dry; an anthropologist looks at America. New York.

43-57   Mekeel, S. A short history of the Teton Dakota, North Dakota Historical Quarterly, 10, 3: 137–205.

43-58   Miranda, F. M. A propósito del método etnológico (carta en respuesta a Don Frederico Schwab), RMN, 12: 24–28.

43-59   Opler, M. E. The character and derivation of the Jicarilla holiness rites, UNMASB, 4, 3.

43-60   Orozco, L. C. Las institucions democráticas de los indígenas Mexicano en la época colonial. Mexico.

43-61   Ortiz, F. F. Las cuatro culturas indias de Cuba. Habana.

43-62   Petersen, W. F. Lincoln-Douglas, the weather as destiny. Springfield, Ill.

43-63   Pierson, D. Acomodaçao e assimilaçåo, Sg, 5, 3: 217–32.

43-64   Pomus, V. I. Buriat Mongolia. IPRNY.

43-65   Posnansky, A. Los dos tipos indigenales de Bolivia y su educación, AI, 3, 1: 55–60.

43-66   Powdermaker, H. The channeling of Negro aggression by the cultural process, AJS, 48, 6: 750–58.

43-67   Raper, A. and Tappan, P. W. Georgia share croppers: "never too old to learn new tricks," ApA, 2, 3: 3–11.

43-68   Reed, S. W. The making of modern New Guinea. APSM, 18.

43-69 Reed, S. W. White influence in the mandated territory of New Guinea and
       Fiji; abstract, GR, 33: 672−74.
43-70 Richardson, F. L. Thirty years of rural reconstruction: the experience of
       Spencer Hatch in Travancore, ApA, 2, 3: 49−58.
43-71 Ritzenthaler, R. The impact of war on an Indian community, AA, 45: 325−
       26.
43-72 Rivet, P. La influencia Karib en Colombia, RIENB, 1, 1: 55−87.
43-73 Rôheim, G. The origin and function of culture. Nervous and Mental Disease
       Monographs, New York. 69.
43-74 Rojas, R. El problema indigena en Argentina, AI, 3, 2: 105−14.
43-75 Roys, R. L. The Indian background of colonial Yucatan. Washington, D.C.
43-76 Schapera, I. Tribal legislation among the Tswana of the Bechuanaland
       protectorate: a study in the mechanism of culture change, LSMSA, 9, 101.
43-77 Shih, K. H. and Tien, J. K. Labor and labor relations in the new industries
       of Southwest China. IPRNY.
43-78 Siegel, M. Creation myth and acculturation in Acátan, Guatemala, JAF,
       56: 120−26.
43-79 Slotkin, J. S. Jazz and its forerunners as an example of acculturation, ASR,
       8: 570−75.
43-80 Slotkin, J. S. Status of the marginal man, SSR, 28: 47−54.
43-81 Speck, F. G. Reflections upon the past and present of the Massachusetts
       Indians, MASB, 4, 3: 33−38.
43-82 Speck, F. G. The Wapanachki Delawares and the English, The Pennsylvania
       Magazine of History and Biography, 67, 4: 319−44.
43-83 Spicer, E. H. Linguistic aspects of Yaqui acculturation, AA, 45: 410−26.
43-84 Steward, J. H. Acculturation studies in Latin America: some needs and
       problems, AA, 45: 198−204.
43-85 Steward, J. H. Acculturation and the Indian problem, AI, 3, 4: 323−28.
43-86 Steward, J. H. Anthropological research needs and opportunities in South
       America, AcA, 1, 1: 20−37.
43-87 Supatmo, R. Animistic beliefs and religious practices of the Javanese
       (mimeo lectures given at Columbia Univ. Naval School for Military Gov-
       ernment and Administration). Southeast Asia Institute.
43-88 Tannenbaum, F. Agrarismo, Indianismo, y nacionalismo; failure of Euro-
       pean civilization to incorporate native culture, Hispan. Am. Hist. R.,
       23: 394−423.
43-89 Tannous, A. I. Acculturation of an Arab-Syrian community in the deep South,
       ASR, 8: 264−71.
43-90 Tannous, A. I. Missionary education in Lebanon: a study in acculturation
       in the village of Bishmizzeen, SF, 21: 338−43.
43-91 Thompson, J. E. S. Pitfalls and stimuli in the interpretation of history
       through loan words, Philological and Documentary Studies, Middle
       America Research Inst., New Orleans, 1, 2: 19−26.
43-92 Thurnwald, R. Origem, formação e transformação de Direito a luz das
       pesquizaz etnológicas, Sg, 5, 2: 171−86 (continued 1944).
43-93 Thurnwald, R. Grade und Spielarten des Wandels der Fremvölker bei der
       Berührung mit Europäern, ArA, 28: 53−60.
43-94 Titiev, M. The Indian problems of Latin America, Michigan Alumnus
       Quarterly Review, 49, 24: 277−83.
43-95 Tower, J. E. and Wolf, W. Ethnic groups in Cullman County, Ala.: influ-
       ence of German settlement. GR, 33: 276−85.

43-96   Useem, J. , Macgregor, G. and Useem, R. H. Wartime employment and cultural adjustments of the Rosebud Sioux, ApA, 2, 2: 1—9.

43-97   Vandenbosch, A. The effect of Dutch rule on the civilization of the East Indies, AJS, 48: 498—502.

43-98   Vlekke, B. Nusantara: a history of the East Indian archipelago. Cambridge, Mass.

43-99   von Hagen, V. W. The Jicaque (Torrupan) Indians of Honduras. Heye Foundation, New York.

43-100 Wagley, C. Notas sobre aculturação entre os Guajajara, Boletin de Museo Nacional, Rio de Janeiro, 2: 1—12.

43-101 Wallis, W. D. Messiahs: their role in civilization. Washington, D.C.

43-102 Warner, R. E. Yaquis of Mexico and their folk literature, Kv, 8, 3: 18—22.

43-103 White, L. A. Energy and the evolution of culture, AA, 45, 3: 335—56.

43-104 White, L. A. Tobacco in New Mexico history, N. Mex. Historical Review, 18, 4: 386—93.

43-105 Whyte, W. F. Street corner society. Chicago.

43-106 Wood, M. M. Russian creoles of Alaska as a marginal group, SF, 22: 204—08.

43-107 Zavala, S. The Spanish colonization of America. Philadelphia.

1944

44-1   Adair, J. The Navaho and Pueblo silversmiths. Norman, U. of Oklahoma Press.

44-2   Aiyappan, A. Iravas and culture change. Bulletin of Madras Gov. Museum, Madras.

44-3   Baldus, H. Problemas indigenistas no Brazil, AI, 4, 1: 9—18.

44-4   Barbeau, M. Totemism, a modern growth on the north Pacific coast, JAF, 57: 51—58.

44-5   Bateson, G. Cultural determinants of personality, in Personality and the behavior disorders, Hunt, J. (ed.), New York: 714—35.

44-6   Beaglehole, E. Character structure. Its role in the analysis of interpersonal relations, Ps, 7, 2: 145—62.

44-7   Bennett, J. W. Culture change and personality in a rural society, SF, 23: 123.

44-8   Bennett, J. W. The development of ethnological theory as illustrated by studies of the Plains sun dance, AA, 46: 162—81.

44-9   Bennett, J. W. The interaction of culture and environment in the smaller societies, AA, 46: 461—78.

44-10 Bennett, J. W. Middle American influences on cultures of the southeastern United States, AcA, 2: 25—50.

44-11 Bermejo, V. La ley y el Indio en el Peru, AI, 4, 2: 106—11.

44-12 Bidney, D. On the concept of culture and some cultural fallacies, AA, 46: 30—44.

44-13 Bonfante, U. and Sebeok, T. A. Linguistics and the age and area hypothesis, AA, 46: 382—86.

44-14 Botelho de Magalhães, A. A. O. Problema la civilização dos Indios no Brazil, AI, 4, 2: 133—248; 4: 233—36.

44-15 Brown, G. G. Missions and cultural diffusion, AJS, 50, 3.

44-16 Buck, P. H. The local evolution of Hawaiian feather capes and cloaks, JPS, 53: 1—16.

44-17 Childe, V. G. Archaeological ages as technological stages, Huxley memorial lecture for 1944, JRAI, 74; 1—19.

44-18 Culwick, A. F. New beginning, RLIJ, 2: 44—49.

44-19 Donauer, F. Auf Apostelwegen in Indien. Einsiedeln.

44-20 Elkin, A. P. Citizenship for the aborigines. Sydney.

44-21 Elkin, A. P. Notes on anthropology and the future of Australian territories, Oc, 15, 2: 85—88.

44-22 Embree, J. F. Community analysis— an example of anthropology in government, AA, 46: 277—91.

44-23 Embree, J. F. Democracy in postwar Japan, AJS, 50: 205—07.

44-24 Embree, J. F. Military occupation of Japan, FES, 13, 19: 173—76.

44-25 Fauset, A. H. Black gods of the metropolis: Negro religious cults of the urban North. Phila., U. of Pa. Press.

44-26 Francolini, B. Bianchi e neri un Africa. Casa Editrice de Dott, Carlo Cya. Biblioteca de Studi Coloniali 11.

44-27 Gillin, J. Cultural adjustment, AA, 46: 429—47.

44-28 Gillin, J. Houses, food and the contact of cultures in a Guatemalan town, AcA, 1, 3: 344—59.

44-29 Grigson, W. V. The aboriginal in the future India, JRAI, 74: 33—41.

44-30 Harris, J. S. Some aspects of the economics of sixteen Ibo individuals, Af, 14: 302—35.

44-31 Hawthorn, H. B. The Maori: a study in acculturation. AAAM, 64.

44-32 Henry, J. and Z. Doll play of Pilagá Indian children. Research Monographs, 4, Amer. Orthopsychiatric Assoc., New York.

44-33 Herskovits, M. J. Native self-government, Foreign Affairs, 22: 413—23.

44-34 Herskovits, M. J. Drums and drummers in Afro-Brazilian cult life, Musical Quarterly, 30: 477—92.

44-35 Herskovits, M. J. Africa and the colonial problem, New Republic, 110: 280—81.

44-36 Hewett, E. L. The evolution of religion, EP, 51, 7: 121—28.

44-37 Hewett, E. L. Man and culture. MPA.

44-38 Hewett, E. L. Man and the state. MPA.

44-39 Hill, W. W. The Navaho Indians and the ghost dance of 1890, AA, 46: 523—27.

44-40 Hogbin, H. I. Native councils and native courts in the Solomon Islands, Oc, 14, 4: 247—83.

44-41 Honigmann, J. J. Morale in a primitive society, CP, 12: 228—36.

44-42 Hopgood, C. R. The future of Bantu languages in Northern Rhodesia, RLIJ, 2: 8—15.

44-43 Humphrey, N. D. Changing structure of the Detroit Mexican family: an index of acculturation, ASR, 9: 622—26.

44-44 Inselmann, R. Letub, the cult of the secrets of wealth. Thesis submitted to the faculty of the Kennedy School of Missions, Hartford Seminary Foundation. (Manuscript).

44-45 Ischer, T. Die Ethnographie hilft prähistorische Objekte interpretieren, Jahrb. d. Schweiz. Ges. f. Urgesch. 124—27.

44-46 Jeffreys, M. D. W. African suicides in the Bamenda division British Cameroons, RSSAT, 30, 2: 135—41.

44-47 Kelly, C. Some aspects of culture contact in eastern Australia, Oc, 15, 2: 142—53.

44-48 Kluckhohn, C. Anthropological research and world peace, in Approaches to World Peace, 4th. Symposium, Conf. on Sci., Philos. and Relig.: 143—52. New York.

44-49 Kluckhohn, C. and Mowrer, C. H. Culture and personality: a conceptual scheme, AA, 46: 1–29.

44-50 Knowlton, G. The Arhuaco Indians, twenty years after, AA, 46, 2: 263–66.

44-51 Kraus, B. S. Acculturation, a new approach to the Iroquoian problem, AAq, 9, 3: 302–18.

44-52 Krieger, A. The typological concept, AAq, 9: 271–88.

44-53 Krige, J. E. The magical thought pattern of the Bantu in relation to health services, AfS, 3: 1–13.

44-54 Kroeber, A. L. Configurations of cultural growth. Berkeley, California.

44-55 Kuer, D. A chapter in Navaho-Pueblo relations, AAq, 10, 1: 75–86.

44-56 Kuper, H. and Kaplan, S. Voluntary associations in an urban township, AfS, 3, 4: 178–86.

44-57 Lester, R. H. Effect of war on Fijian society, PIM, 15, 4: 33–37.

44-58 Majumdar, D. N. The fortunes of primitive tribes. Lucknow.

44-59 Malinowski, B. Freedom and civilization. New York.

44-60 Mekeel, S. An appraisal of the Indian Reorganization Act, AA, 46: 209–17.

44-61 Opler, M. E. Cultural and organic conceptions on contemporary world history, AA, 46: 448–60.

44-62 Orozco, L. C. Manifestations of democracy among Mexican Indians during the colonial period. Natl. Indian Institute, Washington.

44-63 Pierson, D. Herança social, Sg, 6, 1: 26–33.

44-64 Pierson, D. Interação simbólica e não simbólica, Sg, 6, 2: 123–33.

44-65 Redfield, R. The ethnological problem, in New perspectives of peace: 60–84. Chicago.

44-66 Reed, E. Navajo monolingualism, AA, 46, 1: 147–49.

44-67 Rouse, B. I. On the typological method, AAq, 10: 202–04.

44-68 Sanchez, G. I. Mexico in transition, Inter-Americana, 5: 95–97.

44-69 Stewart, O. C. Washo-Northern Paiute peyotism, UCPAAE, 40: 63–142.

44-70 Stewart, W. A. The recent development of crafts and industries in Palestine, Af, 14.

44-71 Thompson, L. Some perspectives in applied anthropology, ApA, 3, 3: 12–16.

44-72 Thompson, L. and Joseph, A. The Hopi way. Chicago.

44-73 Thurnwald, R. Origem, formação e transformação de Direito a luz das pesquizas etnologicas, Sg, 6, 1: 59–68; 6, 2: 156–65.

44-74 Titiev, M. Old Oraibi: a study of the Hopi Indians of Third Mesa. PMAEP, 22, 1.

44-75 Veldt, J. van der. The Catholic missions in the East Indies, KnW, 4, 27: 38–41.

44-76 Vendryes, J. Mana; introduction à l'histoire des religions. Paris.

44-77 Vivo, J. A. Acerca del problema indígena en Hispanoamérica AI, 4, 1: 31–36.

44-78 Warner, W. L., Havighurst, R. L., and Loeb, M. B. Who shall be educated? The challenge of unequal opportunities. New York.

44-79 Willems, E. Acculturation and the horse complex among German Brazilians, AA, 46, 2: 153–61.

44-80 Willems, E. Linguistic changes in German Brazilian communities, AcA, 1, 4: 448–63.

44-81 Williams, F. E. Mission influences amongst the Keveri of southwest Papua, Oc, 15, 2: 89–141.

44-82 Winterbotham, J. M. Africans, European culture, and the English language, RLIJ, 2: 1–7.

1945

45-1   Austen, L. Cultural changes in Kiriwina, Oc, 16, 2: 88—108.
45-2   Baker, S. J. Origins of the words pakeha and Maori, JPS, 54: 223—31.
45-3   Ballinger, M. A scientific approach to the problem of post-war employment
        and the non-European in South Africa, Human Problems in Central Africa,
        Livingstone, N. Rhodesia, 3: 21—32.
45-4   Bavinck, J. H. Christus en de Mystiek van het Oosten. Kampen.
45-5   Beaglehole, E. and P. The study of Maori life, JPS, 54: 235—37.
45-6   Beals, R. L. The contemporary culture of the Cáhita Indians. BAEB, 1, 2.
45-7   Boelaert, E. La situation démographique des Nkundo-Mongo. Centre d'Étude
        des Probl. Soc. Indig., Elizabethville.
45-8   Bourdillon, B. The future of native authorities, Af, 15, 3: 123—28.
45-9   Bourgeois, R. Moeurs et coutumes de Banyarwanda en territoire de Shangugu
        en 1935. Bulletin des Juridictions Indigènes et du Droit Coulounnier Congo-
        lais, 13, 5: 133—58.
45-10   Broom, L. A measure of conservatism, AA, 47, 4: 630—35.
45-11   Cahnman, W. J. France in Algeria— a problem of culture contact, Review
        of Politics, 7: 343—57, South Bend.
45-12   Capell, A. The future of education in Papua, Oc, 15, 4: 277—95.
45-13   Carr, L. G. , and Westez, C. Surviving folktales and herbal lore among the
        Shinnecock Indians of Long Island. JAF, 58: 113—23.
45-14   Carter, G. F. Plant geography and culture history in the American South-
        west. VFPA.
45-15   Clay, G. C. R. History of the Mankoya district. RLIC, 4.
45-16   Collier, J. The U.S. Indian Administration as a laboratory of ethnic rela-
        tions, SR, 12: 265—83.
45-17   Cressey, P. F. Chinese traits in European civilization: a study in diffusion,
        ASR, 10: 595—604.
45-18   Dellicour, M. F. La situation sociale au Congo, BIRCB, 16, 3: 558—60.
45-19   Dollard, J. The acquisition of new social habits, in The science of man in
        the world crisis, Linton, R. (ed.) New York.
45-20   Ekholm, G. F. Stratigraphy and chronology in Middle America, News Letter
        of the Archaeological Society of New Jersey, 13: 14—16.
45-21   Embree, J. F. Applied anthropology and its relation to anthropology, AA,
        47, 4: 635—37.
45-22   Embree, J. F. How to treat the Japanese; a complex issue, N. Y. Times
        Mag., Sept. 9.
45-23   Embree, J. F. Japanese legacy in Asia. Notes, 1, 1, IPRH.
45-24   Fortes, M. The dynamics of clanship among the Tallensi: being the first
        part of an analysis of the social structure of a Trans-Volta tribe. Ox-
        ford U. Press, London.
45-25   Fortes, M. The impact of the war on British West Africa, International
        Affairs, 21, 2: 206—19.
45-26   Fürer-Haimendorf, C. von. The Reddis of the Bison Hills. A study in ac-
        culturation. London.
45-27   García, A. Basis de una política indigenista, AI, 5, 2: 170—76.
45-28   García, A. El indigenismo en Columbia. Genesis y evolución, AI, 5, 3:
        217—34.
45-29   Geddes, W. R. Acceleration of social change in a Fijian community, Oc,
        16, 1: 1—14.

45-30   Gillin, J. Parallel cultures and the inhibitions to acculturation in a Guate-
        malan community, SF, 24, 1: 1—14.

45-31   Gillin, J. Personality formation from the comparative cultural point of
        view, in Sociological Foundations of the Psychiatric Disorders of Child-
        hood: 13—27. Langhorne, Pa.

45-32   Gireaud, M. Le métis Canadien— son rôle dans l'histoire des provinces de
        l'Oest. Travaux et mémoires de L'Institut d'Ethnologie, 44, Paris.

45-33   Gluckman, M. How the Bemba make their living: an appreciation of Richard's
        Land, labour, and diet in Northern Rhodesia, AA, 47: 57—75.

45-34   Goldfrank, E. S. Changing configurations in the social organization of a
        Blackfoot tribe during the reserve period, AESM, 8, 7: 1—73.

45-35   Goldfrank, E. S. Socialization, personality and the structure of Pueblo
        society, AA, 47: 516—37.

45-36   Goodwin, A. J. H. Method in prehistory. South African Archaeological
        Society, Capetown.

45-37   Grant, R. V. Chinook jargon, IJAL, 11, 4: 225—33.

45-38   Greenman, E. F. Material culture and the organism, AA, 47: 211—31.

45-39   Guthe, C. E. , Mead, M. and others. Manual for the study of food habits.
        NCRB, 111.

45-40   Guthrie, M. East Africa's reactions to European culture, JRSA, 93: 488—97.

45-41   Hall, R. A. English loan-words in Micronesian languages, La, 21, 3: 214—
        19.

45-42   Hallowell, A. I. The Rorschach technique in the study of personality and
        culture, AA, 47: 195—210.

45-43   Hallowell, A. I. Sociopsychological aspects of acculturation, in The science
        of man in the world crisis, Linton, R. (ed.): 171—200. New York.

45-44   Haury, E. W. The problem of contacts between the Southwestern United
        States and Mexico, SJA, 1, 1: 55—74.

45-45   Herskovits, M. J. Problem, method and theory in Afroamerican studies,
        AfA, 1, 1: 5—24.

45-46   Herskovits, M. J. The processes of culture change, in The science of
        man in the world crisis, Linton, R. (ed.): 143—70. New York.

45-47   Hewett, E. L. and Dutton, B. The Pueblo Indian world. U. of New Mexico
        Press, Albuquerque.

45-48   Hodgen, M. T. Glass and paper: an historical study of acculturation, SJA,
        1, 4: 466—97.

45-49   Hogbin, H. I. Notes and instructions to native administrations in the B.S.I.P.
        Oc, 16, 1.

45-50   Honigmann, J. J. and I. Alcoholic drinking in an Indian-White community,
        Quarterly Journal of Studies on Alcohol, 5: 576—619.

45-51   Hornell, J. Was there pre-Columbian contact between the peoples of
        Oceania and South America? JPS, 54: 167—91.

45-52   Hsu, F. L. K. Influence of South-Seas emigration in certain Chinese prov-
        inces, FEQ, 5: 47—59.

45-53   Hulstaert, G. Le problème des mulâtres, Af, 15, 3: 129—44.

45-54   Jeffreys, M. D. W. The death of a dialect, AfS, 4, 1: 37—40.

45-55   Kardiner, A. The concept of basic personality structure as an operational
        tool in the social sciences, in The science of man in the world crisis,
        Linton, R. (ed.). New York.

45-56   Kardiner, A. The psychological frontiers of society. Columbia Univ. Press.

45-57 Keesing, F. M. Applied anthropology in colonial administration, in The science of man in the world crisis, Linton, R. (ed.): 373–98. New York.

45-58 Keesing, F. M. Cultural trends in the Philippines, FEQ, 4, 2: 102–08.

45-59 Keesing, F. M. Extension work in Pacific islands, in Farmers of the world, Brunner, E. de S. and others: 19–36. New York.

45-60 Keesing, F. M. Native peoples of the Pacific world. New York.

45-61 Kennedy, R. The colonial administration and the future, in The science of man in the world crisis, Linton, R. (ed.). New York.

45-62 Kimball, S. T. Diversity and change in the culture of non-literate peoples, in Farmers of the world, Brunner, E. de S. and others: 8–18. New York.

45-63 Kluckhohn, C. A Navaho personal document with a brief Paretian analysis, SJA, 1, 2: 260–83.

45-64 Kluckhohn, C. Group tensions: analysis of a case history, in Approaches to national unity, 5th Symposium, Conf. on Sci., Phil., and Religion: 222–43. New York.

45-65 Kluckhohn, C. The personal document in anthropological science, in The use of personal documents in history, anthropology, and society, Gottschalk, L. and others. SSRCB, 53.

45-66 Kluckhohn, C. and Kelly, W. H. The concept of culture, in The science of man in the world crisis, Linton, R. (ed.). New York.

45-67 Kroeber, A. L. A Yurok war reminiscence: the use of autobiographical evidence, SJA, 1, 3: 318–32.

45-68 Kuper, H. The marriage of a Swazi princess, Af, 15, 3: 145–55.

45-69 Kuper, H. Social anthropology as a study of culture contacts, SAJS, 41: 88–101.

45-70 Lantis, M. Applied anthropology as a public service, ApA, 4, 1: 20–32.

45-71 La Violette, F. Americans of Japanese ancestry. Toronto.

45-72 Lee, A. M. Levels of culture as levels of social generalization, ASR, 10: 485–95.

45-73 Leighton, A. H. The governing of men. Princeton Univ. Press.

45-74 Letele, G. L. A preliminary study of the Nguni language on Southern Sotho. New Series, 12, Univ. of Cape Town.

45-75 Linton, R. The cultural background of personality. New York.

45-76 Linton, R. (ed.) The science of man in the world crisis. New York.

45-77 Loomis, C. P. Extension work in Latin America, in Farmers of the world, Brunner, E. de S. and others: 117–37. New York.

45-78 Lowie, R. H. A note on Lapp culture history, SJA, 1, 4: 447–54.

45-79 Malinowski, B. The dynamics of culture change. Yale Univ. Press.

45-80 Malouf, C. and Arline, A. The effects of Spanish slavery on the Indians of the intermountain West, SJA, 1, 3: 378–91.

45-81 Murdock, G. P. The common denominator of culture, in The science of man in the world crisis, Linton, R. (ed.). New York.

45-82 Opler, Morris E. Themes as dynamic forces in culture, AJS, 51: 198–206.

45-83 Powdermaker, H. Review of "the origin and function of culture," by Rôheim, G., AA, 47: 308–12.

45-84 Radin, P. The road of life and death. New York.

45-85 Ramos, A. Die Negerkulturen in de Neuen Welt. Erlenbach-Zürich.

45-86 Ransom, J. E. Writing as a medium of acculturation among the Aleut, SJA, 59, 3: 333–44.

45-87 Reay, M. A half-caste aboriginal community in northwestern New South Wales, Oc. 15, 4: 296–323.

45-88 Redfield, R. Ethnic groups and nationality, AI, 5, 3: 235−45.
45-89 Reichard, G. A. Linguistic diversity among the Navaho Indians, IFAL, 11, 3: 156−68.
45-90 Schapera, I. Notes on the history of the Kaa, AfS, 4, 3: 109−12.
45-91 Scherman, L. India and Kroeber's Configurations of culture growth; tr. by Sheldon, J. G., Am. Oriental Soc. J., 65: 133−44.
45-92 Senter, D. Acculturation of New Mexican villagers in comparison to adjustment patterns of other Spanish-speaking Americans, RS, 10, 1: 31−47.
45-93 Smith, G. H. The missionary and anthropology. Chicago.
45-94 Speck, F. G. The Iroquois, a study in cultural evolution. CISB, 23.
45-95 Speck, F. G. The Iroquois— the historical versus the ethnological view, CISNL, 15, 3: 33−36.
45-96 Spicer, E. H. El problema Yaqui, AI, 5, 4: 273−86.
45-97 Steward, J. The changing Indian, in The science of man in the world crisis, Linton, R. (ed.). New York.
45-98 Strong, W. D. The occurrence and wider implications of a "ghost cult" on the Columbia River suggested by carvings in wood, bone, and stone, AA, 47: 244−61.
45-99 Tannous, A. I. Extension work among the Arab Fellahin, in Farmers of the world, Brunner, E. de S. and others, 78−100. New York.
45-100 Tax, S. Anthropology and administration, AI, 5: 21−33.
45-101 Thompson, L. Logico-aesthetic integration in Hopi culture, AA, 47: 540−553
45-102 Thompson, L. The native culture of the Marianas Islands. BPBMB, 185.
45-103 Useem, J. The changing structure of a Micronesian society, AA, 47, 4: 567−89.
45-104 Villa Rojas, A. La civilización y el Indio, Boletín del Instituto Indigenista Nacional, 1, 1: 53−59.
45-105 Wallis, W. D. Inference of relative age of culture traits from magnitude of distribution, SJA, 1, 1: 142−159.
45-106 Watson, J. B. Historic influences and change in the economy of a Southern Mato Grosso tribe, AcA, 3: 3−25.
45-107 Watson, V. D. An example of rural Brazilian acculturation, AcA, 3: 152−62.
45-108 West, J. Plainville, U.S.A. Columbia Univ. Press, New York.
45-109 White, L. "Diffusion vs. evolution": an anti-evolutionist fallacy, AA, 47: 339−56.
45-110 White, L. History, evolutionism and functionalism: three types of interpretation of culture, SJA, 1: 221−48.
45-111 White, L. The origin and nature of speech, Twentieth Century English: 93−103. New York.
45-112 Widengren, G. Evolutionism and the problem of the origin of religion, Et, 10, 2−3: 57−96.
45-113 Willems, E. Problemas de aculturação no Brasil meridionial, AcA, 3, 3: 145−51.
45-114 Wilson, G. and M. The analysis of social change: based on observations in Central Africa. Cambridge Univ. Press.
45-115 Woolston, H. Process of assimilation, SF, 23: 416−24.

1946

46-1   Altman, G. J. A Navaho wedding, Mk, 20, 5: 159−64.

46-2 Amoo, J. W. A. The effect of Western influence on Akan marriage, Af, 16: 228–37.

46-3 Anderson, J. Maori words incorporated into the English language. JPS, 54: 141–62.

46-4 Angel, J. L. Social biology of Greek culture growth, AA, 48: 493–533.

46-5 Armattoe, R. E. G. The golden age of West African civilization. Lomeshie Research Centre for Anthropology and Race Biology, Londonderry.

46-6 Baldus, H. Akkulturation in Araguaya-Gebiet, An, 41–44: 889–91.

46-7 Barnouw, A. Cross currents of culture in Indonesia, FEQ, 5: 143–52.

46-8 Bastide, R. Contribuição ao estudo do sincretismo católicofetichista, AA, 48: 11–43.

46-9 Beaglehole, E. and P. Some modern Maoris. New Zealand Council for Educational Research, Wellington.

46-10 Beaglehole, E. and P. Contemporary Maori death customs, JPS, 54: 91–116.

46-11 Beals, R. L. Cheran: a Sierra Tarascan village. ISAP, 2.

46-12 Bennett, J. W. The interpretations of Pueblo culture: a question of values, SJA, 2, 4: 361–74.

46-13 Bidney, D. The concept of cultural crisis, AA, 48: 534–53.

46-14 Bidney, D. On the so-called anti-evolutionist fallacy: a reply to Leslie A. White, AA, 48: 293–97.

46-15 Birket-Smith, K. Geschichte der Kultur. Eine allgemeine Ethnologie, Zürich.

46-16 Bolton, C. Lo que quieren los negros, AfA, 2, 3: 77–80.

46-17 Brew, J. O. Archaeology of Alkali-Ridge, southeastern Utah. PMAEP, 21.

46-18 Childe, C. V. G. What happened in history. New York.

46-19 Childs, S. H. Christian marriage in Nigeria, Af, 16, 4: 238–46.

46-20 Clark, G. From savagery to civilization. London.

46-21 Cleene, N. de. Le clan matrilinéal dans la société indigène, hier, aujourd'hui, demain. Institut Royal Colonial Belge, Brussels.

46-22 Comas, J. Social service and anthropology in Mexico, Boletín Inst. Internal. Am. de Protec. a la Infincia, 20: 67–72.

46-23 Cook, S. F. Human sacrifice and warfare as factors in the demography of pre-colonial Mexico, HB, 18, 2: 81–102.

46-24 Cooper, J. M. Anthropology and peace, Catholic Univ. Bulletin, 13, 6: 8, 11.

46-25 Cooper, J. M. The culture of the northeastern Indian hunters: a reconstructive interpretation, PMAEP, 3: 272–305.

46-26 Cooper, J. M. Problems of international understanding, APSP, 90: 314–17.

46-27 Datta-Majumdar, N. The "malaise" of culture, in Snowballs of Garhwal, Folk Culture Series, 1: 3–14. Lucknow.

46-28 Derrick, R. A. A history of Fiji. Suva.

46-29 Eduardo, O. C. Three way religious acculturation in a north Brazilian city, AI, 6: 81–90.

46-30 Elkin, A. P. Conservation of aboriginal peoples whose modes of life are of scientific interest, Mn, 46, 94: 102–03.

46-31 Embree, J. F. Micronesia: the Navy and democracy, FES, 15, 11: 161–64.

46-32 Embree, J. F. Military government in Saipan and Tinian, a report on the organization of Susupe and Churo, together with notes on the attitudes of the people involved, ApA, 5: 1–39.

46-33 Evans-Pritchard, E. E. Applied anthropology (lecture to Oxford Anthropological Society, Nov. 27), Af, 16, 2: 92–98.

46-34 Firth, R. Malay fishermen: their peasant economy. London.

46-35 Forde, D. and Scott, R. The native economies of Nigeria, in The economics of a tropical dependency, Perham, M. (ed.). Nuffield College, London.

46-36 Fuchs, S. Changes and developments in the population of the Nimar district in the central provinces of India, An, 41–44: 46–68.

46-37 Fuchs, S. What some tribes and castes of central India think about God, An, 41–44: 883–87.

46-38 Garrod, D. A. E. Environment, tools and man. Cambridge U. Press.

46-39 Geddes, W. R. Deuba, a study of a Fijian village. PSM, 22.

46-40 Goldfrank, E. S. More on irrigation agriculture, and Navaho community leadership, AA, 48, 3: 473–76.

46-41 Green, A. W. Social values and psychotherapy, JPe, 14, 199ff.

46-42 Greenberg, J. The influence of Islam on a Sudanese religion. AESM, 10.

46-43 Griffin, J. B. Cultural change and continuity in eastern U.S. archaeology, PMAEP, 3: 37–95.

46-44 Grigson, W. V. The aboriginal in the future India, MIA, 26, 2: 81–96.

46-45 Gusinde, M. Beitrag zur Forschungsgeschichte der Naturvölker Südamerikas, Archiv für Völkerkunde, 1: 1–94. Vienna.

46-46 Haring, D. (ed.) Japan's prospect. Cambridge.

46-47 Harper, A. G. Canada's Indian administration, AI, 6.

46-48 Hatt, R. T. Installing a Cayuga chief, CISNL, 15, 6: 65–71.

46-49 Hawley, F. Group-designed behavior patterns in two acculturating groups, SJA, 2: 133–51.

46-50 Hawley, F. The role of Pueblo social organization in the dissemination of Catholicism, AA, 48, 3: 407–16.

46-51 Henry, J. Initial reactions to the Americans in Japan, Jnl. of Social Issues, 2, 3: 19–25.

46-52 Herskovits, M. J. A reply to Dr. Ashley Montagu, AA, 48, 4: 667.

46-53 Hogbin, H. I. Local government for New Guinea, Oc, 17, 1: 38–66.

46-54 Honigmann, J. J. Ethnography and acculturation of the Fort Nelson Slave. YUPA, 33.

46-55 Hornell, J. Water transport: origins and early evolution. Cambridge U. Press.

46-56 Hutton, J. H. Problems of reconstruction in the Assam hills, MIA, 26, 2: 97–109.

46-57 Hutton, J. H. West Africa and Indonesia: a problem in distribution, JRAI, 76: 4–12.

46-58 Infeld, H. F. Cooperative living in Palestine. London.

46-59 Kibbe, P. R. Latin Americans in Texas. U. of New Mexico Press.

46-60 Kluckhohn, C. Personality formation among the Navaho Indians, So, 9, 2 & 3: 128–32.

46-61 Kluckhohn, C. Review of A. L. Kroeber's "Configurations of culture growth," AJS, 51: 336–41.

46-62 Kluckhohn, C., and Leighton, D. C. The Navaho. Harvard U. Press.

46-63 Kroeber, A. L. History and evolution, SJA, 2, 1: 1–15.

46-64 Lam, M. M. Acculturation and the war, SSR, 30: 255–63.

46-65 Lastres, J. B. Algunos problemas modernos de la medicina incaica, RMNL, 15: 33–49.

46-66 Lind, A. A. The impact of languages and the coalescence of the fragments. A preliminary study in the affinities of the Maori language, JPS, 55, 2: 85–110, 175–86.

46-67 Linne, S. Museum news— prehistoric and modern Hopi pottery, Et, 11, 1 & 2: 89-98.

46-68 Lips, J. E. The origin of things. New York.

46-69 Lowie, R. H. Evolution in cultural anthropology: a reply to Leslie White, AA, 48: 222-23.

46-70 Lowie, R. H. Professor White and "anti-evolutionist" schools, SJA, 2: 240-41.

46-71 Macgregor, G. Warriors without weapons: a study of the society and personality development of the Pine Ridge Sioux. Chicago.

46-72 McQueen, H. Vocations for Maori youth. New Zealand Council for Educational Research. Wellington.

46-73 Malherk, E. C. The blingual school: a study of bilingualism in South Africa. London.

46-74 Mead, M. Professional problems of education in dependent countries, Journal of Negro Educ., 15, 3: 346-57.

46-75 Meggers, B. J. Recent trends in American ethnology, AA, 48: 176-214.

46-76 Montagu, M. F. A. Anthropology and social engineering, AA, 48, 4: 666-67.

46-77 Naerssen, F. H. van. Culture contacts and social conflicts in Indonesia. Southeast Asia Institute (translated from Dutch by A. J. Barnouw).

46-78 Opler, Morris E. The creative role of shamanism in Mescalero Apache mythology, JAF, 59: 268-81.

46-79 Osgood, C. Contacto prehistorico entre Sud América y las Antillas, Acta Venezolana, 1, 3: 286-90. Caracas, Venezuela.

46-80 Perham, M. F. (ed.) The economics of a tropical dependency. London. 1946-1948.

46-81 Phan Giang, Literature in Annam; how a popular literature was born of French inspiration, Asiatic Review, 42: 382-84.

46-82 Philipps, T. An African culture of today in the country between the Bantu Negro and the Semitic Arab, An, 41-44: 193-211.

46-83 Pijoan, M. The health and customs of the Misketo Indians of Northern Nicaragua: interrelationships in a medical program, AI, 6, 2: 157-83.

46-84 Pijoan, M. Summa artis. Historia general del arte. Arte precolombino, Mexicano y Maya, 10, Madrid.

46-85 Quimby, G. I. Natchez social structure as an instrument of assimilation, AA, 48, 1: 134-37.

46-86 Radin, P. Japanese ceremonies and festivals in California, SJA, 2: 152-79.

46-87 Rao, P. K. Culture conflicts, cause and cure. Raopura, Baroda, India.

46-88 Reichel-Dolmatoff, G. Las zonas culturales de Columbia y sus elementos constitivos, Ethnologia, 11, 1: 3-17. Bogotá.

46-89 Riesenfeld, A. The swing in Melanesia and some other regions, An, 41-44: 737-56.

46-90 Shropshire, D. W. T. Primitive marriage and European law. A South African investigation. London.

46-91 Speiser, F. Zur Kulturgeschichte Neu-Caledoniens, VNGB, 55: 1-24.

46-92 Spicer, E. H. Social organization and disorganization in an Arizona Yaqui village. U. of Chicago.

46-93 Tatum, R. M. Minnesota trade material in Colorado, SWL, 12, 1: 4-5.

46-94 Taylor, D. Loan words in Dominica Island Carib, IJAL, 12, 4: 213-16.

46-95 Thompson, L. Inquest of a heuristic approach to the study of mankind, Phil. of Science, 13, 1: 53-66.

46-96   Thompson, L. Crisis on Guam, FEQ, 6: 5−11.
46-97   Underhill, R. Papago Indian religion. CUCA, 33.
46-98   Useem, J. Governing the occupied areas of the South Pacific: wartime lessons and peacetime proposals, ApA, 4, 3: 1−10.
46-99   Useem, J. Social reconstruction in Micronesia, FES, 15: 21−24.
46-100 Useem, J. Americans as governors of natives in the Pacific, Jnl. of Social Issues, 2, 3: 39−49.
46-101 Voegelin, E. W. The diffusion of a new folk custom, AA, 48, 2: 290−93.
46-102 White, L. A. Kroeber's "Configurations of culture growth," AA, 48: 78−93
46-103 Willems, E. A aculturacao dos Alemaes no Brasil. Sao Paulo.
46-104 Wonderly, W. L. Phonemic acculturation in Zoque, IJAL, 12, 2: 92−95.

<h2 style="text-align:center">1947</h2>

47-1   Adams, R. F. G. OBƐRIƆKAIMƐ: a new African language and script, Af, 17, 1: 24−34.
47-2   Adams, S. C. Acculturation of the Delta Negro, SF, 26: 202−05.
47-3   Aginsky, B. W. Recent changes in the Pomo family. Paper read at the 46th Annual Meeting of the AAA in Albuquerque.
47-4   Aginsky, B. W. and E. G. A resultant of intercultural relations, SF, 26: 84−87.
47-5   Altman, B. J. The Yaqui Easter play of Guadalupe, Arizona, Mk, 21, 1: 19−23.
47-6   Arquin, F. Reviewing Peruvian crafts, Bulletin of the Pan American Union, 622−26. Washington, D.C.
47-7   Ashton, E. H. Democracy and indirect rule, Af, 17, 4: 235−51.
47-8   Barker, G. Social functions of language in a Mexican-American community, AcA, 5: 185−202.
47-9   Batten, T. R. Problems of African development: part I: land and labor. London.
47-10 Beaglehole, E. Government and administration in Polynesia, in Specialized studies in Polynesian anthropology, BPBMB, 193: 58−74.
47-11 Beaglehole, E. Trusteeship and New Zealand's Pacific dependencies, JPS, 56, 2: 128−56.
47-12 Beckmann, J. Die katholische Kirche in neuen Afrika. Einsiedeln und Köln.
47-13 Belshaw, C. S. Native politics in the Solomon Islands, PA, 20, June.
47-14 Benedict, R. The chrysanthemum and the sword. Boston.
47-15 Berndt, R. M. and C. H. Card games among aborigines of the Northern Territory, Oc, 17, 3: 248−69.
47-16 Bhargava, B. S. Problems of reclamation and reform of criminal tribes, EA, 1, 2: 41−58.
47-17 Bidney, D. Culture theory and the problem of cultural crisis, in Approaches to group understanding, 6th Symposium, Conference on Science, Philos. and Religion, New York: 553−73.
47-18 Bidney, D. Human nature and the cultural process, AA, 49, 3: 375−400.
47-19 Bidney, D. The problem of social and cultural evolution: a reply to A. R. Radcliffe-Brown, AA, 49, 3: 524−27.
47-20 Bogardus, E. S. Japanese return to the West Coast, SSR, 31: 226−33.
47-21 Boultbe, L. A study in continuity and ancient survivals in India and Western Europe, JASB, 2, 1: 15−27.

47-22   Broom, L. Transitional adjustments of Japanese-American families to relocation, ASR, 12: 201—09.

47-23   Burrows, E. G. Hawaiian Americans. The mingling of Japanese, Chinese, Polynesian, and American cultures. New Haven.

47-24   Cato, A. C. A new religious cult in Fiji, Oc, 18, 146—56.

47-25   Childe, V. G. History. London.

47-26   Cook, S. F. The interrelation of population, food supply, and building in pre-conquest central Mexico, AAq, 13, 1: 45—52.

47-27   Cook, S. F. Survivorship in aboriginal populations, HB, 19, 2: 83—89.

47-28   Davidson, D. S. Footwear of the Australian aborigines: environmental vs. cultural determination, SJA, 3, 2: 114—23.

47-29   Devereux, G. Potential contribution of the Moi to the cultural landscape of Indo China, FEQ, 6: 390—95.

47-30   Doroshenko, V. V. Development of written languages among the peoples of the north, American Review on the Soviet Union, 8, 2: 43—51.

47-31   Duff, R. S. The evolution of native culture in New Zealand: Moa Hunters, Morioris, Maoris, Ma, 3, 10: 281—91, 313—22.

47-32   Dyk, W. A Navaho autobiography. VFPA, 8.

47-33   Elkin, A. P. Aboriginal evidence and justice in North Australia, Oc, 17, 3: 173—210.

47-34   Erikson, E. H. Ego development and historical change, The Psychoanalytic Study of the Child, Annual, 2: 359—96.

47-35   Félice, A. de. Influence du milieu américain sur les traditions orales françaises aux États-Unis, ICAP, 28: 247—54.

47-36   Firth, R. Social problems and research in British West Africa, parts I and II, Af, 17, 2: 77—92; 3: 170—80.

47-37   Flannery, R. The changing form and functions of the Gros Ventre grass dance, PM, 20, 3: 39—70.

47-38   Fuente, J. de la. Discriminacíon y negacíon del Indio, AI, 7, 3: 211—15.

47-39   Fürer-Haimendorf, C. Primitive tribes in an Indian state. An account of the progress made in Hyderabad State in assuring the future of its aboriginal inhabitants, Illustrated London News, 211, 5652: 190—93, Aug. 16.

47-40   Garfield, V. E. Historical aspects of Tlingit clans in Angoon, Alaska, AA, 49: 438—52.

47-41   Gibb, H. A. R. Modern trends in Islam. U. of Chicago Press, Chicago.

47-42   Gillin, J. Moche— a Peruvian coastal community. SIP, 3.

47-43   Gillin, J. Modern Latin American culture, SF, 25, 3: 243—48.

47-44   Gluckman, M. Malinowski's "functional" analysis of social change, Af, 2: 103—21.

47-45   Goldschmidt, W. As you sow. New York.

47-46   Goto, M. Diffusion or independent invention? An, 2, 2.

47-47   Greenberg, J. H. Islam and clan organization among the Hausa, SJA, 3, 3: 193—211.

47-48   Grigson, W. V. The challenge of backwardness. Hyderabad-Deccan.

47-49   Grottanelli, V. L. Asiatic influences on Somali culture, Et, 12, 4: 153—81.

47-50   Hadlock, W. S. The significance of certain textiles found at Redbank, New Brunswick, in relation to the history of the culture area, Acadian Naturalist, Bulletin of the Nat. Hist. Society of New Brunswick, 2, 8: 49—61.

47-51   Haekel, J. von. Jugend weihe und Männerfest auf Feuerland. Ein Beitrag zu ihrer kulturhistorischen Stellung, MAGW (Mitt. der Österreich. Gesell. f. Anthropol., Ethnol. und Prähist.), 73−77, 1−3: 84−114.

47-52 Hambly, W. D. Uneasy lies the head that wears a crown, CMNHB, 18, 10: 8

47-53 Harrison, H. S. The origin of the driving belt, Mn, 47: 114−15.

47-54 Heizer, R. F. Francis Drake and the California Indians, UCPAAE, 42: 251−302.

47-55 Heizer, R. F. Historical North Pacific culture influences in the Santa Barbara region, Mk, 21, 5: 150−52.

47-56 Henry, J. Cultural discontinuity and the shadow of the past, SM, 66, 3: 248−54.

47-57 Herskovits, M. J. and F. S. Trinidad village. New York.

47-58 Hesselberth, C. The fall of a culture, Journal of the Illinois State Archaeological Society, 5, 1: 10−13.

47-59 Hogbin, H. I. Native Christianity in a New Guinea village, Oc, 18, 1: 1−35.

47-60 Honigmann, J. J. Cultural dynamics of sex, Ps, 10, 1: 37−48.

47-61 Honigmann, J. J. Witch-fear in post-contact Kaska society, AA, 49: 222−43

47-62 Honigmann, J. J. A new attack on cultural lag; the significance of anthropological knowledge for problems of the psychiatrists, Antioch Rev., 7: 55−63.

47-63 Hulse, F. S. Some effects of the war upon Japanese society, FEQ, 7, 1: 22−42.

47-64 Hulse, F. S. Technological development and personal incentive in Japan, SJA, 3, 2: 124−29.

47-65 Humphrey, N. The Liguru and the land. Government Printer, Nairobi.

47-66 Jacobs, M. Cultures in the present world crisis, HR, 1, 2: 228−39.

47-67 Kardiner, A. and Spiegel, H. War stress and neurotic illness. New York.

47-68 Keesing, F. M. Administration in Pacific islands, FES, 16: 61−65.

47-69 Keesing, F. M. Acculturation in Polynesia, in Specialized studies in Polynesian anthropology, BPBMB, 193: 32−46.

47-70 Keesing, M. Education in Polynesia, in Specialized studies in Polynesian anthropology, BPBMB, 193: 47−57.

47-71 King, A. R. Status personality change in northern Negroes in southern United States, SF, 26, 2: 153−66.

47-72 Kinietz, W. V. Chippewa village: the story of Katikitegon. CISB, 25.

47-73 Kroeber, A. L. A Southwestern personality type, SJA, 3, 2: 108−13.

47-74 Kroeber, A. L. Review of "A study of history," by A. J. Toynbee, AA, 49: 294−99.

47-75 Kunst, J. A hypothesis about the origin of the gong, Et, 12, 1 & 2, 79−85.

47-76 Kunst, J. Once more "a hypothesis about the origin of the gong," Et, 12, 4: 147.

47-77 Kuper, H. The uniform of colour. A study of the white-black relationship in Swaziland. Johannesburg.

47-78 LaBarre, W. Primitive psychotherapy in native American cultures: peyotism and confession, JASP, 47, 3: 301−07.

47-79 Lambert, H. W. The use of indigenous authorities in tribal administration: studies of the Meru in Kenya Colony. SASC, 16.

47-80 Laviosa Zambotti, P. Origini e diffusione della civiltà. Milano.

47-81 Lechler, G. The origin of the driving belt, Mn, 47: 53−55.

47-82 Leighton, D. C. and Kluckhohn, C. Children of the people: the Navaho individual and his development. Cambridge, Mass.

47-83 Levin, R. Marriage in Langa native location. SASC, 16.

47-84 Lewis, G. The beginning of civilization in America, AA, 49: 1–24.
47-85 Lewis, O. Wealth differences in a Mexican village, SM, 15, 2: 127–32.
47-86 Little, K. L. Nende political institutions in transition, Af, 17, 1: 8–23.
47-87 Linton, R. The vanishing American Negro, American Mercury, 64, 278: 135–39.
47-88 Loomis, C. P. Applied anthropology in Latin America, ApA, 6: 31–33.
47-89 Manker, E. The study and preservation of the ancient Lapp culture: Sweeden's contribution since 1939, AA, 48: 98–100.
47-90 Marcelin, E. Les grands dieux du vodou haïtien, JSA, 36: 51–135.
47-91 McBryde, F. W. Cultural and historical geography of southwest Guatemala, SIP, 4.
47-92 McEwen, J. M. The development of Maori culture since the advent of the pakeha, JPS, 56, 2: 173–87.
47-93 Mead, M. The implications of culture change for personality development, AJO, 17: 633–46.
47-94 Miyamoto, S. F. and O'Brien, R. W. A survey of some changes in the Seattle Japanese community since evacuation, Research Studies of Wash. State College, 15, 2: 147–54. Pullman, Washington.
47-95 Mizrahi, H. Recent changes in the life of the Persian Jews, Ed, 3, 1 & 2: 88–90.
47-96 Molina, M. F. Study of a psychopathic personality in Guatemala, Ps, 10, 1: 31–36.
47-97 Morang, D. Modern designs inspired by ancient Indian arts, EP, 54, 11: 270–71.
47-98 Mukerji, D. P. Anthropology and cultural reconstruction, JASB, 2, 1: 28–41.
47-99 Naerssen, F. H. van. Culture contacts and social conditions in Indonesia. Southeast Asia Institute, New York.
47-100 Nicholls, E. G. L. The local authority and its African citizen, RLIJ, 5: 56–61.
47-101 Nooteboom, C. The study of primitive sea-going craft as an ethnological problem, IAE, 45: 216–224.
47-102 Oberg, K. O desenvolvimento da economia dos provos primitivos, So, 9, 2: 164–78.
47-103 Opler, Morris E. Cultural alternatives and educational theory, Harvard Educational Review, 17, 1: 28–44.
47-104 Ortiz, F. Las músicas africanas en Cuba, RAE, 1, 2, 4–5: 235–53.
47-105 Parrinder, E. G. S. Christian marriage in French West Africa, Af, 17, 4: 260–68.
47-106 Patai, R. On culture contact and its working in modern Palestine. AAAM, 67.
47-107 Peckham, H. H. Pontiac and the Indian uprising. Princeton U. Press.
47-108 Pierson, D. and Cunha, M. W. V. da. Research and research possibilities in Brazil with particular reference to culture and culture change, AcA, 5, 1 & 2: 18–82.
47-109 Radcliffe-Brown, A. R. Evolution, social or cultural? AA, 49: 78–83.
47-110 Ramos, A. Introdução a antropologia brasileira, 2: as culturas europieas e os contactos reciais e culturais. Rio de Janeiro.
47-111 Read, K. E. Effects of the Pacific war in the Markham Valley, New Guinea, Oc, 18, 2: 95–116.
47-112 Redfield, R. The folk society, AJS, 52, 4: 292–308.

47-113 Reifen, D. On: Culture contact in modern Palestine, Ed, 2, 3 & 4: 298.

47-114 Riesenfeld, A. Who are the betel people? IAE, 45: 216—224.

47-115 Robin, J. L'évolution du mariage coutumier chez les Musulmans de Sénégal, Af, 17, 3: 192—201.

47-116 Rose, F. Malay influence on aboriginal totemism in northern Australia, Mn, 47.

47-117 Rouget, G. La conque comme signe des migrations océaniennes en Amérique ICAP, 28: 297—306.

47-118 Rouse, I. Ceramic traditions and sequences in Connecticut, Bulletin of the Archaeological Society of Conn., 21: 10—25. New Haven.

47-119 Sachs, W. Black hamlet. Boston.

47-120 Sady, R. R. The Menominee: transition from trusteeship, ApA, 6: 1—14.

47-121 Saenz Poggis, J. Historia de la musica guatemalteca desde la monarquía española hasta fines del año de 1877, ASGH, 22, 1—2: 6—54.

47-122 Schapera, I. Migrant labour and tribal life. Oxford U. Press.

47-123 Schmidt, L. von. Die Volkskunde als Geisteswissenschaft, MAGW (Mitt. der Öst. Ges. f. Anth., Eth. und Präh.), 73—77, 1—3: 115—37.

47-124 Shepherd, R. H-W. and Paver, B. G. African contrasts: the story of a South African people. Capetown.

47-125 Siegel, B. J. The meaning of history in anthropology as exemplified by Near Eastern culture materials, SJA, 3, 1: 50—56.

47-126 Somasundaram, A. M. Segregation or assimilation? MIA, 27, 1: 66—73.

47-127 Speck, F. G. The banished wife and the maid without hands; an European tale from the Mohawk Iroquois of St. Regis, New York, FQ, 3: 312—19.

47-128 Speck, F. G. Notes on social and economic conditions among the Creek Indians of Alabama in 1941, AI, 7, 3: 195—98.

47-129 Spencer, R. F. Spanish loanwords in Keresan, SJA, 3, 2: 130—146.

47-130 Spicer, E. H. Yaqui villages past and present, Kv, 13, 1: 2—12.

47-131 Spoehr, A. Changing kinship systems, FMNHAS, 33, 4: 159—235.

47-132 Stanislawski, D. Tarascan political geography, AA, 49: 46—55.

47-133 Steward, J. H. American cultural history in the light of South America, SJA, 3, 2: 85—107.

47-134 Stout, D. B. San Blas Cuna acculturation: an introduction. VPFA, 9.

47-135 Stout, D. B. Ethno-linguistic observations on San Blas Cuna, IJAL, 13: 9—12.

47-136 Swanton, J. R. The primary centers of civilization, SIR: 367—78.

47-137 Thompson, L. Guam and its people. Princeton (revised edition).

47-138 Thompson, L. and Joseph, A. White pressures on Indian personality and culture, AJS, 53: 17—22.

47-139 Tucci, G. L'afroamericanistica ei soui problemi, Revista di Ethnografia, 1, 3—4: 1—12.

47-140 Useem, J. Applied anthropology in Micronesia, ApA, 6, 4: 1—10.

47-141 Vaughan, B. H. Adjustment problems in a concentration camp, SSR, 32: 513—18.

47-142 Villa Rojas, A. El problema indígena de Mexico, BI, 3: 242—57.

47-143 Vries, D. de. Culturele aspectin van de verhouding Nederland-Indonesie. Amsterdam.

47-144 Wainwright, G. A. Early foreign trade in East Africa, Mn, 47: 143—48.

47-145 Warner, W. L. and Srole, L. Social systems of American ethnic groups, SR, 14: 104—09.

47-146 Warner, W. L. and Low, J. O. The social system of the modern factory. The strike: a social analysis. New Haven.

47-147 Webb, J. H. The cultural front in Honduras, Bull. of the Pan. Am. Union, 81, 10: 558—64.

47-148 White, L. A. Culturological vs. psychological interpretation of human nature, ASR, 12: 686—98.

47-149 White, L. A. Energy and the development of civilization (Radio address; Serving through science, U.S. Rubber Co.), in The scientists speak, Weaver, W. (ed.): 302—05, New York.

47-150 White, L. A. Evolutionary stages, progress, and the evaluation of cultures, SJA, 3, 3: 165—92.

47-151 Whitman, W. The Pueblo Indians of San Ildefonso: a changing culture. Columbia U. Press.

47-152 Willems, E. Cunha: tradição e transição em uma cultura rural do Brasil. São Paulo.

47-153 Willems, E. and Saito, H. Shindô-Renmei, um problema de aculturação, So, 9, 2: 133—52.

1948

48-1   Aiyappan, A. Report on the socio-economic conditions of the aboriginal tribes of the province of Madras. Government Press, Madras.

48-2   Aiyappan, A. Theories of culture change and culture contact, in Essays in anthropology presented to S. C. Roy: 37—49. Calcutta.

48-3   Arboleda, L. J. M. El India en la colonia. Estudio basado especialmente en documentos del Archivo Central del Cauca. Prensas del Ministero de Educatión. Bogotá.

48-4   Arsenio, M. E. Chinese elements in the Tagalog language. Manila.

48-5   Baal, J. van. De westerse bechaving als constante factor in het hedendaagse acculturatie-proces, Indonesië, 2: 102—40.

48-6   Barennes, Y. La modernisation rurale au Maroc. Paris.

48-7   Beaglehole, E. Social and political changes in the Cook Islands, PA, 21: 383—98.

48-8   Beardsley, R. K. Culture sequences in central California archaeology, AAq, 14, 1: 1—28.

48-9   Belshaw, C. S. Post-war developments in the Solomon Islands, FES, 17: 95—98.

48-10 Benedict, R. Anthropology and the humanities, AA, 50: 585—94.

48-11 Bhaduri, M. B. Hindu influence on Munda songs, in Essays in anthropology presented to S. C. Roy: 256—60. Calcutta.

48-12 Billig, O., Gillin, J., and Davidson, W. Aspects of personality and culture in a Guatemalan community: ethnological and Rorschach approaches, JPe, 16: 154—87, 326—68.

48-13 Braidwood, R. J. Prehistoric men. Chicago Nat. Hist. Museum, Popular Series, Anthropology, 37. Chicago.

48-14 Bullen, R. P. Culture dynamics in eastern Massachusetts, AAq, 14, 1: 36—48.

48-15 Burns, A. History of Nigeria (revised edition). London.

48-16 Carothers, J. C. A study of mental derangement in Africans, and an attempt to explain its peculiarities, more especially in relation to the African attitude to life, Ps, 11: 47—89.

48-17   Chamberlain, R. S. The conquest and colonization of Yucatan, 1517—1550, CIWP, 582.

48-18   Chêng, Tê-ch'ao. Acculturation of the Chinese in the United States. Foochow, China.

48-19   Childe, V. G. The dawn of European civilization. New York.

48-20   Cline, W. Notes on cultural innovations in dynastic Egypt, SJA, 4, 1: 1—30.

48-21   Codere, H. Swai'xwa myth of the middle Fraser River: the integration of two Northwest Coast cultural ideas, JAF, 61: 1—18.

48-22   Cohen, A. K. On the place of "themes" and kindred concepts in social theory, AA, 50, 3: 436—43.

48-23   Cuisinier, J. Les Mu'ò'ng. Géographie humaine et sociologie, TMIE, 45.

48-24   Davidson, J. Protestant missions and marriage in the Belgian Congo, Af, 18, 2: 120—28.

48-25   Demeerseman, A. L'évolution de la famille tunisienne, Il, 11: 105—40.

48-26   Drucker, P. Antiquity of the Northwest Coast totem pole, Wash. Acad. Sci. J., 38: 389—97.

48-27   Eisenstadt, S. N. Some remarks on demographic factors in a situation of culture contact, Mn, 48: 101—02.

48-28   Elmendorf, W. W. The cultural setting of the Twana secret society, AA, 50: 625—33.

48-29   Embree, J. F. Kickball and some other parallels between Siam and Micronesia, JSS, 37, 1: 33—38.

48-30   Espinosa Bravo, C. A. The three epochs of the Indian: tawantinsuyo— colony— republic, BI, 8, 2: 164—71.

48-31   Field, M. J. Akim-Kotoku: an oman of the Gold Coast. London.

48-32   Firth, R. Religious belief and personal adjustment (Henry Myers lecture). Royal Anth. Institute, London.

48-33   Foster, G. M. Empire's children: the people of Tzintzuntzan. ISAP, 6.

48-34   Francastel, P. Technique et esthétique, Cahiers intern. de sociologie, Paris, 5: 97—116.

48-35   French, D. H. Factionalism in Isleta Pueblo. AESM, 14.

48-36   Fuchs, S. Changes and developments in the population of the Nimar district in the central provinces of India, An, 41—44, 1—3: 49—68.

48-37   Gamio, M. Consideraciones sobre el problema indígena. Mexico, D. F.

48-38   Gibson, C. The Inca concept of sovereignty and the Spanish administration in Peru. Austin, Texas.

48-39   Gibson, G. D. The probability of numerous independent inventions, AA, 50, 2: 362—64.

48-40   Gillin, J. "Race" relations without conflict: a Guatemalan town, AJS, 53, 5: 337—43.

48-41   Gillin, J. The ways of men. New York.

48-42   Gillin, J. L. and J. P. Cultural sociology. New York.

48-43   Goldfrank, E. S. The impact of situation and personality on four Hopi emergence myths, SJA, 4: 241—62.

48-44   Goldschmidt, W. Social organization in native California and the origin of clans, AA, 50, 3: 444—56.

48-45   Gondal, R. P. Changes in customs and practices among some lower agricultural castes of the Kotah State, EA, 1, 4: 21—28.

48-46   Green, A. W. Culture, normality, and personality conflict, AA, 50: 225—37.

48-47   Greenman, E. F. The extraorganic, AA, 50: 181—99.

48-48 Hawley, F. An examination of problems basic to acculturation in the Rio Grande Pueblos, AA, 50, 4: 612−24.

48-49 Hawley, F. Keresan Holy Rollers: an adaptation to American individualism, SF, 26: 272−80.

48-50 Hoijer, H. Linguistic and cultural change, La, 24: 335−45.

48-51 Hellmann, E. Rooiyard, a sociological survey of an urban native slum yard. RLP, 13.

48-52 Henry, J. Cultural discontinuity and the shadow of the past, SM, 66: 248−54.

48-53 Herskovits, M. J. The contribution of Afroamerican studies to Africanist research, AA, 50, 1: 1−10.

48-54 Herskovits, M. J. Man and his works. The science of cultural anthropology. New York.

48-55 Hill, W. W. Navaho trading and trading ritual: a study in cultural dynamics, SJA, 4: 371−96.

48-56 Hsu, F. L. K. Under the ancestor's shadow; Chinese culture and personality. New York.

48-57 Huot, M. C. Some Mohawk words of acculturation, IJAL, 14, 3: 150−54.

48-58 Jacobs, M. Further comments on evolutionism in cultural anthropology, AA, 50, 3: 564−67.

48-59 Jeffreys, M. D. W. The diffusion of cowries and Egyptian culture in Africa, AA, 50, 1: 45−54.

48-60 Karve, I. Some studies in the making of a culture pattern, in Essays in anthropology presented to S. C. Roy: 206−14. Calcutta.

48-61 Kirchoff, P. Civilizing the Chichimecs, Latin American Studies, U. of Texas, 5: 80−85.

48-62 Kluckhohn, C. and Murray, H. A. (eds.). Personality in nature, society and culture. Harvard U. Press.

48-63 Kosven, M. O. Matriarkhat. Istorija problemy. Moskau - Leningrad.

48-64 Kroeber, A. L. Anthropology (revised edition). New York.

48-65 Kroeber, A. L. White's view of culture, AA, 50, 3: 405−15.

48-66 Kwakume, H. Précis d'histoire du peuple Ewe. Lomê.

48-67 La Farge, O. The Navahos—most hopeful tribe of all, NH, 62, 8: 360−67.

48-68 Leighton, D. and Kluckhohn, C. Children of the people. Harvard U. Press.

48-69 Leroux, H. Animisme et Islam dans la subdivision de Maradi (Niger), Bull., IFAN, 10: 595−697.

48-70 Lewis, O. On the edge of the Black Waxy: a cultural survey of Bell County, Texas. Washington Univ. Studies, St. Louis.

48-71 Little, K. L. The changing position of women in the Sierra Leone Protectorate, Af, 18, 1: 1−17.

48-72 Little, K. Negroes in Britain: a study of racial relations in English society. London.

48-73 Loomis, C. P. and Schuler, E. A. Acculturation of Latin-American students in the United States, ApA, 7, 2: 17−34.

48-74 Lowie, R. H. Social organization (revised ed.). New York.

48-75 Lowie, R. H. Primitive religion (revised ed.). New York.

48-76 Mair, L. P. Modern developments in African land tenure: an aspect of culture change, Af, 18, 3: 184−89.

48-77 Mair, L. P. Australia in New Guinea. London.

48-78 Miller, J. G. Naked cult in Central West Santo . . . New Hebrides, JPS, 56: 330−41.

48-79   Mills, J. P. Some recent contact problems in the Khasi Hills, in Essays
        in anthropology presented to S. C. Roy: 1–10. Calcutta.

48-80   Moore, W. E. Theoretical aspects of industrialization, digest of W. E.
        Moore's Attitudes of native labor toward industrial work, Social Research
        15: 277–303.

48-81   Neumeyer, A. The Indian contribution to architectural decoration in Spanish
        colonial America, The Art Bulletin, 30, 2: 104–21.

48-82   Opler, Morris E. Recently developed concepts relating to culture, SJA, 4:
        107–22.

48-83   Opler, Morris E. Theories of culture and the deviant, in Proceedings of
        the Spring Conference on Education and the Exceptional Child: 8–14.
        Child Research Clinic, The Woods Schools, Langhorne, Pa.

48-84   Palmer, E. N. Culture contacts and population growth, AJS, 53: 258–62.

48-85   Pedler, F. J. A study of income and expenditure in Northern Zaria, Af,
        18, 4: 259–71.

48-86   Perham, M. F. The government of Ethiopia. London.

48-87   Quain, B. Fijian village. Chicago.

48-88   Quimby, G. I. Culture contact on the Northwest Coast, 1785–1795, AA,
        50, 2: 247–55.

48-89   Reay, M. and Sitlington, G. Class and status in a mixed blood community,
        Oc, 18, 3: 179–207.

48-90   Renaud, E. B. Survivals and intrusions in the religion of the prehistoric
        Indians of Mexico, SWL, 14, 2: 22–23.

48-91   Rôheim, G. The origin of the ideal, Samiksa, 2: 1–13.

48-92   Rose, E. Innovations in American culture, SF, 26: 255–72.

48-93   Siegel, B. Currents of anthropological theory and value concepts, SJA, 4:
        199–210.

48-94   Smith, E. R. Appendix III, the effect of war on special groups of children.
        Japanese war relocation center, Hunt, Idaho, in Impact of war on the
        family and children in metropolitan Salt Lake. Salt Lake City.

48-95   Smith, E. W. Plans and— people! A dynamic science of man in the service
        of Africa. London.

48-96   Smith, M. W. Synthesis and other processes in Sikhism, AA, 50, 3: 457–62.

48-97   Spencer, R. F. Social structure of a contemporary Japanese-American
        Buddhist church, SF, 26, 3: 281–87.

48-98   Stent, G. E. Migrancy and urbanization in the Union of South Africa, Af, 18,
        3: 161–83.

48-99   Stewart, O. C. Ute Peyotism, a study of a cultural complex. Univ. of Colo-
        rado, Series in Anth., 1.

48-100 Sundkler, B. G. M. Bantu prophets in South Africa. London.

48-101 Taylor, W. W. A study of archaeology. AAAM, 69.

48-102 Trager, G. L. A status symbol and personality at Taos Pueblo, SJA, 4:
        299–304.

48-103 Thompson, L. Attitudes and acculturation, AA, 50, 2: 200–15.

48-104 Trimborn, H. Indianische Welt in geschichtlicher Schau. Iserlohn.

48-105 Tschopik, H. On the concept of Creole culture in Peru, NYAST, 10, 7:
        252–59.

48-106 Underhill, R. What do whites owe to Indians? BI, 8, 1: 27–34.

48-107 Voget, F. Individual motivations in the diffusion of the Wind River Shoshone
        sundance to the Crow Indians, AA, 50, 4: 634–46.

48-108 Wallis, W. D. Presuppositions in anthropological interpretations, AA, 50,
        3: 560–63.

48-109 Webster, H. Magic, a sociological study. Stanford, Cal.

48-110 White, L. A. The individual and the culture process, Sc, 108, 2813: 585–86.

48-111 White, L. A. Man's control over civilization: an anthropocentric illusion, AM, 66, 3: 235–47.

48-112 White, L. A. Evolucionismo e anti-evolucionismo na teoria etnológica americana, So, 10, 1: 1–39.

48-113 Willems, E. Aspectos da aculturacao dos japoneses no Estado de São Paulo. São Paulo.

48-114 Ydes, J. The regional distribution of South American blowgun types JSA, 37: 275–317.

1949

49-1 Abel, T. M. and Hsu, F. L. K. Some aspects of Chinese personality as revealed by the Rorschach test, JPT, 13, 3: 285–301.

49-2 Adair, J. and Vogt, E. Navaho and Zuni veterans: a study of contrasting modes of culture change, AA, 51, 4: 547–60.

49-3 Aginsky, B. W. and E. G. The process of change in family types: a case study, AA, 51, 4: 611–14.

49-4 Altus, W. D. American Mexican: the survival of a culture, JSP, 29: 211–20.

49-5 Amsden, C. A. Navajo weaving, its technic and history. Albuquerque.

49-6 Armillas, P. Un pueblo de artesanos en la Sierra Madre del Sur, AI, 9: 237–44.

49-7 Baldus, H. Akkulturation im Araguaya-Gebeit, An, 41–44: 4–6.

49-8 Barnett, H. G. Palauan society: a study of contemporary native life in the Palau Islands. U. of Oregon, Eugene.

49-9 Barnouw, V. The phantasy world of a Chippewa woman, Ps, 12: 67–76.

49-10 Bidney, D. The concept of meta-anthropology and its significance for contemporary anthropological science, in Ideological differences and world order, Northrop, F. S. C. (ed.): 323–55. Yale Univ. Press, New Haven.

49-11 Bijlmer, H. J. T. The influence of western contact on primitive peoples in Indonesia and the Pacific, PSCP, 7. Auckland.

49-12 Buck, P. H. The coming of the Maori. Wellington, N. Z.

49-13 Bühler-Oppenheim, K. Zur Geschichte das Tabaks, Ciba Zeitschrift, 116: 4278–84.

49-14 Caplow, T. The social ecology of Guatemala City, SF, 28, 113 ff.

49-15 Caudill, W. Psychological characteristics of acculturated Wisconsin Ojibwa children, AA, 51, 3: 409–27.

49-16 Cavan, R. S., Burgess, E. W., Havighurst, R. J. and Goldhammer, H. Personal adjustment in old age. Chicago.

49-17 Chmielewski, J. The typological evolution of the Chinese language. Kraków.

49-18 Colson, E. Assimilation of an American Indian group, RLIJ, 8.

49-19 Correa, A. A. M. Contacts culturels dans les colonies portugaises d'Afrique, Est. colon.; Rev. da Escola superior colon, 1. 2–3: 99–108. Lisbon.

49-20 Davis, A. L. and McDavid, R. I., Shivaree: an example of cultural diffusion, American Speech, 24: 249–55.

49-21 De Bruyn, J. V. The Mansren cult of Baik, SP, 5, 1: 1–10. (Trans. from TITLV, D 1.83, AF 1–4).

49-22 D'Étienne, J., Villème, L., and Delisle, S. L'évolution sociale du Maroc. Paris.

49-23 D'Harcourt, R. Épidémies chez les Eskimo, JSAP, 48: 184–85.

49-24 De La Fuente, J. Yalalag: una villa Zapoteca serrana. Mexico, D. F.

49-25 Digby, A. Primitive techniques and their influence upon economic organization; summary of papers and discussions at Brighton meeting of British Assn. for adv. of Sci., Mn, 30: 32.

49-26 Digby, A. Technique and the time factor in relation to economic organization, Mn, 50: 16–18.

49-27 Du Bois, C. Social forces in Southeast Asia. U. of Minn. Press, Minneapolis.

49-28 Eisenstadt, S. N. The perception of time and space in a situation of culture-contact, JRAI, 79: 63–68.

49-29 Embree, J. F. American military government, in Social structure: studies presented to A. R. Radcliffe-Brown, Fortes, M. (ed.). London. See also Rejoinder to Collier's reply, HO, 8, 3: 25–26.

49-30 Embree, J. F. The Indian Bureau and self-government, HO, 8, 3: 11–14.

49-31 Fenton, W. N. Collecting materials for a political history of the Six Nations, APSP, 93: 233–38.

49-32 Fenton, W. N. Seth Newhouse's traditional history and constitution of the Iroquois confederacy, Proc., Am. Philos. Soc., 93, 2: 141–58.

49-33 Fortes, M. Time and social structure: an Ashanti case study, in Social structure: Studies presented to A. R. Radcliffe-Brown, Fortes, M. (ed.), London.

49-34 Friede, J. Tres casos de la primitiva aculturación del Indio a la civilizacion europea, Siglo XVII, AI, 9: 245–50.

49-35 Fürer-Haimendorf, C. von. The Raj Gonds of Adilabad. A peasant culture of the Deccan. London.

49-36 Gamio, M. Las necesidades y aspiraciones indígenas y los medios de satisfacerlas, AI, 9: 105–12.

49-37 Garcia, C. J. A. La transculturación indo-española en Holguin, RAE, 2, 4, 8–9: 195–205.

49-38 Gluckman, M. Malinowski's social theories. RLP, 16.

49-39 Gordon, A. I. Jews in transition. Minneapolis.

49-40 Gorer, G. and Rickman, J. The people of Great Russia. London.

49-41 Hatt, G. Asiatic influences in American folklore, Det Kgl. Danske Videnskabernes Selskab. Historisk-Filologiske Meddelelser, 31, 6. Kobenhavn.

49-42 Hawthorn, H. B. Administration and primitive economy, Canadian Journal of Economics, 15: 87–96.

49-43 Hermanns, M. Die Nomaden von Tibet. Wien.

49-44 Herskovits, M. J. and Waterman, R. A. Música de culto afrobahiana, Rev. Estudios Musicales, 1, 2: 65–127.

49-45 Hoebel, E. A. Man in the primitive world. New York.

49-46 Hogbin, H. I. Government chiefs in New Guinea, in Social structure, studies presented to A. R. Radcliffe-Brown, Fortes, M. (ed.). London.

49-47 Honigmann, J. J. Culture and ethos of Kaska society. YUPA, 40.

49-48 Hsu, F. L. K. Suppression versus repression: a limited psychological interpretation of three cultures, Ps, 12: 223–42.

49-49 Joseph, A., Spicer, R. B., and Chesky, J. The desert people: a study of the Papago Indians of Arizona. Chicago.

49-50   Journal of Education, 16, Numéro special consacré aux populations mon-
        tagnardes du Sud Indochinois, Saigon.
49-51   Keesing, F. M. Cultural dynamics and administration, PSCP, 7. Auckland.
49-52   Keesing, F. M. (ed.). Handbook of the U.S. Trust Territory of the Pacific
        Islands. Navy Department, Washington.
49-53   Kluckhohn, C. The limitation of adaptation and adjustment as concepts for
        understanding cultural behavior, in Adaptation, Romano, J. (ed.): 99—
        113. New York.
49-54   Kluckhohn, C. Mirror for man. New York.
49-55   Koppers, W. Die Bhil in Zentralindien. Horn-Wien.
49-56   Koppers, W. Der Urmensch und sein Weltbild. Wein.
49-57   Kroeber, A. L. Values as a subject of natural science inquiry, NASP, 35:
        261—64.
49-58   Kurath, G. P. Mexican Moriscas: a problem in dance acculturation, JAF,
        62: 87—106.
49-59   LaBarre, W. Wanted: a pattern for modern man, MH, 33, 2: 209—21.
49-60   Lanctot, A. Influences réciproques de deux cultures, TRSC, 43: 59—67.
49-61   Lehmann, W. Sterbende Göffer und christliche Heilsbotschaft. Wechselreden
        indianischer Vornehmer und spanischer Glaubensapostel in Mexiko 1524.
        Stuttgart.
49-62   Leighton, A. H. Human relations in a changing world. New York.
49-63   Leighton, A. H. and D. C. Gregorio, the hand-trembler. A psycho-biographi-
        cal personality study of a Navaho Indian. PMAEP, 40, 1.
49-64   Lévi-Strauss, C. Les structures elementaires de la parenté. Paris.
49-65   Linton, R. (ed.). Most of the world: the peoples of Africa, Latin America
        and the East today. New York.
49-66   Lopez de Mesa, L. Perspectivas culturales. Bogotá.
49-67   McCall, A. G. Lushai chrysalis. London.
49-68   Mandelbaum, D. G. (ed.). Selected writings of Edward Sapir in language,
        culture and personality. Berkeley.
49-69   Maquet, J. J. The modern evolution of African populations in the Belgian
        Congo, Af, 19, 4.
49-70   Marvel, T. The new Congo. London.
49-71   Massini, C. C. La historia del arte en la historia de la culturas, Annales
        de Arqueología y Etnología, Mendoza, 10.
49-72   Mead, M. Character formation and diachronic theory, in Social structure;
        studies presented to A. R. Radcliffe-Brown, Fortes, M. (ed.), London.
49-73   Mead, M. Male and female: a study of the sexes in a changing world. New
        York.
49-74   Milligan, E. A. Known migrations of historic Indian tribes, with an intro-
        duction on prehistoric and protohistoric movements in the upper Missis-
        sippi-Missouri area. Bottineau, N. Dak.
49-75   Miner, H. Culture and agriculture. An anthropological study of a corn-belt
        county. U. of Mich. Press, Ann Arbor.
49-76   Miyamoto, N. A note on the Taokas, a Sinicized plain tribe of northwest
        Formosa, MKe, 14, 2: 78—79.
49-77   Monogarova, L. F. The Yazgulemians of the Western Pamirs, SE, 3: 89—
        108.
49-78   Montgomery, J. D. Administration of occupied Japan: first year, HO, 8, 4:
        4—16.
49-79   Montgomery, R. G., Smith, W. and Brew, J. O. Franciscan Awatovi. PMAIP,
        36.

49-80 Mühlmann, W. E. Ethnische Aufsteigassimulation und Rassenwandel, Homo, Stuttgart, 2.

49-81 Mulengreau, G. Vers un paysannat indigène: les lotissements agricoles du Congo Belge. Rapport de Mission, Bruxelles.

49-82 Murdock, G. P. Social structure. New York.

49-83 Murdock, G. P. Social organization and government in Micronesia, PSB, National Research Council.

49-84 Murphy, J. The origins and history of religions. Manchester U. Press.

49-85 Neumann, E. Ursprungsgeschichte des Bewufstseins. Zurich.

49-86 Noon, J. A. Law and government of the Grand River Iroquois. VPFA, 12.

49-87 Okuno, H. The interaction of consanguinity and locality in the formation and 'ramification' of kin-groups in Micronesia, MKe, 14, 3: 28–38.

49-88 Oliver, D. L. Studies in the anthropology of Bougainville, Solomon Islands. PMAEP, 29: 1–4.

49-89 Palthe, P. M. Psychological aspects of the Indonesian problem. Leyden.

49-90 Patai, R. Musha's tenure and cooperation in Palestine, AA, 51, 3: 436–45.

49-91 Prothero, R. M. Bristol Channel coastlands: early cultural contacts, Scottish Aeographical Magazine, 65: 44–54.

49-92 Radcliffe-Brown, A. R. Functionalism: a protest, AA, 51, 2: 320–22.

49-93 Radcliffe-Brown, A. R. White's view of a science of culture, AA, 51, 3: 503–11.

49-94 Reed, K. E. Notes on some problems of political confederation, SP, 3, 12: 229–34; 4, 1: 5–10.

49-95 Reichel-Dolmatoff, G. Los Kogi: una tribu de la Sierra Nevada de Santa Marta, Colombia. Bogotá.

49-96 Reichard, G. A. The Navaho and Christianity, AA, 51, 1: 66–71.

49-97 Ruesch, J. and Bateson, G. Structure and process in social relations, Ps, 12, 2: 105–24.

49-98 Salaman, R. N. The history and social influence of the potato. Cambridge, England.

49-99 Schlosser, K. Propheten in Afrika. Braunschweig.

49-100 Schmidt, W. Der Ursprung der Gottesidee, vols. 8, 9. Wien.

49-101 Schmidt, W. Rassen und Völker in Vorgeschichte und Geschichte des Abenlandes. Wien.

49-102 Schumacher, P. Expedition zu den Zentralafrikanischen Kivu Pygmäen (Twiden). Die physiche und sociale Umwelt der Kivu-Pygmäen. IRCBM, 3.

49-103 Sereno, R. Boricua: a study of language, transculturation and politics, Ps, 12: 167–84.

49-104 Shapiro, H. L. Responsibility of the anthropologist, Sc, 109: 323–26.

49-105 Shimkin, D. B. Recent trends in Soviet anthropology, AA, 51: 621–25.

49-106 Siegel, B. J. Anthropological analysis of shared respect: contributions to a study of revolution, SJA, 5: 351–68.

49-107 Siegel, B. J. Some observations on Pueblo patterns at Taos, AA, 51, 4: 562–77.

49-108 Smith, M. W. Indians of the urban northwest. New York.

49-109 Speck, F. G. The road to disappearance: Creek Indians in Alabama, AA, 51, 4: 681–82.

49-110 Spiro, M. E. Ifaluk: a South Sea culture. PSB, National Research Council.

49-111 Spoehr, A. Majuro, a village in the Marshall Islands. Chicago.

49-112 Steward, J. H. Cultural causality and law: a trial formulation of the development of early civilizations, AA, 51, 1: 1–27.

49-113 Stone, D. Z. The Boruca of Costa Rica. PMAEP, 26, 2.

49-114 Sutherland, I. L. G. Maori revival, in Yearbook of education: 213–21. London.

49-115 Terra, G. J. A. The ethnological affinities of the type of horticulture in Indonesia, Chronikje National, 105, 12: 323–26. Batavia.

49-116 Thurnwald, R. Probleme der Fremdheit, Psycholog. Forschung, 23: 25–68.

49-117 Urvoy, Y. Histoire de l'empire du Bornou. Mem., IFAN, 7.

49-118 Valcarcel, L. E. Supervivencias precolombinas en el Perú actual, RMN, 18: 3–18.

49-119 Van Baal, J. National movements and the problem of acculturation, PSCP, 7. Auckland.

49-120 Van der Kroef, J. M. Prince Diponegoro: progenitor of Indonesian nationalism, FEQ, 8: 424–50.

49-121 Voget, F. Crow socio-cultural groups, ICAP, 29.

49-122 Wagley, C. and Galvao, E. The Tenetehara Indians of Brazil, a culture in transition. CUCA, 35.

49-123 Wallace, A. F. C. King of the Delawares: Teedyuscung 1700–1763. Philadelphia.

49-124 Warner, W. L. A methodology for the study of social class, in Social structure: studies presented to A. R. Radcliffe-Brown, Fortes, M. (ed.). London.

49-125 Warner, W. L., Meeker, M., and Eells, K. Social class in America. Science Research Associates.

49-126 Warner, W. L. and others. Democracy in Jonesville. New York.

49-127 Wassén, H. Contributions to Cuna ethnography. EtS, 16.

49-128 Weitzel, R. B. The Hispanicized Haab of Yucatan. Washington, D.C.

49-129 White, L. A. The science of culture: a study of man and civilization. New York.

49-130 Willems, E. Acculturative aspects of the feast of the Holy Ghost in Brazil, AA, 51, 3: 400–08.

49-131 Zhdanko, T. A. The economy of a Karakalpak collective farm, SE, 2: 35–58.

49-132 Zipf, G. K. Human behavior and the principle of least effort. Cambridge.

1950

50-1   Aberle, D. F. Shared values in complex societies, ASR, 15, 4: 495–502.

50-1a   Aberle, D. F. and others. The functional prerequisites of a society, Ethics, 60, 2: 100–11.

50-2   Almond, G. A. Anthropology, political behavior and international relations, World Politics, 2: 277–85.

50-3   Balandier, G. Aspects de l'évolution sociale chez les Fang, Cah. Int. Sociol. 9: 76–106. Paris.

50-4   Barbeau, M. Indian captivities, APSP, 94: 522–48.

50-5   Barbeau, M. La survivance française au Canada, Les Archives de Folklore, 1949: 67–75.

50-6   Barnouw, V. Acculturation and personality among the Wisconsin Chippewa. AAAM, 72.

50-7   Bascom, W. R. The focus of Cuban santeria, SJA, 6: 64–68.

50-8   Bascom, W. R. Ponape: the tradition of retaliation, FEQ, 10: 56–62.

50-9   Beaglehole, E. Contemporary Maori culture, Philadelphia Anth. Soc. Bulletin, 3, 3: 1–3.

50-10 Beckmann, J. (ed.). Der einheimische Klerus in Geschichte und Gegenwart. Schöneck-Breckenried.

50-11 Bell, R. M. The Maji-Maji rebellion in the Liwale District, Tanganyika Notes, 28: 38–57.

50-12 Belshaw, C. S. Changes in heirloom jewellery in the Central Solomons, Oc, 21.

50-13 Belshaw, C. S. Island administration in the South-West Pacific. New York.

50-14 Belshaw, C. S. The significance of modern cults in Melanesian development, The Australian Outlook, 4, 2: 116–25.

50-15 Berlin, H. La historia de los Xpantzay, Antropología e Historia de Guatemala, 2, 2.

50-16 Berndt, C. H. Women's changing ceremonies in Northern Australia. Paris.

50-17 Berer, L. van. Le cinéma pour Africains. Bruxelles.

50-18 Bidney, D. The concept of myth and the problem of psycho-cultural evolution, AA, 52, 1: 16–26.

50-19 Bouteiller, M. Don chamanistique et adaptation à la vie chez les Indiens de l'Amérique du Nord, JSA, 39: 1–14.

50-20 Bowles, G. T. Point Four and improved standards of living, Ann. Am. Acad., 268: 140–47.

50-21 Brady, C. T. Commerce and conflict in East Africa. Salem, Mass.

50-22 Brandon, S. G. F. The problem of change in the ancient world, Fo, 61, 2.

50-23 Brant, C. S. Peyotism among the Kiowa-Apache and neighboring tribes, SJA, 6: 212–22.

50-24 Bühlmann, W. Die christliche Terminologie als missionsmethodes Problem. Schöneck-Beckenried.

50-25 Busia, K. A. Report on a social survey of Sekondi-Takoradi. London.

50-26 Carr, B. Fifty years of the Eastern provinces. W. Afr. 1753–6: 893–94, 917–18, 943–44, 967–68.

50-27 Carrasco Pizana, P. Los Otomies. Cultura e historia prehispanicas de los pueblos mesoamericanos de habla otomiana, Universidad Nacl. Autonoma de Mexico, Instituto do Historia, 15, Mexico, D. F.

50-28 Carse, M. R. The Mohawk Iroquois. New Haven.

50-29 Carter, G. F. Plant evidence for early contacts with America, SJA, 6: 161–82.

50-30 Carvalho, A. de. Problemas des assimilação, Bol. Geral. das Colón., 26, 305: 21–28.

50-31 Casas, A. E. El problema del Indio, AI, 10: 63–80.

50-32 Chakreverty, N. P. Spread of Indian civilization in Chinese Turkestan, Jour. Bihar Res. Soc., Patna, 36, 3–4.

50-33 Childe, V. G. Prehistoric migrations in Europe. Instituttet for Sammenlignende, A, 20. Kulturforskning, Oslo.

50-34 Codere, H. Fighting with property; a study of Kwakiutl potlatching and warfare, 1792–1930. AESM, 18.

50-35 Collins, J. M. The Indian Shaker church: a study in continuity and change in religion, SJA, 6: 399–411.

50-36 Colson Research Society. Principles and methods of colonial administration. London.

50-37   Cordero, G. J. F. Balance del indigenismo en Cuba, Revista de la Biblioteca Nacional, 1, 4: 61–215. Habana.

50-38   Cossio del Pomar, F. La pintura colonial cusquena, Cuadernos Americanos, 53, 9, 5: 172–83. Mexico, D. F.

50-39   Coughlin, R. J. The position of women in Vietnam. Yale Southeast Asia Studies (mimeographed).

50-40   Dégh, L. The origin of a Székler wedding song; Etnographia, Budapest, 61, 1–2.

50-41   De La Pena, M. T. Problemas sociales y economicos de las Mixtecas. Memorias del Instituto Nacional Indigenista, 2, 1. Mexico.

50-42   Dickson, A. Training community leaders in the Gold Coast: an experiment in mass education, Overseas Education, 22, 1: 8–21.

50-43   Dobyns, H. F. Papagos in the cotton fields. Tucson, Ariz.

50-44   Dube, S. C. Planning for the tribes. Hyderabad.

50-45   Duckham, A. N. American "know how" and Kenya-Uganda farming, E. Afr. Agric. J., 16, 1: 9–15.

50-46   Eberhard, W. The formation of a new dynasty, in Beiträge zur Gesellungs- und Völkerwissenshaft. Professor Dr. Richard Thurnwald zu sienem achtzigsten Geburtstag gewidmet: 54–66. Berlin.

50-47   Embree, J. F. Exchange of persons— directed culture change, a report prepared for UNESCO. Exchange of Persons Division.

50-48   Embree, J. F. Cultural cautions for U. S. personnel going to Southeast Asia. Economic Cooperation Administration (mimeographed).

50-49   Embree, J. F. Rapporteur's report of roundtable discussions on social forces, in South Asia in the world today, Harris Foundation Lectures, Talbot, P. (ed.). Chicago.

50-50   Emperaire, J. Evolution démographique des Indiens Alakaluf, JSA, 39: 187–218.

50-51   Erasmus, C. J. Patolli, pachisi, and the limitation of possibilities, SJA, 6: 369–87.

50-52   Erikson, E. H. Childhood and society. New York.

50-53   Erikson, E. H. Childhood and tradition in two American Indian tribes, in The psychoanalytic study of the child, 1: 319–50.

50-54   Firth, R. The peasantry of South East Asia, International Affairs, 26: 503–14. London.

50-55   Fortes, M. and Evans-Pritchard, E. E. African political systems. London.

50-56   Freedman, M. Colonial law and Chinese society, JRAI, 80: 97–125.

50-57   Gladwin, T. Civil administration on Truk: a rejoinder, HO, 9, 4: 15–24.

50-58   Grandqvist, H. Child problems among the Arabs. Studies in a Muhammadan village in Palestine. Helsingfors, Copenhagen.

50-59   Gunther, E. Westward movement of some Plains traits, AA, 52: 174–80.

50-60   Hall, E. T. Military government on Truk, HO, 9, 2: 25–30.

50-61   Hallowell, A. I. Values, acculturation, and mental health, AJO, 20, 4: 732–43.

50-62   Hallowell, A. I. Personality structure and the evolution of man, AA, 52: 159–73.

50-63   Hanks, L. M., and J. R. Tribe under trust: a study of the Blackfoot Reserve of Alberta. Toronto.

50-64   Heine-Geldern, R. V. Cultural connections between Asia and pre-Columbian America, An, 45: 350–52.

50-65 Heinrich, A. Some present-day acculturative innovations in a nonliterate society, AA, 52: 235–42.

50-66 Herskovits, M. J. American influence in Africa: a problem for ethnohistorical study, Universities in World Affairs, 2: 12–20. New York.

50-67 Hocart, A. M. Caste. A comparative study. London.

50-68 Hodge, F. W. Early Spanish bungling of Indian names, Western Folklore, 9: 153–54.

50-69 Hodgen, M. T. Similarities and dated distributions, AA, 52: 445–67.

50-70 Holmberg, A. R. Nomads of the long bow, the Sirions of eastern Bolivia. ISAP, 10.

50-71 Homans, G. C. The human group. New York.

50-72 Honigmann, J. J. Culture patterns and human stress, Ps, 13: 25–34.

50-73 Hoyt, E. E. Challenge from Guatemala: obstacle to Point Four. Pamphlet, Citizens Conference on International Economic Union, New York.

50-74 Hurt, W. R. and Howard, J. H. Two newly-recorded Dakota house types, SJA, 6: 423–27.

50-75 Jacobs, W. R. Diplomacy and Indian gifts: Anglo-French rivalry along the Ohio and Northwest frontiers, 1748–1763. Stanford.

50-76 Jirku, A. Zum Ursprung des Alphabets, Zeitschr. der Deutschen Morgenländischen Gesellschaft, Wiesbaden, 100, 2.

50-77 Kangudie, P. La famille congolaise marche vers sa destruction, Voix du Congolais, 6, 48: 155–57.

50-78 Keesing, F. M. Some notes on early migrations in the Southwest Pacific area, SJA, 6: 101–19.

50-79 Keesing, F. M. The Pacific island peoples in the postwar world. Eugene, Oregon.

50-80 Kern, F. Ein Spätwerk des britischen Evolutionismus, An, 45: 287–94.

50-81 Kern, F. Mutterrecht einst und jetzt. Theolog. Zeitschrift, Basel, 6: 292–305.

50-82 Kimball, S. T. Future problems in Navajo administration, HO, 9, 2: 21–24.

50-83 King, E. On educating African girls in Northern Rhodesia, Human Problems of British Central Africa, 10: 65–74.

50-84 Kluckhohn, C. and Griffith, C. Population genetics and social anthropology, Cold Spring Harbor Symposia on Quantitative Biology, 15: 401–08.

50-85 Koppers, W. Die historische Ethnologie und der 29 Internationale Amerikanistenkongres, An, 45: 353–54.

50-86 Kühn, H. Das Problem des Urmonotheismus. Akadamie der Wissenschaften und der Literatur. Weisbaden.

50-87 Lambert, H. E. The systems of land tenure in the Kikuyu land unit: part I, history of the tribal occupation of the land. Cape Town. (mimeographed).

50-88 Lampen, G. D. History of Darfur, SN, 31, 2: 177–209.

50-89 Laviosa-Zambotti, P. Ursprung und Ausbreitung der Kultur (Origini e Diffusione della Civiltà. Aus dem Italienischen übersetzt von Ferd. Siebert). Baden-Baden.

50-90 Leeming, A. J. A historical sketch of Victoria, British Cameroons, Nigerian Field, 15, 4: 184–89; 16, 1: 37–45.

50-91 Lembezat, B. Kirdi, les populations païennes du Nord Cameroun, Mem. IFAN.

50-92 Lessa, W. A. Ulithi and the outer native world, AA, 52, 1: 27–52.

50-93   Lezcano, C. G. and García Aller, A. H. Estudio de reactivación económica de una "Zona Tipo." Zona de San Luis, AIEBA, 3.

50-94   Loeb, E. M. The Kuanyama Ambo: an example of how a society generates social controls, ScA, 182: 52—55.

50-95   Lommel, A. Modern culture influences on the aborigines, Oc, 21, 1: 14—24.

50-96   Loomis, C. P. Studies in applied and theoretical social science. Lansing, Michigan.

50-97   Majumdar, D. N. The affairs of a tribe. Lucknow.

50-98   Maude, H. E. The cooperative movement in the Gilbert and Ellice islands, PSCP, 7, Auckland, SP, supplement, May.

50-99   Maude, H. E. Social development in the South Pacific, SP, 4, 5: 73—77.

50-100   Mason, L. The Bikinians: a transplanted population, HO, 9, 1: 5—15.

50-101   Matekole, N. A. The Gold Coast: development in native states, Corona, 2, 12: 446—49.

50-102   Mercier, P. Le consentement au mariage et son évolution chez les Betamm-adibe, Af, 30: 219—27.

50-103   Mitchell, J. C., and Barnes, J. A. The Lamba village: report of a social survey. SASC, 24.

50-104   Mostny, G. Transculturación de las tribus Fueguinas, AI, 10: 221—32.

50-105   Meunsterberger, W. Some elements of artistic creativity among primitive peoples, in Beiträge zur Gesellungs- und Völkerwissenschaft. Professor Dr. Richard Thurnwald zu seinem achtzigsten Geburtstag gewidmet: 313—17. Berlin.

50-106   Mühlmann, W. E. Soziale Mechanismen der ethnischen Assimilation, Abhandlungen des 14 Internat. Soziologenkongresses, 2: 1—47. Rome.

50-107   Nieuwenhuijze, C. A. O. van. The Darul-Islam movement in West-Java, PA, 23: 164—84.

50-108   Opler, M. K. Japanese folk beliefs and practices, Tule Lake, California, JAF, 63, 250: 385—97.

50-109   Opler, M. K. Two Japanese religious sects, SJA, 6: 69—78.

50-110   Ortíz, F. L'Africanía de la música Folklórica de Cuba. Havana.

50-111   Pederson, H. A. Emerging culture concept: an approach to the study of culture change, SF, 29: 131—35.

50-112   Pehrson, R. N. Culture contact without conflict in Lapland, Mn, 51: 157—60.

50-113   Pollenz, P. Changes in the form and function of Hawaiian hulas, AA, 52, 2: 225—34.

50-114   Portères, R. Vieilles agricultures de l'Afrique inter-tropicale, centres d'origine et de diversification variétale primaire et berceau d'agriculture antérieurs au XVIe siècle, Agronomie tropicale, Sept—Oct: 489—507.

50-115   Pos, H. The revolt of the "Manseren," AA, 52, 4: 561—63.

50-116   Price, A. G. White settlers and native peoples. Cambridge U. Press, New York, Melbourne.

50-117   Purseglove, J. W. Kigezi resettlement, Uganda J., 14, 2: 139—52.

50-118   Radin, P. The origin myth of the medicine rite: three versions. The historical origins of the medicine rite. IJAL Mem., 3.

50-119   Raper, A. F., Tsuchiyama, T., Passin, H., Sills, D. L. The Japanese village in transition. GHQ, SCAP, Natural Resources Section, Report 136.

50-120   Redfield, R. A village that chose progress. Chicago.

50-121   Rees, A. D. Life in a Welsh countryside. U. of Wales Press, Cardiff.

50-122 Rinaldo, J. B. An analysis of culture change in the Ackmen-Lowry area. Fieldiana: Anth., 36, 5. Chicago.

50-123 Ritzenthaler, R. E. The Oneida Indians of Wisconsin. Bulletin of the Public Museum of the City of Milwaukee, 19, 1.

50-124 Rôheim, G. Psychoanalysis and anthropology: culture, personality, and the unconscious. New York.

50-125 Röpke, W. Wirtschaft und Kultur, Deutsch Rundsch., 76: 841–48.

50-126 Rüstow, A. Ortsbestimmung der Gegenwart. Eine unversalgeschichtliche Kulturkritik. Erster Band: Ursprung du Herrschaft. Erlenbach-Zurich.

50-127 Schlosser, K. Der Prophetismus in niederen Kulturen, ZE, 75: 60–72.

50-128 Seruvumba, J. Note à propos du mariage indigène en évolution, Bull. Juris. Ruandi-Urundi, 8: 449–54.

50-129 Simpson, C. E. E. B. An African village undertakes community development on its own, Mass Educ. Bull., London, 2, 1: 7–9.

50-130 Slotkin, J. S. Social anthropology. New York.

50-131 Sohier, A. Notes sur l'évolution du mariage des Congolais, BIRCB, 21, 4: 857–68.

50-132 Speck, F. G. and Beck, H. P. Old world tales among the Mohawks, JAF, 63: 285–308.

50-133 Spencer, R. F. Japanese-American language behavior, American Speech, Dec.: 241–52.

50-134 Spiro, M. E. A psychotic personality in the South Seas, Ps, 13: 189–204.

50-135 Stanislawski, D. The anatomy of eleven towns in Michoacán. Inst. of Latin-American Studies 10. Univ. of Texas, Austin.

50-136 Steward, J. H. Area research: theory and practice. SSRCB, 63.

50-137 Stroup, H. H. The contribution of anthropology to social work education, Social Casework, 31: 189–94.

50-138 Termer, F. Über Eingeborenenreservate in America, in Beiträge zur Gesellungs- und Völkerwissenschaft. Professor Dr. Richard Thurnwald zu sienem achtzigsten Geburtstag gewidmet: 325–32. Berlin.

50-139 Thompson, L. Culture in crisis: a study of the Hopi Indians. New York.

50-140 Thompson, L. Action research among American Indians, SM, 70: 34–40.

50-141 Thompson, L. Operational anthropology as an emergent discipline, in Beiträge . . . Thurnwald: 333–44 (as under Termer above).

50-142 Thompson, L. Science and the study of mankind, Sc, 111: 559–63.

50-143 Thurnwald, R. Entstehung und Wandel von Staatsgebilden . . . , St, 44: 53–58.

50-144 Thurnwald, R. Der Mensch geringer Naturbeherrschung. Sein Aufsteig zwischen Vernunft und Wahn. Berlin.

50-145 Thurnwald, R. Psycho-soziologische Völkforschung und Frühgeschichte, in Ur- und Frügeschichte als historische Wissenschaft, Festschrift zum 60. Geburtstag von Ernst Wahle. Heidelburg.

50-146 Tichelman, G. L. Cultural contact met Indonesië, Oost en West 43, 21: 8–9, 12. Amsterdam.

50-147 Tumin, M. M. Dynamics of cultural discontinuity in a peasant society, SF, 29: 135–41.

50-148 Tylden, G. The rise of the Basuto. Cape Town.

50-149 UNESCO. The preservation and development of indigenous arts. Occasional Papers in Education, 8.

50-150 Van der Kroef, J. M. Communism and communalism in Indonesia, FES, 19: 117–21.

50-151 Van der Kroef, J. M. Social conflict and minority aspirations in Indonesia, AJS, 55: 460—63.

50-152 Van der Kroef, J. M. Economic origins of Indonesian nationalism, in South Asia in the world today, Harris Foundation Lectures, Talbot, P. (ed.): 174—281. Chicago.

50-153 Vasey, E. A. Report on African housing in townships and trading centres. Nairobi.

50-154 Vela, D. Noticas del maiz su origen, distribución y relaciones con las culturas indigenas de América, Anthropologia e Historia de Guatemala, 2, 1: 30—42.

50-155 Voget, F. A Shoshone innovator, AA, 52, 1: 53—63.

50-156 Wagner, G. Lafst sich die Richtung von Kulturwandel voraussagen? in Beiträge . . . Thurnwald: 377—92 (as under Termer).

50-157 Wedgwood, C. H. The contribution of anthropology to the education and development of colonial peoples, SP, 4, 5: 78—84.

50-158 White, L. A. Ethnological theory, in Philosophy for the future, Sellars, R. W. (ed.): 357—84. New York.

50-159 Whiting, B. B. Paiute sorcery, VFPA, 15.

50-160 Whorf, B. L. An American Indian model of the universe, IJAL, 16: 57—72.

50-161 Wolff, K. H. Culture change in "Loma," a preliminary research report, Ohio Journal of Science, 50: 53—59.

50-162 Yole, and Mandelbaum, D. G. Pacification in Burma, FEQ, 19: 182—86.

50-163 Zachert, H. Shintō und Staatsführung im neun Japan, in Beiträge . . . Thurnwald: 463—68 (as under Termer).

1951

51-1   Aberle, D. F. The psychosocial analysis of a Hopi life-history. Berkeley, Cal.

51-2   Adams, R. N. Personnel in culture change: a test of a hypothesis, SF, 30, 2: 185—89.

51-3   Arikpo, O. Self-government and the tribal outlook. Nigeria.

51-4   Arndt, P. Religion auf Ostflores, Adonare und Solor. Studia Instituti Anthropos, 1. Wien-Mödling.

51-5   Armillas, P. Tecnologia, formaciones socio-economicas y religion en Mesoamerica, ICAP, 29, 1: 10—30.

51-6   Australian National University. Report of seminar on social processes in the Pacific (mimeo.). Research School of Pacific Studies, Canberra.

51-7   Azemni, A. La famille algérienne devant les problèmes sociaux modernes, Il, 14, 1.

51-8   Barnes, J. A. Marriage in a changing society. A study in structural change among the Fort Jameson Ngoni. Rhodes-Livingston Institute. London, Capetown.

51-9   Bascom, W. R. The Yoruba in Cuba, Nigeria, 37: 14—20.

51-10   Beals, R. L. Applied anthropological research, Sc, 113, supp. 3.

51-11   Beals, R. L. Urbanism, urbanization and acculturation, AA, 53, 1: 1—10.

51-12   Beaucorps, R. de. L'évolution economique chez les Basongo de la Luniungu et de la Gobari. IRCBM, 20, 4.

51-13   Bekker, K. Historical patterns of culture contact in southern Asia, FEQ, 11: 3—15.

51-14   Belshaw, C. S. Recent history of Mekeo society, Oc, 22: 1—23.

51-15 Belshaw, C. S. Wagawaga, an experiment in Oceanic development, SP,
       5, 2: 18−20 (from Corona, Feb. , 1951).

51-16 Belshaw, C. S. Using Papuans in social survey work, SP, 5, 5: 86−88.

51-17 Belshaw, C. S. Native administration in southeastern New Guinea, SP, 5,
       6: 104−09.

51-18 Belshaw, C. S. Social consequences of the Mt. Lamington eruption, Oc,
       21, 4: 241−52.

51-19 Berg, C. C. Der problematiek van het Bahasa-Indonesia-Experiment.
       Jakarta.

51-20 Berndt, R. M. and C. H. The concept of abnormality in an Australian ab-
       original society, in Psychoanalysis and culture, Wilbur, G. B. and
       Muensterberger, W. (eds.). New York.

51-21 Berndt, C. H. and R. M. An Oenpelli monologue: culture-contact, Oc, 22:
       24−52.

51-22 Brahmanand, P. R. Some notes on development problems of backward
       areas, Journ. of the Univ. of Bombay, 20, 1.

51-23 Bodrogi, T. Colonization and religious movements in Melanesia, Acta
       Ethnographica, Budapest, 2: 259−92.

51-24 Brainerd, G. W. The place of chronological ordering in archaeological
       analysis, AAq, 16: 301−16.

51-25 Brand, D. D. Quiroga: a Mexican municipio. ISAP, 11.

51-26 Bright, W. Linguistic innovations in Karok, IJAL, 18: 53−62.

51-27 Bühlmann, W. Psychologisch-religionspädagogische Erwägungen über
       Fragen von Negerschülern, Neue Zeit. f. Missionswiss. , 7, 3: 220−29.
       Schöneck-Beckenried.

51-28 Busia, K. A. The position of the chief in the modern political system of
       Ashanti. London.

51-29 Busia, K. A. Self-government for the Gold Coast. London.

51-30 Caetano, M. Colonizing traditions, principles and methods of the Portu-
       guese. Lisbóa.

51-31 Chaudhuri, N. C. The autobiography of an unknown Indian. London.

51-32 Childe, V. G. Social evolution. New York.

51-33 Coates, W. P. and Z. K. Soviets in Central Asia. Philosophical Library.

51-34 Colson, E. Residence and village stability among the plateau Tonga, RLIJ,
       12: 41−67.

51-35 Comas, J. La "christianización" y "educación" del Indio desde 1492 hasta
       nuestros días, AI, 11: 219−34.

51-36 Comhaire, I. Some African problems of today, HO, 10, 2: 15−18.

51-37 Contreras, R. J. D. Una rebelión indígena en el partido de Totonicapán en
       1820. El indio y la independencia. Guatemala, C. A.

51-38 Cooley, J. S. Origin of the sweet potato and primitive storage practices,
       SM, 72, 5: 325−31.

51-39 Coon, C. S. Caravan: the story of the Middle East. New York.

51-40 Corrêa, A. M. O estudo das populaçôes e o futuro do ultramar, Mensário
       Admin. , 47/48: 13−31. Luanda.

51-41 Cuisinier, J. Sumangat. L'Âme et son cult en Indochine et en Indonêsie.
       Paris.

51-42 Cunnison, I. History on the Luapula: an essay on the historical notions of a
       central African tribe. RLP, 21.

51-43 Deardorff, M. H. The religion of Handsome Lake: its origin and development, in Symposium on local diversity in Iroquois culture. BAEB, 149: 77–108.

51-44 Demeerseman, A. "Tunisie Nouvelle": problèmes social et culturel, perspectives d'avenir rôle des élites, Il, 14, 1.

51-45 Devereux, G. Reality and dream: psychotherapy of a Plains Indian. New York.

51-46 Dittmer, K. Zum Problem des Wesens, des Ursprungs und der Entwicklung des Clantotemismus, ZE, 76: 189–200.

51-47 Dobyns, H. F. Blunders with bolsas. A case study of diffusion of closed-basin agriculture, HO, 10, 3: 25–32.

51-48 D'Orjo de Marchovette, E. Histoire de la chefferie Kongolo. Bull. des Juridictions indigènes et du Droit Coutumier Congolais, 19, 1: 1ff.

51-49 Dozier, E. P. Resistance to acculturation and assimilation in an Indian pueblo, AA, 53: 56–66.

51-50 DuBois, C. Use of social science concepts to interpret historical materials, FEQ, 11: 31–34.

51-51 DuBois, C. and others. Culture contact and culture change in Southeast Asia: a symposium. New York.

51-52 Duchemin, G.-J. Exemples de substitution de mythes avec maintien du rite dans les croyances anémistesa au Sénégal et au Fouta-Djallon, Ie. Conf. int. Africanistes de l'Ouest, 2: 351–53.

51-53 Egami, N. Concerning the ancient history of the mountain region of Altai, KZ, 37, 4: 33–41.

51-54 Eggan, F. Social organization of the western pueblos. U. of Chicago Press, Chicago.

51-55 Elkin, A. P. Reaction and interaction: a food gathering people and European settlement in Australia, AA, 53, 2: 164–86.

51-56 Elkin, A. P. Review of research in social anthropology: Papuan/Melanesian section. South Pacific Commission Project S5 (b), Report 1 (mimeo., publ. by Oxford Univ. Press, 1953).

51-57 Ellis, F. H. Patterns of aggression and the war cult in southwestern pueblos, SJA, 7: 177–201.

51-58 Esenkova, P. La femme turque contemporaine: éducation et rôle social, Il, 14, 3: 55ff.

51-59 Estermann, C. Reflexões sobre educação e instrução entre os povos bantos do Sul. Revista de Ensino, Luanda, Angola, 3.

51-60 Evans-Pritchard, E. E. Social anthropology. London.

51-61 Fenton, W. N. Locality as a basic factor in the development of Iroquois social structure, in Symposium on local diversity in Iroquois culture. BAEB, 149: 35–54.

51-62 Fenton, W. N. (ed.). Symposium on local diversity in Iroquois culture. BAEB, 149.

51-63 Firth, R. Elements of social organization. London.

51-64 Firth, R. Some social aspects of the Colombo plan, Westminster Bank Review, May.

51-65 Friedrich, A. Erkenntnis und Religion, Paideuma, 5, 3: 103–14. Leipzig.

51-66 Fuchs, S. Anthropology and the missions, Word, Hadzor, September: 197–200.

51-67 Garcia, A. Teoria y politica del indigenismo, AI, 11: 281–96.

51-68 Gillin, J. The culture of security in San Carlos: a study of a Guatemalan community of Indians and Ladinos. Middle American Research Inst., 16. Tulane Univ., New Orleans.

51-69   Gluckman, M. The origins of social organization, Human Probl. Brit. Centr. Africa, 12: 1−11.

51-70   Goodenough, W. H. Property, kin and community on Truk. YUPA, 46.

51-71   Guiart, J. "Cargo cults" and political evolution in Melanesia, SP, 5, 7: 128−29 (from Ma, 8, 5).

51-72   Günther, H. E. K. Formen und Urgeschichte der Ehe. Göttingen.

51-73   Hallowell, A. I. The projective technique in the socio-psychological study of acculturation, JPT, 15, 27.

51-74   Harris, Z. S. Methods in structural linguistics. Chicago.

51-75   Haverkamp, H., Maybaum, H., and Weirich, R. Von der Urgeschichte bis zum Entstehen der abendländischen Völkergemeinschaft. Grundzüge der Geschichte, 5. Frankfurt and Bonn.

51-76   Held, J. G. De Papoea—cultuurimprovisator. 's-Gravenhage.

51-77   Helmer, M. Potosi à la fin du XVIIIe siècle, JSA, 40: 21−50.

51-78   Henry, J. Family structure and the transmission of neurotic behavior, AJO, 21: 800−18.

51-79   Henry, J. and Warson, S. Family structure and psychic development, AJO, 21: 59−73.

51-80   Heymans, M., et autres. L'urbanisme au Congo. Bruxelles.

51-81   Hilger, M. I. Chippewa child life and its cultural background. BAEB, 146.

51-82   Hilger, M. I. Arapaho child life and its cultural background. BAEB, 147.

51-83   Hogbin, H. I. Transformation scene: the changing culture of a New Guinea village. London.

51-84   Holas, B. Aspects modernes de la circoncision rituelle et de l'initiation ouest-africaines, Notes Afr., IFAN, 49: 4−11.

51-85   Hoenigswald, H. M. The phonology of dialect borrowing, Studies in Linguistics, 10: 1−5.

51-86   Honigmann, J. J. An episode in the administration of the Great Whale River Eskimo, HO, 10, 2: 5−14.

51-87   Howard, J. H. Notes on the Dakota grass dance, SJA, 7: 82−85.

51-88   Hunt, E. O. W. An experiment in resettlement (Shendam Division, N. Nigeria). Kaduna.

51-89   Iturriaga, J. E. La estructura social y cultural de Mexico. Fondo de Cultura Económica. Mexico, D.F.

51-90   Izikowitz, K. G. Lamet. Hill peasants in French Indochina. EtS, 17, Göteborg.

51-91   Izumi, S. The Quelpart islanders in Tokyo, Mke, 16, 1: 1−25.

51-92   Jablow, J. The Cheyenne in Plains Indian trade relations, 1795−1840. AESM, 19.

51-93   Jäschke, G. Der Islam in der neuen Türkei. Die Welt des Islams, N.S., 1, 1−2. Leiden.

51-94   Jeffreys, M. D. W. The origins of the Benin bronzes, AfS, 10, 2.

51-95   Jones, J. D. R. Native housing in urban areas with special consideration of its social aspects, Race Relations Journal, 18, 2: 96−124.

51-96   Joseph, A. and Murray, V. F. Chamorros and Carolinians of Saipan. Harvard U. Press, Cambridge.

51-97   Kälin, J. Zum Problem der menschlichen Stammesgeschichte, Verhandl. der Schweiz. Naturforsch. Gesellsch.: 59−78. Lucerne.

51-98   Kane, L. M. (ed. and trans.). Military life in Dakota. The Journal of
        Philippe Régis de Trobriand. St. Paul.

51-99   Kaplan, B. A. Changing functions of the Huanancha dance at the Corpus
        Christi festival in Paracho, Michoacan, Mexico, JAF, 64, 254: 383–92.

51-100 Kardiner, A. and Ovesey, L. The mark of oppression, a psychological
        study of the American Negro. New York.

51-101 Karve, I. The cultural process in India, Mn, 51.

51-102 Kattenburg, P. M. A central Javanese village in 1950. Cornell Univ.,
        Southeast Asia program, Data Paper 2.

51-103 Keesing, F. M. Review of research in social anthropology: Polynesian Sec-
        tion. South Pacific Commission Project S5 (a), Report 1 (mimeo., publ.
        by Oxford U. Press, 1953).

51-104 Kluckhohn, C. and Morgan, W. Some notes on Navaho dreams, in Psycho-
        analysis and culture, Wilbur, G. B. and Muensterberger, W. (eds.).
        New York.

51-105 Kluckhohn, F. R. Cultural factors in social work practice and education,
        Social Service Rev., 25: 38–47.

51-106 Kock, G. Die evolutionistische Manatheorie und ihre Kritik, Et, 16: 83–92.

51-107 Koenigswald, G. H. R. von. Indonesian influences in Hawaiian art, BTLV,
        107, 4.

51-108 Koenigswald, G. H. R. von. Über sumatranische Schiffstücher und ihr
        Beziehungen Zur Kunst Ozeaniens, in Südseestudien. Gedenkschrift zur
        Erinnerung an Felix Speiser: 27–50. Basel.

51-109 Kroeber, A. L. Configurations, causes, and St. Augustine, AA, 53: 279–84.

51-110 Kurath, G. P. Social diversity in Iroquois music and dance, in Symposium
        on local diversity in Iroquois culture. BAEB, 149: 109–38.

51-111 LaBarre, W. Family and symbol, in Psychoanalysis and culture, Wilbur,
        G. B. and Muensterberger, W. (eds.). New York.

51-112 Lévi-Strauss, C. Language and the analysis of social laws, AA, 53, 2:
        155–63.

51-113 Lewis, O. Life in a Mexican village: Tepoztlan restudied. Urbana, Ill.

51-114 Linton, R. The concept of national character, in Personality and political
        crisis, Stanton, A. H. and Perry, S. E. (eds.). Glencoe, Ill.

51-115 Little, K. L. The Mende of Sierra Leone: a West African people in transi-
        tion. London.

51-116 Lopatin, I. A. What the people are now singing in a Russian village, JAF,
        64, 252: 179–90.

51-117 Lowie, R. H. Some problems of geographical distribution, in Südseestudien
        Gedenkschrift zur Erinnerung an Felix Speiser: 11–26. Basel.

51-118 McCombe, L., Vogt, E. Z., and Kluckhohn, C. Navaho means people.
        Cambridge.

51-119 Marcozzi, V. Trasformazione progressiva o regressiva nella famiglia
        umana? La Scuola Cattolica, Varese: 121–50, 201–22.

51-120 Margain, C. Los mayas de ayer y hoy: Bonampak, Mexico en el arte, 9:
        36–54.

51-121 Martinet, A. Function, structure, and sound change, Word, 8: 1–32.

51-122 Mayer, P. Two studies in applied anthropology in Kenya. Colonial Research
        Studies, 3, London.

51-123 Mead, M. Soviet attitudes toward authority. New York.

51-124 Mead, M. and Macgregor, F. C. Growth and culture; a photographic study
        of Balinese children. New York.

51-125 Métraux, A. Technical assistance and anthropology, AA, 53, 3: 419—20.

51-126 Métraux, A. Making a living in the Marbial valley (Haiti), Occas. Pap. on Educ., UNESCO. Paris.

51-127 Métraux, A. L'île des Pâques. Paris.

51-128 Mitchell, J. C. A note on the urbanization of Africans on the copperbelt, Human Probl. Centr. Africa, 12: 20—27.

51-129 Montagu, M. F. A. New frontiers in education: developing an harmonic human being, School and Society, 74: 309—11.

51-130 Muensterberger, W. Roots of primitive art, in Psychoanalysis and culture, Wilbur, G. B. and Muensterberger, W. (eds.). New York.

51-131 Mukerjee, R. and others. Inter-caste tensions. Lucknow.

51-132 Nadel, S. F. The foundations of social anthropology. Glencoe, Ill.

51-133 Neville, A. O. The half-caste in Australia, Ma, 4, 7.

51-134 Norbeck, E. Westernization as evident on the Buraku level, Mke, 16, 1: 38—46.

51-135 Oakes, M. The two crosses of Todos Santos: survivals of Mayan religious ritual. Bollingen Series, 27. New York.

51-136 Oliver, D. L. The Pacific islands. Cambridge, Mass.

51-137 Oliver, D. L. Planning Micronesia's future. Cambridge, Mass.

51-138 Olmsted, D. L. Two Korean villages: culture contact at the 38th parallel, HO, 10, 3: 33—36.

51-139 Ortiz, F. Los bailes y el teatro de los Negros en el folklore de Cuba. Habana.

51-140 Otis, L. E. La doctrine de l'évolution. 2 vols. Montreal.

51-141 Pederson, H. A. Cultural differences in the acceptance of recommended practices, RS, 16, 1: 37—49.

51-142 Peuckert, W. E. and Lauffer, O. Volkskunde. Berne.

51-143 Piddington, R. Synchronic and diachronic dimensions in the study of Poly- nesian cultures, JPS, 60, 2—3: 108—21.

51-144 Pierson, D. Cruz das Almas: A Brazilian village. ISAP. 12.

51-145 Plá, C. J. España en la Micronesia, Revista de Indias, Madrid, 11, 43—44.

51-146 Potekhin, I. I. (ed.). Anglo-Amerikanskaia etnografia na sluzhbe im- perializma (Anglo-American ethnography in the service of imperialism). Academy of Sciences. Moscow. Review by Vucinich, A., AA, 55: 110.

51-147 Price-Mars, J. Les survivances africaines dans la communauté haïtienne, Et. Dahomeennes, 6: 5— 10.

51-148 Quimby, G. I. and Spoehr, A. Acculturation and material culture-I, FA, 36, 6: 107—47.

51-149 Radcliffe-Brown, A. R. The comparative method in social anthropology, JRAI, 81: 15—22.

51-150 Raghavan, M. D. The Pattini cult as a socio-religious institution, Ethnol. Survey of Ceylon, 3: 251—61. Colombo.

51-151 Randle, M. C. Iroquois women, then and now, in Symposium on local di- versity in Iroquois culture. BAEB, 149: 167—80.

51-152 Reay, M. Mixed blood marriage in north-western New South Wales, Oc, 22: 116—129.

51-153 Reichel-Dolmatoff, G. Datos historico-culturales sobre las tribus de la antigua Gobernacion de Santa Maria. Instituto Ethnologico del Magdalena, Santa Maria. Bogotá.

51-154 Roberts, J. M. Three Navaho households: a comparative study of small group culture. PMAEP, 40, 3.

51-155 Robinson, W. S. A method for chronologically ordering archaeological deposits, AAq, 16: 293–301.

51-156 Ruesch, J. and Bateson, G. Communication: the social matrix of psychiatry. New York.

51-157 Rüstow, A. Kulturtradition und Kulturkritik, Studium Generale, 4: 307–11. Berlin, Göttingen, Heidelberg.

51-158 Schmidt, W. Das in der 'Dienstehe' abgeloste Mutterrecht, Schweizerisches Archiv für Volkskunde, Basel, 47: 182–91.

51-159 Schmidt, W. Su den Anfängen der Tierzucht, ZE, 76, 2. 1951.

51-160 Schuster, C. Joint-marks, a possible index of cultural contact between America, Ociania, and the Far East. Koninklijk Instituut voor de Tropen. Mededeling 94, Afdening Culturele en Physiche Anthropologie, 39. Amsterdam.

51-161 Simpson, G. E. Acculturation in northern Haiti, JAF, 64, 254: 397–403.

51-162 Slotkin, J. S. Personality development. New York.

51-163 Slotkin, J. S. Early eighteenth century documents on Peyotism north of the Rio Grande, AA, 53, 3: 420–26.

51-164 Snoxall, R. A. How Swahili is changing, East African Inter-Territ. Lang. (Swahili) Committee Bull., 21: 8–11.

51-165 Snyderman, G. S. Some ideological aspects of present day Seneca folklore, PM, 24, 2.

51-166 Sohier, A. La politique d'intégration, Zaire, 5, 9: 899–928.

51-167 South Pacific Commission. The Purari Delta: background and progress of community development. Social development Notes, 7.

51-168 Speck, F. G., Broom, L., and Long, W. W. Cherokee dance and drama. Berkeley and Los Angeles.

51-169 Specker, J. Kirchliche und staattiche Siedlungspolitik in Spanisch-Amerika im 16. Jahrhundert, Missionswissenschafliche Studien: 426–38.

51-170 Spencer, R. F. Problems of religious education in Japanese-American Buddhism, Religious Education, March, April: 1–7.

51-171 Spiro, M. E. Culture and personality, Ps, 14, 1.

51-172 Spoehr, A. The Tinian Chamorros, HO, 10, 4: 16–20.

51-173 Starr, B. The Chorti and the problem of the survival of Maya culture, AA, 53, 3: 355–69.

51-174 Steward, J. H. Levels of sociocultural integration: an operational concept, SJA, 7: 374–90.

51-175 Stewart, B. Some determinants of social change, JSP, 33, 33–49.

51-176 Storme, M.-B. Evangelisatiepogingen in de Binnenlanden van Afrika gedurende de XIXe eeuw., IRCBM, 23.

51-177 Suttles, W. The early diffusion of the potato among the Coast Salish, SJA, 7: 272–88.

51-178 Sutton-Smith, B. The meeting of Maori and European cultures and its effects upon the unorganized games of Maori children, JPS, 60: 93–107.

51-179 Swadesh, M. Diffusional cumulation and archaic residue as historical explanations, SJA, 7: 1–21.

51-180 Tax, S. (ed.). The civilizations of ancient America: selected papers of the XXIXth ICAP. University of Chicago Press.

51-181 Tax, S. Selective culture change, American Economic Review, Papers and Proceedings, 41: 315–20.

51-182 Taylor, D. M. The black Carib of British Honduras. VFPA, 17.

51-183 Theobald, A. B. The Mahdiya: a history of the Anglo-Egyptian Sudan. London.

51-184 Thompson, L. Personality and government. Findings and recommendations of the Indian Administration Research, Ediciones des Instituto Indigenista Interamericano. Mexico, D. F.

51-185 Thurnwald, R. Des Menschengeistes Erwachen, Wachsen und Irren. Berlin.

51-186 Tichelman, G. L. Draaiboek van Nieuw Guinee. s'Gravenhage.

51-187 Tichelman, G. L. Nieuw Guinee, Naar Ruimer Horizon, Amsterdam, 6, 5: 14.

51-188 Tiedke, K. E. A study of the Hannahville Indian Community (Menominee County, Mich.). Michigan State Agricultural Experiment Station, Dept. of Sociology and Anthropology, 360. East Lansing, Mich.

51-189 Titiev, M. Araucanian culture in transition. Occas. Contribs., Mus. of Anth. Univ. of Mich., 15.

51-190 Trager, G. L. Linguistic history and ethnologic history in the Southwest, JWAS, 41: 341−43.

51-191 Traupel, R. Die Entwicklung der schweizerischen Indienne-Industrie, Ciba-Rundschau, 97: 3552−60. Basel.

51-192 Van der Kroef, J. M. Southeast Asia— some anthropological aspects, HO, 10, 1: 5−15.

51-193 Van der Kroef, J. M. Foreign aid and social tradition in Indonesia, FES, 20: 181−85.

51-194 Van der Kroef, J. M. Hinduization of Indonesia reconsidered, FEQ, 11: 16−30.

51-195 Van der Kroef, J. M. The Indonesian minority in Surinam, AJS, 16: 672−79.

51-196 Voegelin, C. F. Culture, language, and the human organism, SJA, 7: 357−73.

51-197 Voget, F. Acculturation at Caughnawaga: a note on the native-modified group, AA, 53, 2: 220−31.

51-198 Vogt, E. Z. Navaho veterans, a study of changing values, Reports of the Rimrock Project Values Series, 1. Cambridge.

51-199 Wallace, A. F. C. Some psychological determinants of culture change in an Iroquoian community, in Symposium on local diversity in Iroquois culture. BAEB, 149: 55−76.

51-200 Wartemberg, J. S. São Jorge d'El Mina. Its tradition and customs. Ifracombe, Eng.

51-201 Weinert, H. Der geistige Aufstieg der Menschheit von Ursprung bis zur Gegenwart. Stuttgart.

51-202 Wilbur, G. B. and Muensterberger, W. (eds.). Psychoanalysis and culture. Essays in honor of Géza Róheim. New York.

51-203 Wolf, E. R. The social organization of Mecca and the origins of Islam, SJA, 7: 329−56.

1952

52-1　　Abbas, M. The Sudan question. London.

52-2　　Adams, R. N. A survival of the meso-American bachelor house, AA, 54: 589−92.

52-3　　Adandé, A. L'évolution de la musique africaine, Notes IFAN, 54: 39−44.

52-4   Alegría, R. E. Origin and diffusion of the term "cacique," ICAP, 29, 2: 313—15.

52-5   Ammar, A. A demographic study of an Egyptian province (Sharqiya) LSMSA, 8.

52-6   Apodaca, A. Corn and custom: introduction of hybrid corn to Spanish American farmers in New Mexico, in Human problems in technological change, Spicer, E. H. (ed.). New York.

52-7   Ashton, H. The Basuto. New York.

52-8   Barnes, J. A. Marriage in a changing society. RLP, 20. New York.

52-9   Bartlett, H. H. A Batak and Malay chant on rice cultivation, with introductory notes on bilingualism and acculturation in Indonesia, APSP 96, 6: 629—52.

52-10 Bascom, W. R. Two forms of Afro-Cuban divination, ICAP, 29, 2: 169—79.

52-11 Bastide, R. La Batuque de Porto-Alegre, ICAP, 29, 2: 195—206.

52-12 Beals, R. L. Acculturation, economics, and social change in an Ecuadorean village, ICAP, 29: 67—73.

52-13 Beckett, W. H. Akokoaso: a survey of a Gold Coast village. LSMSA, 10.

52-14 Belshaw, C. S. Port Moresby canoe traders, Oc, 23: 26—39.

52-15 Belshaw, C. S. Community development in Papua, SP, 6, 4: 374—80.

52-16 Beltrán, G. A. La ethnohistoría y el estudio del negro en México, ICAP, 29: 161—68.

52-17 Beltrán, G. A. Problemas de la poblacíon indigena de la cuenca del Tepalcatepec. México, D. F.

52-18 Beltrán, G. A. El gobierno indígena en México y el proceso de aculturación, AI, 12, 4: 267—97.

52-19 Berlin, H. Los archivos notariales como fuentes para la historia del arte colonial en Latinoamérica, ICAP, 29, 2: 306—12.

52-20 Berndt, R. M. A cargo movement in the eastern central highlands of New Guinea, Oc, 23: 41—65, 137—58 (to be continued).

52-21 Berndt, R. M. and C. From black to white in South Australia. Chicago.

52-22 Bittle, W. E. Language and culture: a comment on Voegelin's view, SJA, 8: 466—71.

52-23 Bliss, W. L. In the wake of the wheel: introduction of the wagon to the Papago Indians . . ., in Human problems in technological change, Spicer, E. H. (ed.). New York.

52-24 Biobaku, S. O. An historical sketch of Egba traditional authorities, Af, 22, 1: 35—49.

52-25 Bock, K. E. Evolution and historical process, AA, 54: 486—96.

52-26 Bogue, D. J. Quantitative study of social dynamics and social change, AJS, 57: 565—68.

52-27 Brodrick, A. H. The tree of human history. New York.

52-28 Brown, P. Changes in Ojibwa social control, AA, 54: 57—70.

52-29 Burrows, E. G. From value to ethos on Ifaluk atoll, SJA, 8: 13—35.

52-30 Caplow, T. The modern Latin American city, ICAP, 29, 2: 255—60.

52-31 Carrera, H. G. Indian adjustments to modern national culture, ICAP, 29, 2: 244—48.

52-32 Casagrande, J. B. Ojibwa bear ceremonialism: the persistence of a ritual attitude, ICAP, 29: 113—117.

52-33 Caudill, W. Japanese American personality and acculturation. Genetic Psych. Mons., 45.

52-34 Cheng, E. Some features of the kinship terminology used in New York
       Chinatown, SJA, 8, 1.

52-35 Cline, H. F. Related studies in early 19th century Yucatecan social his-
       tory, University of Chicago Manuscripts in Microfilm Collection on
       Middle American Cultural Anthropology, 6th Series.

52-36 Cohen, F. S. Americanizing the white man, ASc, 21: 177–91.

52-37 Collins, J. M. An interpretation of Skagit intragroup conflict during accul-
       turation, AA, 54: 347–55.

52-38 Comhaire, J. L. The community concept in the study and government of
       African and Afro-American societies, PM, 25: 41–43.

52-39 Comhaire-Sylvain, S. Land tenure in the Marbial region of Haiti, ICAP,
       29, 2: 180–84.

52-40 Cornell, J. O. Some social and economic aspects of the native problem,
       Jnl. Racial Affairs, 3, 4: 24–31.

52-41 Coulborn, R. Causes in culture, AA, 54: 112–16.

52-42 Daifuku, Hiroshi. A new conceptual scheme for prehistoric cultures in the
       Southwestern United States, AA, 54: 191–200.

52-43 Danielsson, B. The happy island (Raroia, Tuamotus). London.

52-44 d'Arianoff, A. Histoire des Bagesera souverains de Gisaka, IRCBM, 24.

52-45 Decary, R. Les contacts de civilisations et les problèmes fonciers à
       Madagascar, Civilisations, 2: 189–94.

52-46 de Laguna, F. Some dynamic forces in Tlingit society, SJA, 8: 1–12.

52-47 Derrick, R. A. Social processes in the Pacific islands, PA, 25, 2: 176–79.

52-48 Dobyns, H. F. Experiment in conservation: erosion control and forage
       production on the Papago Indian reservations in Arizona, in Human prob-
       lems in technological change, Spicer, E. H. (ed.). New York.

52-49 Dobyns, H. F. Thirsty Indians: introduction of wells among people of an
       arid region, HO, 11, 4: 33–36.

52-50 Donahue, F. M. and Humphrey, N. D. Changing bureaucracy and social
       power in a Chicago Ukrainian parish, HO, 11, 2: 23–26.

52-51 Duckworth, E. H. Badagry: its place in the pages of history, Nigeria, 38:
       145–75.

52-52 Dumas, G. L'urbanisme en Afrique noire, Tropiques, 340: 25–31.

52-53 Eaton, J. W. Controlled acculturation: a survival technique of the Hutterites,
       ASR, 17: 331–40.

52-54 Elkin, A. P. Western technology and the Australian aborigines, International
       Social Science Bulletin (UNESCO), 4, 2: 320–27.

52-55 Erasmus, C. J. Agricultural changes in Haiti: patterns of resistance and
       acceptance, HO, 11, 4: 20–26.

52-56 Erasmus, C. J. Changing folk beliefs and the relativity of empirical knowl-
       edge, SJA, 8: 411–28.

52-57 Erasmus, C. J. The leader vs. tradition: a case study, AA, 54: 168–78.

52-58 Euler, R. C. and Naylor, H. L. Southern Ute rehabilitation planning: a
       study in self-determination, HO, 11, 4: 27–32.

52-59 Firth, R. Notes on the social structure of some south-eastern New Guinea
       communities, Part I: Mailu; Part II: Koita, Mn, 52, 99, 123.

52-60 Foster, G. M. Relationships between theoretical and applied anthropology:
       a public health program analysis, HO, 11, 3: 5–16.

52-61 Foster, G. M. The significance to anthropological studies of the places of
       origin of Spanish emigrants to the New World, ICAP, 29, 2: 292–98.

52-62 Fried, M. H. Land tenure, geography and ecology in the contact of cultures, Am, Jl. of Economics and Sociology, 2, 4: 391–412.

52-63 Gamble, J. I. Changing patterns in Kiowa Indian dances, ICAP, 29: 94–104.

52-64 Gamio, M. Población indo-mestiza, ICAP, 29, 2: 267–70.

52-65 Gardiner, P. The nature of historical explanation. New York.

52-66 Gillin, J. Modern cultural development and synthesis in Latin America, ICAP, 29, 2: 221–23.

52-67 Girard, R. El Popul-Vuh, fuente histórica. Mexico and Guatemala.

52-68 Goggin, J. M. Space and time perspective in northern St. Johns archaeology, Florida. New Haven.

52-69 Goldfrank, E. S. The different patterns of Blackfoot and Pueblo adaptation to white authority, ICAP, 29: 74–79.

52-70 Gough, E. K. Changing kinship usages in the setting of political and economic change among the Nayars of Malabar, JRAI, 82, 1: 71–88.

52-71 Gouilly, A. L'Islam dans l'Afrique Occidentale Française. Paris.

52-72 Gower, R. H. Swahili borrowings from English. Af, 22, 2: 154–57.

52-73 Grader, C. J. Rural organization and village revival in Indonesia, Cornell University, Southeast Asia Program, Data Paper 5, (mimeographed).

52-74 Grahmann, R. Urgeschichte der Menschheit. Stuttgart.

52-75 Gross, F. Language and value changes among the Arapaho, IJAL, 17, 1: 10–17.

52-76 Guiart, J. Report on the native situation in the north of Ambrym (New Hebrides), SP, 5, 12: 256–67.

52-77 Guiart, J. John Frum movement in Tanna, Oc, 22: 165–77.

52-78 Guiart, J. The cooperative called the "Malekula Native Company," a border-line type of cargo cult, SP, 6, 6: 429–33.

52-79 Hallowell, A. I. Ojibwa personality and acculturation, ICAP, 29: 105–112.

52-80 Haring, D. G. Speculations on Japanese communism, FES, 22, 1: 10–12.

52-81 Hawthorn, H. B. (ed.). The Doukhobors of British Columbia. Report of the Doukhobor Research Committee. Univ. of British Columbia.

52-82 Heizer, R. F. and Mills, J. E. The four ages of Tsurai: a documentary history of the Indian village on Trinidad Bay. Berkeley, Cal.

52-83 Hellpach, W. Mensch und Volk der Grossstadt. Stuttgart.

52-84 Henry, J. and Bogg, J. W. Child rearing, culture, and the natural world, Ps, 15, 3: 261–71.

52-85 Herskovits, M. J. Some problems of land tenure in contemporary Africa, Land Economics, 28, 1: 37–45. Madison, Wis.

52-86 Herskovits, M. J. Some psychological implications of Afroamerican studies, ICAP, 2: 152–60.

52-87 Herskovits, M. J. Economic anthropology. New York.

52-88 Hocart, A. M. The life-giving myth and other essays. London.

52-89 Hodgen, M. T. Change and history. VFPA, 18.

52-90 Holmberg, A. R. The wells that failed: an attempt to introduce a stable water supply in Viru valley, in Human problems in technological change, Spicer, E. H. (ed.). New York.

52-91 Honigmann, J. J. Intercultural relations at Great Whale river, AA, 54: 510–22.

52-92 Hori, I. Diffusion and change of culture, MKe, 17, 2: 56–60.

52-93 Hoselitz, B. F. (ed.). The progress of underdeveloped areas. Chicago.

52-94 Hoyt, E. E. Certain social and cultural aspects of technological development in British East Africa, Zaïre, 6: 487–90.

52-95 Hoyt, E. E. The needs of east African workers, HO, 11, 2: 27—28.

52-96 Hutton, J. H. Caste in India. New York.

52-97 Jackson, G. P. Some factors in the diffusion of American religious folk-songs, JAF, 65: 365—69.

52-98 Jewell, D. P. A case of a "psychotic" Navaho Indian male, HO, 11, 1: 32—36.

52-99 Jones, J. D. R. Administration of South West Africa: welfare of the indigenous population, Race Rels, Jnl., 19, 1: 3—21.

52-100 Kaberry, P. M. Women of the grass-fields: a study of the economic position of women in Bamenda, British Cameroons. London.

52-101 Kamma, F. C. Messianic movements in western New Guinea, Int. Rev. of Missions, 41: 148—60. London.

52-102 Keesing, F. M. The Papuan Orokaiva vs. Mt. Lamington: cultural shock and its aftermath, HO, 11, 1: 16—22.

52-103 Kern, F. von and others. Historia Mundi: ein Handbuch der Weltgeschichte in zehn Bänden. Band I. Bern.

52-104 Kerr, M. Personality and conflict in Jamaica. Liverpool.

52-105 King, A. R. Changing cultural goals and patterns in Guatemala, AA, 54, 1: 139—142.

52-106 Kluckhohn, C. and others. Value theory, in Toward a general theory of action, Parsons, T. and Shils, E. (eds.). Cambridge, Mass.

52-107 Kroeber, A. L. and Kluckhohn, C. Culture: a critical review of concepts and definitions. PMAEP.

52-108 Kroeber, A. L. The nature of culture. Chicago.

52-109 Kubler, G. The Indian caste of Peru, 1795—1940. A population study based on tax records and census reports. ISAP, 14.

52-110 Landheer, B. Mind and society. Epistemological essays on sociology. The Hague.

52-111 Lantis, M. Eskimo herdsmen: introduction of reindeer herding to the natives of Alaska, in Human problems in technological change, Spicer, E. H. (ed.). New York.

52-112 Le Grip, A. Le Mahdisme en Afrique Noire, l'Afrique et l'Asie, 18: 3—16. Paris.

52-113 Lehmann, F. R. Das Tswana—Dorf auf der Farm Epukiro der Römisch—Katholischen Mission in Südwestafrika, ZE, 77: 83—115.

52-114 Leon, L. A. Historia y extinción del cocaismo en el Ecuador. Sus resultados, AI, 12: 7—32.

52-115 Leonard, O. E. Bolivia: land, people and institutions. Washington, D. C.

52-116 Lesser, A. Evolution in social anthropology, SJA, 8, 2: 134—46.

52-117 Lévi-Strauss, C. Race and history. UNESCO, Paris and New York.

52-118 Levy, J. F. The structure of society. Princeton.

52-119 Lewis, O. Urbanization without breakdown: a case study, SMo, 75, 1: 31—41.

52-120 Lewis, O. The effects of technical progress on mental health in rural population, AI, 12, 4: 299—308.

52-121 Loeb, E. M. The function of proverbs in the intellectual development of primitive peoples, SM, 64: 100—04.

52-122 Macmillan, A. and Leighton, A. People of the hinterland: community interrelations in a maritime province of Canada, in Human problems in technological change, Spicer, E. H. (ed.). New York.

52-123 Mair, L. Land tenure on the Gold Coast, Civilisations, 2: 183—88.

52-124 Mair, L. P. Political developments in Africa, SP, 6, 1: 284–90.

52-125 Mair, L. P. Native administration in Central Nyasaland. London.

52-126 Mandelbaum, D. G. Soldier groups and Negro soldiers. Berkeley, Cal.

52-127 Mandelbaum, D. G. Upset in Nepal, in The story of our time, Grolier
Society, New York: 114–16.

52-128 Mandelbaum, D. G. Technology, credit and culture in an Indian village, HO,
11, 3: 28.

52-129 Manners, R. A. Anthropology and "culture in crisis," AA, 54, 1: 127–33.

52-130 Marie-André du Sacré-Coeur, Soeur. Évolution de la famille en Afrique
noire, C.R. Acad. Sci. Col., 12: 287–302.

52-131 Marquard, L. Peoples and policies of South Africa. London.

52-132 Maude, H. E. The colonisation of the Phoenix islands, JPS, 61, 1–2: 62–
89.

52-133 Mayanja, A. M. K. Chronology of Buganda, 1800–1907, trans. from Kagwa's
Ebika, Uganda Jnl. 16: 148–58.

52-134 Mendoza, V. T. El alumbramiento en el México de antaño y de ogaño, ICAP,
29, 2: 316–28.

52-135 Mendoza, V. R. R. de. La bruja en México, ICAP, 29, 2: 285–91.

52-136 Mennesson-Rigaud, O. Étude sur le culte des Marassas en Haïti, Zaïre,
6: 597–621.

52-137 Metge, J. The Maori population of northern New Zealand, New Zealand
Geographer, 8, 2: 104–24.

52-138 Métraux, R. Some aspects of hierarchical structure in Haiti, ICAP, 29,
2: 185–94.

52-139 Miles, S. W. An analysis of modern Middle American calendars, ICAP,
29, 2: 273–84.

52-140 Miner, H. The folk—urban continuum, ASR, 17: 529–37.

52-141 Mitchell, J. C. A note on the African conception of causality, Nyasaland
Jnl., 5, 2: 51–58.

52-142 Montagu, C. A. On being human. New York.

52-143 Morioka, K. Acceptance of Christianity (Protestantism) in the Japanese
rural community, MKe, 17, 2: 1–14.

52-144 Mühlmann, W. E. Entwicklung und Geschichte, Archiv. f. Kulturgesch.,
Münster-Köln, 34: 107–29.

52-145 Murdock, G. P. Anthropology and its contribution to public health, Am.
Jnl. Pub. Health, 42: 7–11.

52-146 Nadel, S. F. Witchcraft in four African societies: an essay in comparison,
AA, 54: 18–29.

52-147 Nett, B. R. Historical changes in the Osage kinship system, SJA, 8, 2:
164–81.

52-148 Norris, H. T. Tuareg nomadism in the modern world, Afr. Affairs, 51:
152–55.

52-149 Opler, M. E. The Creek "town" and the problem of Creek Indian political
reorganization, in Human problems in technological change, Spicer, E. H.
(ed.). New York.

52-150 Opler, M. E. and Singh, R. D. Two villages of eastern Uttar Pradesh (V.P.),
India, AA, 54: 179–90.

52-151 Opler, M. E. and Singh, R. D. Economic, political and social change in a
village of north central India, HO, 11, 2: 5–12.

52-152 Orr, K. G. Change at Kincaid: a study of cultural dynamics, in Kincaid, a
prehistoric Illinois metropolis, Cole, F.-C.: 293–359. Chicago.

52-153 Osborne, H. Indians of the Andes: Aymaras and Quechuas. London and Cambridge, Mass.

52-154 Parker, M. Social and political development in Kenya urban society, Probl. Afr. Centrale, 5, 15: 12—19. Bruxelles.

52-155 Paton, W. F. The native situation in the north of Ambrym (New Hebrides), SP, 6, 5: 392—96.

52-156 Phillips, A. Recent French legislation concerning African marriage, Af, 22, 1.

52-157 Piddington, R. Maori child welfare: the cultural background, The New Zealand Child Welfare Worker's Bulletin, October.

52-158 Price-Mars, J. Les processes d'une culture, ICAP, 29: 142—52.

52-159 Pritchett, J. P. Historical aspects of the Canadian métis, ICAP, 29, 2: 249—55.

52-160 Radcliffe-Brown, A. R. Structure and function in primitive society. London.

52-161 Richardson, S. A. Technological change: some effects on three Canadian fishing villages, HO, 11, 3: 17—27.

52-162 Riley, C. L. The blowgun in the New World, SJA, 8: 297—319.

52-163 Rhodes, W. Acculturation in North American Indian music, ICAP, 29: 127—132.

52-164 Rousseau, J. and M. Le dualisme religieux des peuplades de la forêt boréale, ICAP, 29: 118—26.

52-165 Rubio, A. La economia y la vivienda rural e indigena en Panama, AI, 12: 55—70.

52-166 Santiana, A. Los Indios Colorados (Tsàtchila). Declinar de su existencia. Quito.

52-167 Sasaki, T. and Adair, J. New land to farm: agricultural practices among the Navaho Indians . . . , in Human problems in technological change, Spicer, E. H. (ed.). New York.

52-168 Sayles, L. R. A case study of union participation and technological change, HO, 11, 1: 5—15.

52-169 Schapera, I. Tribal legislation among the Tswana of the Bechuanaland protectorate. LSMSA, 9.

52-170 Schapera, I. Anthropology for the administrator, Jnl. of African Administration, 3, 2: 57 ff.

52-171 Schebesta, P. Die Negrito Asiens, I. Geschichte, Geographie, umwelt Demographie und Anthropologie der Negrito. Vienna.

52-172 Schmidt, W. Eine neue Erklärung der Exogamie, An, 47: 659—64.

52-173 Schmidt, W. Entstehung der Verwandtschaftssysteme und Heiratsregelungun, An, 47, 5—6: 767—83.

52-174 Schmitt, K. and Osanai, I. Wichita kinship, past and present. Norman, Oklahoma.

52-175 Schuster, C. V-shaped chest-markings: distribution of a design-motive in and around the Pacific, An, 47, 1—2: 99—118.

52-176 Seder, T. A. Old World overtones in the New World. UPMB, 16, 4.

52-177 Seumois, A. V. Introduction à la Missiologie. Neue Zeitschrift für Missionswissenschaft, Supp. 3. Schöneck-Beckenreid.

52-178 Sharp, L. Steel axes for stone-age Australians, HO, 11, 2: 17—22.

52-179 Shimkin, D. B. Industrialization, a challenging problem for cultural anthropology, SJA, 8, 1: 84—91.

52-180 Siegel, B. J. Suggested factors of culture change at Taos Pueblo, ICAP, 29: 133—142.

52-181 Singh, R. D. The village level: an introduction of green manuring in rural India, in Human problems in technological change, Spicer, E. H. (ed.). New York.

52-182 Slotkin, J. S. Some basic methodological problems in prehistory, SJA, 8: 442—43.

52-183 Slotkin, J. S. and McAllester, D. P. Menomini peyotism: a study of individual variation in a primary group with a homogeneous culture. APST, 42, 4.

52-184 Smith, M. G. A study of the Hausa domestic economy in northern Zaria, Af, 22: 333—47.

52-185 Smith, E. W. Kenya: a community development project (Kitui), Corona, 4: 267—68.

52-186 Spencer, R. F. Native myth and modern religion among the Klamath Indians, JAF, 65: 217—25.

52-187 Spicer, E. H. (ed.). Human problems in technological change. New York. (Includes introduction and three papers by the editor.)

52-188 Spindler, G. D. Personality and peyotism in Menomini Indian acculturation, Ps, 15: 151—59.

52-189 Spindler, G. and Goldschmidt, W. Experimental design in the study of culture change, SJA, 8: 68—83.

52-190 Spindler, L. S. Witchcraft in Menomini acculturation, AA, 54: 593—610.

52-191 Spoehr, A. Time perspective in Micronesia and Polynesia, SJA, 8: 457—65.

52-192 Stern, T. Chickahominy: the changing culture of a Virginia Indian community, APSP, 96, 2: 159—225.

52-193 Stewart, D. D. Cheyenne—Arapaho assimilation, Phylon, 13, 2: 120—26.

52-194 Stewart, O. C. Southern Ute adjustment to modern living, ICAP, 29: 80—87.

52-195 Streib, G. F. An attempt to unionize a semi-literate Navaho group, HO, 11, 1: 23—31.

52-196 Strong, W. D. Cultural resemblances in nuclear America: parallelism or diffusion, ICAP, 29, 1: 271—79.

52-197 Sun, E-tu Zen. Results of culture contact in two Mongol-Chinese communities, SJA, 8, 2: 182—210.

52-198 Sutherland, I. L. G. Maori and European, JPS, 61, 1—2: 136—55.

52-199 Swadesh, M. Unaalig and Proto Eskimo IV: diachronic notes, IJAL, 18, 3: 166—71.

52-200 Talbot, D. A. Contemporary Ethiopia. New York.

52-201 Tax, S. (ed.). Acculturation in the Americas. Chicago.

52-202 Tax, S. (ed.). Heritage of conquest: the ethnology of Middle America. Glencoe, Illinois.

52-203 Tax, S. Penny capitalism: A Guatemalan Indian economy. ISAP, 16.

52-204 Teicher, M. I. Anthropology and social work, HO, 10, 3: 22—24.

52-205 Thurnwald, R. The role of political organization in the development of man, with suggested applications in the New World, ICAP, 29, 1: 280—84.

52-206 Tichelman, G. L. Teveel dynamiek om Bataks te zijn, Oost en West, 45: 7 ff. Amsterdam.

52-207 Trimingham, J. S. Islam in Ethiopia. London.

52-208 Tolstoy, P. Morgan and Soviet anthropological thought, AA, 54, 1: 8—17.

52-209 Tschopik, H., Jr. On the identification of the Indian in Peru, ICAP, 29, 2: 261—66.

52-210 Tumin, M. M. Caste in a peasant society: a case study in the dynamics of caste. Princeton, N. J.

52-211 UNESCO. Social implications of technical change, International Social Science Bulletin, 4, 2.

52-212 Useem, J. South sea island strike: labor—management relations in the Caroline Islands, Micronesia; democracy in process: the development of democratic leadership in the Micronesian islands, in Human problems in technological change, Spicer, E. H. (ed.). New York.

52-213 Van Baal, J. The Nimboran development project, SP, 6, 8: 492–99.

52-214 Van der Kroef, J. M. Society and culture in Indonesian nationalism, AJS, 58: 11–24.

52-215 Van der Kroef, J. M. Patterns of western influence in Indonesia, ASR, 17, 4: 421–30.

52-216 Voget, F. Current trends in the Wind River Shoshone sun dance, BAEB, 151, 42.

52-217 Voget, F. Crow socio-cultural groups, ICAP, 29: 88–93.

52-218 Vogt, E. Z. Water witching: an interpretation of a ritual pattern in a rural American community, SM, 75: 175–86.

52-219 Wagley, C. The folk culture of the Brazilian Amazon, ICAP, 29, 2: 224–30.

52-220 Wagner, G. Aspects of conservatism and adaptation in the economic life of the Herero, Sociologus, 2, 1: 125. Berlin.

52-221 Wallace, A. F. C. The modal personality of the Tuscarora Indians as revealed by the Rorschach test. BAEB, 150.

52-222 Wallace, E. and Hoebel, E. A. The Comanches: lords of the south plains. Norman, Okla.

52-223 Wallis, W. D. Values in a world of cultures, AA, 54, 1: 143–46.

52-224 Waterman, R. A. African influence on the music of the Americas, ICAP, 29, 2: 207–220.

52-225 Watson, J. B. Cayuá culture change: a study in acculturation and methodology, AAAM, 73.

52-226 Xabregas, J. O amendoim na alimentação dos indígenas de Angola, Mensário Admin., 55–56: 51–57.

52-227 Zborowski, M. and Herzog, E. Life is with people: the Jewish little-town of eastern Europe. New York.

52-228 Zerries, O. Die kulturgeschichtliche Bedeutung einiger Mythen aus Südamerika über den Ursprung der Pflanzen, ZE, 77, 1: 7–56.

16/2